# SEX AND THE CITADEL

## Intimate Life in a
## Changing Arab World

## Shereen El Feki

Chatto & Windus
LONDON

Published by Chatto & Windus 2013

2 4 6 8 10 9 7 5 3 1

Copyright © 2013

Shereen El Feki has asserted her right under the Copyright, Designs
and Patents Act 1988 to be identified as the author of this work

First published in Great Britain in 2013 by
Chatto & Windus
Random House, 20 Vauxhall Bridge Road,
London SW1V 2SA
www.vintage-books.co.uk

Addresses for companies within The Random House Group Limited can be
found at: www.randomhouse.co.uk/offices.htm

The Random House Group Limited Reg. No. 954009

A CIP catalogue record for this book
is available from the British Library

ISBN 9780701183165

The Random House Group Limited supports the Forest Stewardship
Council® (FSC®), the leading international forest-certification organisation.
Our books carrying the FSC label are printed on FSC®-certified paper. FSC is
the only forest-certification scheme supported by the leading environmental
organisations, including Greenpeace. Our paper procurement policy
can be found at: www.randomhouse.co.uk/environment

Printed and bound by CPI Group (UK) Ltd, Croydon, CR0 4YY

*For my parents*

*I swear by God there is a need to know this subject; those who do not know it, or make fun of it, are ignorant, stupid, of little understanding.*

—'Umar Muhammad al-Nafzawi,
*The Perfumed Garden* (fifteenth century)

*Let us admit, once and for all, that sex is the basic principle around which all the rest of human life, with all its institutions, is pivoted.*

—Magnus Hirschfeld, *Women East and West: Impressions of a Sex Expert* (1935)

# Contents

## A Note on Language

A few years ago, I was invited to visit a foundation for women's rights in Cairo. The staff and I talked in English, which they spoke far more fluently than I did Arabic. At the end of an impressive tour, however, I tried to rise to the occasion. "Thank you," I struggled in my very best Arabic, "for inviting me to your woman's center." There was an awkward pause and some curious looks from my hosts, but the moment quickly passed, and with the hospitality that Egyptians are famous for, we parted with handshakes and smiles all around.

It wasn't until later, when some Egyptian friends burst out laughing as I told them the story, that I discovered the source of the confusion. "But, Shereen, you thanked them for visiting their center for sluts!" Through a subtle mispronunciation of the Arabic word for "woman," I had put their organization into a different line of business altogether.

Such adventures in Arabic have made me all the more conscious of helping readers to get it right. So in this book, where Arabic words are transliterated into English, I have followed the gold standard of the *International Journal of Middle East Studies;* for simplicity's sake, however, diacritical marks have been omitted. Two Arabic letters that have caused me plenty of trouble over the years, including the episode above, are represented by ' for *'ayn* and ' for *hamza*.

When I'm talking about Egypt, I've sometimes parted ways with *IJMES,* transliterating words to capture local pronunciation. So it's *ahwa* instead of *qahwa,* Gamal instead of Jamal, and so on. There are, inevitably, exceptions to this exception. For example, where Arabic words have made their way into English, they are not italicized and I have opted not to Egyptianize them in most cases—that means "hijab," instead of *hegab,* for instance. The same applies for plurals. Where words have crossed into English, I use *s;* otherwise, I have retained the original Arabic plural form. So that's "fatwa" and "fatwas" (not *fatawa*); *faqih* and *fuqaha'* (not faqihs). I have also used the common English spelling for names of places and well-known people, past and present.

# Introduction

"What is it?"

Six pairs of dark eyes stared at me—or rather, at the small purple rod in my hand.

"It's a vibrator," I answered, in English, racking my brain for the right Arabic word. "A thing that makes fast movements" came to mind, but as that could equally apply to a hand mixer, I decided to stick with my mother tongue to minimize what I could sense was rising confusion in the room.

One of the women, curled up on a divan beside me, began to unpin her hijab, a cascade of black hair falling down her back as she carefully put her headscarf to one side. "What does it do?" she asked.

"Well, it vibrates," I added, taking a sip of mint tea and biting into a piece of syrupy baklava to buy myself some time before the inevitable rejoinder.

"But why?"

How I came to be demonstrating sex toys to a coffee morning of Cairo housewives is a long story. I have spent the past five years traveling across the Arab region asking people about sex: what they do, what they don't, what they think and why. Depending on your perspective, this might sound like a dream job or a highly dubious occupation. For me, it is something else altogether: sex is the lens through which I investigate the past and present of a part of the world about which so much is written and still so little is understood.

Now, I grant you, sex might seem an odd choice, given the spectacle of popular revolt playing out across the Arab world since the beginning of this decade, which has taken with it some of the region's most entrenched regimes—in Egypt, Libya, Tunisia, and Yemen for starters—and is shaking up the rest. Some observers, however, have gone so far as to argue that it was youthful sexual energy that fueled the protests in the first place.[1] I'm not so sure. While I've often heard Egyptians say their fellow countrymen spend 99.9 percent of their time thinking about sex, in the heady days of early 2011, making love appeared, for once, to be the last thing on people's minds.

Yet I don't believe it was entirely out of sight. Sexual attitudes and behaviors are intimately bound up in religion, tradition, culture, politics, and economics. They are part and parcel of sexuality— that is, the act and all that goes with it, including gender roles and identity, sexual orientation, pleasure, intimacy, eroticism, and reproduction. As such, sexuality is a mirror of the conditions that led to these uprisings, and it will be a measure of the progress of hard-won reforms in the years to come. In his reflections on the history of the West, the French philosopher Michel Foucault described sexuality as "an especially dense transfer point for relations of power: between men and women, young people and old people, parents and offspring, teachers and students, priests and laity, an administration and a population."[2] The same is true in the Arab world: if you really want to know a people, start by looking inside their bedrooms.

Had it not been for the events of September 11, 2001, I might never have opened that door. I was working at *The Economist* when the world turned. Having trained as an immunologist before becoming a journalist, I was on the health and science beat, far removed from the great political debates of the day. From these sidelines, I had a chance to sit back and watch my colleagues grapple with the complexities of the Arab region. I saw their confidence in Anglo-American might and exuberance in the early afterglow of the war in Iraq gradually turn to doubt, then bewilderment. Why weren't Iraqis rushing to embrace this new world order? Why did they rarely follow the playbook written in Washington and London? Why did they behave in ways so contrary to Western expectations? In short, what makes them tick?

For me, these are not questions of geopolitics or anthropology; this is a matter of personal identity. The Arab world is in my blood: my father is Egyptian, and through him my family roots stretch from the concrete of Cairo to cotton fields deep in the Nile Delta. My mother comes from a distant green valley—a former mining village in South Wales. This makes me half Egyptian, though most people in the Arab region shake their heads when I tell them this. To them there is no "half" about it; because my father is wholly Egyptian, so am I. And because he is Muslim, I too was born Muslim. My mother's family is Christian: her father was a Baptist lay preacher, and her brother, in a leap of Anglican upward mobility, became a vicar in the Church of Wales. But my mother converted to Islam on marrying my father. She was not obliged to; Muslim men are free to marry *ahl al-kitab,* or people of the Book—among them, Jews and Christians. For my mother, becoming Muslim was a matter of conviction, not coercion.

I was born in England and raised in Canada long before "Muslims in the West" was a talking point. There were a few of us at school (I grew up in a university town near Toronto), but I never thought much of it. Then again, I was brought up with an icing of Islam on an otherwise Western lifestyle: my only observances were steering clear of pork and alcohol and learning *al-Fatiha*—the opening chapter of the Qur'an—which my parents had me recite before our very British Sunday lunches. As the sole Muslims on the block, we were always the first to put up Christmas lights, and Easter never passed without a clutch of chocolate eggs.

As for Egypt, each year we would visit my grandmother Nuna Aziza and a vast circle of aunts, uncles, and cousins. We were the outliers: my mother was the only Western woman (*khawagayya,* in Egyptian Arabic) to have married into the family, and during my childhood, we were the only members living outside of Egypt. So between my father's prestige as the eldest son and my own exotic pedigree, I basked in the spotlight. My *nuna*'s apartment was a shrine to our tiny branch of the family in exile; amid the plastic plants and the frolicking shepherds and coy maidens in petit point, our photos were crammed onto coffee tables and consoles, whose delicate gilded legs seemed unequal to the weight of so much grand-motherly affection. Growing up, I came to love Egypt and respect Islam, but I never thought to go beyond the surface.

Back in Canada, many of my father's Egyptian friends ques-tioned his decision not to raise his only child more strictly in the faith. I was not taught salat, the Muslim ritual of prayer, nor did I study Arabic. It was not for want of conviction on my father's part. He is a devout Muslim who prays five times a day and recites the Qur'an every morning, from memory; he's a hajji, having gone on pilgrimage to the holy cities of Mecca and Medina; he scrupulously observes the fast during Ramadan and never fails to pay zakat, or alms for the poor. But my father saw his friends push Islam and their own Arab upbringing on their children—particularly their daughters—like a vaccine against the perceived ills of the West. More often than not, however, what these parents saw as a dan-ger, their children embraced as an opportunity, many turning away from a religious and cultural heritage that seemed to them like too much strong medicine. My parents, on the other hand, gave me the freedom to come to my religion and my roots on my own terms and in my own time.

That moment came after September 11. Like so many others who straddle East and West, I was impelled to take a closer look at my origins. That I chose sex as my lens is unusual—but under-standable, given my background. Part of my job at *The Economist* was writing about HIV, and that included the grim task of report-ing on the state of the global epidemic. Each year, UNAIDS, the United Nations agency in charge of tracking the disease, issues updates full of daunting statistics. What always grabbed my atten-tion were not the huge numbers of those living with HIV in sub-Saharan Africa, Eastern Europe, and Asia but the tiny ones in the Arab region, where the prevalence of infection was only a fraction of what it was elsewhere. How, in an era of mass migration and instant access, could one part of the world stay seemingly immune to HIV? Was it possible that people in the Arab region were simply not engaging in risky behavior—that there was no needle sharing or contaminated blood supplies or unsafe sex?

As I started to ask questions, I began to tumble into the gap between public appearance, as reflected in official statistics, and private reality. While many people were busy reassuring me that HIV was not, and could never be, the problem in the Arab world that it was elsewhere, I was meeting whole families who were infected and was hearing the increasingly urgent pleas of those working quietly to stop the epidemic in its tracks. The more I looked, the more I realized that the main wedge between appearance and reality was sex: a collective unwillingness to face up to any behavior that fell short of a marital ideal, a resistance buttressed by religious interpretation and social convention.

In broad strokes, this sexual climate looks a lot like the West on the brink of the sexual revolution. And many of the same underlying forces that drove change in Europe and America are present in the modern Arab world, if only in embryo: struggles toward democracy and personal rights; the rapid growth of cities and a growing strain on family structures, loosening community controls on private behavior; a huge population of young people whose influences and attitudes diverge from those of their parents; the changing role of women; the transformation of sex into a consumer good through economic expansion and liberalization. Add to that greater exposure to the sexual mores of other parts of the world brought about through media and migration. All of which raises the question: As political upheaval convulses the region, is a sexual shake-up next in line?

Because of their essential differences in history, religion, and culture, the West is no guide to how change will play out in the Arab world. Development is a journey, not a race, and different societies take different paths. Some destinations are, however, more desirable than others. I believe that a society that allows people to make their own choices and to realize their sexual potential, that provides them with the education, tools, and opportunities to do so, and that respects the rights of others in the process is a better place for it. I do not believe this is fundamentally incompatible with social values in the Arab world, which was once more open to the full spectrum of human sexuality and could be so again. Nor need this irremediably clash with the region's dominant faith: it is through their *interpretations* of Islam that many Muslims are boxing themselves and their religion in.

This book is the story of those who are trying to break free: researchers who dare to probe the very heart of sexual life; scholars who are reinterpreting traditional texts that currently constrain choices; lawyers who are fighting for more equitable legislation; doctors who are trying to relieve the physical and psychological fallout; religious leaders who are brave enough to preach tolerance where they once talked of damnation; activists who are on the streets trying to make sex safe; writers and filmmakers who are challenging the limits of sexual expression; bloggers who are forging a new space for public debate. And it is also the story of those who oppose them; the shifting political landscape of the Arab region, after decades of stasis, is opening new opportunities for both.

It took more than a thousand days to assemble these stories, and, like *One Thousand and One Nights,* these tales lead into each other in often unexpected ways. In chapter 1 they help us to understand how sexual attitudes in the East and West have shifted over time. In chapter 2, they illuminate the trouble with marriage, in and out of the bedroom. In chapter 3 they show us the sexual minefield of youth, and in chapter 4, they point to ways of navigating safe passage through it with sex education, contraception, and abortion— and what to do when the trigger is pressed, as in the case of unwed motherhood. Chapter 5 examines the many shades of sex work in the region and the prospects for those involved. In chapter 6 we look at those who break the heterosexual mold and how they themselves see the way forward. Finally, chapter 7 takes a wide-angle view of the current state of affairs and considers how a fairer and more fulfilling sexual culture might develop in the coming decades. For all the predicaments these stories highlight, this isn't another book about what's wrong with the Arab region. It's about what's right: how people on the ground are solving their problems in ways that often look different from responses elsewhere in the world. This is not an academic tome, nor a slice of Arab exotica. It is, in the end, an album of snapshots from across the region taken by someone trying to better understand the region in order to better understand herself. Those looking for an encyclopedia, or a peep show, should search elsewhere.

So far, I have talked about the Arab world as a collective entity, as if one could generalize about twenty-two countries, three hundred fifty million people, three major religions, dozens of religious sects and ethnic groups. The term Middle East is even more of a geographical blender, mashing together not only the Arabic-speaking countries of North Africa, the Arabian Peninsula, and the eastern Mediterranean but also non-Arab Turkey, Iran, Afghanistan, and occasionally Pakistan thrown in for good measure. While there are essential similarities in sexual attitudes and behaviors across Arab countries, there are also important differences in how societies are—or are not—tackling these challenges. Such distinctions transcend sexuality and are clearly reflected in the different trajectories of political change prompted by the popular uprisings of this decade.

So from now on, specifics. This book is centered on Egypt, and in particular Cairo, whose population represents the length of the country and the breadth of a vast social spectrum. Personal history aside, Egypt is a natural focus because it is the most populous country in the Arab region, because of its strategic geopolitical importance, and because it retains formidable political, economic, social, and cultural influence across the region. When I started my journey, few in the area—outside of Egypt, that is—agreed with me. Pivot of the Arab world for centuries, almost sixty years of post–World War II military dictatorship had sorely diminished Egypt, while its neighbors rose in economic, political, and cultural prominence. Egypt had been written off as a lost cause, a country plagued by poverty, narrow-minded Islamism, crumbling infrastructure, cultural decline, rampant corruption, and political sclerosis. Or, as my taxi driver in Rabat, Morocco's capital, put it, with devastating simplicity: "Egyptians, so egotistical. And for what?"

Egypt, they said, had lost the plot. But once its millions rose up against the regime, the same voices heralded it as a beacon of transformation across the region. Farther afield, protesters from Wall Street to Sydney have tried to bring Egypt's uprising home. Since 2011, worldwide solidarity protests, the nervousness in Western capitals, the anxiety of Arab leaders, and continuous global media coverage have amply demonstrated that what happens in Egypt still matters, not just for its own citizens but for the rest of the world as well. Egypt has rediscovered its geopolitical mojo, and in the process it has gained a long-term opportunity to reshape its society, including its sexual culture—shifts that its neighbors will be watching closely.

On many of the tough issues of sexuality, models for change lie close to home. This is a question of pragmatism, not chauvinism. While substantial progress on issues of sexuality has been made elsewhere in the Global South, and there are impressive lessons to learn, it is only natural that Egyptians should more readily appreciate, and adopt, change when they see it in a more easily identifiable package. And so I have looked to Morocco and Tunisia in the west and to Lebanon in the east, which offer models for Egypt in dealing with at least some of its collective sexual problems. I have also traveled through countries in the Gulf—United Arab Emirates, Qatar, and Saudi Arabia, among them. This region has considerable influence on Egyptians through media, money, and migration and has powerfully shaped (or warped, some would argue) Egypt's social and sexual attitudes over the past half century. And you will hear voices from other parts of the Arab region whose situations shed light on Egypt's state of affairs.

"Excuse me if I sometimes do no more than hint at the names of the heroes of my anecdotes, and do not mention them more explicitly. . . . It is enough for me to name only those whom naming does not harm, and whose mention brings no opprobrium either upon ourselves or them; either because the affair is so notorious that concealment and the avoidance of clear specification will do the party concerned no good, or for the simple reason that the person being reported on is quite content that his story should be made public, and by no means disapproves of it being bandied about."[3] This disclaimer comes from Ibn Hazm, a Muslim philosopher in Spain in the tenth and eleventh centuries, whose famous treatise, *The Ring of the Dove,* is a user's guide to falling in, and out of, love. A millennium later, I have followed the same policy: if it's first name only, then that name has been changed.

I was a scientist before I became a journalist, and this book reflects that training. Wherever possible, I have complemented personal stories with hard data; as vice-chair of the Global Commission on HIV and the Law, a body established by the United Nations to advocate for legal reform, including laws regulating sexuality, around the world, I was given privileged access to both. Such information is difficult to come by in the Arab region because research on sexuality here is still scarce. Many pressing questions have yet to be addressed, and results have, as often as not, ended up in a locked drawer.

The goal of this book is to help change that, as part of what millions across the Arab world are hoping will be a new era of openness and intellectual freedom. To this end, *Sex and the Citadel* is accompanied by a website, www.sexandthecitadel.com, where you can find a wealth of additional facts, figures, and findings on the topics at hand, as indicated in the endnotes. I encourage readers not only to visit the site but also to contribute to it by posting related news, events, and research, in Arabic, English, or French. The site aims to be a clearinghouse for information on sexuality in the Arab region and, along with this book, a resource for all those who wish to understand the past, the present, and to collectively forge a better sexual future for coming generations. *Sex and the Citadel* is by no means the last word on sex in the Arab world, but it is an early step at a turning point in the region's history, for others to take forward.

*Cairo, November 2012*

# SEX AND THE CITADEL

# 1

## Shifting Positions

*Whoever abandons his past is lost.*

—My grandmother, on remembering
where you came from

Every journey across Cairo is a moving lesson in history. I'm not talking about its ancient monuments or medieval souk, its colonial villas or twenty-first-century skyscrapers. Nor even the extraordinary fashion plate of its twenty million–plus inhabitants: men in turbans and galabiyas (traditional robes) alongside boys in well-worn jeans and trendy T-shirts; women in abayas and niqabs (long cloaks and face veils), cultural imports from the Gulf and signs of a time of rising religiosity, shoulder to shoulder with girls in the latest Western fashions and freely flowing hairstyles.

What I focus on when I jostle through the city—aside, that is, from the treacherous sidewalks and mile-high curbs—is street signs. Not just because getting lost in Cairo can cost you hours, but because these dark blue plaques, with their splashes of white calligraphy, say so much about the country's past. In a single stroll downtown, you can pass under the Sixth of October Bridge, commemorating Egypt's face-saving attack on Israel in the 1973 war, to the glory of the pharaohs on Ramses Street, before turning the corner onto Twenty-Sixth of July Street, marking the overthrow of Egypt's last monarch. Then it's back to the Napoleonic invasion along Champollion Street, named after the man who deciphered the Rosetta stone, before hurtling into Tahrir (Liberation) Square, a souvenir of Egypt's 1952 revolution against British occupation and autocratic rule.

*Tahrir* is now doing overtime. In the winter of 2011, hundreds of thousands of Egyptians converged on this otherwise traffic-gnarled, pollution-saturated pedestrian death trap in the heart of Cairo, demanding nothing less than national transformation. Tahrir Square was the epicenter of Egypt's popular revolt against the thirty-year rule of President Hosni Mubarak. While the uprising spread far and fast throughout the country, it was Tahrir Square that caught the world's attention, the experiences of millions of protesters televised, tweeted, and blogged in real time. Tahrir Square turned into an eighteen-day revolutionary reality show as protesters dug in, camped out, and fought back against their own Big Brother, the Mubarak regime. "We are one Egypt," the people shouted, as decades of frustration with business as usual brought rich and poor, Muslims and Christians, men and women, parents and children, together in a single, focused front. The achievement of Tahrir Square wasn't just its grand political movement but the tiny personal battles fought and won against the frictions wearing down Egyptian society: between religions, classes, sexes, and generations.

In the years to come, the success of Egypt's recent uprising will, in large part, be judged by how these millions of miniature victories are transplanted from the hothouse of Tahrir Square to the cold realities of everyday life. This is true of the rest of the Arab region as well, where nations are working their way through the political upheaval that began this decade. To fully appreciate whatever flowering may follow, we need to know the ground on which these gains take root. And one of the rockiest places to look is sexual life.

In today's Arab world, the only widely accepted, socially acknowledged context for sex is state-registered, family-approved, religiously sanctioned matrimony. Anything else is 'ayb (shameful), *illit adab* (impolite), haram (forbidden)—a seemingly endless lexicon of reproof. That vast segments of the population in most countries in the region are having a hard time fitting this mold—young people who can't afford to marry, career women who don't conform to gender expectations, men and women who engage in same-sex relations, those who sell sex to make ends meet—is increasingly recognized, but there is widespread resistance to any alternative.

Even within the marriage bed, sex is something to do, not to discuss. Such collective unease with sex makes tackling the fallout—including violence, infection, exploitation, dysfunction, conjugal dissatisfaction, and profound ignorance—all the more difficult. "In the Arab world, sex is the opposite of sport," one Egyptian gynecologist explained to me. "Everyone talks about football, but hardly anyone plays it. But sex—everyone is doing it, but nobody wants to talk about it."

Growing up in the Arab region, you are taught to steer clear of the "red lines": taboos around politics, religion, and sex that are not to be challenged in word or deed. But these lines are not isolated strokes. They flow and mingle like calligraphy; if you efface some of the script, the meaning of the rest changes. The "Arab Awakening," that began this decade took a chisel to the red line of politics and started the long process of chipping away at received wisdoms: that the people of the Arab region are, by their religion, culture, and tradition, ill suited to democracy; that they would never challenge authority; that their fear of instability trumps their desire for change and its attendant uncertainties; that they cannot handle freedom. Now that those fetters are breaking, it is only natural to ask if other taboos will follow.

Since the uprising, Cairo has become a vast billboard for human rights. "Freedom," "justice," and "dignity" are just a few of the catchwords in the graffiti wallpapering the city. But extending these same rights—as well as equality, privacy, autonomy, and integrity—to the sexual lives of all citizens is another matter entirely. In practical terms, "sexual rights" means the freedom to access sexual and reproductive health services and to generate, share, and consume ideas and information about sexuality. It is the right to choose your own partner and to be sexually active, or not, in consensual relations. It is the freedom to decide whether you want to have children, and when; it is the right to control your own body and the liberty to pursue a satisfying, safe, and pleasurable sexual life. And all this without coercion, discrimination, or violence—a tall order anywhere in the world.[1]

Sexual rights are integral human rights; they are not some lesser set of entitlements that you can take or leave and still claim to respect another's freedom and humanity. The exercise of "sexual citizenship"—the power to make one's own decisions and demand accountability from those in authority, irrespective of color, class, creed, gender, or sexual orientation—is more than a reflection of a democratic system. It is a means of building one, by anchoring these principles at the core of human existence, where they can, in turn, shape attitudes and actions in the other domains.

But "sexual rights" are a minefield in the Arab world; for many people, they are shorthand for a Western social agenda, meaning homosexuality, free love, prostitution, pornography, and the slippery slope toward undermining Islam and "traditional" Arab values. Such differences are reflected in World Values Surveys, which gauge attitudes on a wide range of issues in more than ninety countries. When two American academics, Ronald Inglehart and Pippa Norris, looked at the results from surveys conducted from 1995 to 2001, they found that the greatest difference of opinion between the Islamic countries polled (which included Morocco, Jordan, and Egypt) and the West (North America, Australasia, and Western Europe) was over not democratic values but rather gender roles and sexuality—the acceptability of abortion, divorce, and homosexuality, for example. There has been little change in these positions in subsequent waves of World Values Surveys.[2] As the authors concluded, "The cultural gulf separating Islam from the West involves Eros far more than Demos."[3]

## TRADING PLACES

Sex has long been a divide between the Arab world and the West. Today, the former seems busy denying the flesh, while the latter appears content to let it all hang out. What is often overlooked in these mutual recriminations, however, is that such positions are fluid; at other times in history, East and West traded places.[4] Two journeys made in the first half of the nineteenth century—one by a Frenchman, the other by an Egyptian—illustrate this shift.

In 1849, Gustave Flaubert, author of *Madame Bovary* and other classics, traveled the length of Egypt, from Alexandria south to Wadi Halfa in Sudan. Aside from Luxor's ancient ruins, Flaubert wasn't much impressed by monuments. ("Egyptian temples bore me profoundly," he recorded in his diary in March 1850.)[5] Nor was he particularly interested in his official mission: to collect information for France's Ministry of Agriculture and Commerce. ("Near me, about ten millimeters away, are my ministerial instructions, which seem to be waiting impatiently for the day I'll use them as toilet paper," he wrote to a friend back in France.)[6]

For a man of Flaubert's romantic tendencies and wide appetites, commercial fact-finding was an unsatisfactory occupation. What really interested the budding author was people at their earthiest and most intimate. Luckily for Flaubert, Egypt gave him a "bellyful of colors" in this respect.[7] But it was another part of his anatomy that did most of the touring. Fresh off the boat, Flaubert spent a night in a brothel with Turkish prostitutes whose "shaved cunts make a strange effect—the flesh is as hard as bronze, and my girl had a splendid arse," as he reported home.[8]

Flaubert proceeded to fuck his way up the Nile. He wrote at length of the prostitutes in the southern village of Esna, and especially of his time with Kuchuk Hanem, "a tall, splendid creature, lighter in coloring than an Arab . . . her skin, particularly on her body, is slightly coffee-colored. When she bends, her flesh ripples into bronze ridges. Her eyes are dark and enormous . . . heavy shoulders, full, apple-shaped breasts."[9] Flaubert's visit to Hanem's house of pleasure featured music and striptease (a bare-all version of a traditional Egyptian dance called the bee) in addition to the business at hand: "I went down with Safia Zoughairah [one of Hanem's colleagues]. She is very corrupt, writhing, full of pleasure, a little tigress. I stain the divan. [And then] the second bout with Kuchuk. I felt her necklace between my teeth as I clasped her shoulders. Her cunt corrupted me like rolls of velvet. I felt ferocious."[10]

When Flaubert wasn't having sex, he was observing it at almost every turn. Cairo's bawdy street life caught his imagination: skits about whores and buggering donkeys; children playing, the girls "making imitation fart sounds with their hands"; a boy pimping his mother ("If you'll give me five *paras*,* I'll bring you my mother to fuck. I wish you all kinds of prosperity, especially a long prick").[11] In addition to the common round of mosques and pyramids, Flaubert did some unusual sightseeing. In Kasr al-Ainy Hospital, where my own family still practices medicine, he toured the syphilis ward; on cue from the doctor, the male patients "stood up on their beds, undid their trouser belts (it was like army drill), and opened their anuses with their fingers to show their chancres."[12]

Not that this deterred Flaubert from same-sex adventures. As he wrote to a friend: "Here it is quite accepted. One admits one's sodomy, and it is spoken of at table in the hotel. Sometimes you do a bit of denying, and then everybody teases you and you end up confessing. Travelling as we are for educational purposes, and charged with a mission by the government, we have considered it our duty to indulge in this form of ejaculation. So far the occasion has not presented itself. We continue to seek it, however."[13] Flaubert's research included taking in a performance of Cairo's male prostitute-dancers ("charming in their corruption, in their obscene leerings and the femininity of their movements, dressed as women, their eyes painted with antimony") and an interesting time at the hammam, where the masseur "lifted up my *boules d'amour* to clean them, then continuing to rub my chest with his left hand he began to pull with his right on my prick, and as he drew it up and down he leaned over my shoulder and said 'baksheesh, baksheesh,' "† an opportunity Flaubert declined because the man wasn't young or handsome enough for his tastes.[14]

Today, Flaubert and other nineteenth-century commentators on Arab sexual culture rank high on the Orientalist hit list. Orientalism, once a neutral term used to describe the study of the Arab region and parts farther east, became something of an insult after Edward Said published his book of the same title in the late 1970s.

---

*An old unit of currency, one-fortieth of a piastre, today the smallest denomination of Egyptian currency.
†A tip.

In it, he took generations of Western scholars to task for projecting the Arab region through their own prism of racial and religious prejudices and political interests, making Orientalism "a Western style for dominating, restructuring, and having authority over the Orient."[15] The result, according to Said, was the transformation of the Orient into a "living tableau of queerness," including its sexual mores, thereby asserting Western superiority and justifying Western hegemony over the region and its peoples. Said was particularly critical of Western commentators and their sexed-up accounts of Arab life, cruising the colonies for kicks they could not get in the straitlaced climate of home.

While Flaubert and his contemporaries found much to applaud in the apparent sexual ease of the East, some Arab visitors admired aspects of Europe's sexual culture for the opposite reason. In 1826, Rifaʻa Rafiʻ al-Tahtawi, an Egyptian imam, arrived in Paris for the start of a five-year stay, part of a forty-strong delegation of Egyptian students sent to learn the language and pick up other useful knowledge. Al-Tahtawi was one of the more apt pupils, an accomplished writer and translator who would later be a leading light in educational reform back home. His record of this state-sponsored junket is part insightful observation, part *Idiot's Guide to Europe*. Al-Tahtawi was enormously curious and wrote about everything from politics to restaurants, gala balls to slaughterhouses. There were aspects of French character he applauded (punctuality, honesty, and gratitude) and those he disdained (indulgence in personal pleasures, as well as a greater faith in philosophers than in prophets).

Al-Tahtawi generally took a dim view of relations between men and women in his home away from home. "Among French women there are those with great virtue and others who display quite the contrary. The latter are in the majority since the hearts of most people in France, whether male or female, are in thrall to the art of love."[16] Nor was he particularly impressed by their stand on premarital relations, which they considered "part of the [human] faults and vices rather than a mortal sin."[17] Nonetheless, al-Tahtawi seemed to have a soft spot for the ladies, those "paragons of beauty and charm," and pinned much of the blame for their failings on the weakness of their men, who, in his opinion, gave them too much sway.[18]

While their relations with women might be questionable, al-Tahtawi had nothing but praise for Frenchmen's strong stand on interactions with one another. "They do not have any propensity towards the love of boys or the celebration of its pursuit. This is a lost sentiment among them and one that is rejected by their nature and morals. Among the good qualities of their language and poetry is that they refuse to extol homosexual love. Indeed, in French it is highly inappropriate for a man to say, 'I fell in love with a boy.' This would be considered repugnant and troublesome."[19]

Al-Tahtawi went on at length about French zero tolerance on this point. "The French consider homosexuality to be one of the most disgusting obscenities. As a result, they only very rarely mention it in their books, and when they do it is always in veiled terms. One will never hear people talking about this."[20] In his account, al-Tahtawi noted that the French aversion to homosexuality was the "one [thing] they truly have in common with the Arabs."[21] This is something of a whitewash, though, given how well documented same-sex relations were in nineteenth-century Cairo, not just by curious foreigners like Flaubert, but by local chroniclers as well.[22]

What's interesting, in this ebb and flow of history, is how stereotypes have changed. The Arab world, once famous in the West for sexual license, envied by some but despised by others, is now widely criticized for sexual intolerance. It's not just Western liberals who hold this view. It has also become a keynote in some of the "Islamophobic" discourse of conservatives in America and Europe, the self-proclaimed last stand in the battle between "Western" values and the depredations of "radical" Islam, particularly as they relate to the rights of women.[23] And the West, once praised by some in the Arab world for its hard line on same-sex relations, is now seen by many as a radiating source of sexual debauchery from which the region must be shielded. Perceptions, however flawed, are shaped by position. Western views of Arab sexuality, and vice versa, have shifted in part because attitudes within their respective societies have also changed.

What happened in the Western world is common knowledge. I am too young to have lived through the sexual revolution, but I understand how dramatic a break it was from the past through stories of my mother's youth. When she was growing up in the 1930s to '50s in rural Wales, sex was never discussed, but everyone knew that good girls waited until marriage. In an age before the Pill, in which contraception was hit-or-miss and abortion illegal and complicated to procure, this was as much a question of practicality as morality. When my mother was a teenager, contact with young men was strictly supervised, curfews were rigorously enforced, and chaperones were in full force at village dances. Homosexuality was a deep, dark secret and my mother, who was once propositioned by a female teacher, was all the more stunned because she had never heard of such behavior.[24]

My Egyptian friends under forty are astonished by this history. Having been brought up on American movies, then music videos, and now the Internet—all post–sexual revolution—they simply cannot believe that Western society was once as conservative about sexual matters as theirs is now. The parallels are striking; taboos against premarital sex, masturbation, homosexuality, unwed motherhood, abortion, and a culture of censorship and silence, preached by religion and enforced by social convention, are as strong in today's Arab world as they were in my mother's youth.

But they are equally surprised when I tell them stories from my father's youth in Cairo of the 1930s to '50s or regale them with my Egyptian grandmother's riper sayings—anecdotes and proverbs that weave through this book and reflect sexual attitudes and antics not far off Flaubert's descriptions, however much anti-Orientalists might protest. "What is fascinating is that our Arab ancestors were not like us, and their attitude about sex was one full of freedom and openness," wrote Salah al-Din al-Munajjid, one of the first modern Arab historians to take a good look at the region's sexual heritage, comparing even my father's day to ages past. "They were never embarrassed when speaking about women and about sex or when writing about them. I believe that this great freedom of theirs is the cause of this strictness we find today."[25]

## DECLINE AND FALL

What accounts for this reaction? How did the Arab world get itself into such a twist over sex? In search of answers, I went to see the man who quite literally wrote the book on the subject. Abdelwahab Bouhdiba, a Tunisian sociologist, is best known for his 1975 work, *Sexuality in Islam.* There had certainly been books on the subject before, and there have been plenty since, but Bouhdiba's work is arguably the most popular, translated into more than half a dozen languages.

Through his reading of the Qur'an and hadiths—accounts of the words and deeds of the Prophet Muhammad—and other sources, Bouhdiba argued that matters of the flesh in general and sexuality in particular are not just compatible with Islam but essential elements of faith. "The exercise of sexuality was a prayer, a gift of oneself, an act of charity," he wrote. "To rediscover the meaning of sexuality is to rediscover the meaning of God, and conversely."[26] But somewhere along the line, Arabs lost this spiritual dimension: "This open sexuality, practised in joy with a view to the fulfillment of being, gradually gave way to a close, morose, repressed sexuality. . . . Furtive, secretive, hypocritical behavior assumed an ever more exorbitant place. . . . All freshness, all spontaneity were eventually crushed as if by some steamroller."[27] To get back on track—politically, socially, economically, and spiritually, as well as sexually—Bouhdiba reckons a dramatic rethink is in order: "To emerge from this malaise we must at all costs rediscover the sense of sexuality, that is to say, the sense of the dialogue with the other partner, and the sense of the faith, that is to say, the sense of the dialogue with God. . . . For sexuality properly performed is tantamount to freedom assumed."[28]

In his brown corduroy trousers and houndstooth jacket, with

a neatly knotted tie and clipped grizzled hair, Bouhdiba doesn't come across as a sexual radical. He looks and sounds, with his carefully chosen words and thoughtful pauses, more like a university professor—which is exactly what he was before he retired. "I am not a man of provocation. . . . My style is restrained, a style in which I say shocking things, but with a lot of discretion," he told me. It has proved a successful formula: *Sexuality in Islam* was well received, even in the Arab region. For all the book's academic acclaim, Bouhdiba's most gratifying review came from an unexpected quarter. "I was at Djerba [in southern Tunisia]," he recalled, "waiting to leave for Tripoli [in Libya] by boat. Someone said, 'Bouhdiba? Author of *Sexuality in Islam*?' and began to embrace me. He was a professor at the University of Sarajevo. He said he had translated my book by candlelight, with a rifle in one hand and a pen in the other. He sold two thousand copies in fifteen days. He said, 'I found two things in the book: pride in our belonging to an open religion and a joie de vivre—two things we badly need today.'"

As Bouhdiba points out, both were in ample supply during the Abbasid Empire, whose golden age lasted from the eighth to the tenth centuries and whose power once stretched from the shores of the Mediterranean to the borders of India. Baghdad, its capital, saw a flourishing of Arab thought and culture the likes of which the region has yet to see again. The city was home to Bayt al-Hikma (House of Wisdom), a famous library, and its scholars helped to rescue the classics of Greek and Persian thought from oblivion. The giants of mathematics, medicine, astronomy, chemistry, and engineering of the age provided broad shoulders on which subsequent generations would stand. The Abbasid period was a time of lively religious debate, when several of the main schools of Islamic jurisprudence (*fiqh*), the foundation stones of law in the Arab world, were established and when independent religious interpretation (*ijtihad*) flourished. The arts blossomed—including works of a highly sexual nature.

There is a long and distinguished history of Arabic writing on sex—literature, poetry, medical treatises, self-help manuals— which has slipped out of sight in much of the Arab world. Many of these great works were by religious figures who saw nothing incompatible between faith and sex. Indeed, it behooved these men of learning to have as full a knowledge of sexual practices and problems as they did of the intricacies of Islam. There is nothing academic about their writing: with surprising frankness, and often disarming humor, these works cover almost every sexual subject, and then some. There is precious little in *Playboy, Cosmopolitan, The Joy of Sex,* or any other taboo-busting work of the sexual revolution and beyond that this literature didn't touch on over a millennium ago.

Bouhdiba sees this sexual open-mindedness as part and parcel of the intellectual blossoming of the age. At their zenith in the early Abbasid period, the Arabs were a confident and creative people, and open thinking on sexuality was a reflection of this. "It was not a coincidence that at the height of Islamic culture there was a flowering of sexuality," Bouhdiba says. "It is a synthesis of all domains. The rehabilitation of sexuality is the rehabilitation of science within the rehabilitation of Islam." Today, however, there is a deep vein of denial that these elements are connected, and plenty of people who want to pick and choose their history, taking what is now considered the respectable face of the Arab golden age—science and technology, for example—and leaving the rest behind. But Bouhdiba believes these facets are inseparable.

It's easy to read too much into Arabic erotic literature. Did its openness really represent society at large, or just the notions of the sexually sophisticated elite? After all, many of the most famous books of Arabic erotica were written for rulers. Bouhdiba is convinced that these books say something more broadly about the spirit of the age. He invokes religion to illustrate his point: "These elites were never denounced by the masses; their societies accepted them more or less, maybe not actively but passively. It's a little like Sufism, which represented an elite but was eventually accepted. Sometimes they were treated as heretics, sometimes they were whipped, but at the end of the day, they represented a deep current in society." There's no doubt in Bouhdiba's mind that these works were widely consumed: "These books were written for princes; they circulated among the people."

By the end of the nineteenth century, such frank and often celebratory writing on sexuality had all but dried up. Bouhdiba believes this sexual hibernation is just one element of a broader intellectual decline that gained momentum during the colonial period: "Since Bonaparte, we've witnessed a negative evolution of Muslim societies. Especially over the past half century, since the collapse of Nasserism and nationalism [following the defeat of Arab forces in the 1967 Six-Day War with Israel], our societies have been on the defensive, in the process of closing in on themselves," he notes, especially so when it comes to the key elements of family, women, and home.

There's an expression in Egypt that neatly sums up this state of affairs: *'uqdit al-khawaga,* or foreigner complex. It's a feeling of inferiority to the West, and it took off in 1798, when Napoleon invaded Egypt. In an operation reminiscent of the 2003 war in Iraq, Napoleon came to Egypt promising to liberate a people oppressed by a cruel and capricious military dictatorship—in this case, an imported military caste called the Mamluks. The Mamluks were supremely confident of victory over the French: after all, the last encounter they recalled with Europe—the Crusades—did not end well for the visiting team. This time around, however, the French, with their superior technology and tactics, crushed the Mamluks in what could best be described as "shock and awe." Although things rapidly unraveled for Napoleon after that, this victory on Arab soil marked a new phase of engagement, in which the Arab world rapidly lost ground to the West, with waves of European colonial expansion that began with the French invasion of Algeria in 1830 and washed over Egypt in 1882 with British occupation.

In asking themselves why Europe was in the ascendant, Arab thinkers of the late nineteenth and early twentieth centuries began to wonder if their proclivities—especially homosexuality—were connected to their descent. The Abbasid dynasty, once masters of the Islamic universe, lost their grip by the tenth century; while some of these writers saw its sexual ease as a symptom of decline and fall, others considered it a direct cause.[29] As Arab intellectuals came to see themselves through foreign eyes, some historians argue, they also started to rewrite their own sexual history according to a European script.[30]

This rewriting gained pace with the emergence of Islamic fundamentalism. The foundation of the Muslim Brotherhood—by Hassan al-Banna in 1920s Egypt—was, in large part, a response to colonial occupation, and again invoked sexual immorality as one of the reasons for the country's slide. Al-Banna believed that Egypt had lost its independence because its people had lost their way from Islam and that the only way forward was a return to shari'a, or Islamic law. Islamism, in its many modern strains, takes a hard line on sexuality, often framing it in opposition to the West. One man who helped to shape these views was Sayyid Qutb, a teacher and writer who joined the Brotherhood in the 1950s and quickly rose to prominence. He fell from grace, along with the rest of the Brotherhood, during the era of President Gamal Abdel Nasser; Qutb was imprisoned and eventually hanged in 1966.

While behind bars, Qutb wrote a number of books that became manifestos for some of the brands of red-hot Islamic fundamentalism to emerge in the second half of the twentieth century. His ideas have traveled farther than his name. You may have never heard of Qutb, but you are probably familiar with his thinking, thanks to al-Qaeda; Ayman al-Zawahiri, éminence grise of the organization and successor to Osama bin Laden, was deeply influenced by Qutb's work.

While Qutb's views were forged in the crucible of Nasser's prisons, they were informed by a trip to America in the late 1940s. As a staunch opponent of British rule in Egypt, Qutb was suspicious of Europeans and their influence on Egyptian culture and values long before he ever set foot in the West. His visit to America gave him a firsthand look at a Western society, and the more he saw of it, the more it confirmed his views. "America is not special, but a branch from the satanic tree and the corrupt plant," he wrote to friends back in Egypt in 1949.[31]

In a blaze of fiery criticism that swept through letters, articles, and books, Qutb lambasted American "primitiveness"—a base, savage society devoid of any spiritual or moral foundation and obsessed with material gain. Qutb was appalled by the sexual freedom—"licentiousness," as he called it—of Americans, which greeted him the moment he set sail. En route to New York, a beautiful, scantily clad, and highly intoxicated woman appeared at his cabin door looking for somewhere to spend the night. "Her bodily charms were very tempting," said Qutb, but her invitation came hot on the heels of his shipboard embrace of greater Islamic devotion, so Qutb cast her aside.[32]

Such sexual adventures continued on land. Even in Greeley, Colorado, the small town he visited, young women had open ideas about sex, as one college student enlightened him: "The sex question is not a question of morals, it is only a biological question. And when we look at it from this angle, we discover that using words like sin and virtue, good and bad in describing this is putting it in the wrong place; and if you do that, it seems very amusing to us."[33] For his part, Qutb was more aghast than amused. Everywhere he turned, he saw bodies on display: men showing off their muscles, and women flaunting their assets. Even the churches, according to Qutb, were banking on sex. Pastors were keen on the regular attendance of pretty girls to bring in the boys and fill up the pews, and at church dances "arms circled arms, lips met lips, chests met chests, and the atmosphere was full of love."[34]

Not only was such activity far from halal (that is, permitted under Islamic law) in Qutb's opinion, the American approach to sex also stripped it of its moral and spiritual dimensions, reducing it to a physical sensation, like everything else in that material-mad society. The upshot of such debauchery, he predicted, was the "complete extinction" of America: families torn apart by divorce and the young addled by drugs, booze, and sexual "deviance," leading to wholesale depopulation as reproduction ground to a halt. "I have seen films which talk about jungle life . . . the males jumping on the females and females jumping on the males, couple by couple, and group by group . . . this big sex-mad forest, these feverish bodies and hungry looks, animal fun," he wrote. "It is exactly here in America as in the jungle, except the jungle is not full of factories, labs, schools and bars."[35]

## BACK TO BASICS

Qutb's framing of the West as a cesspit of sexual chaos and moral decay—a sort of reverse Orientalism—is echoed in the rhetoric of many Islamic conservatives today. To guard against such contamination, Qutb argued, Muslim societies must go back to the ways of the founding fathers of Islam, the *salaf*—or rather, an interpretation of the time of the Prophet.

Decades of dictatorship in Egypt have worked wonders to strengthen this conservative streak. People turned to Islam, and its social and political organizations, not only as a solace from the growing struggles of everyday life and a provider of the essential goods and services that the state singularly failed to supply, but also as a form of protest and an opportunity for civic engagement in a country whose political regime left little space for either. This culminated in the resounding victories of Islamist candidates in many of the region's first elections after the uprisings, from parliaments to professional syndicates, in those countries that directly experienced insurrection—notably Egypt and Tunisia—as well as in some of those indirectly affected, including Morocco and Kuwait.

Understanding Islamism in its many forms is a science in itself. But in practical terms in post-Mubarak Egypt, it's easiest to think of it in terms of strength and speed. The most obvious face is the extrastrong, ultrafast Salafi movement, which has been gaining ground in Egypt over the past few decades but officially "came out" after the 2011 uprising, beards and face veils flowing. These men and women are in a hurry to reshape Egypt according to their understanding of Islam, one heavily influenced by religious currents in the Gulf, and that includes a recasting of laws in line with their strict interpretation of shari'a.

Sex is something of a preoccupation for Salafis. "I am afraid for the nation, that they go for lust and destroy themselves," Mahmoud al-Masry warned me. Al-Masry is a celebrity Salafi, a smiling shaykh whose jolly face and cheerful manner can be seen on religious TV channels across Egypt and the wider Arab world. We were sitting in his expensive villa in a gated compound on the outskirts of Cairo—sugarcoated fire and brimstone having proved a lucrative line of business. Al-Masry takes a dim view of *ikhtilat*—that is, mixing of the sexes—to which he ascribes a host of ills, including adultery, disease, and sexual exploitation. But we managed to meet all the same because his wife, a sparky mass-communications graduate who works as his business manager, served as our chaperone.

"I believe that the woman is like a diamond, to be preserved. We do not suppress or oppress the woman—I want to protect her," al-Masry said, his wife nodding vigorously. "If you leave her, she could be lost because she is simple and emotional; she could be hurt by anybody." In al-Masry's book, that means yes to veiling, if at all possible; yes to wives obeying their husbands in all worldly affairs; and no to women working unless strictly necessary, certainly not with men and definitely not in positions of authority. "A people will never succeed if they are led by a woman," al-Masry told me, quoting a popular—and debatable—hadith. "The emotional part is affecting the very most of her, so if she is a judge or a ruler, at that time she will rule with her emotions and that would be unjust to the people."

Al-Masry and his Salafi peers seem to have little faith in their fellow Muslims. From the way they talk, men and women are brimming with lust, due in no small part to globalization, that will spill into communal chaos unless the sources of temptation are removed. Indeed, the dust had barely settled on Tahrir Square before self-appointed Salafi God squads—modeled along the lines of Saudi Arabia's infamous religious police, the Commission for the Promotion of Virtue and the Prevention of Vice—were on the streets trying to close down hair salons, cover up statues, and terrorize hand-holding couples. Such antics variously amuse and enrage the majority of Egyptians outside the Salafi movement. Should they ever get their act together, however, these ultraconservatives have the potential to be more than just a joke or an irritation, thanks to their newfound political presence in the post-Mubarak landscape.

How much political influence the Salafis will ultimately have depends on the real heavy hitters in the new order, the Muslim Brotherhood and their flagship political party, Freedom and Justice. "We are different to the Salafis only in the way we go about implementing [these ideas]," said Ali Fath al-Bab, a senior figure in the Brotherhood's leadership and a longtime member of Parliament. "We have the same background and knowledge, but they do not have experience in political life." The Brotherhood has plenty of that. Through four generations of persecution, through uprisings and crackdowns, the Muslim Brotherhood has been honing its skills, and now, after sweeping the first post-Mubarak elections, it sits at Egypt's political center.

Given Fath al-Bab's long-standing membership in the Brotherhood, I prepared for our meeting at one of Cairo's trendy cafés carefully, interlacing my fingers as I saw him approach, the better to resist the impulse to shake his hand—a lesson I learned the hard way, having once sent an Egyptian imam into a temporary state of paralysis with just such a hearty greeting. I needn't have bothered. Fath al-Bab enthusiastically took my hand, and the chair beside me, and by the time his latte arrived, he had spelled out much of the Brotherhood's current thinking on pressing issues in gender and sexual rights.

Compared with the fast-track Salafis, Fath al-Bab and his like-minded colleagues see themselves as a slow-acting remedy for Egypt's ills. For them, it is social change first—through education, economics, and other fundamental reforms—legal change second. This gradual approach, he said, comes with an impressive pedigree. "In the Prophet Muhammad's day, there were many houses for prostitution. But he did not ban them immediately; he left them until they changed and they themselves stopped it." Egypt's Muslims are not yet ready for shari'a, Fath al-Bab said, and until that time, there's no point in passing laws, as the Salafis urge, just for them to be broken. But this softly-softly approach is at odds with the views of others in the Brotherhood who believe that Egypt is ripe for Islamic law. For all their internal differences, however, the bottom line is the same. "Freedom and equality are our principles, but within borders or limits set by Islam and society," Fath al-Bab told me. "Freedom within a frame" is how many inside the Brotherhood and out describe their dream of Egypt's new order. But I wonder which, in the end, will be cut to size: the canvas of people's thoughts and actions or the frame that aims to contain it?

## "SEXUAL MISERY OF THE MASSES"

"Shari'a is a text that can be interpreted in the sense of sexual liberty or in the sense of repression. If the politicians decide on sexual liberty, then the Islamic scholars will find a way." This is how Abdessamad Dialmy answers that question. He's a Moroccan sociologist and one of the few in the Arab world to specialize in sexuality. Over the past four decades, Dialmy has explored the full spectrum of attitudes and activities in the region—from sex work to homosexuality to the role of sex in Islamic fundamentalism. There are easier ways to make a living, by his own admission: "The Arab researcher in this field gets little recognition for his hard work . . . suffering from loneliness, exclusion, intimidation and persecution."[36]

As we sat on the terrace of a bustling café in the heart of Rabat's Ville Nouvelle, in the shade of the chestnut trees, I asked Dialmy how he came by his unusual calling. "I read Wilhelm Reich in 1971. I was twenty-two years old, teaching at high school. I was already married, a petit bourgeois, with a house and dog," he told me. "When I read this book, it shook me, it really shook me. Because of this book, I divorced my wife. I understood that marriage is really a prison."

Wilhelm Reich was one of the most provocative, and eccentric, thinkers of the twentieth century. His seminal book, *The Sexual Revolution,* first published in German in 1936, was an indictment of "bourgeois sexual morality" and the capitalist institutions that maintained it, including marriage. Dialmy responded to Reich's "idea of revolution, attack on traditional morals, to be free, to live one's sexuality," as he put it, by leaving everything to his wife and heading to France to continue his studies—in and out of class. "Really, I lived. I practiced [sex] every day with different women. It was crazy," he recalled.

When he returned to Morocco in the mid-1970s, Dialmy went on to complete a doctorate in women's sexuality and continued his work as a sexual "militant." "I lived that revolution in my personal life; it was possible at that time," he said. Today, things are different, in Egypt as in Dialmy's homeland. "In the seventies, we had liberal thought about sexuality in Morocco among intellectuals in the leftist parties. Their practices were not as liberal; their talk was ahead of their behavior. Now it is reversed. Now they [the people] have very liberal practices, but they are not as open in their thinking."

Reich had a theory about that, one that goes some way to explaining the recent sexual history of Egypt and its neighbors. He began his career as a psychoanalyst in Vienna, alongside Sigmund Freud, and saw enough sexual unhappiness pass through the clinic to last a lifetime. What's the point, Reich asked, in tackling such confusion one patient at a time when society was mass-producing these hang-ups faster than he could ever treat them? As a result, Reich started looking beyond his couch to broader social conditions. What he saw looked a lot like the sexual terrain of today's Arab world: sex outside of marriage roundly condemned; young people, unable to get jobs, afford marriage, or find moments of privacy, reduced to furtive relations without adequate contraception or sufficient information, storing up sexual problems for later life; women whose sexual needs, beyond reproduction, were ignored or suppressed, held to double standards of virginity before marriage and chastity ever after, even in the face of miserable, unsatisfactory unions from which there was little escape, given the trouble and stigma of divorce. Abortion outlawed, masturbation condemned, sexual education suppressed—in short, "sexual misery of the masses."[37]

Why do people put up with this? Reich asked. With not just sexual repression but economic and political subjugation as well? Instead of throwing off their shackles, why do they accept, and even embrace, authoritarian regimes? Reich thought he had an answer, one in which sex went hand in hand with politics and economics and with religion and tradition to keep the ruling class in power and the people in their place.

An authoritarian system needs submissive subjects, and Reich reckoned that the most efficient factory for the latter was the patriarchal family, in which power relations between the head of state and his people are mirrored in the ties between the head of the family and his dependents. "The authoritarian state has a representative in every family, the father; in this way he becomes the state's most valuable tool," Reich wrote. "He in turn reproduces submissiveness to authority in his children, especially his sons."[38] The most effective way for a father to keep his children in line, Reich argued, is by clamping down on their sexual urges from day one. The institutions of the authoritarian system give fathers a helping hand in constraining the sexual freedom of their charges: the emphasis on marriage, which keeps women in check; the church, which condemns nonprocreative and extramarital sex as a sin against God; and schools, which ram home the message of sexual abstinence for youth. The result, Reich concluded, is paralysis of "the rebellious forces because any rebellion is laden with anxiety; it produces, by inhibiting sexual curiosity and sexual thinking in the child, a general inhibition of thinking and of critical faculties. In brief, the goal of sexual suppression is that of producing an individual who is adjusted to the authoritarian order and who will submit to it in spite of all misery and degradation."[39]

The repressive systems in Reich's sights were capitalism and fascism, but he considered sexual suppression to be the hallmark of any dictatorship. The first step to wholesale social reform was to make people aware of their sexual subjugation, he believed, and with that consciousness would come action. His ideas are interesting in the context of Egypt and many of its Arab neighbors, because they might explain, at least in small part, why people tolerated lousy government for so long. Sexual repression arguably played a role in keeping Egyptians at home for years, though sexual awareness— even in an era of mass media and instant communication—was not, in the end, what brought them into the streets. Anger at injustice, corruption, poverty, inequality, and many other failings of the old regimes was what drove these uprisings; sex was just one of frustration's many channels.

Addressing society's sexual dilemmas will be an important part of building a better order across the Arab region, according to Dialmy. "We need to talk about the right of the individual to a sexual life, to sexual pleasure," he told me. "If we want to have a real democracy, these will be important." Or, as his hero, Reich, put it: "No freedom program has any chance of success without an alteration of human sexual structure."[40] Reich cautioned would-be revolutionaries that the one does not inexorably follow the other. You can change the political system, but that doesn't mean the sexual order changes with it. But if you don't change the sexual order of things, freedom will never stick.


RACE TO THE POLE


In Egypt's emerging new order, a liberal minority, whose thinking is along the lines of Dialmy's, and a conservative majority, on the same page as Fath al-Bab, are fighting it out in all domains. This includes the vexed question of personal freedoms, especially as they relate to "morals"—whose definition has tended to be limited to women and sexuality, as opposed to broader questions of political, economic, and social justice. Sex is one of the easiest ways to discredit political opponents in the post-Mubarak period, accusing liberals of promoting "foreign"—that is, Western—ideas about sexual freedom, and Islamists of peccadilloes and perversions, from curb-crawling to necrophilia.

"In a world in which frustration, aggression and anxiety have become everyday conditions," Bouhdiba observed, "hyper-sexuality and religious Puritanism are certainly convenient ways of escaping our responsibilities and masking our failures."[41] In his view, "when a society is confronted with difficulties, it returns to its origins, or it destroys them. The two great poles of political evolution [in the Middle East] are Mustafa Kemal [Ataturk] in Turkey, who wanted to break everything, and Abdulaziz Ibn Saud [the founder of Saudi Arabia], who wanted to return to his roots. These are the two poles between which Muslim societies now find themselves."

Which pole they will gravitate to is the big question. Bouhdiba believes that in the end social change within the region will come not from a dramatic clash—burning bras and gay pride marches, for example—but rather through a long-running contest of ideas, which he calls societies of cultural competition, not cultural conflict. To those now in power tempted to sweep sex under the prayer rug, he says: "You are misreading the cultural and juridical history of our region. Lean on these elements in the quiet understanding that [in addressing these issues] you are not doing things against the religion." But he also has words of caution for those who think the way forward is a trail blazed by the West: "We need to talk about AIDS, IVF, new sexual behavior, abortion. These are problems, but we need to talk about them in the propriety of the Qur'an. Unfortunately, the Western models [of sexual expression] don't teach this, flaunting [sex] in the cinema, in the street."

For Bouhdiba, the future of the Arab region, in and out of the bedroom, lies in fully comprehending its past. "Personally, I am a believer," he says, "and it is because of that I think about my faith. Faith today is not the faith of yesterday. What does it mean to be a Muslim, what does it mean to be a believer, in sexuality, in charity, [in other elements of Islamic life]? To be a believer today is not to reproduce the old messages but to understand these messages and incorporate them into behavior that fits the demands of today. To redesign—that's the big idea."

The Arab region began this decade with a political big bang; how that will shape, and in turn be shaped by, sexual life is an open question. The intimate order of today's Arab world is like our solar system: marriage is the sun, whose gravitational pull holds the whole together; around it are planets in ever-distant orbits, from premarital sex to sex work to same-sex relations, the final frontier in the dark reaches of the cosmos. To understand this universe, we need to explore it. So let us begin at its fiery core: married life.

# 2
## Desperate Housewives

*A woman said to her daughter, "I am happy that you are now respectably married." Her daughter replied, "I wish, Mother, that I could return to the days of living scandalously."*

—My grandmother, on marriage

When I moved to Cairo in 2008, I was introduced by a mutual friend to Azza, an Egyptian woman who offered to help me with my Arabic. For all her good humor and intellectual curiosity, Azza was, at first, a little surprised by the sort of vocabulary I was looking to learn; I'm sure I'd be equally suspicious if a student of mine showed such a marked interest in the English words for genitalia, or abortion, or sundry acts of sexual violence. Given what I knew about local sensibilities, I decided to say little about my research, thereby giving Azza the impression that my interests were purely recreational and reinforcing local notions of what happens when good Egyptian girls go West.

As we got to know each other, however, and I talked more about my work, Azza was intrigued. Although a little shy at first, she quickly started asking questions and talking about her own experiences. Soon I was being introduced to family and friends as "*Doctura* Shereen, the lady who studies reproductive health and marital relations"—polite longhand for "sex." This turned out to be the ultimate calling card, an open sesame onto a treasure trove of sexual culture.

Each week brought new tales of sexual angst from Azza and her circle, like a modern-day *One Thousand and One Nights:* the neighbor who caught her husband, in their bedroom, having phone sex with her friend; the sister who found porn on her husband's laptop and, to his horror, turned the tables by uploading racy photos of herself; the older brother who divorced his wife by text message when she refused to put out and who has now taken another, sexier quasi-official wife; the younger brother who, when his bride showed some initiative on their wedding night, hauled her out of bed and made her swear on the Qur'an that she had no previous experience; the sister-in-law whose husband's lovemaking is so brief and brutal as to almost constitute sexual assault.

Azza is one of eight siblings whose married lives mirror the changes that Egypt, along with many of its Arab neighbors, has experienced over the past half century and the tensions that exploded onto the streets in the uprisings of 2011. Now in her forties, Azza is a child of the *infitah,* the "open-door" policy introduced by President Anwar Sadat in the early 1970s. Under his predecessor, Gamal Abdel Nasser, much of Egypt's economy was appropriated by the state in the name of national development. Sadat began rolling back this policy, opening Egypt's economy to the global market, a process that accelerated under the three-decade rule of his successor, Hosni Mubarak.

Some people have become very rich as a result of the *infitah;* according to one estimate, 10 percent of the population controls almost 30 percent of the national income, while more than 20 percent live on less than two dollars a day.[1] It was these superrich who found themselves in trouble during the uprising because of their tight ties to the Mubarak regime, and many in prison thereafter on corruption charges. Meanwhile, the poor are still with us, and there's no quick fix to Egypt's vast economic divide.

Azza and her family are somewhere in the struggling middle. They are, materially speaking, much better off than her grandparents, who started life in the family village, the *'izba,* in the countryside west of Cairo; like almost half of Egypt's population, most of Azza's family now live in the city. They are also more educated: Azza and her siblings all attended university—the beneficiaries of Nasser's policies opening higher education beyond the elite. Unfortunately, the supply of jobs has not kept pace with the surge in graduates, and their education has not kept up with the demands of the market: while official statistics put unemployment in the low double digits, unofficial estimates suggest that the real figure is closer to double that, hitting university graduates hardest. Even Egyptians with jobs are finding it tough to make ends meet, what with annual inflation hovering in the double digits as well.

These seismic shifts in Egyptian society are rocking Azza's marital bedroom, although the earth most certainly does not move when she and her husband make love. "He can have an erection, then two minutes later . . . " Azza pursed her lips, imitating a deflating tire. "Now he is afraid to come near me. We used to make love once every five days. Now it's been more than a month." Azza's husband was eventually persuaded to see a doctor and came back with a clean bill of health. She wonders if their problems might be related to her work.

Like a quarter of Egyptian women her age, Azza has a job, in her case one that earns almost three times as much as her husband's, since she is with a foreign firm, while he's a midlevel employee in a sluggish state-owned company. She covers most of the household bills, and there are a lot of them. Azza and her family are caught up in Egypt's burgeoning consumer culture; what with private school fees (something of a necessity, given the poor state of government schools), sporting club memberships (not exactly a luxury, with how little public space there is in Cairo to safely exercise), mobile phones, and new clothes for three kids, it takes at least two incomes just to keep up. The five of them live in a modest two-bedroom apartment in one of the high-rise eyesores that have sprung up over the past decade as Cairo has expanded into the desert. They'd like to move—sleeping arrangements aren't doing much for Azza's love life since she and her husband share a bedroom with their youngest child—but Cairo's property prices have soared over the past decade, putting the next rung on the housing ladder all but out of reach.

Azza belongs to a generation, and a class, of women in a bind. On the one hand, she has benefited from Egypt's push to educate women; more than 70 percent of Egyptian women are now literate—that's tripled since Azza was born—and half have gone on to secondary school and beyond.[2] She has more rights under the law—at least on paper—than her mother did when she was Azza's age, and many more than are accorded to women in most of Egypt's neighboring states: if Azza wants to travel, for example, she can get her own passport, without needing her husband's permission, and she can pass her Egyptian citizenship to her children. But there are plenty of catches to these hard-won rights, and men still have much more scope than women when it comes to laws, on the books and in practice.[3]

For all the gains made by Azza and her peers, there is a strong streak of patriarchy in Egypt, reinforced by the rise of Islamic conservatism since the 1970s, that has conspired to keep women in what is seen by many as their religiously sanctioned place. "[My husband] doesn't like that I work with foreigners," said Azza, "but he likes my money. He doesn't like that I earn more than him, that I make most decisions about money or the kids." He's not alone: a recent national survey of Egyptian adults found that while around 60 percent are in favor of women working outside the home, more than three-quarters of those polled—including a majority of women—believe that when work is scarce, it's men who should get the jobs. While almost half of those surveyed in an earlier poll agreed that the more satisfying marriage is one in which both husband and wife work and take care of the kids, in practice working women like Azza end up doing double duty, at home and on the job.[4]

Traditionally, women have played an important role in decision making inside Egyptian homes; my grandmother, for example, was a force to be reckoned with on the domestic front (though, like many wives today, she made sure my grandfather was seen to have the final say).[5] No matter the balance of power behind closed doors, there is, as we saw in the previous chapter, a pronounced reluctance in many quarters to see women flex these muscles in public; more than half of those surveyed in yet another recent national poll rejected women working as judges, mayors, or the president.[6] And so, while Azza's job is an economic necessity, her professional success is putting a strain on her marital relations—in and out of bed.

Meanwhile, Samar, Azza's cousin, has troubles of her own. Her husband, a small-businessman, had just returned from a trip to Italy. When Azza was a child, Egyptians rarely traveled abroad; today that's changed. Samar's husband was full of praise for Italy, particularly its slim, elegant women, whom he has taken to comparing with his wife, to her face and not in her favor. Since then, Samar, a stay-at-home mom, has been trying to spruce herself up and shed some pounds, at considerable expense; Cairo is full of weight-loss clinics, gyms, and plastic surgery centers ready to nip and tuck bodies into shape—a shape now increasingly modeled on the honed curves of Lebanese bombshells like Haifa Wehbe, a pop singer and Pan-Arab pinup girl. But there's only so much Samar can do with her naturally ample form. If that weren't enough, her husband now complains that she is boring in bed. Samar is not sure what exactly that means; as far as she knows, there's only one position—flat on your back, braced for action. She assumes, or rather hopes, he's drawing his standards from porn DVDs and the Internet, rather than from real-life, real-time experience.

## LAUNCHPAD FOR LIFE

Marriage is the bedrock of Egyptian, and Arab, society, considered the natural and desirable state by more than 90 percent of Egyptians, regardless of age, sex, or education.[7] The drive to wed is, in large part, propelled by family pressure and fueled by religion. The Qur'an is big on matrimony, exhorting believers to tie the knot as quickly and as simply as possible: "Marry off the single among you and those of your male and female slaves who are fit [for marriage]. If they are poor, God will provide for them from His bounty: God's bounty is infinite and He is all knowing."[8] The Prophet too encouraged Muslims to marry: "Whoever marries safeguards half of this faith; let him fear God for the second half" is one of many hadiths on the subject.[9]

That being said, booty, as well as duty, comes into play. In Islam, sex is channeled into regulated structures, one of which is marriage. This connection is enshrined in language. The same word in classical Arabic, *nikah,* applies to both marriage and sexual intercourse; in Egyptian street slang, *niik,* an abbreviated form, means "to fuck." Sex outside these regulated contexts constitute *zina,* that is, illicit relations—an offense that crosses the line of acceptability (*hadd*) in Islam. In shari'a, the penalty for *zina* is death by stoning for married partners and one hundred lashes for the unmarried— provided four eyewitnesses testify or there is an uncoerced confession. And so in Egypt—indeed, across the Arab world—marriage opens the door to a socially sanctioned (and therefore more regular) sexual and reproductive life. It is also the gateway to adulthood and a little more independence from your family. If finances permit, marriage gives you a free pass out of your parents' home, and the green light to set up your own semiautonomous breakaway state.

All of which helps to explain one of the more curious placards held by a young man in Tahrir Square during the uprising of 2011. GO, it ordered President Mubarak, I WANT TO GET MARRIED. Matrimony might seem an odd demand for a revolutionary, but if you understand what has happened to marriage in Egypt over the past few decades, it makes perfect sense.

In my grandparents' day, marriages were by and large arranged by the family, within the family—usually between paternal cousins. Today, however, around half of married Egyptians under the age of thirty say they met their spouses through a friend or relative; for university students and graduates, these sorts of personal networks are now the main way to find a mate.[10] In my own family, for example, my uncle married a cousin, and my father was once engaged to his cousin as well. But in my generation, despite my grandmother's best-laid plans that had all her grandchildren paired off like passengers on the ark, none of us intermarried. Yet tradition still counts for something: around a third of Egyptians under thirty—mainly poor, young, rural, less educated, and from the more conservative south of the country—still marry a relative.[11]

In opinion polls, respectability appears to trump romance when it comes to choosing a mate: in a recent national survey of Egyptian youth under thirty, for example, more than three-quarters of women (and 90 percent of men) cited "polite"—that is, well brought up—as the most important feature in a spouse, with "religious" a close second; "educated" and "love and understanding between husband and wife" came further down the list.[12] But such results require careful reading in Egypt and across the Arab region; depending on the issue at hand, people will often say what they think they should in opinion surveys—especially when it's the government asking the questions—rather than what they actually believe. Anecdotally, there is plenty of evidence to suggest that young women and men, across the region's great divides, are indeed looking for love, among other criteria, when it comes to matrimony.

Getting married in Egypt is like sending a rocket to the moon—there are several stages that have to fall away before you get into orbit. Families are the fuel for liftoff. One friend, a successful businesswoman in Cairo, gave me the lowdown. "If you want to get married, there are certain places to go, and certain routes to take. You wanna make sure this guy is marriage material," she warned. "It has to be through family; so his mom, his aunt, his sister, somebody. His family has to know and your family has to know. This way is formal, like no messing around."

The engagement phase begins when parents publicly acknowledge a relationship and give their blessing to the couple spending time together; in more liberal households, this means time alone as well. Engagement is a flexible arrangement; I know women who have been through multiple fiancés, without turning a hair—family involvement being a necessary, but no longer sufficient, condition to reaching your destination. Mission Marriage moves into higher orbit with *katb al-kitab* (writing the book), the formal Islamic marriage ceremony; this tends to be a small family affair in which the union is officially recorded by a *ma'dhun,* or marriage notary. Finally there is the *farah,* or public wedding celebration. It is considered bad form to consummate a union at any point before the *farah,* though I know plenty of couples who have prematurely fired their boosters after *katb al-kitab.*

Should friends, family, or neighbors fail to produce a marriageable prospect, then it's time to bring in the experts. *Khatba,* professional matchmaker, is a long-established calling in Egypt and the wider Arab world. While less than 1 percent of married Egyptian youth in Egypt say they met their spouses through paid intermediaries, you wouldn't know it from a visit to an "office for the facilitation of matrimony," or a marriage bureau, in downtown Cairo.[13] Under a photo of the Ka'ba,* a large table held hundreds of photos of men and women, some smiling, some serious, attached to papers scrawled with personal details. "In an average day I see forty cases, equally males and females, all over the age spectrum, from eighteen to seventy," said Amr Abdel Megeid, a cheerful man in his forties, as he pointed to the mountain of applications beside him.

Abdel Megeid set up his matchmaking business in the early 1990s. He takes a dim view of newfangled approaches like online matchmaking. "The Internet is full of irregularity," he sniffed. "On the Net, you can get temporary relations, but if you are serious, you come to us." For a modest joining fee (and escalating payments as matches progress toward matrimony), applicants can fill out a form with their details and what they're looking for in a prospective spouse, and then Abdel Megeid and his colleagues set to work. "We have the specifications in the files, and I match them from my experience, according to age, occupation, and other factors," he explained, taking into account that women in Egypt tend to marry up in terms of education, wealth, and age. In the getting-to-know-you phase, meetings are under the bureau's watchful eye; while women usually come with a relative, men tend to turn up alone, reflecting their greater personal ambit.[14] "After introductions, we are still involved to stop men taking advantage. If we have suspicion, we kick them out," he said.

Social change in Egypt is good for business, according Abdel Megeid. He's well-placed to know; with a university degree in sociology, he sees matchmaking as part of the big picture, filling in gaps

---

*The black cubic structure at the center of Masjid al-Haram, the great mosque in Mecca, and Islam's holiest site, around which Muslims walk seven times as part of the ritual of pilgrimage.

that have opened as the connective tissue between individuals and the state has broken down. "One of the biggest problems in Egypt," he said, "has been the gulf separating the ruling system and the people. There are no lines of communication between them. The decisions to deal with people's problems are taken in a vacuum. The communication roads are all blocked, except when you can get to the rulers through intermediaries." He sees this gap in politics reflected in private life: "The blocked lines of communication lead to a lot of problems. For example, you could depend on your friends for help [in the old days]. Now everybody has his own problems and does not have time to help you. The relationships are all governed by self-interest. This leads to a vicious circle of deterioration."

Abdel Megeid's marriage bureau is benefiting from a widespread anxiety, in Egypt and across the Arab world, over the decline and fall of matrimony. In Egypt, government announcements on the number of unmarried people over thirty (more than one million, according to the 2006 census) stoke frantic talk about erosion of family values.[15] Dig a little deeper into the statistics, however, and the panic finds some relief: marriage rates, which fell by a third from the early 1950s to the mid-2000s, have climbed back in recent years, and the vast majority of Egyptians are married—around 90 percent by the age of thirty-five.[16]

It's not so much that people aren't marrying as that they are marrying later. The average age at marriage in Egypt stands at around twenty-nine for men and twenty-four for women, three years later than what is considered optimal by young people themselves.[17] These delays in marriage—dubbed "waithood" by one expert—are now seen in many countries in the region.[18] The extreme example is Tunisia, where the median age has crept up over the past twenty years, to early thirties for men and late twenties for women.[19]

Today's delays in marriage are a distinct shift, in Egypt as in most of the region, from a tradition of near-universal teenage marriage for women. My own grandmother was considered well past her nubile prime, and lucky to have married my grandfather, at the age of eighteen; two of my aunts married at sixteen, but their daughters and granddaughters, who are working university graduates, married in their early or middle twenties. National statistics reflect this trend: today roughly a quarter of young Egyptian wives are married by eighteen, compared with around a third in their mothers' generation.[20]

In many quarters, satisfaction at the decline of early marriage—good for women's empowerment, as well as a brake on population growth—has been replaced by rising moral alarm. Premarital relations are not such a pressing issue if most young women are married a few years out of puberty (and young men by their midtwenties). Moreover, for women in Egypt and its Arab neighbors, having a husband is key: a woman's social value is still tied to her status as a wife and mother, no matter how accomplished or professionally successful she might be. In recent years, the phenomenon of 'unusa—spinsterhood—has become the stuff of Facebook groups, blogs, best-selling books, and TV series. As they say in Egypt, "The shade of a man is better than the shade of a wall."

Ask Egyptian men why they are waiting to get married and they have a ready answer. "The problem now is that the society is very materialistic," says Abdel Megeid. "Money comes first; we lost our old principles." Aspiring grooms and newlywed husbands are a little more blunt in their assessment. "The families of the ladies are so stupid," one recent university graduate told me, himself just married. "They ask for too much—for shabka [jewelry], the golden things, the diamond solitaire, stuff like this. Plus an apartment, plus the guy has to get all the home appliances, plus the mu'akhkhar (if they get divorced he has to write on the contract that he's going to pay this amount) plus the mahr [money given by the groom to the bride], plus, plus, plus, plus, plus," he said, taking me through the conventional checklist of items expected of the groom in order to get the go-ahead from his intended's family.

This is not the first time, however, that Egypt has been in a flap over marriage and blamed it on economics. In the early decades of the twentieth century, middle-class men were also complaining about their inability to marry—too little income, too much unemployment, too many demands from brides' families. A newspaper of the day opined: "It is indisputable that the vast majority of young men are poor. Before they can think of marriage, they must think of making a living. If that is impossible then they are forced to neglect marriage."[21] Such grievances are strikingly similar to today's complaints, and were similarly bound up in broader concerns about economic policies, moral values, consumerism, and Westernization.

Like their great-grandfathers, today's grooms bear the brunt of matrimonial costs. The financial responsibility of men within marriage is enshrined in Islam: "Husbands should take good care of their wives, with [the bounties] God has given to some more than others and with what they spend out of their own money."[22] More recently, this balance of payments has redistributed slightly: for couples under thirty, the groom and his family are picking up just under 60 percent of the costs, with the bride's family covering the rest; brides themselves chip in around 5 percent of the total outlay—no surprise (tradition aside) given how few young women have regular employment.[23]

Expectations have puffed up over the years. Those critical of today's matrimonial excess often cite a hadith in which the Prophet encouraged a poor man to marry even though the only *mahr* he could offer his prospective bride was to teach her the chapters of the Qur'an he had learned by heart.[24] When my parents married in the 1960s, my father brought a refrigerator and a set of cutlery to the union; their *mahr* was twenty-five piastres (roughly five cents now), which my mother carries with her to this day. But those were the lean years of Nasser's regime; today a fridge and a fork no longer cut it when it comes to matrimony. The average cost of marriage in Egypt—excluding housing—ranges from around EGP 20,000 (just over USD 3,300) in the poorest families to just under EGP 60,000 in the wealthiest echelons of society.[25] All in all, this is an enormous investment; according to one analysis, it would take the poorest cohort of men and their families a scripturally significant seven years to save enough to marry.[26]

Egyptians under thirty say the biggest hurdles to tying the knot are the cost of housing, furnishings and finding a job to pay for all of it. When asked the best way to overcome these barriers, more than half looked to the government to step up—or step down, in the case of the protester in Tahrir Square with his pro-marriage placard.[27] Various schemes have been tried in Egypt and across the region—some government funded, others charitable concerns—to ease people into matrimony, a policy favored by the Muslim Brotherhood and like-minded groups. These include subsidized group weddings, which are arguably more popular with journalists looking for a colorful story than with brides looking forward to their big day.[28]

Few governments, however, have mounted quite as concerted an assault on singletons as those in the Gulf. The United Arab Emirates Marriage Fund, for example, provides grants of AED 70,000 (USD 19,000) to low-income grooms (those earning less than AED 19,000 a month).[29] To appreciate how much—or rather, how little—this will buy a groom, I took a trip to a bride show in Abu Dhabi. The event assembles hundreds of exhibitors, from wedding dress designers and jewelers to chocolatiers and makeup artists, under one football-stadium-size roof. My curiosity was as much personal as professional. I too was planning a wedding—my own, in fact. My fiancé and I had settled on a simple affair, with fewer than a hundred guests, and I was keen to see how my own modest arrangements stacked up against local celebrations. At the show, I quickly ran into Salwa and Annous, two sisters in their twenties from Abu Dhabi. Annous was getting married in a couple of months, and they were busy selecting photographers and checking out designer abayas, blithely unaware of how much the wedding might cost.

One group that knows the numbers by heart is Carnation, a Dubai-based events organizer. Business is booming across the UAE, in the "season," which runs October to April. The cost of a wedding can easily run into millions of dirhams—and that's just for the venue, food, entertainment, and decorations. Weddings of the ruling families of the emirates can cost tens of millions of dirhams and have thousands of guests—which some young Emiratis complain is setting an impossibly high standard and ramping up expectations among brides and their families.[30]

Even less exalted weddings are big productions in the Gulf region; five hundred guests is a discreet event in Carnation's books—mine barely registered on their scale. In the UAE, these guests, and those costs, are spread over two separate parties. Weddings in Egypt (and much of the rest of the Arab world, for that matter) are now largely mixed occasions, where men and women mingle over dinner and dancing. Not so in the Gulf, where the tradition of separate male and female parties—which was common in Egypt in my grandparents' day—continues. Wedding planners described the men's celebration as a relatively low-key event, with a simple dinner and some local music; by midnight, the party is essentially over. The women's gathering, however, is a much longer and more lavish affair, with an elaborate dinner, a lineup of singers that can include famous names flown in from the entertainment centers of Cairo and Beirut, and blinding quantities of bling. At the bride show, wedding organizers were strutting their stuff with full-scale mock-ups of wedding decor in what can best be described as the bordello school of interior design: enough gold, gilt, crystal, velvet, jewels, feathers, flowers, beads, lace, and satin to bring on an attack of luxury-induced Stendhal syndrome.

By comparison, Carnation's display was positively restrained. Osama Mistal, a company manager, and I sat on a vast white quilted leather sofa, fur rugs at our feet, bathed in a soft pink glow, looking down a catwalk where, on the night of the wedding, the bride would parade after making a dramatic late entrance. Her dress is obviously a star attraction, and from the gowns doing a brisk trade at the show (AED 35,000 on up), opulence-meets-decadence was very much the fashion: bare shoulders, plunging necklines, and open backs. Female guests, particularly the more nubile among them, are also dressed to kill, revealing their assets in what is essentially a showroom for future brides, giving prospective mothers-in-law at the party a good look at what they might snag for their sons. Around midnight, the groom and his close male relatives turn up briefly on the women's side. The women then party on after the couple has disappeared to a local hotel before jetting off to some distant destination. (In a slick yet slightly optimistic exhibit, South Korea was marketing itself at the show as a honeymoon hotspot.)

As Mistal explained, it's not just the wedding that is breaking the bank for men these days: "There is gold, the dress, the house, the furniture, gift items to the bride during the engagement like perfume, watches, clothes . . . so many ways to spend money." The Gulf states have opened themselves to the full force of global capitalism, so it's no surprise that status should now be tied to possessions, and that weddings have become a celebration of conspicuous consumption. "Where you [in the West] were, is where we are now," Mistal observed. "Before twenty years [ago], children, what they need? They go to school and come back. Now they need separate room, and laptop and games, the mobile. There are so many requests. So everything becomes more and more and more."

Forty years ago, before the UAE and other countries in the Gulf began to ride a fossil-fuel wave of prosperity, today's lavish outlays were out of reach for most families. The mothers and grandmothers of today's brides remember their own simpler weddings, in which finding enough food and feeding the poorer members of the tribe were the primary concerns.[31] Some of those traditions live on in today's weddings, with a global gloss that makes them more expensive than ever. Weddings may have moved from desert encampments to five-star hotels, for example, but camel is still on the menu, only now you need a whole caravan for a legion of guests.

But it's in the brides themselves that this mixture of old and new is most pronounced. Annous is a good example. She's marrying at twenty-two and has finished university—a rarity in earlier generations, who married in their teens and were mothers, often several times over, by her age. Today, however, women vastly outnumber men in higher education in the UAE and are increasingly carving space for themselves in the workplace.[32] Annous speaks excellent English, is widely traveled, and is up-to-date with the latest movies and fashion in the Gulf and the West. Yet her father chose her bridegroom, a distant relative whom she has met only once; her recently married older sister saw her husband for the first time at their own wedding. This is not unusual in the UAE. Research shows that arranged marriages, usually to first cousins, remain the norm there, where the financial and social benefits of keeping it all in the family are seen to outweigh the well-known medical risks to children of such consanguineous unions.[33]

Annous prefers to rely on her father's judgment in choosing a husband, though she is aware of how couples meet and mate in the West. I asked if she wouldn't prefer to have a "love story"— Egyptian shorthand for an unarranged marriage. "If he is from the family, you feel it's okay," she said. "If they get married from love, they divorce. We know some women, they get married by love story; even if they continue [in the marriage], it's all problems in our culture. If it's a relative, it's better."

Even so, brides today are a lot pickier than they used to be. In Islam, a woman has the right to refuse a prospective husband, although in practice plenty lack the opportunity to exercise it. Salwa, however, belongs to a new generation that is flexing its muscle on this point. She has turned down a number of offers because she's waiting for the right man: moral, respectable, hardworking, polite, and definitely not married to another woman. I know some young career women in the Gulf who choose to become a second wife, which gives them the perks of marriage and motherhood as well as time for a career, while leaving the full-time occupation of cooking, cleaning, and otherwise maintaining a husband to wife number one. But Salwa doesn't see it that way, and it's this assertiveness that some think is at the heart of the UAE's marriage problems.

Emiratis are practically an endangered species in their own country; more than 80 percent of the population are foreigners brought in to build the nation. While the planners meant this to be the building of skyscrapers and a diversified economy, it has come to include forming families as well: about a fifth of Emirati men are now married to foreign women, mainly from other Arab countries and Asia.[34] Less than a tenth of Emirati brides take a foreign husband, but that figure is also rising, aided by a recent change in nationality laws that, as in Egypt, allows women to pass citizenship—and all the material benefits that go with it—to their children.

The official discourse blames the phenomenon of foreign marriages on economics: foreign brides don't have status-conscious families breathing down a groom's neck for the wedding of the century and the house of a lifetime.[35] And so marriage has become part of the national push to preserve Emirati identity and to combat perceived family fragmentation. But as Salwa and thousands like her demonstrate, there are clearly other forces at work in the marriage stakes, ones no amount of money will dispel.

Back in Egypt, the uprising saw a number of on-the-spot weddings in Tahrir Square, as couples sought to mark the occasion and show their revolutionary colors by breaking with the excesses of the ancien régime. "This is the new Egypt," one man, insistent on marrying his fiancée the next day, told his prospective in-laws. "We don't need all that stuff," he said, referring to the trappings of marriage. But while Egypt struggles toward what many hope will be a new order, the big wedding is still in fashion, albeit on a less lavish scale. In the short term, this degree of restraint has more to do with economic uncertainty and a reluctance to reveal one's wealth too publicly, out of a newfound fear of being targeted for violent crime in the security vacuum that opened after the uprising, as well as a desire to avoid suspicion of ill-gotten gains through association with the former regime, than it does with any postmaterialist change of heart. There are, of course, couples who want to get off this material merry-go-round altogether, but it is hard to stop the ride. One prospective bride, a middle-class university student in Cairo, listened in awe as I described my own arrangements: my fiancé and I splitting the bill between ourselves; my symbolic twenty-five cent *mahr* and a pair of pearl earrings as *shabka;* newlywed bliss in a tiny rented apartment, with no car, few appliances, and little furniture to our names. "Wow, that's way cool," she said admiringly. "You could never do that in Egypt."

## A SIMPLE AFFAIR

Such is the desire to steer clear of *zina* that, even if a big white wedding is not in the cards, couples will go to considerable lengths to bring their sexual relations into Islamic alignment. In addition to "official" marriage, whose many bells and whistles include government paperwork, there are a number of "unofficial" forms of matrimony permitted in Islam: some are state registered, some not, but they generally check a minimum number of boxes to make them Islamically sound. Just because they are halal, however, doesn't necessarily make these unions socially acceptable.

Arguably the most straightforward of these arrangements is *zawaj mut'a* (pleasure marriage), in which a couple agrees to a time-limited union, ranging from hours to years, with physical intimacy generally part of the package. In *mut'a* marriage, it can be as easy as reciting a few lines to make a contract stick. Nor is divorce necessary, since these unions are on a timer from the start. Women walk away with the money they were given upon marriage. While "temporary" wives are not entitled to inherit from their husbands, children born of the union have, in theory, the same rights as those from an official marriage provided their fathers acknowledge paternity.

*Mut'a* marriage is allowed in Shi'i, but not Sunni Islam. At least not anymore, having been abrogated during the early years of the Islamic empire—a point of considerable debate ever since.[36] Today, *mut'a* marriage is practiced by Shi'i Muslims in their Arab heartlands—Iraq, Lebanon, and Bahrain among them—although reliable statistics on such arrangements are hard to come by.[37] Research shows a variety of motives, among them, young people searching for space to get to know one another and married men and divorced or widowed women—the latter now common in war-ravaged Iraq—looking for sexual gratification with an Islamic cover in economically straitened circumstances. Although religiously accepted, a *mut'a* union does not enjoy the same social prestige as, nor the full legal rights of, official marriage—and is not something a woman with a reputation to keep would likely put on her résumé. This is because *mut'a* marriage is not about settling down and starting a family; it makes no attempt to varnish its sexual purpose.

Even more controversial is Egypt's spin on informal marriage: *zawaj 'urfi,* or customary unions. Over the past few decades, *'urfi* marriage has become a lightning rod for anxieties about sexual morality in particular and social collapse in general. Customary marriages, which are not recorded by the state, used to be the way of much of matrimony in Egypt until the 1930s, when government registration was required. *'Urfi* marriage continued in my father's day, but it was rare, practiced mainly by widows fearful of losing their husbands' pensions on remarrying, actors and artists with a taste for the unconventional, and middle-class men trying to have it all—sleep with their secretaries, salve their consciences, and keep it a secret from their wives.

More recently, however, *'urfi* marriage has trickled down to the youth in Egypt and elsewhere in the Arab region.[38] Just how common it has become is a matter of speculation; no one knows for certain because modern-day *'urfi* marriages tend to be secret, unlike those in my great-grandparents' day. In Egypt, figures attributed to "official sources" range from tens of thousands to hundreds of thousands of such marriages a year. As with anxiety over unmarried women, such numbers fuel public panic but research tells a different story. In a study of more than forty-five hundred Egyptians aged eighteen to thirty, at most 6 percent of university students were estimated to be in such relationships; the real frequency lies somewhere between what young people are willing to admit to and what their elders greatly fear.[39]

"A lot of my friends have *'urfi* marriage," Laila, a soft-spoken undergraduate in media studies at one of Egypt's leading universities, told me. She has firsthand experience: as a teenager, Laila entered into an *'urfi* marriage with a man ten years her senior. They told their friends but kept it from their families. It was a simple pro-

cess: Laila signed a preprinted form that her boyfriend provided—
she has little recollection of what it specified, and in any case, she
didn't keep a copy. Laila's *'urfi* arrangement was positively bureaucratic compared with more exotic forms: "blood marriage," in
which the couple seal their contract with pinpricked fingers, "tat-
too marriage," and other inventive vows.[40]

Official marriage was never going to be an option, Laila said. She
comes from an upper-middle-class family, with educated parents,
and was attending a private foreign-language school when she met
her boyfriend, one of Egypt's millions of drug users. "I knew this
relationship would not continue and my parents will not accept
an addict," she told me. Besides, her boyfriend was keener on *'urfi*
than formal marriage. "He encouraged me because he doesn't want
to feel responsible. In *'urfi* marriage, all the essential things in a
normal marriage are not required of him."

From the beginning, Laila was under no illusions about the
Islamic-acceptability of her arrangement. But that's not why she
did it. "In my religion, I know it's not halal, but it's a sign of commitment," she explained. "It's for the couple. It's a paper that's
worth nothing, but they think it is something that connects them."
She was clear in her mind on this. "I know that my religion does
not accept *'urfi* marriage; I am doing it to make me feel better, but
I know it's not right. In my religion, marriage is about more than
having pleasure. It's a journey in life and it's two persons coming
together. . . . Maybe parents, they want to see a good life for their
kids and that's why they don't accept it."

Laila holds a harder line on *'urfi* marriage than do some of
Egypt's Islamic scholars. The religious permissibility of *'urfi* takes
us back to the heart of what makes a marriage in Islam. The minimal set of requirements depends on whom you ask. Some scholars
argue that an intent to settle down and start a family is key. Others
argue that *ishhar,* or public announcement, is central to making a
marriage Islamically sound; some insist that the consent of a
woman's *wali* (official guardian) is vital. But other scholars maintain that all it takes to make a real marriage in Islam is an offer,
acceptance, *mahr* (which can be as little as the couple agrees—

or none at all, if the bride consents), and two witnesses—a *wali* is not required, provided a woman is mature and knows her own mind.[41]

Aside from religious objections, criticism of *'urfi* marriages in Egypt also centers on their ambiguous legal status. Although they are not officially registered, courts have the power to grant women divorce from *'urfi* marriage so long as they can provide evidence (witnesses or a written contract) that the union existed—a paradoxical situation in which the state is essentially liberating women from something it doesn't recognize in the first place. Women have no rights to financial support during or after *'urfi* marriages, including inheritance, and the children of such marriages can find themselves in an awkward position.[42] As a result, *'urfi* marriages are generally presented as a raw deal for women.

But some women see *'urfi* marriage differently; Suhaila, a widow in her early thirties living in Cairo with a young daughter, is one of them. Suhaila seems to have it all: education, money, looks, and a bright personality. So it's no wonder that one of Azza's brothers, a married man with teenage kids, fell for her at first sight. To pursue their relationship, the couple entered into an *'urfi* marriage, at Suhaila's request. For her, this arrangement offers the benefits of attractive male companionship, as well as the protection of a man about the house, without the material complications of an official marriage.

In Azza's family, her brother's *'urfi* marriage is anything but secret, having had a written contract, a lawyer, and two witnesses. But it's the basis of seemingly endless discussion—or rather, dispute—among family members. Not surprisingly, Azza's official sister-in-law is unhappy with the arrangement, but there's not much she can do when her husband disappears to Suhaila's apartment for much of the week. Most of his brothers and sisters are upset; to them, this is just thinly disguised adultery. And while Suhaila is holding most of the cards in this relationship, she's not revealing her hand: her friends and daughter have been told this marriage is official.

Their union is closer to yet another Islamic spin on matrimony: *zawaj misyar,* or so-called ambulant marriage. These arrangements are creating quite a stir in the Arab region, particularly in Saudi Arabia. They are akin to official marriage in the sense that, in some countries, they are registered with the state with full documentation, as well as witnesses, and the wife and any children resulting from the marriage have the same rights of inheritance as they would in an official marriage. One key difference, however, is that during the union the husband does not necessarily have to financially support his *misyar* wife, who remains at her original home. In Egypt, *misyar* marriage has been endorsed by an edict from Dar al-Ifta, the government body that issues fatwas—that is, legal opinions from Islamic authorities—to the dismay of women's rights groups, who consider it a lesser form of marriage that gives women few entitlements.[43]

At the end of the day, debates over informal marriage, in its evolving forms, are not really about haram or halal, or even legal rights. Informal marriages, particularly among young people, are widely seen as both a symptom and a cause of family breakdown. Because they usually take place without parental knowledge, let alone consent, they subvert social convention and circumvent family control. Therein lies a large part of the problem, because they challenge patriarchal authority—troubling to the family and, by extension, to the state as well. Some describe *'urfi* marriage as an innovative middle ground between the perceived sexual laxity of the West and traditional Islamic codes, offering women more latitude than conventional matrimony. But the majority of people appear—at least in public—to be less enthusiastic about alternative unions: in a national survey of Egyptian youth, for example, fewer than 10 percent of men and women under thirty thought *'urfi* a solution to Egypt's marriage problems.[44] Most people I know in such marriages regard them, at best, as a temporary fix until they can get the real thing; the day has not yet dawned when informal marriage is widely considered a lifestyle choice rather than a last resort.

## PILLOW TALK

For all the effort Egyptians make to get married, all is not well in the conjugal bed. The pressure-cooker atmosphere of recent years—which blew in the protests of 2011—continues to build in married life. For Azza and her circle, this means less-than-steamy relations; what research there is on the sex lives of Egyptian couples and their counterparts across the region shows she and her friends are not alone.[45]

Lackluster lovemaking is positively un-Islamic. There are plenty of stories about the sayings and doings of the Prophet Muhammad that extol the pleasures of sex for husbands and wives. "Let none of you come upon his wife like an animal, and let there be an emissary between them," the Prophet is reported to have said. "What is this emissary, O Messenger of God?" a clueless believer asked. "The kiss and [sweet] words," he replied.[46] According to another account, the Prophet ranked peremptory foreplay and failure to sexually satisfy one's partner among serious male deficiencies. Indeed, the Prophet's regular advice on the nitty-gritty of sexual life featured prominently in medieval Christian attacks on the new faith, whose unabashed sensuality was seen as a cunning ploy to win converts and undermine Christianity's more austere official line, which exalted virginity, chastity, and monogamy. "It is impossible that he who excites his people to sensual things rather than to spiritual ones would be a true messenger of God," sniffed a thirteenth-century Spanish philosopher.[47]

One woman out to breathe that pioneering spirit back into marital relations is Heba Kotb, the Arab world's best-known sex therapist. "You have just one life. We don't have a lot of time in this world. And we practice sex, so let's practice it in a good way," she enthused. "Let's transform it into the dynamo of our life and our happiness." Kotb and I first met at her clinic in a trendy part of Cairo. "For now, I'm booked three months in advance. Daily, I see between ten and twenty [patients]. In the summer [when Egyptians living abroad, and Arabs from elsewhere in the region, visit Cairo], it's usually a mess," she told me. Her Egyptian patients come from all classes, locations, and age groups; although women are traditionally expected to head into sexual hibernation at meno-pause (*sinn al-ya's* in Arabic, "age of despair"), Kotb's clientele also includes a sprinkling of those well past retirement.

Patients were not always as forthcoming. When Kotb first set up shop in 2001, the few people bold enough to seek help were wary about putting in an appearance. "In the very first days of my practice, privacy was very important to them. The man would ask whether he would be seen in my office or not [and], if there's another patient on the day, whether there would be a space so that they would not overlap. It was a very sensitive issue," she recalled. "For now, no. They are waiting outside, ten to fifteen patients at the same time, and they have no problem to be seen by each other. Things change."

This change is in part due to Kotb herself. In 2006, she burst into Arab households with *Kalam Kabiir* (*Big Talk*), a weekly TV series on sexual problems broadcast by one of Egypt's private sat-ellite channels. The show's dozen or so episodes openly ventured into areas where other presenters had feared to tread—online porn, oral sex, and wedding night jitters, among them. For just under an hour, a soberly suited Kotb, her hair and neck fully covered by a hijab, dispensed advice on various topics, her lengthy monologues relieved by the occasional guest expert and an imam giving an Islamic take on the issue at hand, be it masturbation or voyeurism.

Kotb's show mirrored her experience with patients. Back at the clinic, it's clear that the region's sexual dynamo is out of order. "Husbands and wives, they don't know they should communicate about what they want sexually. They don't know that sexuality is something we can discuss," she observed. "They are full of the idea that this is an instinct. It's an instinct only in animals, but we as people—praise be to God almighty—we need to communicate."

Kotb described a typical consultation to me: "It's a nice couple. They want the wife to be happier, [so] they come together. He says she is not interested in sex—she's not spontaneous. Then they get into mutual accusations. [She says] all he wants is his pleasure and it's over in five minutes—he's selfish." Kotb spends a lot of time getting couples back to basics. "I teach them techniques, Masters and Johnson, Kinsey. Using pictures in a book or on the computer, I am showing them: here is something called the clitoris, here is the labia, try . . . this is sensitive to this and that . . . friction transverse, longitudinally, circular, et cetera." Over the course of half a dozen sessions, Kotb encourages couples to explore their bodies. "Sometimes I give them exercises: go and get to know yourself and each other. Then come back and tell me. If they tell me it looks like this, I know they went and did it, they are not lying." It's not just anatomy and physiology on the syllabus; Kotb spends a lot of time with her clients working on psychology as well—getting men to understand the fine art of wooing their wives in and out of bed.

As for women, some cases require overtime. In her practice, Kotb sees a lot of vaginismus—three or four patients a day with a condition that makes them seize up during intercourse, rendering penetration painful if not impossible. There is plenty of research from Egypt to show that female sexual dysfunction is a common enough condition. One study of almost a thousand married women—mainly high-school-educated housewives—in a region north of Cairo found that nearly 70 percent had some sort of sexual dysfunction; of those, around half reported low desire and difficulties reaching orgasm, and roughly a third said they had trouble with arousal or pain on intercourse.[48] A comparable study of women in southern Egypt found equally high rates of sexual dysfunction: over half of the women surveyed said they were sexually dissatisfied.[49] But one woman's disappointment can be another's fulfillment. Other research in Egypt has shown that for some women, the fact that their husbands are enjoying themselves in bed is how they define their own sexual pleasure—for them, having their own orgasm simply doesn't enter into the equation.[50]

Kotb, however, has noticed a change in the women turning up at her clinic over the years. Earlier it was mainly husbands dragging in their wives for consultation; after the uprising, she found the situation reversed. "Women are more courageous now to accuse their husbands of not being good [in bed]. It is the spirit of the revolution—I have to reject, I have to refuse, I have to say no [I am not the one to blame]," she told me. "Today I had a couple, he is not asking her for sex, only once a month. When he approaches, sometimes he loses his erection, so she is starting to talk: 'I don't accept this relation. We are like brother and sister living together here, and you have to do something about yourself.'"

Kotb's advice to couples is shaped by her faith. "I love Islam," she told me. "I admire the religion. In radical Christianity, sex is not a good thing, even within marriage. But this is not logic; people find themselves desiring something, and they couldn't get attached to that religion, so they start to get out of that religion. In Islam, it's the contrary: sex is something that is advised, that is pushed to[ward]. . . . This makes people more religious and more loving to this religion, which is giving them all this space, which is giving them all this pleasure—and also the reward in this life and the hereafter."

Kotb is in her forties; like many Egyptians of her generation, she became interested in Islam at university. "I started to be religious not very early in my life. I was brought up in a very liberal house; I was wearing a swimsuit until after I got married." Her husband, whom she met at medical school, came from an even less observant background, but together, she said, "we decided to make ourselves and our future families better than our older families, so we started to read about religion, to study Qur'an, to get it by heart." It was around this time that Kotb decided to put on hijab, much to her parents' dismay—at the time, headscarves were something for servants, not aspiring surgeons.

Her career in sexology came later. An early opportunity passed her by when the only class on the subject in her entire course of studies at Cairo University Medical School was canceled because of freak bad weather. But a second chance appeared unexpectedly, after graduation. As a working mother, Kotb decided to forgo a career in surgery for something less time intensive: forensic medicine. She began working on the sexual abuse of children—both victims and perpetrators—and it was through this that she developed her interest in sexuality. In the course of her research on sexual abuse, Kotb became one of Egypt's first sex surfers. "I started reading about sexuality," she recalled, "getting some books from abroad. Then the Internet was extremely fresh; it was [newly] wrapped. It was very hard to get a free line on the Internet, but my mother-in-law knew someone in the army, so I was going to a forbidden [classified] area to get onto the Net to get information about sexuality." A doctorate from the United States on sexuality in Islam topped off her training, and in Cairo she began to build her patient roster, which now extends to several Gulf states, and a following among Muslims in Canada as well.

Kotb is obviously an inspiration to some; I've seen strangers come up to her in public to thank her for her show. How many of these fans are actually following her advice is another matter; many of the women I've asked have the same relationship to Kotb's programs that I do to cooking shows—interesting in theory, but not something we could ever do in practice. "I like Heba Kotb," one married woman in her early twenties in a working-class neighborhood of Cairo told me, "because she explains everything in a modest and useful way. I watch it always, but my mother does not like her. I heard from her [Kotb] that I need to ask for my sexual rights. But I cannot apply that because my husband will not agree or will feel that I am rude."

To be sure, Kotb's advice seems daring to many by today's standards. Given recent fatwas forbidding oral sex or nudity between the conjugal sheets, her suggestions on how to spice up spousal relations have earned her conservative opponents. But on closer inspection, Kotb is hardly a radical—something that puts her in the crosshairs of other, more liberal sexologists across the region. She is, for example, an implacable opponent of premarital sex, on psychosexual as well as religious grounds. And for all her talk of women exerting their God-given sexual rights, it's still men first in Kotb's book. "For wives, I want to say that a man's sexual needs are different than a woman's. Instead of being a passive recipient of sex, try to be an active partner," she advised. "He is exposed to many temptations outside the home. Be available to please him and do not give him a reason to make a choice between you and hellfire."[51]

The advice of Kotb and other Islamically inflected sex therapists pales in comparison with the full-blooded approach of the past. Take, for example, the *Encyclopedia of Pleasure*. We know little about its author, 'Ali ibn Nasr al-Katib, other than where and when he wrote: Baghdad in the late tenth or early eleventh century. That's a pity, because he sounds like just the sort of man I'd like to meet.

The *Encyclopedia* is truly breathtaking. Short of cybersex and porn videos, its forty-three chapters cover every conceivable sexual practice: heterosexual, homosexual (male and female), bisexual, animal, vegetable, and mineral—you name it, it's all there. Section titles "On the Kinds and Techniques of Coition," "On Jealousy," "On the Advantages of a Nonvirgin over a Virgin," "On Increasing the Sexual Pleasure of Man and Woman," and "Description of the Nasty Way of Doing It and Lewd Sex" give you some idea of its vast scope. 'Ali ibn Nasr's message is clear: sex is God's gift to mankind and we are meant to enjoy it. While the book's intent is serious, its style is not only arousing but very often hilarious. I attracted plenty of dirty looks from fellow readers in the rare book room of one London library as I squirmed and guffawed my way through stories like this:

> Hubba al Madaniyyah, for instance, said that one day she went out of the bath accompanied by a boy who had a puppy. It so happened that the puppy, seeing her vulva and vaginal lips, went between her legs and began to lick her organ. She lowered her body to give the animal a better chance of performing its job. However, when she had reached an orgasm, she fell down heavily upon it and could not raise herself until the helpless animal had died from heavy pressure.[52]

Much of the *Encyclopedia* is drawn from earlier writers, Arab and foreign, and it includes a liberal sprinkling of advice from female authorities.[53] The *Encyclopedia* is full of women—concubines, slave girls, prostitutes and wives—with full-throttle sex drives. The sexual insatiability of women was a well-established theme long before 'Ali ibn Nasr came on the scene. The Qur'an tells the story of the wife of a Pharaonic court official, better known as Zuleika, who attempted to seduce the prophet Joseph, then a young and handsome slave. When he refused her advances, she claimed that he was the seducer, but her lie was exposed when people noticed that his shirt was torn from the back, proving that he had been fleeing her, not the other way around.[54]

Rather than try to curb female sexual drive, however, the *Encyclopedia* goes to great lengths to advise readers on how to fulfill it. It begins with unabashed romance—love letters "full of sweet words, nice poems," not to mention patience, kindness, and tact, as well as the occasional gift. The book shows considerable insight into female character, offering the following counsel to bewildered lovers:

> It should also be known that it is in a woman's nature to get angry with a man without any reason whatsoever. When she does, the man should put up with her because she will return to her normal condition of her own accord. Moreover, a woman is of such a nature that she may be under the delusion that a man is guilty and so establishes his guilt without investigation. When the woman gets angry and treats the man unkindly as a result of her delusion, he should be wise enough to put up with her and not take her delusion seriously.[55]

The *Encyclopedia* also shows a fine appreciation of female physiology, giving detailed classifications of women's libidos and types of orgasms. The ultimate prize, according to its author, is simultaneous orgasm, which will guarantee "everlasting" love, or so he assures readers, and the book is full of handy hints on how to reach this goal. French-kissing and cunnilingus are also on the to-do list, and as if this weren't female-friendly enough, further recommendations include plenty of postcoital conversation and cuddling—the sign of civilized lovemaking, he says.

It is tempting to contrast Azza and her peers, with their sexual hang-ups, to the freewheeling, fun-loving women of the *Encyclopedia*. It is, however, important to remember that this is not some medieval Masters and Johnson; 'Ali ibn Nasr is telling tales, not taking a compass to female sexual response. His stories may be exaggerated, or even fabricated, but that's not the point. What's remarkable about his work, seen through twenty-first-century eyes, is not whether women actually behaved in this way in the eleventh century, but the fact that it was considered desirable that they should express their sexuality—at least in private—and that it was socially acceptable to write about it in such a free, frank, and detailed fashion.

## SCENES OF A SEXUAL NATURE

This spirit lives on, at least in fiction. Some of the most sexually expressive writing in the Arab world these days is not just about women but by them as well. Across the region, female writers have been letting loose on paper for decades: Nawal El Saadawi, the famous Egyptian feminist now in her eighties and her literary daughters, novelists Hanan al-Shaykh from Lebanon and Ghada Samman from Syria, as well as younger women like Samar al-Muqrin, a Saudi writer, and Mona Prince, an Egyptian novelist, are just a few of those tackling both the pains and the pleasures of female sexuality.[56]

When it comes to pushing the boundaries of sexual expression, few revel in it as publicly as Joumana Haddad, a Beirut-based poet and writer, newspaper editor, and publisher. "When I'm excited, whether physically or intellectually, I always say I have an erection," she told me matter-of-factly as we sat in her office at *An-Nahar,* one of Lebanon's leading newspapers. "Writing is an orgasmic act of ejaculation. Although I have a female body, and I like it, I also have a lot of masculinity in me. And I also love it. We are all hybrids, a mixture of genders and races and nationalities and lands, it is too limiting and narrow-minded to stick to just one category."

If you were to breathe life into an Arab man's wildest dreams, and deepest fears, about female sexuality, you'd end up with something very close to Haddad. Physically, she's the epitome of desirability through the ages: flashing black eyes, flowing locks, and promising curves. 'Umar Muhammad al-Nafzawi, the fifteenth-century Tunisian author of *The Perfumed Garden,* one of the best-known books of Arabic erotica, neatly summed up her appeal: "When she comes towards you, you are fascinated, when she walks away, she murders you [with desire]."[57] Mind you, al-Nafzawi also thought the ideal woman should keep quiet, stay at home, and live for her husband as "her sole reliance," a lingering stereotype Haddad rails against in her autobiography, subtitled *Confessions of an Angry Arab Woman.*

Al-Nafzawi's belief in women's powerful sexual drive is closer to the mark when it comes to Haddad. "It's the way I conceive of the world, through sexuality," says Haddad. "Even when I write, I always say I write with my body, with my fingernails. I'm not a sensual person; I'm a sexual person," she explained. Haddad's half a dozen books of Arabic poetry ooze this essence. Take *Lilith's Return,* for example, a work that invokes the legendary first wife of Adam, famous for her ego and libido. Lilith and Haddad were made for each other, and the resulting verse is full-frontal: "From the flute of my two thighs my song rises. / Rivers stream out of my lust. / Why would the tide not rise high / when a smile glitters between my vertical lips?"[58]

Haddad wrote her first poem at eleven, and sexuality has been a long-running theme. "I have always been what you would call, whether sympathetically or disapprovingly, a 'bad girl,' " she wrote in her autobiography. "I used to think that only two things were worth doing whenever I had the chance of being alone: reading and masturbating."[59] The first, at any rate, she indulged with ado-lescent expeditions into the far reaches of her family's bookcase. "I was brought up in a conservative family," she told me. "My father, who was a great intellectual but very traditional, used to hide all these dangerous books on the upper shelves. I always used to wait for them to go out, and I put a chair and I climbed, because that's where all the interesting things are. I wanted to see *Histoire d'O, Emmanuelle,* Marquis de Sade, Henry Miller."

For a long time, Haddad felt more comfortable reading, and writ-ing, about these subjects in French or English. She only came to them in Arabic in her twenties. It's a familiar story among writers, academics, and activists, as Haddad explains: "There are things we can say in English or in French that if we hear them in Arabic, we go [gasp]. But there is this distance that the other language allows you, and it's an escape. And I don't want to escape; I want to face these words and confront them."

Haddad took a very public stand in 2008 with the launch of *Jasad.* It's a glossy quarterly magazine devoted to exactly what it says on the cover—*jasad* means "body" in Arabic. Its combination of essays, reportage, reviews, and art is not all about sex; topics ranging from addiction to tattoos also get a look. But sex forms a big part, from the logo, with its dangling handcuff, to the content: early issues included a special section on the penis, an essay in praise of masturbation, a dossier on sexual violence, and a gallery of sexually explicit artwork. Coverage is both regional ("Insight into Incest Cases in Syria") and international ("This Is How They Fuck in China"). And there are regular columns—"My First Time" and "His Body, Her Body"—in which Arab writers bare all.

The women who contribute to *Jasad* are as outspoken as their male counterparts. "No, it's definitely not easy to be a woman who writes without compromise in an Arab country," Haddad noted. "And this is why every woman writer is swamped by a slew of patriarchal accusations. How many times, for example, have steamy sex scenes in a novel penned by a woman become an excuse for denigration and rumour about that woman writer's sexual life and adventures?"[60] She sees women speaking out on sex as an essential step toward their intellectual emancipation. "It might seem that I am putting subversive/erotic literature above all other genres, and that is definitely not my aim," she points out. "But a woman writing erotic/explicit literature in the Arab world is claiming freedom as a vital necessity, as opposed to many Arabs who view it as a luxury."[61]

The public response to *Jasad,* and to Haddad, has been mixed. Social conservatives condemn her assault on conventional moral-ity, while sexual rights advocates lambast her as a skin-deep radical who makes a big deal about her sexual defiance but whose challenges to social strictures are superficial and, coming as they do from one of the elite, do not reflect the restrictions facing the vast majority of women. For her part, Haddad criticizes those who "are zealous to preserve the hymens of the eye, the nose, the ear, the throat, of language, of the imagination and of dreams, and of anything else they can dream up to protect."[62] Yet *Jasad* is not censored in Lebanon and is widely distributed across Beirut, albeit wrapped in plastic and slapped with an ADULTS ONLY sticker; elsewhere in the region, circulation is by subscription only.

"I'm receiving lots of insults, threats, and stuff like that: I'm corrupting new generations; these are not our values; I'm importing values of the West and the East; God will punish you—you know, the usual stuff," she says. The threats are financial as well as physical: advertisers shy away from *Jasad*—something that baffles Haddad, given how well sex sells elsewhere in Lebanon, and makes publishing a struggle. Nonetheless, *Jasad* also has fans. "I have folders in all my e-mail accounts called '*Jasad* Congrats' and '*Jasad* Insults,'" Haddad told me. "And I can tell you that the '*Jasad* Congrats' is a lot bigger than the '*Jasad* Insults.'"

Haddad is an unusual woman when it comes to sex, in that she openly says what she does, and vice versa. And this despite conservative roots. "I've been brought up in a Catholic school: you have sex just to have babies and that's it. I should have had a whole country by now." She laughs. She married twice, the first time when she was nineteen—her route to independence, she says. She had a relationship with the man who was to become her second husband before she was quite through with the first. "So I'd been living in 'sin' even before I got divorced. And even after I got divorced, I've been traveling everywhere with him, going to parties with him, socializing together like a couple. All people knew we were lovers. I loved it. We got married on a technicality." Not surprisingly, her marriage is a little unusual. "We decided not to live together. We are both free-spirited. When I say this, people look at me as if I am coming from Mars. What kills a relationship is not only the decayed institution of marriage, but living together, the lack of breathing space, confusing love with ownership."

Haddad takes an equally unconventional approach with her two sons, from her first marriage. She encourages her kids to pick up *Jasad,* although to her regret, they are not big readers. "Sometimes I think I should have hidden some books on the top shelves and told them, 'Don't go there,'" she says. But unlike her own parents, who preferred silence on the subject of sex, she has made a point of talking it through with her boys.[63] I can't think of many mothers in the Arab region who would feel comfortable advising their sons on safe sex, but it's no big deal for Haddad. "And now I am insisting on condoms and safety awareness," she added, recalling one mother-son chat. "He was so alert and informed. 'Don't worry, Mum, I'm going to put on five, one after another!'"

Although Haddad is bending some boundaries in her personal and professional lives, the big picture is unchanged. *Jasad,* her poetry, and her translations of foreign erotica are opening a sliver of space for sexual expression—but that's still largely on paper and mainly for a cultured elite; so few people in the Arab world read novels or poetry these days that censors are not as concerned with sexual content in print as they are with it on-screen or even on canvas. Haddad's goal is not wholesale social reform, but to rehabilitate Arabic language and literature. "If you go back to the tenth and eleventh centuries, you would find wonderful texts in Arabic, even obscene. And that talked about the body in such a wonderful way. And then something happened; there is a missing link. Starting in the seventeenth and eighteenth centuries, we started going backward, with a few ups and downs," she lamented. "How did we get from that early high point of liberty, of talking about sex so naturally, to our constipated present-day reality? I wonder." Haddad often asks herself: "When did we start sliding down the hill of taboos?"[64]

## GOING DOWN

It was somewhere on this downward slope that I came to be explaining the finer points of clitoral vibrators to Azza and her sisters. If you know only Arabic, don't have the money to consult a specialist, and lack easy access to the Internet, your options for explicit advice on sexual matters are limited—all the more so if you're a woman. Unlike Haddad and her feisty literary sisters, Azza and her circle were at a loss. In their desperation for details, they turned to me for help. "*Ya* Shereen, they have so many problems," Azza said. "They are not satisfied with their husbands, but they don't know what to do." I thought toys might add some fun, even though some sex therapists are firmly against them. "I don't recommend them for Middle Eastern people," Kotb warned me. "They would be attached to toys and just let down their wife, and the other way around. If I had toys in my own office, I would be a millionaire. I am always for sex with Islam; in the days of the Prophet Muhammad, people were the happiest, over their history, sexually. And there were no toys." Interestingly, sex toys do not feature prominently in the long history of Arabic erotic writing, for all their treatment of almost every other sexual practice under the sun.[65]

Just finding suitable toys turned out to be a task in itself. Although there are a couple of shops in Cairo that discreetly sell a few items, supply is sporadic; one shop owner described to me the customs gauntlet he has to run to bring back, tucked away in his suitcase from overseas trips, even the few subtle vibrators he has in stock. In any case, Azza would rather die than be caught buying this stuff in public, so I asked her and her sisters to look on the Web and give me a list of items I could pick up on my next trip abroad. They struggled with the assignment. Part of the problem was timing, as Ramadan had begun and they were reluctant to delve into such worldly matters, given the prohibition on sexual intercourse during the hours of fasting.[66] The bigger obstacle, however, was their complete confusion at the online world of adult entertainment. For all Azza's near-perfect English and the lavish product illustrations, they simply could not make sense of a "buzzing clit bunny with twirling shaft beads" and similar devices.

Together, we worked our way through the catalog. Dildos were out; Azza warned against anything too phallic, which might make husbands feel dispensable. Interestingly, lubricants were not required, but flavored massage oils were high on the list. Ben-wa balls—essentially a pair of Ping-Pong balls inserted into the vagina for strengthening and stimulation—posed a particular problem. "How do you get them out?" Azza asked. "Well, there's a string attached. You remove them just like a tampon," I explained. But it turns out that Azza and her circle don't use tampons. Traditional beliefs about the impurity of menstrual blood, and the perceived health risks of letting it linger in the body, make tampons an unpopular choice with many women. But there was more to it than that. "My friend wanted to try them before she was married, but her mother wanted to kill her: 'You will lose your virginity!'" Azza said. But surely, after a couple of kids each, this was no longer an issue for Azza and her friends? "They are afraid to touch this area. My sister-in-law says when she washes down there after sex, she has fear. This area is always forbidden us, even after marriage."[67]

One item Azza and her friends were on top of was lingerie. Before I left, Iman, her sister-in-law, showed us her latest purchase: a pair of red lace crotchless underpants. Azza was agog. "So do they work?" she asked eagerly. "Yes, he loves them." Iman smiled, recalling her husband's response. Iman bought her astonishing undergarment in downtown Cairo, in one of the many tiny lingerie boutiques that line its once-grand boulevards. While the shop-windows are provocative, the sheer luridness of the stock inside is breathtaking. Mere words cannot do justice to the fevered imaginations that would create thongs adorned with plastic scorpions or a bra whose daisy-decorated cups play a tinny version of "Old MacDonald Had a Farm" on contact.[68]

When I went shopping for my own trousseau, I was a little surprised to find myself in the company of so many *muhajjabat,* women wearing hijabs. If these women cover their bodies as a sign of Islamic piety, what are they doing buying such frankly tarty stuff? The lingerie designer whose elegant, filmy creations I chose for my own honeymoon (sadly for my husband, a world away from the chocolate-coated G-strings of the region's "eat-me" school of design) explained the seeming contradiction to me. "Here, women are bottled up about sex. All women, in spite of the culture, are afraid their husband will run after another woman. So that's why, even if they are conservative, they need to seduce their man," she said. "So long as there is sex, there will always be this market. There is no [financial] crisis in lingerie."

On reflection, it stands to reason; it is because women like Azza are bound by conservative codes of Islamic modesty that they buy such over-the-top underwear in the first place. You might argue that outrageous lingerie is just another tool of male oppression, turning women into frilly, frothy sex objects, but Azza and her circle don't see it that way: lingerie is one of the few means at their disposal to signal their sexual desire.

To help them make the most of this desire, I also picked up some British "instructional" DVDs during my overseas shopping expedition; even if they couldn't understand the earnest Open University–style voice-overs, at least the women would get the gist from the curiously unarousing videos of couples demonstrating various positions and techniques. But choosing the right DVDs was a problem, because the more I watched, the more I began to appreciate the boundaries of sexual life in the modern Arab world. One video, for example, encouraged couples to caress over a glass of wine—something the *Encyclopedia* covered more than a thousand years ago. But Islam takes a strong stand on alcohol, and while this certainly doesn't prevent followers from knocking back a glass, the conservative Islamic climate that surrounds Azza and her friends means they are in no position to suggest it to their husbands.

"Sex out-of-doors has its own special appeal," the narrator enthusiastically observed. "Seaside sex comes high on any list of romantic settings," the voice-over continued, as shots of a naked couple making passionate love in the water flashed across the screen, "though the realities of mixing sand and sex are rather more sobering." Too right. While the DVD was referring to sand in uncomfortable places, the realities of sex on the beach in Dubai, for example, can run to three months in prison, as one British couple discovered in 2008. The only appeal this was going to have for Azza and her friends was the kind you make to overturn a conviction for public indecency.

Beyond holding hands, or an arm over the shoulder (more visible—in Cairo, at any rate—after the uprising), public displays of affection between men and women are generally frowned upon in Egypt. This public reserve can translate into a private awkwardness as well; while Azza's husband is the cuddly kind, her sisters complain that, honeymoon over, their spouses rarely show them much physical or emotional affection, and there is precious little companionship on offer. *Ana bahibbik* (I love you) is the catchphrase of a million sappy songs and music videos that saturate urban Egypt, but in Azza's experience it's not something spouses say beyond the bed. "I swear, no one of my friends, her husband says 'I love you.' Only the first year of marriage. They feel that this is shame, to say 'I love you.' Men feel they are very weak when they say 'I love you,' and women feel they are begging."

So much for the Arab lover of twenty-first-century romance novels. *The Sultan's Virgin, Bedded by the Desert King, The Sheikh and the Pregnant Bride,* and variations on the theme are big sellers in English-speaking markets. The Arab hero is predictably tall, dark, and handsome—sometimes a carefree playboy, sometimes a caring surgeon or daring secret agent—with a brooding arrogance and explosive virility. Think Heathcliff in headdress. The heroines are pale beauties, usually American or English, occasionally with Arab roots of their own. They are also feisty, full of "Western" ideas about love, freedom, and equality that their Arab suitors, despite having lived and loved across Europe and America, imperiously reject.

The first desert romances, which appeared in the early 1900s, were full-blooded; the most famous, E. M. Hull's *The Sheik,* was the inspiration for Rudolph Valentino's screen icon and includes a lively prelude to serial rape: "Her body was aching with the grip of his powerful arms, her mouth was bruised with his savage kisses. She clenched her hands in anguish. 'Oh, God!' she sobbed, with scalding tears that scorched her cheeks. 'Curse him! Curse him!' "[69] And so on, fade to black. Today's books continue the list of human rights abuses, including abduction and forced marriage. But the sex is more explicit, and rapturously consensual. "With crazy, unbelieving joy she stroked the marvelous body, felt how the strong back, the clenching buttocks, the powerful shoulders and thighs moved under her hands, felt how the hard masculine sex moved within her. . . . At last more pleasure than her system could hold burst through her." So the story goes in *Sheikh's Honour.*[70]

At first glance, these books seem to turn Orientalism on its head: the soft, pliant women of the harem, once the mainstay of male fantasies of the East, swapped for their hard, insatiable masters. But it's the same old story of unfettered desire, no matter who's penetrating whom. Today's desert hero is an unvarnished sex object, his physique and technique described in luxuriant detail. Some critics argue that the genre's enduring appeal simply perpetuates the notion of a submissive East, as Western heroines break their Arab seducers through the power of love, turning them into tidy, monogamous partners.[71] (When I mentioned this theory to my parents, my mother nodded sagely. "Ah, yes, just like I did with your father"—to which my father simply snorted.)

Taming of the sheikh: that might be a Western woman's fantasy, but is it really what Arab women want? I gave a few books to Azza and friends to find out. It took Azza several weeks to get through just under two hundred pages of *The Sheikh's Defiant Bride;* secrecy, not fluency, was the stumbling block. "I couldn't possibly let my husband, or my children, see me reading this." She laughed.

"Oh my God, do they really think Arab men are like this?" was the unanimous reply. Some scoffed at descriptions of the hero's beauty, "the magnificence of his honed, muscular body." "I've been to the Gulf and I haven't seen anyone like this," one friend told me. "They are usually overweight. They eat junk; the only exercise they do is race their four-by-four cars." Azza was surprised at the way these books describe the sexual prowess of the Arab hero, famous "for his ability to pleasure a woman until she could be pleasured no more. Then and only then would he take his own release."[72] Azza shook her head in disbelief: "Five minutes, and it's only his pleasure." Forget French-kissing, forget foreplay: "He kisses her et cetera? That's not true—it's one minute only. After kissing, it's straight to sex, then he sleeps, then he watches TV."

Her voice dropped to a whisper: "Men, in Egypt, in the Gulf, they always want to have sex in the wrong place." It turned out Azza was talking anatomy, not geography— more specifically, anal sex. "They think after ten minutes, she is wider, so he's not happy. That's why he wants the other way. Women don't get pleasure from this, only men."

## A SORE POINT

Heterosexual anal intercourse is generally considered haram by Sunni Muslims, while some Shi'i authorities allow it, albeit reluctantly. Its permissibility has been a matter of lively debate among religious authorities since the birth of Islam. The Prophet Muhammad, who had to grapple with this issue among his followers, is said to have been pretty clear on the subject: "Cursed is the one who has sex with a woman in her anus."[73] Nonetheless, anal sex continued in the Arab world, as is clear from the great works of erotica like the *Encyclopedia,* which quotes women on its manifest advantages: "Love is a lock and anal intercourse is the key to it."[74] Today, some Sunni scholars who condemn the practice invoke a verse from the Qur'an: "Your women are [like] your fields, so go into your fields whichever way you like."[75] By analogy to planting a seed and watching it grow, they argue that non-procreative anal sex between husband and wife is therefore off-limits. On the other hand, those who seek to justify the practice—at least in their own minds—maintain that if this is the way a man wants to "go into his field," so be it.

Just how common anal sex is among married couples is difficult to ascertain. The few studies to have probed this sensitive spot yield predictable results: wives say it is exceedingly rare, while a substantial proportion of husbands claim to have done it with their spouses.[76] Somewhere between female modesty and male vanity lies the real figure. Back in Egypt, there's plenty of anecdotal evidence to suggest that anal sex is an issue for married women. Even some of Azza's country cousins, who still live in the ancestral village, have been complaining about their husbands' demands; their men never used to ask for anal sex, these women say, until they went to work in the Gulf.

If true, this is one of the more unusual exports from that part of the Arab region. Around two million Egyptians are working in the Gulf—more than half of them in Saudi Arabia.[77] Over the past four decades, their numbers have soared as a growing supply—thanks to an expanding population and rising unemployment back home— has met the rising demand of Gulf economies. These workers are overwhelmingly male; less than 10 percent of Egyptian migrants to the Gulf are women, and even this minority is a source of considerable unease among Egyptians, who fear their countrywomen will be debauched by the locals. In 2007, for example, the Egyptian government temporarily stopped issuing permits to Egyptian women looking to work in Saudi Arabia as domestic help after reports surfaced of the sexual abuse of Asian and African workers.[78]

Migration to the Gulf is not a lifelong commitment; Egyptian workers stay, on average, five years. Aside from the billions of dollars these migrants send home annually, there are also "social remittances"—that is, attitudes and practices migrants have picked up abroad. Some experts argue that ideas about the role of women or domestic violence change little on migration to or return from the Gulf—those who are conservative have their ideas confirmed, and those who have a more liberal stance develop a greater appreciation of the relative social freedoms of home. But others see a definite change, among them Ayman Zohry, an expert on Egyptian migration. He comes from a village in Sohag, in Upper Egypt, where a large proportion of the men go to the Gulf for work. "When I was in the village thirty years ago, not all the women were covered. Today, even girls in school cover their hair, although this is not required by [religious] law," he told me. "The people were very open. My aunts used to pray wearing a galabiya which only went to their knees; now they wear a Saudi abaya." It's not just dress that has changed. "Even twenty years ago, when I went back to the village to visit, my female relatives treated me as if we were Europeans, hugging me; now they don't. Many women won't even shake hands with a man."

Zohry reckons these changes are, at least in part, the result of migration and that this has, in turn, changed the way people in the village see Islam and, therefore, aspects of life governed by it. "They not only consider Saudi the Holy Land, but Saudi religious institutions have become their Al-Azhar," he said, meaning that they seek religious guidance from voices that espouse a more conservative interpretation of Islam rather than from Egypt's historic Islamic authority. To his mind, this brand of Islam has brought a "harem mentality," as he calls it, to the village. "Everything is explained by sexual parts. The body of the woman is the main concern in Salafi [a conservative form of the religion]. But when you hide a part, you focus on the hidden part."

Whether anal sex is one of these newfound parts, as Azza's cousins attest, is hard to tell. There are plenty of sexual stereotypes across the Arab region, and one of them is that men in the Gulf are into each other, so to speak, and that sodomy is par for the course, no matter which sex is in the bed. Pinning down the ratio of fact to fiction in this particular stereotype isn't easy. Over in Jeddah, I asked a few doctors if women there were also on the receiving end of husbands' "misplaced" attentions. "We see anal [sex]. It is growing," one gynecologist told me. "It's there; we cannot do statistics, but it is obvious." A telltale sign is women showing up at the clinic suffering from anal fissures—that is, tears due to excessive force. "Some of the ladies complain about the husband. Even in Islam it is not allowed; they are considered divorced if they do this," the physician said. "They manage it with the fatwa of Shi'a. Some people say it is allowed during the period of menstruation. They try to manipulate this fatwa according to what they want."

On this point—that is, sex during menstruation—the Qur'an clearly states that it is "a painful condition, so keep away from women during it. Do not approach them until they are cleansed; when they are cleansed, you may approach them as God has directed you."[79] This taboo has made its way into folklore: in Egypt, for example, menstrual blood is considered impure, and men have traditionally stayed clear of vaginal sex during a woman's period for fear that it would make its way inside their own bodies and cause damage.[80] There are, however, plenty of other Islamically sanctioned ways to get it on during menstruation, as recommended by religious authorities through the ages.

As for anal sex among patients, the Saudi doctor pointed to other forces at work. "I think some of the males [with] young females, they are not allowed to touch her from the vagina, [so] they do it from the other side. They have girlfriends, and they do it from here. And when they go [get married], they maybe want to do it the same with the wife. They apply religion to bad actions." This gynecologist put the blame firmly on the media: "Definitely, the sexual films, they change [things]. Even the young females, they are different now; they know everything about sex, in detail, better than my mother, and better than me, and I am a physician. Unfortunately, they get it from the wrong way. They take it from the films. Films, it doesn't mean this is actual life."

To shift the focus (or rather, locus) of sexual activity, Azza and her friends are prepared to try just about anything. A few have considered surgery to tighten up their vaginas, but at an estimated EGP 2,000 a procedure, it's a squeeze on their household finances. There are, however, more economical alternatives.

Zizi is a sprightly woman in her midtwenties who owns a beauty parlor on a run-down side street in one of Cairo's new suburbs. Her two-chair salon is a tidy, cheerful spot, the walls decorated with torn-out pages of magazines showing the latest hairstyles—tresses as long and glistening as her own. Zizi gets several dozen clients a week—all *muhajjabat* in this part of town—and there are always a couple looking for something a little special.

"A lot of women complain that their husbands want not-from-the-front [anal] sex and they do not want that. Nowadays, men want strange things and ask their wives to be ready the whole time to make sex," she told me. Like the Saudi gynecologist, Zizi is clear, in her mind at least, where the source of the trouble lies: "Many things become strange now because of the Western [porn] clips, like some men practice sex with two women in front of each other, and ask other men to do that with their wives if they have trouble performing."

Zizi sees such sexual demands as a rising source of conflict, within spouses as well as between them. "Men watch Western songs and [video] clips, but at the same time they want their wives to be good mothers and care for kids. Many women come to my shop and say that they hate making oral sex. . . . Women think if they do that, they are impolite, and from here the problems start. Men think that if their wives refuse to do that, they are less than Western men in the videos, which pushes them to practice that with bad girls."

Oral sex appears to have been practiced in *jahiliyya,* the period before the coming of Islam, in what is now western Saudi Arabia. And although not as prominent as other sexual practices, fellatio and cunnilingus also make an appearance in the great works of Arabic erotica. Today, however, thanks to foreign porn, oral sex is seen as a Western import. Although I have heard many women in Egypt talk with distaste about going down on their husbands, and vice versa, it has been endorsed as halal by one of Islam's most prominent scholars, Yusuf al-Qaradawi. "Muslim jurists are of the opinion that it is lawful for the husband to perform cunnilingus on his wife, or a wife to suck her husband's penis [fellatio], and there is no wrong in doing so. But some say if sucking leads to releasing semen, then it is Makruh [blameworthy], but there is no decisive evidence [to forbid it]," he opined.[81]

In the meantime, all this female anxiety is good for business. Among Zizi's specialties is a vaginal-tightening mixture, consisting of almond oil, *shabba* (alum, a well-known astringent that causes tissues to contract temporarily—hence the tightening effect), and warm water, which she recommends a client "put inside her down [there] to make it narrow." This recipe has a long tradition. Most books from the golden age of Arabic erotica touch on the impor- tance of well-honed genitalia, with a wide selection of remedies. "We should not feel embarrassed to talk about the enlargement of the penis, the narrowing of the vagina and increasing the pleasure of coition, for such subjects are relative to reproduction," advises one twelfth-century treatise, *A Jaunt in the Art of Coition.*[82] "Many an ugly woman was preferred to a beautiful one only because the former had a narrow vagina and the latter had a wide one," it counsels readers. "Therefore, the narrowing and warming of the vagina is necessary indeed."

Such recipes are, however, the least of Zizi's repertoire. She also does a brisk trade in *'amal,* or magic. Magic has a long history in Egypt and across the Arab region. While Islam comes down hard on some kinds of magic (also known as *sihr*), "white" magic—the kind that Zizi practices—is an accepted part of popular religion. Even educated people like Azza and her circle firmly believe in its power: one of the reasons Zizi's salon is so tidy is that clients— Azza included—insist on taking their cut hair with them just in case someone uses it as *'atar,* a personal item on which *'amal* is done.

These women should know, since they are busy asking Zizi to do the same to others. "I earn a lot making *'amal.* Sometimes they give me two hundred pounds [thirty-three dollars] for one," she notes. Her most popular item is a *hijab*—which, in this case, means "amulet" to keep husbands faithful. It is an intimate affair: "I ask only for the underwear [of the husband] and other things. I read specific Qur'an verses depending on the women's problems. Usually I read the Yusuf verse,* especially for women complaining about their husbands. I tell them to put it [the *hijab*] under the pillow or under their mattress. They do that because they want their husbands to see them and listen to them only."

Zizi picked up her skills from her mother, who in turn learned them from her own mother, when the family was living in a rural area south of Cairo. She says the *hijab* are effective, according to customer feedback, though she can't speak from personal experience. "I never tried *'amal* or *hijab* before because I had a love story with my husband. I am married for more than five years and knew him for two years before marriage. That is why I don't need *'amal.*"

---

*Chapter 12 of the Qur'an, featuring the story of Joseph and Zuleika.

She shares her philosophy with customers, free of charge. "I see that women who come to my shop are not happy to practice sex with their husbands because all of their lives they are raised that sex is haram and shame, which I do not believe. I say that women should show their husbands that they are interested in sex and happy to do it with them in order to decrease problems with their husbands."

With that in mind, and back in Cairo after my travels, I met with Azza and her sisters. They were certainly curious about the assorted devices in the foreign aid package I had assembled, and there were gales of laughter as we went through the vibrators, massage oils, and other items. Three of the sisters were single, and although they were boldest in asking questions, there was no way Azza—who's the eldest—was letting them take any of the stuff home for further research. The married sisters—Azza, Iman, and Wisam—were just as interested, though wary of how their husbands might respond to such innovation in the bedroom. Indeed, a couple of Azza's other relatives, who had hoped to attend our gathering, were prevented by their husbands from leaving the house in the first place. Several times an hour, Azza had to break away to take calls on her mobile from anxious menfolk wondering what their women were up to. "I can't believe it. He keeps asking, 'What is she [Shereen] saying? What are you doing?'" Azza fumed after yet another call from her brother. "They go out every night and do I don't know what. But the moment we have something to do for ourselves, they complain."


MEN ON TOP


What men want is an interesting question. While there is a growing body of research on married women's sexuality, husbands in the Arab region are more of a mystery when it comes to hard evidence on sexual attitudes and behaviors. This may seem a curious gap, given just how dominant men are in societies across the region; in Arabic, this masculine authority even has a name—*qawama.* But it is this very dominance that has, until recently, made married men a sideshow when it comes to research on sexuality. This work has tended to focus on problems—violence, disease, exploitation—in populations at risk. Framed this way, married men—pillars of the patriarchy—don't exactly fit the mold of a vulnerable group. The very word for masculinity—*rujuliyya*—is a relatively new coinage in Arabic, and it is only in the past few years that masculinity studies, looking at how men define themselves and are defined in society, has started to take root in the Arab region.[83]

The menfolk of Azza's circle seem conflicted when it comes to sex—like so many of their countrymen, as emerging research shows. On the one hand, they are obviously keen to maintain their authority on the home front and see it as their manly role to lead their wives in intimate affairs. On the other hand, one or two of the husbands were quite clearly discouraged by their spouses' sexual passivity—for its impact on her pleasure, as well as how it rebounds on their own. They described their struggles to talk through these issues with their wives—a communication gap that, on further probing, appeared to extend well beyond the bedroom. And yet, when a couple of the wives tried to close the distance by showing some sexual spark, their men found this disconcerting, some even describing it as shameful.

Aside from notions of female virtue, this lukewarm response has its origins in a long-standing male concern: impotence. In Egypt, this sexual anxiety starts for many men on their wedding nights, with the fear that they will be *markhi,* or limp. Studies from across the region show that upward of 40 percent of older men may be suffering from some degree of erectile dysfunction, with younger ones also feeling the pinch.[84] There are a number of reasons that men are failing to make the grade in the bedroom. Some are physical, among them complications arising from diabetes or hypertension and smoking, all frequent among Egyptian men. The fear of impotence has even been pressed into the service of public health: recent warnings on Egyptian cigarette packs show a picture of an upright cigarette wilting, its ash about to fall like an avalanche, accompanied by a sobering prediction: "Smoking over a long time weakens marital relations."

Other causes, some Egyptians believe, involve darker forces at play. There is a well-known phenomenon in Egypt called *rabt*, which makes men *marbut*. In English, *marbut* literally translates to "tied up," but in Arabic it doesn't mean "to be busy"; quite the contrary, in fact. *Rabt* renders a man unable to perform in bed because his brain is not sending the right signals to pump blood into the penis for an erection, so the thinking goes. While this might sound like a plausible hypothesis for a new erectile dysfunction drug, it's the root cause of *rabt* that is a little more difficult to tackle in a test tube. According to local beliefs, *rabt* is caused by mischievous *jinn,* or spirits, summoned by someone with a grudge—a neglected first wife or ex-girlfriend, perhaps—that bewitch a man's brain and put him out of action. (Women too can be affected by *rabt,* experiencing symptoms including a vice-like clamping of the legs preventing penetration, bleeding during intercourse, and, my favorite, missing-vagina syndrome, in which a husband cannot find his wife's relevant parts.)[85]

While they were happy to talk about relieving *rabt,* the traditional healers I met were reluctant to go into details about how it is cast in the first place. "It's called *suflii,*" Zizi told me, referring to a type of "low," or black, magic that causes harm to others—as opposed to the white magic she was practicing. "It's very dangerous. I do not do this kind of thing," she said. Zizi hinted that if I were in need of such dark arts, I might try a Coptic priest instead. "It's done in the churches, not only for Christians but also for Muslims," she whispered. Zizi's advice is shaped by an enduring prejudice among Egyptian Muslims that shady practices are the preserve of their Christian cousins. This is a reflection of ongoing tensions between the two faiths, which have historically lived in relative harmony but have in recent years come into bloody conflict. Generally speaking, these clashes are fueled by power and politics, but are very often ignited by some sex-related incident, be it the alleged rape of a Muslim girl by a Christian man (or vice versa) or the incendiary topic of intermarriage between the two faiths.

*Suflii* aside, rather less mystical are findings from a handful of medical studies that show that most cases of honeymoon impotence are due to psychological factors, the majority of those related to "performance anxiety."[86] That men should be suffering a sort of sexual stage fright is perfectly understandable. Matters surely have not been helped by the economic, political, and social pressures building up during the long, sluggish years of the Mubarak regime, which have put men on the defensive—against women, against the government, against each other. Men too are carrying plenty of societal expectations. One male friend, in his early twenties, neatly summed it up: "Being a man is a privilege, but it's also a terrific pressure." Moreover, given how little formal sex education young Egyptians receive, how little practical experience they bring to marriage, and how keen they are to prove their manhood, it is a wonder they manage to consummate these unions at all.[87]

Whatever the reason, the upshot is men with their tackle in a twist. Azza's husband described how a discreet inquiry around the office revealed twenty of his colleagues with sexual difficulties, ranging from premature ejaculation to none at all. Some blamed it on the economy, others on pollution, but after much discussion they concluded it was a Western-Israeli plot. According to the office consensus, there are secret agents all over Cairo wearing special belts that emit some sort of spray or beam to neuter Egyptian men, thereby weakening the nation and reducing population growth. What's protecting the agents themselves from such malign effects was not considered; perhaps they are women, or men kitted out in special Western-Zionist underpants to shield them from the blast?

It's easy to scoff at such notions, and impotence is indeed the butt of a thousand jokes. But for Egyptian men, this is no laughing matter. In Egypt's patriarchal culture, male self-worth is bound up in the ability to provide for women—materially, but sexually too, which for many men is a straightforward affair: erection, then ejaculation. Failure in this department can have serious domestic consequences: in shari'a, impotence is grounds for divorce. Many Egyptians believe that when it comes to virility, the grass is greener across the class divide. Some educated women I know speak wistfully of the potency of lower-class men, though they are talking from stereotype, not personal experience. Yet poorer men generally think that the rich are better endowed in the virility stakes.

A case in point is Mustafa, a small, balding forty-year-old taxi driver in Cairo. "I like doing it," he volunteered during a ride home late one evening. He raised his hands to imaginary reins and started making the sort of *tchk-tchk* noises riders do to get the horses going—which was almost endearing, but for the fact that we were in a car, not a calèche, and racing down the Nile Corniche at seventy kilometers an hour with his hands off the wheel.

It was clear that Mustafa was talking about sex, and he proceeded to elaborate on his habits: "Twice a day—once in the morning, once in the evening," he said matter of factly. When I suggested that Egyptian men were struggling with impotence and needed Viagra, he was incensed. "No, no, I am natural, no Veeagra," he shouted, knocking on the top of his metal-clad meter to give me a sense of just how nature had made him.

Viagra is available from almost any pharmacy for around EGP 10 a tablet, without a prescription, prices having fallen precipitously after the uprising; it is also possible to pick up local generic versions with such imaginative names as Virecta and Vigorama. Viagra was initially banned in Egypt in the late 1990s, but has become so much a part of the culture that it serves as an alternative currency in some circles. I know of one man who carries a pocketful of the real thing, picked up in America, for baksheesh; the pills are especially useful, he says, for bribing bureaucrats to finish paperwork on time. Whether the drop in price, as well as Egypt's drive to root out corruption from the system in the wake of the uprising, will cut down on this gray—or rather, blue—trade remains to be seen. Quite aside from their transactional value, such drugs have also proved a popular wedding gift among male friends, even young ones.

Viagra-free Mustafa was, nonetheless, looking for a little help. "I want another wife. I want sex, three times, four times [a day, presumably]. If I had more money, good food, then yes." To his mind, money helps relieve the worries, but diet is key: Egyptians are convinced that the more protein men eat, the greater their potency. I was curious as to how his wife felt about all this. "Nothing, she can say nothing. No sex twice a day and I say, I will have *'urfi* marriage," he explained, then turned round to me in the backseat. "Would you like to sit up here?"

Mustafa's faith in food is borne out by the freezer section at my local supermarket in Cairo. Come Thursday nights, the carts are lined up around the seafood, as middle-class, middle-aged couples snap up bags of frozen Malaysian prawns.[88] Egypt imports several billion dollars' worth of lobster and shrimp a year. I thought this was some passing crustacean craze until Azza explained to me that her husband insists on buying them every week in the belief that it will make him stronger in bed; no sign as yet, she said. Around the corner, a fast-food joint called Cook Door is selling "Viagra sandwiches," whose active ingredients, such as they are, include crabsticks and prawns. At Cook Door you can have your Viagra fried or, for the health conscious, grilled; I tried the latter and it was delicious, if not libidinous. This is only one of a number of "natural" remedies for sexual performance. Among the most popular is *gargiir,* or garden-variety arugula, which is the aphrodisiac of choice for poorer Egyptians outside the Viagra-popping, shrimp-scoffing classes. "If women knew the benefits of *gargiir,* they would plant it under their *siriir* [bed]," as the saying goes.

In twenty-first-century Cairo, and across the Arab region, people still turn to herbalists and perfumers for sexual problems and receive much the same remedies as they have for centuries. One of the busiest purveyors is the Egyptian House of Perfumes, with branches across Cairo, including one bustling outlet downtown. Its sign proudly advertises an inventory of a thousand and five varieties, and on first inspection, that doesn't seem far off the mark. It's a tiny shop, covered ceiling to floor in jars, drawers, boxes, and bags, stuffed with herbs, roots, and mysteriously colored liquids, and erupting onto the pavement in barrels, bowls, and sacks of grains and powders. A thousand different odors blend into a sensory hum, a stray note of sandalwood or cumin breaking away from the olfactory noise like a single voice rising above the din of the street outside.

On the Saturday morning I visited, the place was packed, money flying in and out of a drawer in a small cash desk in the corner. Young, old, rich, poor—they all come here: a twentysomething in a neat hijab asking for lemon oil shampoo; a middle-aged lady, her frazzled hair uncovered, looking for *mughat,* a root that stops post-partum bleeding; and an obviously affluent silver-haired man in a safari vest asking for "ah . . . the usual thing." Muhammad, the manager, smiled, wiped his hands on his jeans, and handed the man his order.

The "usual thing," it turns out, is help for sexual dysfunction. Muhammad gets up to twenty people a day coming in for assistance. He's worked in the shop for fourteen years, and the numbers looking for relief in sexual matters have risen, he says, men and women, young and old. And not just from Egypt either; the company gets orders from the Gulf as well, thanks to TV advertising.

"May God help you," Muhammad said to the man departing with his usual. Muhammad sees his job as spiritual as well as physical: "If God gave somebody knowledge and he kept it from people, God will punish him for that." In Muhammad's opinion, there's nothing strange or sacrilegious about invoking a higher power when helping people with their sex lives, provided they meet certain criteria. Women who come in for *gamagim* (an abortifacient made from animal skulls that looks like dried truffle chips) have to bring their husbands or guardians or show a doctor's prescription. And he asks those looking for sexual stimulants if they are truly married, though for grooms-to-be he makes an exception. In any case, Muhammad practices tiered pricing: the more devout you are, or at least appear to be, the less you pay, so *munaqqabat*—women who veil their faces—are in luck.

With a university degree in commerce, Muhammad is an educated man, and he knows his history. The shop's recipes are inspired by *Medicine of the Prophet.* This book, written in the four-teenth century by the Syrian theologian Ibn Qayyim al-Jawziyah, is Islam's premier guide to wellness, combining injunctions from the Qur'an and hadith with medical advice to promote both physical and spiritual health.[89] On the sexual front, the House has two popular prescriptions. One consists of *gilingan* (galangal, a rhizome), along with dried alfalfa, arugula, and a few other ingredients to boost male performance. According to Muhammad, the advent of Viagra has made this item even more popular because "the chemicals in Viagra, if you use for ten years, it is too much. All Egyptians know this, which is why they come here because this you can use every day." The second recipe combines palm tree and flower pollen (for energy), ginseng, ginger, cinnamon, and white pepper (to heat up the blood) and can be used by both men and women, one teaspoon twice a day.

Muhammad offered to prepare the latter for me, and darted about the shop, opening drawers and climbing ladders, throwing in a scoop of brown powder here, a pinch of green powder there, and a dash of some yellow stuff. He then added the whole mixture to a pot of honey. Honey is key to most of these recipes for reasons clearly stated in the Qur'an, in a chapter called "The Bee": "From their bellies comes a drink of different colors in which there is healing for people. There truly is a sign in this for those who think."[90] Some forms of honey, like that from Yemen, are considered aphrodisiacal in their own right and are popular wedding gifts in the Gulf.

While Muhammad recited verses of the Qur'an, he stirred this concoction into a thick, gooey paste. He pulled a tiny amount away from the jar, like taffy, and offered me some with clear instructions: I had to say *bismillah* (in the name of God) before taking it. So I did, and it tasted like sweet, spicy halva. "God gives some people certain knowledge. This is built on the fact that if you pray to God, he will respond to you and you will get the cure through somebody like myself," he explained. That may well be, but I doubt I have the stomach to take a spoonful of this stuff twice a day. No problem, though: Muhammad offers his customers a money-back guarantee.


MEANS OF REPRODUCTION


Impotence is just one of many reasons a married couple may fail to launch—that is, produce a baby by their first wedding anniversary.

While there is a trend among educated, professional couples to put off having their first child for a couple of years after marriage, the majority of Egyptians try to have a baby immediately; less than 1 percent of married women use birth control before their first pregnancy.[91] A mere month after my wedding, several Egyptian friends asked whether I was expecting. Aside from the fact that Egyptians generally adore children, such solicitude is also pragmatic; many women will tell you that having a child—two to three is now considered optimal by young couples—is important for keeping a husband from taking another wife.[92] As my grandmother used to say, "Clip your bird or it will fly the coop."

Roughly one in eight Egyptian couples is infertile, on par with the global average.[93] Yet in Egypt, as in most of the Arab world, when couples run into problems conceiving, suspicion almost always falls on wives. And so it was that Iman, our lady of the lurid lingerie, was sitting on my sofa, shyly examining a vibrating cock ring. A year into marriage, Iman was still not pregnant—a rising source of concern for the whole family. She was hoping a little more excitement in the bedroom might make intercourse more productive. Iman had already consulted a number of doctors, who immediately put her on fertility treatment, contrary to best medical practice, given that she's still in her twenties and that the new couple was just warming up. Iman had been pricked, probed, and pumped up with hormones before anyone thought to check out her husband.

Siring a child is important to men in Egyptian society, and chinks in the armor of fertility are hard to admit. "When I started here eight years ago, I could not have imagined how much male factor infertility there is," says Amira Badr al-Din Mehany, head of the embryo lab at the assisted reproduction unit of Al-Azhar University. Al-Azhar is one of the world's oldest universities, established in the tenth century, and is associated with the famous mosque of the same name; on its doorstep is Khan al-Khalili, Cairo's famous souk. Outside the university gates are winding alleys and shaded caravansaries, where from tiny stalls wares have been peddled for more than a millennium. Step inside the unit's surgical wing, however, and you hurtle through the centuries to the cutting edge of fertility treatment.

Gowned and gloved, Mehany and I were talking through surgical masks in a sterile lab, looking through a window at an operating theater, where a surgeon was extracting eggs from a patient. We watched as tubes of straw-colored fluid were passed through a hatch into the lab, decanted into a petri dish, and whipped under a microscope. A technician peered down its lens and rattled off numbers. "Three here," she shouted. "Five more here," she announced, counting eggs in the harvest.

Al-Azhar's infertility unit specializes in ICSI, or intracytoplasmic sperm injection. This technique helps give sperm not quite fit for purpose a microscopic push into an egg. Across the lab, another technician was turning dials and manipulating two probes under a microscope, one holding the egg in place and the other injecting it with sperm. Mehany offered to let me watch, and tried to attach a tiny Panasonic TV to the microscope so I could see the moment of conception on-screen. Unfortunately, the connection wasn't working; the only thing we could get on the TV was a fuzzy rerun of *Noor,* a hugely popular Turkish soap opera from 2008 that had women across the Arab world swooning at its handsome leading man and longing for the romance and companionship generally lacking in their own marriages.[94]

I asked Mehany what might account for the high rate of male infertility in Egypt. "I don't know, maybe the pollution," she replied. "And yes, the smoking." Her colleagues had other ideas. "It's the genes," one of them told me. Egypt has a high rate of consanguineous marriage—as do many other countries in the region—which raises the odds of genetic defects being passed on to children. But that's not what he was talking about. "Yes, the jeans," he explained, "lead to elevating the temperature of the testicles, so it damages the testes."

Aside from theories of fashion-induced infertility, others at the unit speculated that life on the farm, and specifically exposure to agricultural chemicals, might account for the large number of fallahin, or small farmers, turning up. I could see them thronging in the waiting rooms, men and women dressed in galabiyas. Al-Azhar has an excellent reputation in ICSI, but that's not the only reason poor patients flock there. There is no shortage of private IVF clinics in Egypt, but the cost of a single cycle of treatment runs to EGP 10,000. At Al-Azhar, treatment is a third the price, and those that social workers deem in need of financial assistance receive further discounts. "Sometimes when couples come and they admit they don't have money," says Mervat Mohamed, a professor at the unit, "we think why they need children [if] they can't [even] afford dressing well? Very, very poor. But one of the ladies, she told me, 'I hope I can be pregnant, and when I deliver, I want to pass through this procedure'—just to feel that she is pregnant, that you are a woman." In Egypt, a childless woman is called *maskiina* (pitiful one); the idea that a married woman might be childless by choice is unthinkable to most people.

Test-tube baby making is never easy, but there are additional challenges in Arab countries. Semen, like other bodily fluids, is considered ritually impure in Islam, and ablutions are required of both men and women after sexual intercourse (which explains why, in poorer parts of Egypt where neighbors live in close quarters and often share bathrooms, women will often make a big show of taking a shower—proof positive that their husbands still desire them). Women douche almost immediately after sex; having to wait prone for at least half an hour after ejaculation, on the advice of the infertility specialist in order to promote conception, can be disconcerting.[95]

The bigger problem, however, is getting a sperm sample in the first place. Many men consider masturbation deeply troubling, and they blame such practices for their infertility. The permissibility of masturbation is something that religious scholars have been grappling with for over a millennium. Al-Shafi'i, founder of one of the major schools of Islamic jurisprudence in the eighth and ninth centuries, said it was haram, drawing on a verse of the Qur'an that specifies believers as those who, among other things, "guard their chastity except with their spouses or their slaves—with these they are not to blame, but those who seek [to go] beyond this are exceeding the limits"—and that includes your own hand.[96] Some jurists disagreed: Ibn Hanbal, for example, founder of another school, argued that masturbation was preferable to adultery and therefore allowed, especially for travelers, prisoners, and others lacking lawful sexual partners; some of his followers even permitted it for women.[97] Other religious scholars have compared masturbation to a Muslim breaking the fast during Ramadan because of illness, something that is permitted in Islam; by the same token, they considered masturbation the necessary release of the otherwise harmful pooling of semen in the testicles.[98] On the whole, however, religious scholars have weighed in against the practice, invoking hadiths, that, for example, exclude masturbators from God's mercy on the Day of Judgment, fast-tracking them to hell.[99]

As a result, having to produce a semen sample for infertility treatment—usually in the clinic bathroom—is problematic for many. The Al-Azhar unit deals with this discreetly, with a room tucked away on a side corridor to make users a little more comfortable. "It happens here many times, we ask him to get a sample and he stays all the day without getting [it]," Mohamed explained. Al-Azhar University is affiliated with one of the oldest and most respected religious institutions in the Muslim world, and Mohamed is a refined, soft-spoken woman in a hijab. So I felt a little awkward asking her if the unit gives patients a helping hand, with pornographic magazines or videos. But she answered without hesitation: "We don't give them material. We give him the private room and sometimes his wife. He knows the way to do it; he has the instruction before he comes to the clinic. We are not like outside [clinics, where they provide] these sex movies. We don't provide them with anything, except the cup."

Islam also sets limits on how far assisted reproduction can go. In Egypt, techniques that involve a couple's own gametes—artificial insemination, in vitro fertilization, and ICSI—are okay; sperm or egg donation and surrogacy are unacceptable.[100] Al-Azhar laid down the law in a 1980 fatwa, which has set the tone for Sunni Muslims throughout the Arab world.[101] The reasoning, according to Sunni authorities, is that reproduction is between a husband and wife; the use of anyone else's gametes is analogous to *zina,* and the child born of such a union would be illegitimate. The overriding concern here is *nasab*—a child's relatedness to the paternal bloodline—which determines everything from whom a woman can sit with unveiled to rights of inheritance. As a consequence, such techniques are for married people only—a widow, for example, wanting to use her dead husband's frozen sperm or their embryos from earlier cycles of IVF, can have a hard time arguing her case.

But none of these technological advances have helped Iman. Three years into marriage, she was still waiting to conceive. She and, belatedly, her husband had been given clean bills of reproductive health; the trouble now was lack of opportunity. The tips and toys from our session had long since spent their meager worth, and by the time the revolt rolled around, she and her husband rarely slept together, he finding greater satisfaction in surfing the Net for porn and chatting up women on Facebook, for all the governmental attempts to block, even criminalize, such online entertainment. Beyond the bedroom, their marriage was on the rocks—and she was trying to reconcile herself to the prospect of his taking another wife to provide him with children. A truly downcast Iman came to rue the day she attended the sex toy talk. She pinned the blame firmly on *hasad,* the evil eye: having spoken openly about her newlywed bliss at our meeting, she reckons the envy of her sisters is the cause of her reproductive distress.


## STRIKING OUT

Back at the coffee morning, Wisam, another of Azza's sisters, sat quietly on the divan, like a shadow. Unlike the other women, whose carefully coordinated hijabs, tunics, and trousers were a blaze of color, she was dressed in black and gray. When Wisam did speak, it was in a crushed voice, with barely enough energy to describe her fatigue and low libido. As a stay-at-home mom of a young son,

Wisam was looking for something to restore her interest in life in general and sex in particular. But the source of her lassitude turned out to be something beyond boredom in the bedroom.

Like a third of Egyptian women, Wisam was on the receiving end of domestic violence. The beatings and verbal assaults started a couple of years into her eight-year marriage. Around 10 percent of married women in Egypt also experience sexual abuse; Wisam is among them, her husband pushing her into intercourse, irrespective of his state or her mood. Intimate partner violence is a common phenomenon across the Arab world, and what statistics do exist undoubtedly underestimate the scale of the problem.[102] Wisam is in many ways typical: abuse starts early, and younger women without a job and financially dependent on their husbands are particularly vulnerable. While abuse rates are highest among poor, illiterate women, education does not necessarily protect them; both Wisam and her husband are college graduates.

One of the challenges in dealing with intimate partner violence is the extent to which women in Egypt, and many of their peers in the region, not only accept but actually condone it. In the national survey of ever-married women in Egypt, for example, around a third said a husband is justified in beating his wife if she goes out without telling him or neglects the kids; a quarter think she is asking for a hiding if she refuses him sex.[103] Young Egyptians take a similarly hard line.[104] Some will invoke Islam, saying the Qur'an allows men to discipline their spouses and obliges wives to put out: "Righteous wives are devout and guard what God would have them guard in their husbands' absence. If you fear high-handedness from your wives, remind them [of the teachings of God], then ignore them when you go to bed, then hit them. If they obey you, you have no right to act against them: God is most high and great."[105] But these verses are subject to interpretation, and certainly do not justify the violence many women experience.[106] At the heart of wife battering is Egypt's patriarchal culture, where men are men, violence is part of the package, and a woman is raised to put up with it, her obedience in exchange for his financial maintenance. For much the same reason, little is known about the reverse situation, in which wives assault husbands, in part because it is undoubtedly rarer than wife abuse, but also because the very idea of a turning of the tables in this way goes against prevailing notions of masculinity.

Across the Arab region, there are attempts to break this bargain. In Egypt, for example, shelters, hotlines, and free counseling and legal services, as well as a national ombudsman on women's issues and a network of nongovernmental organizations working to put violence against women on political and personal agendas, have sprung up in recent years. But there are plenty of practical limitations to these initiatives—including a lack of awareness on the part of potential beneficiaries.[107] Wisam, an educated woman living in the capital, simply did not know that such services were available; those in farther flung parts of the country are ill placed to avail themselves of assistance, even if it were readily at hand.

Acceptability is the issue. Wisam, like most women, preferred to keep the problem in the family. Surprisingly, her sisters advised her to leave her husband; studies show that, more often than not, women counsel others to stay put, in part because of practical considerations, such as finances and child custody, and in part because they too have bought into the system and therefore tend to blame women who break with the cycle of endurance and spousal pacification.[108] In Wisam's case, however, it was her brothers, fearing for the family's reputation and their own authority, who advised her to return to her husband.

When the abuse continued, Wisam took the unusual step of trying to file charges with the police. The law in Egypt is not exactly a woman's best friend when it comes to domestic abuse. Although Egypt ratified a number of international agreements on human rights that cover violence against women, including the Convention on the Elimination of all Forms of Discrimination Against Women (CEDAW), and its constitutions over the years have included plenty of fine words about the rights of women and men, there is, as yet, no specific law covering domestic violence. Marital rape is even trickier, as it has no standing in Egyptian law, despite years of effort by women's rights organizations to get some protection on the books.[109] When Wisam tried to press charges under Egypt's general assault laws, the police refused to file the case, saying it was a man's right to discipline his wife.

But Wisam, in her early thirties, was unwilling to take this lying down. After years of trying to find employment, Wisam finally landed a low-level job at a call center with one of Egypt's mobile phone companies. And when she did that, she decided to get a divorce.

Though increasingly accessible to women, divorce is far from socially acceptable. In Egypt and across the Arab region, there is widespread nervousness over what is seen as a wave of marital breakdown, particularly among middle-class newlyweds, whose irreconcilable differences often come down to complaints of loving fiancés turned into control-freak husbands and laments that new wives are too independent and lack "old-school" attentiveness. Depending on where you look, however, official statistics don't necessarily support gloomy predictions about divorce-induced social disintegration.[110] In Egypt, for example, the divorce rate has been running at between one and two divorces per thousand people for the past decade, which is actually lower than in 1960.[111] It may seem there is more divorce about, in part because rates are significantly higher than the national average in some parts of the country—Cairo, for instance—and because marital breakups have become more public, as divorced women increasingly come out of the shadows.[112]

One divorcée squarely in the spotlight is Mahasin Sabir. She's the creator and a host of Motalakat (Divorced Women's) Radio and Facebook page. Based in Zagazig, a town north of Cairo, Motalakat has thousands of followers across the Arab world and beyond. The titles of its programs—among them *Misunderstood and Mistakes, Mother in the House,* and *Your Son as You Raise Him*—give you some idea of the preoccupations of the audience, women and men who regularly interact with Sabir via e-mail, Instant Messenger, and Facebook.

"I want to change the look for divorced women," Sabir told me. "The woman who wants divorce is not a bad one. The woman who wants divorce is not a hooker, goes to sleep with anyone. Here in our society, they look to the woman like that; in the courts, the lawyer, the justice man [judge], they look to the woman that she is easy to take. I want to speak to the society, the men and women. Sure, you have a girl [daughter] who is divorced, or a mother who is divorced: look to the woman who is divorced in a human way." Her grim assessment is borne out by research: in the national survey of Egyptian youth, roughly two-thirds of young men and women said that divorcées are not respected in society.[113]

Sabir speaks from the heart. After two years of unhappy marriage, she spent another four trying to break free of her husband. In the interests of her young son, she prefers not to speak publicly about the reasons for her divorce. However, she's happy to talk about its repercussions, which is why she started blogging on her experiences in 2008, the largely positive response to which—mainly from men—led her to start Motalakat Radio.

In her early thirties, Sabir lives with her son, mother, and brother. Relations have never been good with her mother, who was vehemently opposed to Sabir's divorce. But Sabir chooses to stay close so that her son will have a sense of belonging. "I don't want to lose the soul of my family, but so many times I want to be on my own," she said. This family safety net is one of the reasons women, in particular, are reluctant to marry without their parents' approval, since many divorced women have few alternatives to moving back home if they fall out of wedlock. "A single woman to live alone? Disaster!" She laughed. "Here in our society, it is not good if she comes back late—that is to say, nine p.m.—in the family house. So many divorced women think they will not go [out], not work, to keep the image they are polite and good women."

Part of the problem is the stereotype of a divorcée as a sexual predator, on the prowl for men (and that means other women's husbands) to slake her lust. "They have something [the idea] here she can go with any man. She is not a girl [virgin] anymore, so [it is] easy to have sex with anyone," Sabir told me. "Men and women have stupid ideas. If she wants to go with another man, she can go early; she will not wait to be with him at night. You deal with an idiot society." She is not expecting enlightenment anytime soon.

"Revolution did not change the society view of divorced women. Not now; maybe after two centuries."

Sabir reckons that attitudes toward divorce in Egypt are less tolerant now than in her parents' day. "People are more closed-minded about divorce than before. We have Wahhabi;* that is something too bad. They make our society so closed-minded; they are a disaster in our society. Egypt used to be [about] culture, art, so many beautiful things, but the Wahhabis and the [TV] channels for them, they make people think of religion, but in a bad way. They take from religion something not right."

Such Islamic objections have been fueled by the introduction into Egyptian law of *khul'*, which allows a woman to unilaterally divorce her husband, provided she gives up her financial rights and pays back her *mahr,* among other conditions. It is one of three types of divorce in Egypt, the others being *talaq,* in which a man says "I divorce you" three times and registers this with a marriage notary, and fault-based divorce, in which wives can brave Egypt's tortuous legal system to split from their husbands on the grounds of desertion or maltreatment.[114] According to Sabir, most men prefer to be dragged through the courts, which can take years, thereby deferring alimony payments and having to leave the family home to the ex-wife and kids. In the meantime, husbands can take other wives, official or not, while women are frozen in place and cannot move on unless they are formally released from marriage. Divorcées *can* go on to remarry: for all the stigma associated with divorce, they are an attractive prospect to some men, since second-time brides are not looking for all the trappings of a white wedding and a first marriage. And so *khul'* offers women a way out, though it is a hard bargain for those without independent means and considerable patience.

When it first entered the books in 2000, *khul'* sparked a fierce debate about the rightful role of women and unmasked a deep well

---

*Wahhabism is an ultraconservative interpretation of Sunni Islam that originated in what is now Saudi Arabia in the eighteenth century; today it's gone global, thanks to the Saudi powerhouse it helped to create.

of male anxiety. In the wake of the uprising, conservative opponents of *khul'* have tried to limit the practice, finding new ammunition in the association of the law with the old government. Even more damning in their eyes is its connection with the former first lady, Suzanne Mubarak, who, quite aside from being part of a discredited regime, was active in promoting what many see as a Western women's rights agenda undermining traditional Islamic values—although *khul'* has its origins in Islam in the first place.[115]

No matter how they get out of their marriage, Sabir believes the upshot for women is a no-win situation: "[If she instigates proceedings], she is [a] bad woman, she is [an] evil woman, she broke the tie of the family. She told her husband to divorce [her], so she is [a] bad woman. From the other [side, if] the man divorces the woman, they say about her she is a loser woman, she can't keep her house, she can't keep her husband and keep him happy. They want her to be a clown for him, like the song, Elton John, 'Don't Go Breaking My Heart.'"

At Motalakat Radio, divorcées are keen to talk about feelings, while their male counterparts are mainly focused on money, and how they are going to make ends meet after the breakup and its attendant financial obligations. I asked Sabir if the audience ever spoke about sex as a contributing factor to marital breakdown, given inflated expectations going into marriage and communication problems thereafter. "Half of the women want to be divorced because [they are] not happy sexually. [But] they are scared to speak about that. First from society, scared from their families, scared from their children," she explained. "If her son asks her, 'My mother, why did you divorce my father?' I think he will not accept that [if she explains it was for sexual reasons]. He is a boy in Arabian society, and he has no experience of sexual life and [does] not know that is very important to human beings. He will not understand his mother. She is scared to lose her son, her family." It is the old double standard, Sabir explained. "So the woman is scared to talk about this. But a man goes and gets another wife; he gets to be very happy, with a woman, two or three. But she [does] not have this right. She has to be sad, unhappy, and [accept] bad treatment and just live to raise her children. Society wants her to be like that. She can't say, 'I have a sexual right—I want to be happy'; if she says that, they will say she is a bad woman."

Sabir herself married after a whirlwind romance of three months. She met her husband at the supermarket. "It was a love story like movie cinema. You feel that this is the one who is your soul mate. Everything is white and pink, and after that you get shocked." Her lively voice sank. "I was in love with him so, so much. And after marriage, I suffer from him so much." In Egypt, they have a saying: "Marriage is like a watermelon; you only know how it is inside once you cut into it." So I asked if she thought the personal, and sexual, freedom of the West to engage in premarital relationships, giving partners a chance to get to know each other, might have saved her this pain. Sabir was skeptical that "open relationships," as she calls them, before marriage might mitigate divorce thereafter: just look at Madonna and her many husbands, she told me. In her eyes, the benefit of a Western approach lies elsewhere. "It's about the treatment after marriage. . . . Sure, in the West, it is more better than here in Arab society because the men [there] are scared to treat women in [the] wrong [way]. He grows up and his parents and his society teach him to respect the women. Here in Arab society, the things [do] not go in this way. Men grow up and the society and the family teach him you have to treat a woman in a bad way, and he start[s] with his sister, his mother, and then his wife. . . . I think there is some men, they have got the idea they are men, [and] the woman is some weak creature."

Wisam is proving otherwise. When her husband refused to release her, she tried *khul'*, only to be told by lawyers that such cases had all but frozen in the courts. So Wisam opted for de facto *khul'*, paying off her husband and renouncing any claims to further support, in the hope of finally persuading him to divorce her. Though she will likely win her freedom, there is trouble ahead. Since 2005, divorced women in Egypt have been entitled to retain custody of their children until they are fifteen, at which time the court gives kids the choice of which parent to live with. When they no longer have custody, divorced women also lose the right to live in the matrimonial home. But Islamic conservatives have long objected to this legal amendment and want to lower the age of custody.[116] If such a law were to pass, Wisam might end up paying for her freedom with her son.

As for Azza, the uprising had an unexpected impact on her marriage. Her husband, once so perfunctory in bed, became an attentive lover. Azza wasn't sure how long he could keep it up—the attentiveness, that is—but she was happy while it lasted. "He changes a lot. He reads a lot on this topic, in an Islamic way, do this and do this and this, will make your wife happy." Azza smiled. "Always he sends me articles about how I can satisfy my desire." He also started to take better care of himself, struggling to spruce up his looks in line with the designer-stubbled, finely chiseled Arab man of a thousand fashion and grooming ads. Azza reckoned that her own greater knowledge of sex, sparked by years of discussing my work, had made a difference, along with her relative strength within their marriage. "After I met you, he tries to make it fun and happy with me. Maybe because I earn more than him, maybe I will leave him and go to another man. Maybe. He thinks that this is the way to attract me."

Azza and her family and friends are just a drop in the sea of matrimony in Egypt and the Arab world. For all their conjugal woes, that's not to say there aren't happily married couples across the region—of course there are. But read any newspaper, flip through any women's magazine, watch any talk show, or surf any website from the Arab region and you'll find people talking about the trouble with marriage. It's hard to see how democracy can flourish in a society if its constitutional and cultural cornerstone in the family is so undemocratic. Bringing the values of democracy to marriage, including equality of personal freedoms, will be the work of a generation at least. Changing laws, on paper and in practice, to put women on an even level with men is only part of it. Empowering women to realize these rights is important, but so too is working with men so that they not only accept but embrace equal opportunities within marriage as a reflection of their faith, not a violation of it. There is no shortage of worthy reports and laudable projects on the ground to address gender inequality in the Arab region, but few have yet tackled the sexual confusion at the heart of many a marriage.

In the best-case scenario, a new climate of openness in Egypt and across the Arab region may prompt people to question accepted truths in personal as well as political life. Taking some of the heat off couples, through better economic prospects and less day-to-day oppression, may go some way to improving relations between husbands and wives. When men feel less threatened by the world outside, when they feel they have choices in life beyond the well-worn path of their fathers and their fathers before them, they may, perhaps, be more prepared to accept alternative roles for women in various domains, including the bedroom.

But all this will take time, and there are limits to how far the new order will reach. I don't expect marriage to go out of fashion in Egypt or its Arab neighbors anytime soon. For the foreseeable future, matrimony will remain the only publicly accepted context for sexual activity, however troubling this may be for either party. Or as Abdessamad Dialmy, whom we met in the last chapter, neatly put it: "A driver's license is permission to drive; in the Arab region, marriage is a license to fuck." But what of the tens of millions of young people across the region who don't, or can't, pass that test? What's a single Arab to do?

# 3
## Sex and the Single Arab

*The honor of a girl is like a match; it only lights once.*

—Egyptian proverb

"To be, or not to be?"

I was standing in the middle of a *milyuniyya*—one of those mass protests in Tahrir Square that had become a regular feature of downtown life after the uprising. It was a dramatic departure from Cairo as I knew it, even a year before. Egypt is a country for old men, who call the shots in virtually all domains, from family matters to affairs of state. But in Tahrir Square, it was young people in charge: self-appointed guardians manning the barricades, checking IDs, and patting us down for weapons; medical students handing out surgical masks against the waves of tear gas; young men battling army and police in the side streets; and the thousands of teenagers and twentysomethings milling around in an atmosphere part rave, part political rally.

"To be, or not to be?" A woman, her hijab made out of an Egyptian flag with its eagle strategically centered on her forehead, emerged from the crowd and was at my elbow, repeating her question.

"What?" I asked, thrown off balance by the unexpected Shakespeare and the surrounding spectacle. Beside me, a couple of young men and a woman were sprawled on the pavement, smoking hashish. A young imam, dressed in traditional robes and a turban, stopped to tell them off, but they, in turn, told him to mind his own business. Just in front of me, a young woman was fielding a call from her mother, reassuring her that all was well and parrying her pleas to come straight home. Meanwhile, young couples were strolling hand in hand, an intimacy that used to be confined to the shadows, not paraded in broad daylight.

Such public defiance was astounding in a culture driven by convention and conformity. Were these the stirrings of a social revolution?

"That is the question," the woman answered to my silence, before melting back into the crowd.

I had come to the square to talk to young people about sex, how the fight for political freedoms might translate into their personal lives. Sally Al Haq, a teenage literature student and self-confessed "social rebel" from a provincial university, was all for change. "Yeah, sure, there are people in the square, they have their very free sexual life. It's okay," she said. "I agree with all of this and I respect this mentality." Unlike many young Egyptians, Al Haq was a great reader, with a special interest in feminist literature, and a fan of French erotica. "I read about Paris '68: 'It is forbidden to forbid.'" She smiled as she quoted a slogan from those famous student uprisings. "These guys, like, really made a difference in their personal life and even in the society and in the political life. I wish we will have that here."

As we wove through the crowds, Al Haq led me to the center of the square, across a tangle of guy wires and through a forest of makeshift tents, to meet Amr El Wakeal, a medical student and fellow member of a new youth political party. The two friends were from neighboring towns, and the same conservative background, but their views on sexual freedom were a world apart. "Sex is a bad topic. I give you an advice: for your safety, don't speak here [about] this topic," El Wakeal kindly warned me. I was a little surprised, given the reputation of the Tahrir campsite as something of a mini Woodstock, all sex, drugs, and rock 'n' roll. "I will not lie to you. You will find two tents in all these may have that. They will be very liberal, socialist, they can accept that, but their percentage is very few," El Wakeal said. He pointed to his own tent, where a handful of men and women were seated on the ground, sheltering from the unseasonable cold, and to his fellow squatters beyond. "All these tents, they can't do that. Most are from the countryside, and the poor. If anyone finds that [men and women are having sex], it will be a big disaster." He shook his head. "This not our manners, or our ethics. In Egypt, we are Arabs, we are conservative, we are religious, we believe in the marriage institution." El Wakeal was aghast at the suggestion that the political liberation he and his colleagues were fighting—and, in recent days, dying—for might one day free Egyptians from all fetters, including sexual. "No one, no one will accept that. This is not the freedom we are aiming for. The political revolution will need a social revolution, but not a sexual [one]." He shook his head again. "No, no, no. Not in a hundred years."

There are an estimated 100 million people across the Arab world between the ages of fifteen and twenty-nine; they represent almost a third of the region's population, making it home to one of the biggest youth bulges on the planet.[1] The political and economic grievances of Arab youth are no secret, exploding in protests across the region since 2010. But their intimate lives and desires are still largely hidden from view. In Egypt, a minority of women and men in their teens and early twenties are (or have been) married; given the pressure on couples to reproduce, it's safe to assume they've had sex. What the single ones, who constitute the vast majority of youth, are getting up to is more of a mystery, because asking detailed questions about the sex lives of the nation's unmarried young people isn't easy. I know because I've tried.

In 2009, the Population Council, an international research group, launched a survey in Egypt of more than fifteen thousand people aged ten to twenty-nine, going door to door to ask about their lives at school and home, work and play. Sex was one of the issues the council wanted to explore, so I joined a team crafting the questionnaire. Local experts dealing with young people gave us a long list of topics on which they were eager to see hard, nationally representative data. How many kids were masturbating regularly? How often were they cruising Internet sex sites? How many were engaging in phone sex? Did they know where to get reliable help and information on sexual health? How many were exchanging sex for gifts or money? And what about same-sex relations? Truly everything you wanted to know but were afraid to ask.

We settled for an indirect approach: instead of asking kids about their own sexual experience, we included questions about their close friends, in the hope that this would at least open a statistical window on the scale of premarital relations. In the end, however, even that was too much; the government, which authorizes and administers household surveys, refused to give permission for questions on premarital sexual activity, except for one: "Have you heard of a girl/boy of your age having a relation with boys/girls?" Unfortunately, this phrasing was too vague to elicit particularly meaningful results.

Now why would officials bother to censor questions on youth sexual activity? At least two possible explanations come to mind. One is that premarital sex is forbidden in Islam. The Qur'an is clear on this point: "Those who are unable to marry should keep chaste until God gives them enough out of His bounty."[2] The standard Islamic response to sexual privation is a spot of hunger to focus the mind and dampen the libido. Such guidance comes directly from a hadith in which the Prophet Muhammad is said to have advised: "O young men, those among you who can support a wife should marry, for it restrains eyes from casting [evil glances], and preserves one from immorality; but those who cannot should devote themselves to fasting for it is a means of controlling sexual desire."[3] Given early marriage in ages past, the Prophet was talking about fasting for a couple of weeks, not well into your twenties and beyond. "[The] principles of Islamic shari'a are the main source of legislation," according to the Egyptian constitution, which was suspended after the uprising—and political wrangling over a new one gave little chance of this provision softening, much to the disappointment of reformers looking for a fresh start in a secular state. While Egypt, unlike many of its Arab neighbors, has no explicit law against premarital sex, there are, on paper at least, other charges that can be brought against those who take the plunge before marriage.[4] So perhaps the government balked at asking questions about religiously impermissible and legally doubtful activity.

An alternative and, frankly, more likely explanation is that the state had little interest in what people get up to in bed—at least not on moral grounds. What most concerned those in power was staying in power, and that meant not handing ammunition to the opposition—namely, the Muslim Brotherhood. The last thing the government needed was to be administering a national questionnaire suggesting (let alone discovering) that young people, and in particular unmarried women, were—shock, horror—engaged in premarital relations. While it was possible to survey the sexual lives of young people on the margins—street kids, for example—mainstream Egyptian youth were off-limits as far as the government was concerned.[5] Now that the Muslim Brotherhood and its more conservative cousins are a resurgent force in Egyptian politics, any shift in policy would be a welcome surprise.

Not all countries in the Arab region are as coy when it comes to probing youth sexuality. Where researchers have been able to field surveys (and communicate the results)—Tunisia, Morocco, Algeria, Lebanon, and Jordan, among them—a pattern emerges: a third or more—often much more, depending on the population—of young men say they are sexually active before marriage (generally making their debut in their mid- to late teens and taking multiple partners along the way), while upward of 80 percent of young women say they themselves are not.[6] This, of course, raises the question as to whom exactly all these young men are having sex with. The reality is that surveys underestimate female premarital activity because women are reluctant to admit to such behavior. Those youth who surveys show are engaged in "sexual contact" of various descriptions are taking few precautions, leaving themselves wide open to pregnancy and sexually transmitted infections. As for the rest of the Arab region—particularly countries in the Gulf—research is only now starting and detailed facts and figures on the sexual behavior of unmarried people are still hard to come by. Faced with this gap, I turned to one of the region's most famous feminists for advice on how to get a handle on the sexual lives of Arab youth. "I don't believe in surveys in the Arab world at all, because people lie," she told me. "It's simple. You can just target important blogs and other stuff on the Internet and you have much better results."

## NET EFFECT

Enter Marwa Rakha, Egypt's agony aunt for the online generation. "Walking media" is how Rakha has described herself; she's been dispensing personal advice and spiky social commentary in print and on TV, radio, and the Internet since the mid-2000s. Women like Tahrir Square Sally consider her an inspiration. "Many girls were liberated because of Marwa Rakha. She helped and supported them, because of her very strong presence in the social networks. These wild women, they make a difference in the younger genera- tion," she said admiringly. Every week brings Rakha e-mails and Facebook messages from lovelorn, angst-ridden youth across Egypt and the wider Arab world, seeking her counsel on everything from straight-up premarital sex and conjugal life to sadomasochism and stalking. If you want to know about sex and the single Arab, talk to Rakha.

Rakha's standard disclaimer to correspondents is that she's nei- ther a physician nor a therapist. "It's just that I've been in so many relationships. So I know where it's going, so I can tell people," she explained as we sat on dusty plastic chairs at a sidewalk café in Borsa, Cairo's colonial-era financial district, now pedestrianized in a brave attempt to claw back some space from the relentless traffic. "Every story I hear relates to something in my life. I've been in their shoes and I understand their fears."

Rakha started out as a successful, but ultimately dissatisfied, marketing executive. "I was really bored, and this kind of boredom led me to all sorts of relationship problems, starting with picking the wrong guy, to plaguing the guy, to nagging the guy, to building a whole world around the guy, to eventually [being] just heartbroken in no time." From such experience, she began helping friends in similar straits, who encouraged her to publish her advice. "When I saw my name on [my first article], I panicked. Should I publish that? It's like stripping naked in the street. I can't tell people I've

had my heart broken that bad, and I can't tell people that I've suffered that much. I just can't."

Rakha overcame her reservations, however, and began blogging
in 2005; in what was then a new trend in Arabic publishing, these
soul-baring posts were collected in her first book, *The Poison Tree*.
From there her career took off, with magazine columns, her own
show on satellite TV, and a regular gig on Internet radio, as well
as a website, a Facebook page, and tweets followed by thousands.
Rakha tells it as it is and has little time for those who want her to
soften the line. "I'm not an entertainer. I don't go out there to strip
to entertain the guests. I have a mission and I have a message, and
if we are not on the same wavelength, so be it."

Rakha's openness, let alone the details of her own dating history, marks her as a taboo breaker in Egyptian society. "Her face
is unveiled and she's on her way to untying her hair" is how my
grandmother used to describe daring women of her own generation.
Rakha is often mistaken for—or rather, accused of being—a foreigner, her unconventional attitudes rendered all the more alien by
her fair complexion, hijab-free chestnut curls, and perfect English.
"A lot of people think I have lived all my life in the States and that
I come here with a Western culture trying to change our culture."
Rakha took a long draw on her shisha. "I'm a typical middle-class
girl. I'm not *bint balad awi* [hoi polloi]. And I'm not the elite thing.
I'm somewhere in between."

Now in her late thirties, Rakha found religion in her youth, in
the late 1980s. "I was veiled for six years, when I was fifteen until I
was twenty-one. I didn't know it was part of Islam or Qur'an. I just
put it on and I looked nice. And I had all those nice colorful scarves
that would accentuate my eyes. How could I know it was religious?
At the time, it was quite unheard of. It wasn't like now at all." She
laughed. "Then I got really, really religious. Like really religious.
No TV, no pictures on the wall, no this and no that. I became kind
of an extremist in my life. I was listening to this shaykh [on cas-
sette tape]. I was one of his devout followers. It was fear, fear of
God. The tapes I had were all, 'You're gonna die.' He used to tell

us that women who are not veiled are gonna be in hell and they're gonna be hanging from their hair. Two years fashion, and the other was this."

By the time Rakha reached university, the fundamentalist appeal had started to fade, and after graduation she removed her hijab. "In my last two years of college, I got busy with my studies and reports and stuff. So I kind of loosened up a bit and I wasn't listening as much [to the tapes] as I was before," she said. "And then after I graduated [and] I got my first job, it just felt wrong. It was like I was wearing something that was very conservative but I was the person talking to you now. I was a mismatch."

By then, she also had a boyfriend, a further catalyst for change. Although, as we've seen, it's hard to get a statistical grip on such relations in Egypt, an evening stroll along the corniche in Cairo or Alexandria, weaving between canoodling couples, is enough to show that young people are not waiting for marriage to get to know the opposite sex. But just how carnal is their knowledge? Does having a boyfriend also mean you're having sex? Rakha set me straight on middle-class Cairo's mating rituals. "For a growing number of men, sex is an expectation in a relationship; if she doesn't agree, he's going to move on to another girlfriend. But for others, it's still a test." These men, she said, will make overtures—try to hold a woman's hand or grab a kiss—as part of their assessment. "You fail if you've had relationships." Rakha sighed. "They want to make sure she's never had, and she never will."

That's not to say that women don't. "Of course it happens all the time," Rakha continued. "Making out, kissing, cuddling, having all those little getaways. Boyfriend-girlfriend is happening, always happening. Everything still happens, they just throw dust on it." The Internet has made hooking up a lot easier for the minority of young Egyptians who are online, part of a rising tide of surfers post-uprising.[7] "Even those girls who don't go out, they're online, chatting with four or five men at the same time," says Rakha. She should know: Rakha spent a year on Adult Friend Finder—"the world's largest sex dating site and swinger personals community," so it describes itself—exploring how Egyptians, hundreds of thousands of whom are registered on the website, meet and mate in cyberspace (though not without risks, given that popular police pastime, Internet entrapment). Posing as "Jenny," she was swamped with requests from Egyptian men, and women, looking for fantasy role-play, group sex, or other spice lacking in their relations in or out of marriage.[8]

In Rakha's opinion, virtual cruising is not some elite diversion. Men who can't afford a computer at home can go to an Internet café. Women, whose movements are more often supervised and circumscribed by their families, lack this easy access. In Egypt, while more than half of young men say they use the Internet outside the home, over 80 percent of young women have their connection under the family gaze—although their wealthier peers across the region, with their own rooms and laptops, have a little more latitude. For those lacking such privacy, there's the mobile phone, prize possession of more than half of young men and around a third of young women in Egypt, with near blanket ownership among the most educated and wealthiest urban youth.[9] Technology-assisted flirtation is a Pan-Arab phenomenon. Indeed, in more overtly segregated societies, like that of Saudi Arabia, Bluetooth has proved a boon to those looking for a little action: just head to the mall, switch your phone to "discoverable" mode, and wait for the messages to pour in.[10]

Just how connected youth are in Egypt and across the Arab world became clear during the uprisings that began this decade, when social media—from Facebook to text messaging—mobilized millions, even as governments tried to pull the plug on the networks.[11] The foundation for this electronic outpouring was laid in less tumultuous times, in bedrooms and Internet cafés across the region. Connectivity has soared since 2011; Egypt's Facebook generation is no longer just young people but their parents as well. A "robot leash" is how some women describe their mobile phones, which allow anxious parents to keep regular tabs on their movements. Nonetheless, technology allows young people at least a chance to slip family moorings, if only in cyberspace, and in the wake of the uprisings, a growing number are testing the waters of personal and sexual expression.

A case in point is Aliaa Elmahdy, the "Nude Photo Revolutionary," whose blog shot to international notoriety when she posted photos of herself naked.[12] Although pictures of Arab women baring all are easy enough to find online, Elmahdy gave her unveiling a distinctly political spin, lashing out at a culture of censorship and "echoing screams against a society of violence, racism, sexism, sexual harassment and hypocrisy." Rather than remain anonymous, Elmahdy tweeted her name, thereby revealing her identity as a middle-class student at Egypt's elite American University in Cairo. The photos themselves, more Victorian postcard than Victoria's Secret, nonetheless excited a firestorm of interest, with more than a million hits in a couple of days. As if that weren't enough of a shock for local audiences, Elmahdy let it all hang out in an interview with CNN, in which she discussed losing her virginity, living with her boyfriend (a well-known Egyptian blogger and former political prisoner), fighting with her parents, and being an atheist.[13]

Comments on the photos swung from hellfire damnation to enthusiastic congratulations for taking charge of her own body and challenging the limits of expression, the attacks vastly outweighing the applause. A political youth movement said to be associated with Elmahdy quickly moved to squelch all rumors that she was a member and condemned her actions as a government plot to undermine their "liberal" reputation.[14] Meanwhile, a group of young conservative lawyers lodged a case with Egypt's prosecutor general to punish Elmahdy and her boyfriend for violating shari'a, corrupting society, and tarnishing the spirit of Tahrir Square.[15] "Asking for sexual freedoms, they are giving the uprising a bad name," said the group, calling for the full force of the law to be applied.[16] The Elmahdy affair was reminiscent of an episode just two years earlier, in which a hapless Saudi Arabian in Jeddah talked frankly about his sex life on Pan-Arab satellite TV and ended up sentenced to five years in prison and a thousand lashes for "publicly boasting of sin."[17]

Such public displays attract enormous attention because they remain so rare: research across the Arab region shows that even in the virtual world, social constraints still apply, especially to women.[18] And no matter how daring they are online, how far women will go off-line depends on what they're looking for, says Rakha. "There's a big difference between a wife and a girlfriend. If you're going to be a wife, and you have sex before marriage, you have a problem. You have sex before marriage, he's not going to marry you. Because you're loose, because you're easy. Most of the girls in the A [upper] class I know, they would do everything with a guy, except for intercourse." That everything includes what one Egyptian friend described to me as a "blue job" (which turned out, on further inquiry, to be fellatio). And where researchers have been able to ask the question—in Morocco, Algeria, and Tunisia, for example—anal and superficial sex appear to be common enough practices among single Arabs as well.[19]

## CUT AND CHASTE

Keeping women on the straight and narrow is more than a matter of "just say no"; in Egypt one common tool of enforcement is female genital cutting.[20] It is an ancient custom, dating into the Pharaonic period, well before the arrival of both Christianity and Islam.[21] Fast-forward to the twenty-first century and the practice is still widespread; according to the 2008 national survey of ever-married Egyptian women under fifty, more than 90 percent have been circumcised.[22] Egyptians sometimes call the practice *tahara,* which means "purification," but it is often referred to in English as female genital mutilation (FGM). Between these poles of beauty and butchery lies a more neutral term, *khitan al-inath,* which translates to "female circumcision," but what we're talking about here is a more complicated business than a quick snip of the foreskin. FGM can take many forms, but the standard procedure in Egypt is removal of the skin covering the clitoris, usually along with the clitoris itself, and often taking the neighboring tiny flaps of flesh as well.[23] Girls generally go under the blade around nine to twelve years of age, with little warning, let alone consent. Depending on the skill of the practitioner, what's left is a smooth opening to the vagina and vivid, often jagged, memories for many women.[24]

"I'm having my daughters done next week," Umm Muhammad told me as we sat in her tiny, tidy living room drinking bottles of 7Up. Umm Muhammad lives with her handyman husband, her twentysomething unmarried son, and two young daughters in a two-room apartment on a dusty side street in Helwan, a suburb south of Cairo. Helwan is not exactly leafy: in the distance I saw what looked like gleaming towers looming over the scrappy main thoroughfare, but these turned out to be the smokestacks of the town's famous cement works. Umm Muhammad is in her forties, a substantial figure in a plain blue galabiya and green hijab. She's quietly good-humored, but she runs a tight ship. There's no satellite dish to the family TV, and their aging PC does not have an Internet connection because, her son grumbles, his mother doesn't want him watching "bad things"—meaning porn.

As Umm Muhammad bustled about, her friend Magda—a small, lively woman, like a tiny sparrow in her neat brown gown and headscarf—filled in the details. Magda is the neighborhood expert on FGM, because it's a large part of how she makes a living. She's a twenty-first-century *daya,* an untraditional traditional midwife. Historically, the *daya* was the mainstay of women's health in Egypt, but with the growth of the medical profession, much of a *daya*'s job—delivering babies, dealing with gynecological problems— has passed to doctors, particularly in urban areas. This includes FGM: three-quarters of girls under seventeen in Egypt have been circumcised not by a *daya* as in older generations but by a doctor or nurse.[25] This is largely the consequence of anti-FGM campaigns, which stressed the associated health risks: infection, uncontrolled bleeding, severe pain, even death. As a result, parents have turned to what they consider a safe pair of hands—a physician's—and found a willing set of practitioners, who, if not convinced on moral or social grounds, were understandably happy to supplement their meager public sector incomes with upwards of EGP 100 (USD 16) per procedure.

Magda learned to circumcise at the local medical clinic, where she worked as a nurse's aide when her husband died, leaving her to support one young daughter and another on the way. When the resident doctor left the district, she took her tools and set herself up as a *daya*. She is proud of her professional approach to the business of FGM, which begins with a careful diagnosis. "A lot of women come to me to ask me for advice and to circumcise their daughters. I see the girls and I say if she needs it or not after I check her. If the lips of her sexual part are big like leaves and the shape is not good, she needs the operation." Part of the concern here stems from a belief that uncircumcised, flapping labia may make penetration, and therefore conception, more difficult. "I commonly use a *mash-rat* [scalpel], and I first give her *bing* [anesthetic], because I am a nurse, not like the others who cut with primitive tools," she continued. Magda speaks from experience close to home. "My [eldest] daughter had the operation twice: the first time was not beautiful, so I took her to the doctor and he told me she needs to clean the shape, the place, so it was done [again]. My second daughter, who is studying nursing, I did her by myself because I learnt and I had the experience."

The drive to circumscribe FGM has been running for decades in Egypt, but it picked up speed around 1994, the year Cairo hosted a pivotal international conference on population and development, one of the first concerted efforts to put sexual and reproductive rights on the international agenda. To mark the event, CNN broadcast a now-infamous video of an actual circumcision, which made for extremely queasy viewing.[26] Since then, millions of dollars have been poured into fighting FGM, with nationwide campaigns assisted by an army of international agencies and local NGOs. National task forces were formed, fatwas were handed down, and the airwaves hummed with talk shows and TV commercials, reaching almost three-quarters of Egyptian women, trying to persuade them to break with FGM.

The legal standing of FGM makes little difference to the ladies of Helwan. The deaths in 2007 of two girls during FGM in as many months put pressure on the Mubarak government to take action beyond the bans and restrictions that had been issued, and ignored, for decades. The following year, the government forced a law across fierce parliamentary opposition from representatives of the Muslim Brotherhood to punish those performing FGM (and by extension, parents, as their accomplices) with a fine of up to EGP 5,000 and two years in prison. Magda is skeptical that law on its own can do much to deter the practice. As with so much of the legislation relating to women and children passed during the Mubarak regime, the law is suspected by Magda and other FGM supporters of having more to do with outside influence than homegrown attitudes. To her, FGM is a private matter, not an affair of state. "In the villages, people make circumcision a lot and do not put in mind the government decisions. I believe there is no need to prevent circumcision. I see they [the government] want to do that [ban the practice] to be like Western countries."

Law aside, FGM is traditionally a quiet affair, without the noisy celebrations that mark male circumcision. And so, Magda reckons, if doctors know and trust a family, they will be happy to pocket the money and do it under the table; unless something goes seriously wrong during the procedure, no one will be the wiser. But doctors, even freshly minted ones, are often as staunchly supportive of the practice as their clients.[27] As a recent medical graduate explained to me, physicians themselves are under extreme pressure, from both fellow practitioners and local communities, to do the job. In any case, the law allows FGM on the grounds of "medical necessity," which leaves physicians plenty of wiggle room. And if all else fails, mothers can always find a *daya* in a far-flung village—back to where it all began.

Those who support FGM believe they have God on their side. Magda and Umm Muhammad are convinced that the practice is obligatory for Muslims: "Gad al-Haq [former head of Al-Azhar] said that girls should be circumcised, and I believe and trust him." Magda invoked an oft-cited hadith in which the Prophet Muhammad is said to have advised a woman in Medina who performed female circumcision: "Do not cut too severely as that is better for a woman and more desirable for a husband." However, there is considerable debate around the meaning and authenticity of this hadith—none of which shakes the two women's belief in it.[28]

There are, however, religious authorities who oppose the practice. Leaders of the Coptic Church, for example, have staked a dramatic defense of girls under the knife. "What a look of fear and panic they will have in their eyes, what a horror . . . blood . . . bleeding and severe pain! It is a grave hazard to their present and to their futures when they marry and give birth. Therefore, we must take a decisive and firm stand against this harmful practice . . . from the Christian perspective—this practice has no religious grounds whatsoever," say church authorities.[29] The message is clearly getting through; today FGM rates are significantly lower in Egypt's Christian communities than among their Muslim counterparts.[30]

Shaykh Ali Gomaa, the Grand Mufti and Egypt's second highest official Islamic authority, is similarly dismissive: "Genital circumcision of women is a deplorable, inherited custom . . . it has no basis in the Qur'an with regard to the authentic hadith from the Prophet. . . . Therefore, the practice must be stopped in support of one of the highest values of Islam, namely to do no harm to another without cause."[31] But such big guns were often dismissed as mouthpieces of a government in hock to the West and a foreign agenda to undermine traditional values. To the intense frustration of anti-FGM activists, there are plenty of local imams who support FGM, themselves often under community pressure to hold the line.[32] And so Magda and her neighbors carry on cutting with a clear conscience, religion buttressing a tradition under attack.

Magda's strong attachment to FGM is about more than just genital aesthetics. If this were merely a question of appearances, it might be easier to change attitudes. But Magda thinks of the clitoris—"below," as she calls it—as a protopenis that must be cut in order to curb women's sexual desire. Circumcision, according to this logic, makes a girl "cool," quenching the fires of female lust. If the clitoris is not tamed, then girls, like boys, will seek sex before marriage, and married women will make sexual demands of their husbands—both of which could be marriage killers, so the thinking goes. "It's shame in our culture to ask our husbands for sex; I cannot imagine that a woman does that. Western countries are not like us," Magda told me. "In the hot weather, below [is] aching and that's why [a woman] should be circumcised. What is the case if her husband died or divorced her, is she going to pull men from the cafés?" Magda would no doubt be surprised to hear the results of a recent study of Cairo commercial sex workers that found that the majority said they had been circumcised.[33]

The connection Magda makes between FGM and female chastity is not some fringe belief. According to the recent national survey of ever-married women, more than a third of women and men are convinced that the practice prevents illicit sexual relations.[34] Or, as they sometimes say in Egypt: "The circumcised woman is a woman with a broken wing."[35] This is the sort of thinking that anti-FGM commercials have targetted when they ask, "Who says FGM is for a girl's chastity? The chastity of a girl is how you raise her. . . . Morals are a girl's only protection." No need to say protection against what, since everyone watching knows the enemy: untrammeled female desire.

This popular connection between FGM and sex cuts both ways. Those trying to stamp it out argue that circumcision impairs women's sexual fulfillment. "All types of FGM that are practiced in Egypt deprive a woman of the full pleasure during legitimate sexual relations," according to one former head of the Egyptian Medical Syndicate, the national doctors' union. "This can create bad feelings in the marital relationship which we know to be the basis of the human race and an important sign of intimacy. Thus the relations become a source of misery and conflict instead of being a source of happiness, understanding and delight."[36] The trouble is the evidence. What research there is on FGM and sexuality in Egypt has yielded mixed results. In a number of studies, circumcised wives have reported diminished libidos and less sexual activity, fewer orgasms, and less pleasure in intercourse than their uncircumcised counterparts, while other research has found little impact, at least in those women with lesser forms of FGM.[37]

One woman trying to make sense of all this is Mawaheb El-Mouelhy. A leading authority on women's sexual and reproductive health in Egypt, she has studied the connection between FGM and sexual pleasure in two poor parts of the country: a Cairo slum called Manshiat Nasser and two villages in the governorate of Minya in Upper Egypt. "Most women who shared their personal experience said that sometimes they experience sexual pleasure and on other occasions they did not; and that their pleasure is independent of circumcision," El-Mouelhy and her colleagues concluded.[38] The problem with conventional ways of examining sexual pleasure, say these researchers, is the emphasis on measuring performance—how often, how many, how strong. In their opinion, this doesn't work for looking at women's sexual pleasure in Egypt, because their enjoyment is bound up in broader questions of family life: how are the kids, are the bills paid, and—critically—are their husbands happy in bed.

The men in the study were conflicted on FGM. On the one hand, they consider it their God-given duty as men—their *qawama*—to protect their women, body and soul. Part of that responsibility is to deliver a virgin bride to any prospective groom, an uphill battle, in their opinion, thanks to the temptations of modern life. Added to that is their desire to be in the driver's seat when it comes to sex in their own marital beds. And so, to them, circumcision is a good thing because they feel it makes women more manageable. "My wife is circumcised, she is used to my style," said one study participant. "However, the uncircumcised wife wants sex all the day, so I would have to take pills [Viagra]. If I did not have sex one day, she might have someone [else] to satisfy her."[39]

For all this emphasis on male authority, when it comes to FGM, fathers tend to step aside, leaving the decision to cut, or not to cut, to mothers and grandmothers. In the communities studied, it was generally assumed that all girls had been circumcised, and so men hardly ever asked their wives whether they themselves had undergone the procedure. When pressed on the issue, many men admitted that, truthfully, they wouldn't know one way or the other. But that is changing, thanks to globalization—more specifically, porn. Now that men can see what uncircumcised women look like, it just serves to confirm what they have always believed: uncircumcised women—particularly Westerners—are sexually uncontrollable, and FGM is essential to keep women in check. "We are afraid if we don't circumcise females, because as we see in the satellite channels, a female can have sexual contact with three men at the same time, and yet it is not enough for her," one of the men in the study commented, reflecting the views of many.[40]

On the other hand, for these men, marriage is their big sexual breakthrough. "Sexual happiness represents 50% of marital happiness," according to one young man.[41] Anything that diminishes that experience is a problem. "I will tell you frankly, I got married six months ago, my wife takes a long time to come on and I do not know why," said a Muslim religious leader from Manshiat Nasser. "I asked one of the shaykhs who knows about health/medicine, he asked me if my wife's organ [clitoris] is long, I told him no it is short [circumcised], he told me this is why she takes a long time and he advised me to play a little and shake it before being together; it worked."[42] A minority of men in the study were acutely aware of the disadvantages of FGM, but practically speaking, the decision to circumcise was out of their hands.

The bottom line is that the connection between FGM and sexual pleasure is far from cut-and-dried. "It's more complicated here than the 'Western' idea that the clitoris is so important, and that you can't experience sexual pleasure without it," El-Mouelhy explained. Research in Egypt has shown that many women tend to dissociate the clitoris from climax; they consider it a driver of desire but a bit player, at best, in orgasm.[43] In El-Mouelhy's opinion, some basic lessons in anatomy and physiology could go a long way to helping people understand what the clitoris can, and cannot, do. But if anti-FGM campaigners want to use sex as an argument in abolishing the practice, El-Mouelhy and her colleagues recommend that they address such messages to men, who are more focused on the mechanics of sex and may be more receptive to these ideas than are women, who see sexual pleasure in a broader context and often have a take-it-or-leave-it attitude when it comes to the clitoris and sexual fulfillment.

That being said, decades of campaigns, decrees, and declarations have made a perceptible dent in FGM. While nearly all women in Egypt over the age of forty-five have been circumcised, around 80 percent of those between fifteen and seventeen have been cut.[44] That's a national average; if you look in certain populations, the figures are substantially lower, especially in wealthier circles and urban areas and among the children of mothers educated to secondary school or beyond.[45] According to the national survey, over a third of ever-married women under fifty think FGM should be stopped; that may not sound like much, but it is more than double the response from the mid-1990s, and disapproval rates are even higher among young, educated, urban women.[46] As one thirtysomething mother of three in Minya remarked, "I will not do anything to my daughter. Ever since we watched this on TV, I have made up my mind." Should efforts continue at this clip—by no means assured, given the ascent of Egypt's Islamists—it's expected that less than half of eighteen-year-olds will be circumcised by 2025.[47]

## VIRGIN GROUND

Just because FGM is declining doesn't mean that premarital sex is any more acceptable in most quarters. Across the Arab world, female virginity—defined as an intact hymen—remains what could best be described as a big fucking deal. Just how big was demonstrated by a furious debate in the Egyptian parliament in 2009 over an "artificial hymen" from China—essentially a small plastic bag filled with red fluid, designed to simulate the resistance, and bleeding, of defloration. News that it might be making its way onto the Egyptian market was enough to send some parliamentarians into a frenzy and provided a convenient stick with which to poke the Mubarak government. "It will be a blot on the conscience of the NDP [the now-disbanded National Democratic Party] government if it allows these membranes to enter," a representative of the opposition Muslim Brotherhood warned, arguing the product was a dire threat to Egyptian womanhood, tempting "vulnerable souls into committing vice."[48] Despite the best efforts of several young women I know to find them, I have yet to meet anyone who has actually managed to buy one of these fake hymens on the local market.

The Qur'an makes no mention of the hymen (*ghisha' al-bakara,* in Arabic) per se, but it does talk at length about private parts and the importance of protecting them from view. While virginity is, in principle, gender-neutral in the Qur'an, female virgins get special billing, the Virgin Mary coming in for particular praise.[49] Then there are the *hur,* the perpetual virgins of paradise, "maidens restraining their glances, untouched beforehand by man or jinn," whom Muslim men will marry as a reward for a righteous, God-fearing life, so the faithful believe.[50] According to hadith, the Prophet is said to have joked with a newly married companion that he might have had more fun with a virgin than the "mature woman" he took as his wife.[51] Female virginity became yet another tool to keep women in line, all the easier to enforce through its intimate connection to family honor, making it a matter of collective concern rather than a private affair.

Opinion polls show the line on virginity, in word if not in deed, holding firm, even in countries, such as Morocco and Lebanon, with a reputation within the Arab world for sexual openness.[52] There are certainly some women who don't care and some men for whom virginity is not a deal breaker. "I have a friend of mine who did it," Rakha told me. "Before she got engaged, she confessed to her fiancé that she slept with two guys. And he married her. One of the few very respectable guys." But I've met plenty of women across the region who distrust such seeming liberality, fearing their premarital experiences will come back to haunt them when marriage turns rocky and their sexual histories are thrown back in their faces. As my grandmother used to say, "The woman who trusts a man is like a woman who stores water in a sieve."

In my experience, more men fall into the camp of Kassim, a Cairo pharmacist. "I'm twenty-nine years old. I've passed through university; those were the days. I've seen lots of girls and I've been with lots of girls, that's a fact. Actually, they were my passion. After you finish class or lab, let's go and find some girls," he recollected with a smile. But it's not a given that getting a girl will get you laid, as Kassim explained. "Normally, in Egypt, let's say 80 percent [of unmarried couples] no, not sex, but just having fun. They put themselves into the frame we are boyfriend and girlfriend, we can do whatever we can do, but not intercourse," he observed. Kassim paused for a moment, lost in thought, then corrected himself. "Sometimes, yeah, it reaches intercourse. [But] it's not for a fact if you have a girlfriend, you're gonna have sex. No, this is never the fact."

This is a source of frustration for young men, keen to get some sexual know-how before their wedding nights. "Normally, men seek for experience before marriage. I'm not gonna talk about [religiously] strict people, naive people; I'm talking about a normal person," Kassim noted. "I would rather have this experience, at least let's say how to kiss, how to unbuckle the bra by one hand, those are skills. I would rather do this instead of getting married, and I'm all of a sudden, Whoops, we need some help from some other third party. It's a shame to ask one of my friends what to do."

Kassim, who studied abroad, managed to pad out his sexual résumé with an Italian girlfriend, whom he contemplated marrying, though their relationship eventually foundered. However, he drew the line on premarital sex with the woman he eventually wed, the sister of one of his friends. "As an Egyptian, she has to be a virgin," he insisted. Why the difference? "If she's foreign, it puts the girl into a different classification other than Egyptian women. If it's fine with me, [then] it's fine with my parents, my family; they have nothing to do with this [decision]," Kassim explained. "[But] if I marry an Egyptian girl from an Egyptian family, this is where my mother and father come."

And how. In Egypt, virginity can be very much a family affair, thanks to *dukhla*. The word means "entry" and refers to defloration of the bride on her wedding night. *Dukhla baladi,* so-called "country-style" defloration, was a time-honored custom in Egypt, for Muslims and Christians alike, in which the *daya* would pierce the bride's hymen with her finger or a razor wrapped in a white cloth, with the groom looking on (or taking the lead) and mothers in attendance. The bloodstained *laf al-sharaf* (sheet of honor) would then be shown off to nearest and dearest to demonstrate that the family had kept its good name and duly delivered a virgin bride to the groom.

When my father was a boy, visits to the family farm in the Nile Delta, north of Cairo, were punctuated by post-*dukhla* celebrations for women in the village. There was a special song, "Bride, You Have Whitened the Gauze"—that is, honored the family—sung by female relatives and friends as they paraded from home to home with the bloodstained sheet, collecting presents for the couple, laughing and ululating in celebration. Even as a child, my father knew exactly what had happened—it was a joyous event to be shared by all, not some shameful sex-stained episode to conceal.

In recent decades, however, a new kind of wedding night ceremony has gained traction: *dukhla afrangi*. *Afrangi* comes from the Arabic word for "Frank," the term used to describe Europeans in the medieval period, and in days gone by, it was Egyptian shorthand for anything new or foreign. *Dukhla afrangi* essentially pushes bystanders out of the marriage chamber and replaces a finger with an exclusively male member to break the hymen—that is, straight-up sexual intercourse. The bloodstained sheet or handkerchief, however, remains part of the program, to be shown to the bride's family and other concerned parties. Then there is what you might call *dukhla afrangi* 2.0, which is what happened to one young woman I know, a scientist in her midtwenties who recently married. In the run-up to the big day, the prospective groom was bombarded with calls from her father, a Cairo lawyer, who insisted that his son-in-law text him right after the defloration to let him know that his daughter had bled as expected. The steady stream of calls and messages reminding him of this duty made the groom so anxious that he tried to take his bride to the cinema, instead of the honeymoon suite, on their wedding night to avoid the situation altogether. In the end, the newlyweds managed to consummate their union as required, the groom having turned off his phone. Undeterred, her parents turned up the next day to collect the sheet of honor. While slightly more private, *dukhla afrangi* still piles on the pressure: on brides to prove their virginity and on grooms to demonstrate their virility—far from easy, given the wedding night jitters discussed earlier.

As for old-style *dukhla baladi,* personal accounts make it sound about as pleasant for the women at the center of the ceremony as their circumcision was years before, and particularly traumatic for those with hymens that don't break as anticipated. Indeed, there are voices that condemn *dukhla baladi* as a form of sexual violence against women, a sort of family-sanctioned rape. From an Islamic perspective, some consider the practice haram on a number of grounds, among them that it violates the penis-meets-vagina definition of legitimate sexual intercourse. And for those who hold such notions dear, it also undermines the value of virginity, reducing what should be a focus on broader questions of morality and conduct to a bit of anatomy and a late-night performance.

Nonetheless, some young women in Cairo use *dukhla baladi* to their advantage. Among them are poor working women whose daily forays outside their communities, inevitably bringing them into contact with strangers, put their honor into question; others, whose families migrated to the big city, find themselves relative outsiders and unknown quantities to the families of their perspective husbands. For any woman whose personal history is in doubt, *dukhla baladi* is a form of exoneration, as well as a trade-off for a little more personal freedom, so long as she is prepared to demonstrate her virginity in so public a fashion.[53] Indeed, research suggests that *dukhla baladi* is actually more common in poor neighborhoods of Cairo than it is in some rural areas, contrary to notions of the "modernizing" effect of the city. This is in part because the economic and social realities of urban life mean that families are unable to exercise the same vigilance over their daughters, and in part because many inhabitants of these neighborhoods, originally migrants from the countryside, find themselves clinging to rural traditions as the city's powerful tide rushes in.[54]

That *dukhla* of any description persists in Egypt is because family honor is still bound up with female virginity; it's possible that as family ties unwind, or as personal freedoms come to be recognized in an emerging democratic order, this tight association might weaken, and that virginity will become a private affair, between husband and wife only, as it is among some couples I know. This day will be some time in coming, however. In the meantime, mothers still invest enormous mental energy in putting the fear of a ruptured hymen into their daughters, warning them off anything that might breach that all-important membrane, be it masturbation or the ubiquitous water hose, found in bathrooms across the Arab world for washing "down there," according to Islamic custom.

If such traditional methods fail in protecting a hymen, newer measures are available. Hymen repair is the stuff of overheated headlines across the Arab region, often taken as evidence of the moral decline of today's youth. In Egypt it's hard to get a firm grip on the number of such procedures: one doctor, working at a women's hospital in a poorer quarter of Cairo, says she sees two cases a week. The quick-fix approach is a stitch across the vaginal opening, which, like the Chinese fake hymen, offers a fair imitation of resistance and bleeding on intercourse. The procedure costs around EGP 200 and lasts a couple of days; more elaborate interventions are said to run from EGP 700–2,000, the monthly income of a lower-middle-class family. There are other costs too: women gynecologists talk of male colleagues taking advantage of such patients, extorting sexual favors in exchange for keeping the operation secret.[55]

Restoring virginity—or rather, the appearance of it—is not a uniquely modern concern. Egyptian folklore is full of stories of the quick-handed *daya* helping a "virgin" bride out of a tight spot with a bottle of red dye or a pigeon's giblet stuffed with blood on the wedding night; the *Encyclopedia of Pleasure,* for example, offers many handy hints on the subject. In Egypt, hymen repair is not illegal, but it is widely considered shameful or indeed haram. In recent years, a lively debate has broken out among religious authorities in Egypt and the wider Arab world over the permissibility of the procedure. According to one school of thought, hymen repair is forbidden by Islam for a number of reasons, among them that it deceives husbands, opens the possibility of mistaken paternity (if the "repaired" bride has already conceived from a previous relation), unnecessarily reveals a woman's private parts, and pushes her down the slippery slope of easy-to-conceal illicit sex.[56]

However, other Islamic voices argue that hymen repair is permissible because a missing hymen is not, in itself, proof positive of adultery according to shari'a. Moreover, denying a woman access to hymen repair impairs her chances of marriage, which could lead her to channel her sexual energy into unlawful relations. Such authorities also argue *satr al-'ird,* the Islamic principle of protecting a woman's honor from public speculation, so long as concealment does not cause wider social harm. Among them is Shaykh Ali Gomaa, who issued a controversial fatwa in 2007 permitting hymen repair in a wide range of circumstances beyond rape and other "accidental losses," though he drew the line at "women known for promiscuity."[57]

Hymen repair puts some physicians in a quandary. Should they participate in what could be considered deception of the husband, or is it their obligation to help a woman who might otherwise find herself in extremely hot water if her previous experience is discovered? Are they complicit in a procedure that buttresses the patriarchy and the double standards around virginity, or are they giving women more personal freedom by helping them around these social restrictions? For some practitioners, the question is emotional, not intellectual. "A young woman has been led into error, or has made a mistake—to rebuild her life from scratch, I approve that she does it," one Cairo gynecologist explained. "I can't morally judge someone who comes to me. When I have ten women who appear for a consultation, I sympathize with at least nine of them. They're suffering, and I am of a mind to help these girls."[58]

There are women's rights advocates who argue that hymen repair surgery might put itself out of business by tearing right through the Arab world's membrane fixation: if men can't tell a real hymen from a reasonable facsimile, what is the point of *dukhla*? One day, perhaps. For now, though, stories of hymen repair are simply pumping up social anxiety: I know of Egyptian men who, in the face of tradition and whispering about their own prowess, will wait a couple of days after the wedding to consummate the union, having read that the effects of hymen repair will wear off by then and all will be revealed.

Gynecologists across the Arab region receive plenty of anxious young women looking to get their hymens checked, some horrified to learn that what they thought were "incomplete" relations with boyfriends—that is, withdrawal before penetration—have, over time, in fact broken their membranes, or that their hymens were not as "elastic" (that is, bendable, rather than breakable) as they wishfully believed. But virginity testing can take other, more disturbing forms. Among them is the "virginity certificate"— a physician-signed testimonial that the virgin bride is the genuine article. Premarital examinations are common across the Arab region to test for sexually transmitted infections, such as HIV and hepatitis, and—because of the high rate of consanguineous marriage—some inherited disorders as well. In a number of countries, including several in the Gulf, such tests are legally mandated; while they raise a number of ethical issues (among them the right to privacy, and the freedom to marry, whatever the results), studies from across the region show they are widely supported by prospective newlyweds.[59] In some cases, however, grooms and their families take tests one step further, asking for the bride to be certified as intact before consummation—or after, should she not bleed as expected. Such tests can be emotionally scarring and are certainly ethically charged, not just for the woman on the examining table but for the doctor asked to take a look.[60] Virginity testing is also considered by some to be un-Islamic, yet another violation of the principle of *satr al-'ird*.

Virginity testing can also be a tool of political control. In the wake of the Egyptian uprising, several female protesters were forcibly subjected to virginity tests authorized by the military. Officials argued that the tests were to prove that these unmarried women, who had been camping out in Tahrir Square, were not virgins, just in case they later brought charges against the army for sexual assault. The reality is that such tests are just another instrument in the torturer's toolkit. Sex is a source of shame, which makes it a powerful tool of subjugation—be it the humiliation of male prisoners in Abu Ghraib prison or violence against female protesters in uprisings across the Arab region, packing a one-two punch of disgracing women and, by extension, their menfolk as well.[61] In this particular case, the results of such testing could help to shore up prostitution charges, as well as serve as grounds for blackmail should unmarried women prove not to be virgins—all ways of discrediting protesters and discouraging any others who might be tempted to follow their lead. One of the women tested decided to strike back and filed a lawsuit against the military, but she found herself up against the same old obstacles in achieving redress from Egypt's post-Mubarak regime.[62] Interestingly, it was forced testing under the microscope in this long-running legal battle, rather than the value of virginity itself, or why it should be relevant to what is essentially a political matter.

There are, nonetheless, a small but rising number of voices that publicly question the fixation on female virginity and the blanket condemnation of premarital sex. Marwa Rakha is among them. "I am attacked a lot about my view on the subject of sex and sexual relations before marriage," she wrote to one correspondent. "I am not against it, and I also see that it is a natural thing in the stages of knowing other people. Just as people know each other emotionally, mentally and they talk about their principles, their thoughts and their beliefs, so it is imperative that they get near sexually."[63] For her, this is not an issue of religion or morality but a question of personal freedom, particularly for women.


## BREAKING AWAY

Key to realizing that freedom is negotiating independence within the family. It's clear that young people in Egypt and across the Arab region are deeply attached to their families, even as these shrink from extended to nuclear units and members scatter across cities, countries, and continents, as my own family has. This umbilical cord is, in large part, financial. In Egypt, for example, the vast majority of unmarried people (and around 40 percent of married couples) under the age of thirty live with their families; given that unemployment is running in the double digits, this means many are tied to them economically as well.[64]

All-in-the-family has practical implications for your love life: in most households, it's almost inconceivable to bring home a date unless it's of the edible variety, especially since only a small minority of youth in Egypt have their own bedrooms. A hotel is generally too expensive for most young people, and most will ask to see a marriage certificate as well, unless you can slip a suitable sum under the reception desk. If you want to get intimate, your best bet is to have a friend with his own apartment, or car, or it's back to the corniche for some alfresco fumbling.

This material dependence takes subtle forms. In a society that runs on *wasta*—connections—your family's name and influence are important to getting on in life. This I know from personal experience: when my Western upbringing and can-do independence withered on contact with Egyptian bureaucracy, I had to call in my family to have a few words and promise a few favors to get things done.[65] As my grandmother used to say, "The one who has a back [family support] will not be punched in the stomach."

But there is a deep emotional component to this connection as well. The Qur'an exhorts believers to honor their mothers and fathers: "We have commanded people to be good to their parents: their mothers carried them, with strain upon strain, and it takes two years to wean them. Give thanks to Me and to your parents—all will return to Me" is just one of many verses on the subject.[66] This family connectedness is borne out by research across the Arab region, which shows the strength of young people's sense of family identity and affiliation.[67] How the uprising—and the experience of millions of young men and women out on the streets, night after night, defying political authority—will affect relations with parental authority is an interesting question. *Hurriyya* (freedom) has become the rallying cry of many a youngster talking back to parents on household chores or trying to extract a larger allowance. For older youth, however, this is a more complicated negotiation.

Al Haq spoke for many I've met when she described the tightrope act between her personal freedom and her family. "Me and Mom are very close. She believes in what I am doing, and she admires me. But every single time I say something that's not all that common in society, she is like, 'What about the society? What about the family?'"

Al Haq argued with her mother for days to be allowed to come to Tahrir Square from their town in the countryside north of Cairo. "I wanted so much to be there, to join my friends, and just to see what the hell they are doing with Egypt. In my generation, I never felt like I am in a home. So it was for me, the revolution, this feeling [of] belonging to a country. It was very beautiful, very strong; I was dying to feel this. Egypt is ours, not for Mubarak, not anyone's Egypt except us." Al Haq sneaked away, and although her mother was furious, she eventually relented. But there are limits to how far Al Haq is willing to push her newfound liberty. "I live my life freely and am not afraid of anyone. I just won't tell Mom that I have a boyfriend and I am enjoying my life with him. Just because that will hurt her much and it will be very shocking for her. And I don't want to lose people from my family."

In my experience, few young people see a link between their rebellion against the head of state and openly defying the heads of their families—at least not yet. But some are clearly making the connection. Tarek Salama is a journalist turned activist working on sexual rights—not exactly a popular subject in Egypt. "The first time in my life to go out and protest was on the twenty-fifth of January," he said. "I used to believe protests were nothing and that they will lead us nowhere." But the events of 2011 have changed his life, professionally and personally. "For me, as an activist, there are many decisions that I wouldn't dare to take before the twenty-fifth of January, because of politics, because of society, because of my family situation," he told me as we sipped coffee quite literally a stone's throw from Tahrir Square, on a side street that was the scene of fierce clashes between young protesters and security forces. "For example, I don't think, if it wasn't for the twenty-fifth of

January, I would be able to sit with you at this table and talk about sexuality. Because I would have been scared. Now I am not afraid of this fight."

Nor is it elders and betters anymore. "I used to be this kind of shy person, and respectful of old people," Salama said, readjusting his chunky black-framed glasses. "But when I discovered we got rid of Mubarak—he was eightysomething—this somehow destroyed the old figure in my imagination. So somehow I became aggressive and sharp, even if the person is much older than me, when I find that all that they say is shit." The uprising has left Salama both disillusioned and enlightened. "Most of the people who fucked us up through the revolution were older. Most of the people I took as idols and icons really let me down. When I found them collapsed, I discovered that this has nothing to do with the age, nothing to do with experience; it has to do with whether the person is true to him or herself, and that's what matters to me."

For their part, I heard parents complain, time and again, before the uprising about their children's lack of maturity. "I always used to say before, this generation has nothing to do but stay on their computers and play," one father in his fifties, a former army general, lamented to me. The 2011 uprising, spearheaded by the country's youth, changed that. He and his twentysomething daughter spent days in Tahrir Square, a bonding experience that altered his opinion. Many older Egyptians, my own relatives included, have been rattled by recent events and find change hard to accept. Not the general, though. "I was very wrong," he told me, no easy thing for an Egyptian man, and father, to admit. "At the beginning I was very surprised by the demonstrators, the decency, the civilized way they presented their ideas. This generation has proved to me that they have plans for the future and they know how to work for it."

Subsequent events have taken some of the gloss off that admiration. Making way for young blood—be it in political or domestic decision-making—is a long-term process. Whether young people will be given a chance to take the lead, and have the wit to use it well, is another story. One test of this new entente cordiale will be how easy young people—particularly young women like Al Haq—

find it to strike out on their own in the years to come. Al Haq's mother now allows her to stay alone in the family flat in Cairo, for example, something that was out of the question before the revolt. But this freedom doesn't come easy: leaving your parents' place is less a rite of passage and more an ordeal by fire for the minority of unmarried people across the region who can afford it. "If you go to any shaykh and say, 'There is this girl and she moved out,' they will say, 'Ah, bad girl!' She would be, like, cursed and damned," says Rakha.

She should know. Life changed for Rakha when she started working in her early twenties. "When I earned my first salary, I realized having my own money makes me happy. And it gave me this little freedom that even if I want perfume or a dress, I don't have to go to my mom and get her approval for what I'm going to be wearing," she told me. "This is where the independence started. I'm not happy where there is a man; I'm happy when I do things for myself."

By her late twenties, Rakha had decided to get her own apartment. "My mom thought if I move out, I'm gonna fail and I'm gonna move back home. So she let me go, and she was shocked I survived," she recalled. "When I was home, I didn't do anything. I slept until eight [p.m.] and then I went out with my friends. Moving out, the house has to be clean. It's a whole different thing. I was ready for it. Thing is, I didn't want this package with a man. I needed to just do it on my own."

Such self-reliance is more of a black mark than a badge of honor for Egyptian women, in Rakha's opinion. "For a man, there is usually a question mark: 'Why did you leave your parents'?' If a man replies, 'Because I wanted to grow up, because I wanted to learn to be responsible,' that's perfectly fine in the society. But most men don't want to move out; they want somebody to cook and clean for them. It's the girls here who want their independence; they want to prove themselves apart from their socially accepted posts." Rakha is all too familiar with this sort of thinking, which starts at home. Parents are worried about keeping up appearances, and daughters who fly the coop are accused of shirking filial responsibility. "I'm going to tell you my mom's version of it," says Rakha. "First of all,

she feels I'm ungrateful. Like, instead of being with her, and supporting her, and comforting her, I moved out. My counterargument
always was, 'What if I got married? I would leave you.' 'But that's
because you're married.' So what—now I'm being punished for not
being married?"

When I meet an intelligent, ambitious, and professionally successful woman over thirty-five in Egypt—indeed anywhere in
the Arab region—I don't expect her to be wearing a wedding ring.
While the vast majority of young women in Egypt are married by
their late twenties, the proportion of those still single at thirty or
older is more than three times higher among those who have gone
on to higher education than those with less than a high school
diploma.[68] Some unmarried women I know would happily consider
a Western spouse (provided he was of the same religion), while others have turned to their faith and a fatalism that allows them to
chalk up their single status to God's will. But many of them have
simply given up on their countrymen as husband material. There
are a number of social and economic factors to account for this state
of affairs, but Rakha has a straightforward answer. "When women
got educated—college, university, whatever—their brains opened
up. Men, they go through the same process, but it's like their brain
is somewhere and their career is somewhere else," she said. "So
you meet this great guy, this successful guy, glamorous guy, well-
educated guy, traveled guy, but in his head, he's still stupid guy."

She was careful to define her terms. "Someone my age or older,
he's a complete piece of shit. Traditional and baggage, shit everywhere. Insecure; 'I hate women, they're so bad, controlling'; intim-
idated by anything, everything." Rakha gets a lot of e-mail from
anxious men across the country, and she has a ready explanation
for their behavior: "All the shit that they do [is] out of fear. They
are scared. Scared little boys. That goes from the age of thirteen
to thirty. Scared of everything, scared of being judged. Scared of
being rejected. Scared of saying or doing the wrong thing. Scared
of being dumped. Scared of being cheated on. They all have these
insecurity issues. Everywhere." What this means, in the mating
game, is a mismatch between prospective husbands looking to con-

trol and prospective wives searching for autonomy—one reason for the growing ranks of unmarried women.

## BATTLE OF THE SEXES

These tensions go beyond private relations. *Taharrush jinsi*—or sexual harassment, ranging from ogling and lewd remarks to flashing, public masturbation, and outright physical assault—plays out on the streets of Egypt and across the Arab world. The recent national survey of Egyptians aged ten to twenty-nine found that more than half of young women living in towns and cities had experienced sexual harassment—mainly salacious comments from strangers.[69] But there is plenty of evidence of far more violent incidents, and not just on dark, deserted streets but in jam-packed daylight. Visible minorities—Sudanese refugees, Asian domestic workers, Western tourists—are particularly vulnerable, their harassers egged on by stereotypes of sexed-up foreign females.

Cairo is a concentrate of Egypt, so it's no surprise that sexual harassment is most extreme in the capital. It was here that the phenomenon first made the headlines in the mid-2000s, and over the years public celebrations—particularly religious holidays—have become something of a free-for-all for sexual harassers, notorious for swarms of young men cornering passing women.[70] Now sexual harassment and assault even feature—along with political unrest, dodgy water, and dangerous driving—in foreign governments' travel advisories on the hazards of visiting Egypt.[71]

*Mu'aksa,* or male flirtation, used to be a gentler sport. "*Ya helwa, ya gamila*" ("You sweet, beautiful thing") and "*Ya amar*" ("You are like the moon") were the sorts of honeyed phrases my aunts and cousins used to hear in downtown Cairo and Alexandria in the 1960s and '70s. Then there is the Egyptian equivalent of a wolf whistle, also used to attract cats, a soft hissing noise like a tire leaking air—not, to my mind, a particularly promising association for a man on the make. Today, however, the come-ons are a lot less courteous: "*Ya labwa* [You bitch]" is how one of my friends, in full hijab and modest attire, was greeted by a carful of young men when she stopped at a traffic light. "How I wish I had two beds so I could sleep with you twice."

Many people pin the blame for such "impolite" behavior, as Egyptians call it, on economics: unemployed youth with time on their hands and sex on their minds, thanks to TV and the Internet; parents working round the clock, or fathers toiling in the Gulf, leading to a breakdown in family surveillance and moral upbringing. Without marriage, and therefore an easy sexual outlet, this libidinous energy is spilling onto the streets, so conventional thinking has it. At the same time, the argument goes, women are increasingly in the public domain, and men are being provoked beyond endurance by their daring dress and bold behavior. Not surprisingly, with this sort of wisdom doing the rounds, many men believe that women actually welcome these attentions.[72]

It's not just self-confessed harassers who subscribe to a blame-the-victim philosophy: more than 60 percent of the most highly educated women in the national youth survey, and three-quarters of their least literate counterparts, believed that "provocatively dressed" women are asking for it.[73] Although more than 90 percent of young women in Egypt cover up—over their heads, up to their necks, and down to their wrists and ankles—there are plenty of ways to sex up this uniform: eye-catching headscarves in fantastical arrangements; layers of makeup; flashy wrapround sunglasses; tight jeans and curve-molding tunics, Lycra being God's gift to Arab men.[74] These *dolce hegabbanas* are deftly upending today's conservative rules, technically covering up their *'awra* (parts of men's and women's bodies to be concealed from public view, according to Islamic principles) and buying themselves a little more freedom from parents, all the while flaunting their femininity. And yet, as these young women wistfully recall, their mothers and grandmothers were able to go out with flowing hair and far more flesh on display—short skirts, bare arms—and pass unmolested.

For all this subtle subversion, many women are reluctant to defy convention and mention incidents of sexual harassment to their families, let alone report them to authorities.[75] There are a variety of reasons for such reticence: some blame themselves for the harassment; others worry about damage to their reputation by admitting they have been hassled and about its attendant consequences, including being grounded by their parents. Moreover, many fear that police will not take them seriously, partly because it is difficult to provide proof of hit-and-run harassment, and partly because it has often been the police themselves who are the perpetrators.[76]

For all these obstacles, sexual harassment is one of the taboos now openly discussed in Egypt. There are a number of innovative campaigns to help women report incidents, deal with the fallout, engage young people of both sexes in community projects, and teach the next generation—especially boys—that hassling women does not make you more of a man.[77] A small but growing number of women, emboldened by the uprising, have used existing laws on public indecency and sexual assault to turn the table on their assailants. There are also efforts by NGOs to secure a law explicitly criminalizing sexual harassment, although the experience of Tunisia and Algeria with legislation already on the books shows that legal loopholes are hard to close and that cultural change can be slow to follow. "Sometimes when we come to change the mentality of the people, we feel we move the sea with a cup," joked Nehad Abu Komsan, a Cairo-based lawyer and head of the Egyptian Center for Women's Rights, a leader in the fight against sexual harassment.

One of the ways Abu Komsan and fellow campaigners have been able to move this sensitive topic out of the shadows is by taking the sex out of sexual harassment, making it a question of personal safety and government failings, rather than a question of women's rights, which raises hackles with social conservatives. "We [are] not attacking men because they are bad people harassing women. We [are] not blaming society because it's an ignorant society and say in the public what they not do [in private]," she explained. "You can attack the government if you are not happy with their policies: 'It is your fault. You are not interested in people's security; you're interested about political security.' But if you want to make social change, don't attack the people." While some worry that sexual harassment may be used by Islamists to curtail women's freedoms, others are concerned that the state might exploit this framing of the issues in terms of security and policing to strengthen its power in the name of protecting women, with the bonus of clamping down on political opponents in the process.[78] But until there is a climate in Egypt where such issues can be addressed in terms of personal freedoms and rights, this approach is better than nothing. "It is about packaging," Abu Komsan told me. "As they say, 'You can put poison in a very nice glass and people will take it very happily.'"

Abu Komsan and others argue that Egypt's epidemic of sexual harassment is more a function of political and economic oppression—which has men lashing out at those next down the line in the patriarchy—than an explosion of sexual frustration. Certainly, recent events have shown that when men feel a sense of empowerment and purpose, their behavior toward women shifts dramatically. Until 2011, mass gatherings of young men were dangerous territory for women. And yet in the marches in Tahrir Square, where tens of thousands gathered to protest against authoritarian regimes, past, present, and future, I and other women found ourselves able to move freely—well, as freely as you can in a revolutionary throng—as men made way and listened with respect. When I was running from tear gas, there were men helping me to safety, not taking advantage of easy prey. That's not to say there was no sexual harassment of women in Tahrir Square—there was, for all the utopian myth that surrounds the 2011 uprising. As long as the youth in Tahrir were united in a pressing common goal, men and women worked well together, but as soon as that purpose drained from the square, a carnival atmosphere prevailed and the sexual harassment returned. On one of these occasions, I watched, horrified and unable to help, as a crowd of young men cornered a young woman in a hijab, pinned her up against a railing, and tore off her clothes. Under normal circumstances, men usually stick to the sidelines when women are harassed, but in this case a few were trying to rescue her, handing over their own clothes to cover her up and carrying her out of the mayhem.

Tipping the balance from harassment to cooperation isn't easy.

But Abu Komsan is confident that, in the long run, the revolt will lift Egypt out of its decades-long malaise and that symptoms like sexual harassment will shift from a chronic condition to a sporadic complaint. "What is it the revolution gave? It gives people a powerful feeling that they are able to control their life and make their own decisions. Before, most of us Egyptians were very depressed and feeling they are not human. [I'm] not talking about human rights, just being human. Revolution gives people a sense of victory and dignity and hope. Definitely, this makes their behavior better."

Better remains to be seen. But when it comes to intimate life, will it be any different? For all her hopes, Al Haq was doubtful of change beyond those who had already broken the rules. "I believe the one who was rebel before the revolution will be more rebel after the revolution. It happened for me and it happened for many friends. Maybe they won't still be able to face the society in what they are doing, but in their social circles, they will be okay, 'Yes, I do this; I am not regretting it.'" Those who publicly defy convention—like the Nude Photo Revolutionary—are largely seen as aberrations, not trendsetters. "It won't happen in this society, a real freedom of sexual life and freedom of expression, except [when] the people are really educated," Al Haq said. "It won't come for years and years." Salama was similarly doubtful. "Girls sleeping out in the square with boys, that's a social aspect of the revolution. But this is not a social revolution. The social phase of the revolution is just starting. For these changes to take place, it's going to need much time."

And yet there are countless private rebellions playing out across the land, even if those at their heart don't see them as such. "Revolution is for political matters, but not in thinking. Tradition has no relation with revolution," Amany sighed, sinking into the shadow of a hypostyle hall. She and I met at one of the many ancient temples dotting the countryside between Luxor and Aswan, where I was on a break from the crush of Cairo and Amany was on the job as a guide. As we wandered past obelisks and statues, she shared her impressive knowledge of history and her own story of quiet uprising.

Amany is in her late twenties and comes from a lower-middle-class family in Upper Egypt. Al-Sa'iid, as the south of the country is known in Arabic, is a famously conservative region, but times are changing. Egyptian parents increasingly want to have daughters as well as sons; they also see the value of sending their girls on to higher education, even if that means far afield, in part because educated (but not *too* educated) young women are thought to have a greater chance in the marriage stakes and to make better wives and mothers. And so Amany, who is the bright spark of her five siblings, was allowed to go away for university, but once student days were over, she had to move back home. Unlike many young Egyptians, however, she has a lucrative job, which makes her the family breadwinner now that her father is retired. Amany may hold all the financial cards, but her parents still call the shots. Every couple of weeks her mother produces a suitor, in the hope of seeing her daughter married. But Amany refuses all comers for one simple reason: she's secretly married already.

Five years ago, Amany met Hossam, a former soldier and her brother's friend, who comes from the north of Egypt. Hossam was quickly smitten, Amany told me, and duly appeared with his parents in tow to ask for her hand. Here Amany paused her story for a moment to show me a hieroglyph. "This is the symbol of eternal life," she explained, pointing to an ankh. "It also represents the unity of Upper and Lower Egypt." Sadly, no such union was in the cards for Amany and Hossam. Her parents refused him because he makes less money than their daughter and would therefore drain an income that otherwise flows to them. But their objections were also geographical. "They do not trust a lot in the men of Lower Egypt. It seems that if they [the couple] have a kind of trouble, maybe he will leave her and he will go to live up there [in the north] and marry another woman. Not peace enough in their mind," she explained. As far as Amany is concerned, though, Hossam's provenance is an asset. "He has a more open mind. He trusts me; he does not mind that I work with other men," she said, comparing him favorably with her local suitors. "He is the type of the man, if you are not talking, he can read your eyes. It looks like he had a trip through my mind. He understands me. You can't find this type of man nowadays."

After three more years and two more tries with her parents, Amany decided to take matters into her own hands. "I found no hope of the family anymore. They will never change their mind. So I said it's my choice, let me do my choice." As the 2011 uprising drew to a close, she and Hossam traveled north, far from the prying eyes of home, and signed an 'urfi marriage contract in a lawyer's office. For Amany, sleeping with Hossam was inconceivable without it. "We had secret marriage because we wanted to make it right before my God. Because we are Muslims, we do not want to do something that is haram." But it was equally unimaginable to her to openly defy her parents and enter into an official marriage without their consent. "I don't like to put my family in a critical situation. I have to obey them. I have to do all of my best to make them happy more than me," she said. "And for reputation, their reputation, not my reputation. My father is now retired, but all of the time he is in the mosque, the famous man of religion. He is a man with a good position. [If I marry without his consent], they will say he has a very impolite girl."

As we passed by tales of "beautiful meetings" between gods and goddesses inscribed on the temple walls, Amany told me about her less-than-beautiful life with Hossam, sneaking out of her parents' place in quiet hours to catch some time with him at his tiny rented flat across town. As far as she is concerned, discretion is a matter of life and death. "My parents, if they find out, they will kill me. Really. It happened in my family. The sister of my grandmother, she had a relation, and they took her and one day . . . " Amany drew her hand across her throat like a knife. Honor killings are a shadowy subject in Egypt, and no one is quite sure of the scale of the problem.[79] But for Amany it is far from a dying practice; the story is kept alive in her family to keep the girls in line.

Like many young women I've met, Amany is caught between defiance and regret. She is quietly furious with her parents for driving her to this situation, but she is also torn by guilt. "I am now deceiving my family," she told me sadly. "My family trust me, and I am using their trust not in a good way. I used to be so honest all of the time. I used to tell them everything happening in my life. But this thing I can't say." Amany's reticence is compounded by the fact that she no longer believes her 'urfi marriage is Islamically sound. "I read on the Internet, some people say it is 100 percent halal, some people say 20 percent halal. So I don't know. I told [Hossam] we need to stop to doing anything together [having sex], because maybe what we did is haram. I don't like to continue in haram again: I have to feed poor people; I have to pray a lot; I have to go to hajj. Maybe God will forgive me."

Amany has few hopes that her family will come around, or that Hossam will find a job in Egypt's struggling economy. "I don't like to think what will happen in the future. I don't like to make myself to be sad. Keep it for God," she said. Amany spoke as if the uprising had already passed her by, too late to make much of a difference in her life. But she has high hopes that any daughter of hers will one day benefit, and she is clear on what she, as a mother, will do. "I will never give something to my kids that makes me hard with my family. I hurt a lot from them, [because] they are thinking in a different way," Amany said, her voice breaking. "But I will be able to understand my daughter, what she is thinking, because I am in that experience before. I will let her to choose the person that her heart chooses and her feelings choose."

Whether Amany and her generation will, in fact, behave any differently from their parents in matters ranging from family life to Egypt's political future is the big question. Opinion polls suggest that on many issues—particularly as they relate to gender and sex—young people across the Arab region are even more conservative than their elders. But talk to these same youth in private and they express dreams and desires that belie such stern appearances. Young Egyptians—especially young women—continue to walk a fine line between public conformity and private fulfillment. But for one spectacular moment, in the uprising of 2011, public and private aligned.

The postrevolutionary reality has not turned out as many had hoped, and old men are once again in charge, having deftly out-maneuvered their less experienced sons and daughters. But just because they are not out in front does not mean these youth are out of sight; if they play the next decade right, study their societies, build their knowledge, and hone their tactics, then they could well bring about the change that Amany dreams of for herself and her children—starting, as we'll see in the next chapter, with a few foundation stones.

# 4

# Facts of Life

*A clever woman can spin yarn with a donkey's thighbone.*
—My grandmother, on making the most
of what you're given

In a blood-red basement in Cairo, I walked in on a beautiful young woman on the phone, talking sex. "Trust us," she wrapped up with a caller. "We are dealing with people from different levels. No one will know anything." It's a pity he could only hear her voice, because she really was a sight: flawless olive skin and full red lips, her beautifully manicured fingers brushing back a lock of thick, glossy hair from jet-black, almond-shaped eyes. Imagine Nefertiti on toll-free. It was a quiet night, she told me; usually, there are around forty calls a day. A lot for masturbation, she said. Oral sex too, and anal intercourse from time to time.

Now, if you have a mobile, and money, in the Arab world, it's not hard to find a woman willing to provide a little aural stimulation. A good place to start is the back channels of your TV. For those tuned to an obliging satellite, surfing the far-flung spectrum brings a wave of dial-in sex ads, much to the public fury of Islamic conservatives who threaten to pull the plug. Many of these ads are foreign—Turkish, German, Thai—but there is plenty on offer in Arabic as well: Arab Sex Club, Arab XXX, Arab Babes. It's a fairly standard service: still shots of busty, ivory-skinned nudes in various states of arousal, playing with themselves or going down on each other. For the more traditionally inclined, some of the women are wearing hijabs or niqabs—and nothing else. In a rare display of Pan-Arab unity, the flags of most countries in the region flash across the screen, accompanied by local numbers. The sound track features sample conversations—"Ah, ah, *habibi,* more, more" and similarly encouraging words.

Back in Cairo, however, that lovely young woman at the end of the line was part of a more specialized service. She's a doctor working with Shababna (Our Youth), a telephone help line to answer young people's questions about health in general and sex in particular. Six days a week, twelve hours a day, two physicians—one male, one female—are standing by to answer calls and texts from across the country. "You can't imagine the misinformation available. It's tremendous," said Mamdouh Wahba, a grandfatherly gynecologist based in Cairo, who founded Shababna. Wahba is head of the Egyptian Family Health Society, an NGO specializing in reproductive health, and has spent much of the past decade trying to dispel the fog of youthful confusion over sex and reproduction. It's no joke, but you can't help laughing with Wahba when he recalls some of the misconceptions he's had to deal with: "They don't wash underwear of girls and boys together just in case they get pregnant. Of course the menstrual blood is rotten blood that the body has to get rid of every month; if you don't have your period, you are poisoned." And then there is the stern warning that some girls, especially those from rural areas, receive on the perils of drinking tea and coffee, thought to excite them into unseemly behavior. Not to mention that old chestnut, masturbation (known as *al-'ada al-sirriyya,* or "the secret habit," in Egyptian Arabic) and its perils, including blindness, madness, impotence, and God's wrath.[1]

At their tiny call center, Rania and her colleague, Ahmed, were at the ready, laptops fired up to surf the Web for additional information should young callers tax their already impressive body of knowledge.[2] These two take their jobs very seriously. "We still have a taboo around our sexual life. As a community, we believe this is our culture. And this is a big problem in our society," said Ahmed. Rania is proud of her job: "I am here to provide service to young people, and to change wrong ideas about relationships, especially in Egypt." Still, she preferred not to talk about her work in any great detail off the job: "I don't tell my family. I just say I talk to teenagers about their problems."

Those problems come fast and furious for youth—especially young women—who move beyond the social nucleus of sex within marriage. People are quick to blame them for religious or moral laxity, but to my mind, the real failing lies in the gap between the rhetoric toward, and the reality of, Arab youth. Over the past decade, there has been no end of official statements, glossy reports, multimillion-dollar projects, and high-profile conferences extolling the power and possibilities of the region's young people. Yet those in authority, from parents to presidents, have failed to provide their sons and daughters with the basic tools of empowerment in key aspects of their lives, including that most private part—sexuality.

The fear is of the slippery slope: if young people were actually given accurate and accessible information to understand the risks and rewards of sexual life, if condoms and abortion were more easily available, if illegitimacy were less of a stigma, then this would speed the way toward *zina*—no matter the international evidence to the contrary. On this downward journey, it's not just the ends, but the means as well that have come to be seen as haram; so that's no to sexual education and condoms and abortion in many people's minds, despite the scope of permissibility within Islam. While parents are clearly concerned about the influence of "modern life" on their young, from the sexual content of movies and the Internet to the decline of extended family surveillance, they are equally anxious about providing young people with the information and services to make sense of it all.

The central deficit here is trust, the absence of which is a feature of authoritarian regimes—from national politics to personal life. As the largest demographic cohort, young people are seen, and increasingly heard—as recent political upheavals clearly demonstrate—but they are not necessarily to be trusted, especially when it comes to making decisions about their own lives. I know from my own family just how fiercely protective Egyptian parents can be, but that is not the same as preparing children for life, particularly when it comes to the means of reproduction. If democracy is, one day, to take root in Egypt and across the region, then young people need access to the tools of transformation—and the faith that they will use them well—in all areas of life, including sexuality.

Education is the place to start. When I ask teenage and twenty-something friends and family about their priorities for change in the coming years, education (along with employment) tops the list, and their anecdotes of classroom calamity are supported by surveys in Egypt and across the region.[3] "In the government school, it's not just bad, it's the worst education ever," one Cairo business school student turned protester told me, her hijab flapping in indignation. "The problem is the teacher, the way they deal with students, the equipment. It was awful, awful. Those years, I want to take those years off my life." Her frustration is reflected in the grim standing of Egypt's educational system in international rankings and by the countless reports on its shortcomings, among them underpaid staff, overcrowded facilities, stultifying curricula, and the unequal opportunities for those who can afford private tuition and those stuck with what the public system can provide. The winding down of Egyptian education is, in many ways, a mirror of the country's fortunes over the past sixty years, from the high hopes of Gamal Abdel Nasser's opening it to the masses to today's mass failure.

Among the sorriest subjects in the schoolroom is "reproductive health," as sex education is delicately called in Egypt.[4] Few can forget the fiasco of their near brush with the topic: that infamous lesson on reproductive anatomy that teachers are supposed to deliver in biology class but are often too embarrassed to communicate, instead sending students—especially girls—home to read on their own. Sexual topics are also covered in religion class, but it's more dos and don'ts in the proper practice of Islam than practical advice for the modern teenager. Studies show that only a tiny fraction of young people in Egypt, including those in the wealthiest and most educated circles, get their information on puberty and reproduction from the classroom.[5]

Egypt is not unique in its discomfort with sexual education; there are plenty of other countries, developed and developing, that are squeamish about, if not downright hostile to, teaching youth about sex, even in its most mechanical, least arousing aspects.

However, Egypt, like most of its Arab neighbors, has ratified a number of international agreements, among them the Convention on the Rights of the Child, which enjoin nations to provide young people with accurate and adequate information on sexual and reproductive life—though such agreements are under scrutiny by Islamists in the post-Mubarak period.[6] In my father's day, there were no such global covenants, but nor was learning about sex a big deal. Even citified families like ours preserved the umbilical cord to the ancestral village, and my father learned the facts of life from long talks with country cousins and by keeping a close eye on farmyard animals.[7] With the shift away from the land, however, few young urban Egyptians have access to nature's classroom anymore.

Parents are proving a poor alternative. For all their dependence on family, most young people I know in Egypt—indeed, across the Arab region—operate on a "don't ask, don't tell" basis with their parents when it comes to love and sex. According to the recent national youth survey, a majority of young women cite family— that is, mothers or aunts—as their main source of information on puberty and reproduction, but only around 5 percent of young men consult their elders on such matters, preferring to rely on friends, who are in much the same boat.[8] The upshot is that men, the most sexually active as youth, are also the ones with the least access to reliable information. Not that parents are a particular font of wisdom on sexual and reproductive matters; in Egypt and its Arab neighbors, studies show that many mothers and fathers, for all their desire to be closer to their kids than they were with their own parents, are either themselves sketchy on the details or hesitant, for various reasons, to broach the nitty-gritty.[9] Almost half of young men and women surveyed in Egypt claim to be dissatisfied with the information they're receiving.[10]

## SEX ON-SCREEN

Although reluctant to admit as much in official surveys, many young Egyptians are, unsurprisingly, gleaning their scattered fragments of sexual knowledge from TV and the Internet—movies and, in particular, porn being prime resources. In Cairo, for example, it is easy enough to find sexually explicit material, especially if you're a man, illegal though it is. For those without the bandwidth—or privacy—to view online, there's always the possibility of a trip downtown to a kiosk selling blockbuster CDs and DVDs, and a bit on the side. Even more convenient, you can send and receive short clips on your phone, thanks to Bluetooth and Egypt's ever-expanding mobile network. But the locally produced material I've seen has a homemade feel to it—poor lighting, bad staging, and muffled sound. There isn't much professional-quality porn from the region these days.[11]

Mainstream movies are another story. "Let me show you something." I was looking at the Nile from an expensively furnished apartment in one of Cairo's high-rises, my gaze drifting downriver, when my host called me back to admire a different watery view. He popped a disc into his DVD player, and a giant flat-screen TV suddenly filled with the video of a voluptuous woman in a shower, water cascading down her long black hair. It was Marwa—a Lebanese pop star—usually seen revealing her talents in assorted music videos. But never quite as exposed as this, naked and clutching her luxuriant breasts, eyes flickering up at the camera.

The scene was from a movie called *Ahasiis* (*Feelings*), which played in cinemas in Egypt and across the Arab region in 2010. The film portrays sexual frustration and infidelity from the perspective of four women, complete with lashings of melodrama. "In the movie I discuss the issues of men who practice sex with their wives without preparing women before and this leads them to betray their husbands," the director Hani Girgis Fawzi told me as we sat in his living room, watching outtakes. There were a lot of them: a couple making out at the beach, another embracing in bed, and endless showers—ritual ablutions serving as useful cinematic shorthand for sexual relations. In the final release, there was no frontal nudity, no lingering kisses, and some pretty tame nods to intercourse, but sexy stuff nonetheless compared with movies of a few years earlier. "I cut maybe half of the scenes and they [the national censors]

made [rated] the film only for adults and there was someone standing in front of cinemas to check IDs. Particularly for this movie,
there are very strict rules." Fawzi sighed, his HEAVY METAL T-shirt
crumpling. "I do not know why especially me and my film."

While other countries in the region have their own film industries, Egypt is the center of big-budget production, churning out
movies and soap operas that saturate screens big and small across
the Arab world. Over the past decade, Egyptian cinema has increasingly depicted sex—not the act itself, so much, but many of its associated taboos, including premarital relations, sexual harassment,
and sex work. And this against a backdrop of official censorship,
religious conservatism, and a political regime not exactly famous
for freedom of expression.

These films diverge from the fashion of "clean cinema," a recent
trend in Egyptian filmmaking. In the 1960s and '70s, sex was a part
of cinema, and it was no big deal—bedroom scenes, sexual themes,
and plenty of female flesh.[12] But with the rise of Islamic conservatism at home, as well as new audiences in the oil-rich, socially
conservative Gulf states, came a tendency in mainstream Egyptian cinema to eschew sexual subjects and risqué material (though
extreme violence, including slapping female stars clear across
the screen, is apparently clean enough to escape such scruples).
Actresses made a song and dance of rejecting roles that required
revealing costumes and so-called hot scenes; some went so far as
to give up acting altogether, putting on hijabs and beating a high-
profile retreat from cinema.[13] Clean cinema came in for a polish
with the rise of the Muslim Brotherhood and Salafis after the 2011
uprising and their push to edify Egyptian popular culture—that is,
strip sex from movies, TV series, and music videos.

How far filmmakers can go in Egypt is, in large part, dictated by
official censorship. To receive government approval to record and
release a movie in Egypt, filmmakers have to submit their scripts,
and final edits, to the censorship bureau. The law exhorts censors
to generally uphold "public order, public morals and the supreme
interest of the state." Various ministerial directives have fleshed
out the details, prohibiting the presentation of "sin and sinful acts

or drug use in a way that encourages people to imitate them. . . . exciting sexual scenes that will offend polite behavior, as well as expressions and gestures which are impolite," not to mention "calls to atheism or debasing heavenly religions" among other offenses."[14]

While such regulations would appear to guarantee a halal ending, in practice, this charter gives the censor, and therefore filmmakers, considerable latitude. Ali Abu Shadi, a film historian and former national censor, gave me a rundown of hot-button topics: "Religion, then sex, then politics is the order of elements to be considered when cutting." There's no question that religion is the touchiest subject of all, and the highest religious authorities in the land—Al-Azhar and the Coptic Church—are given a chance to weigh in. Abu Shadi gave me an example of what happens when faith and sex collide on-screen. "A movie came to me in my office to censor and the story was about a *munaqqaba* [veiled woman] who runs a prostitution ring and chooses her assistants and clients through the mosque," he explained. "I know the niqab is not a religious requirement, but to insult this group would be disastrous and provoke a backlash. I haven't refused any movie on the basis of sex, but this one I did because of the niqab."

As for sex pure and simple, the red lines are clear, said Abu Shadi. "I would never accept or permit any movie with scenes of sex or showing bodies of men or women," he noted. "But I could accept it if the woman were covered under bedsheets." Yet Abu Shadi sees the censor's role not as limiting a filmmaker's scope for expression but rather expanding it—what he called "creativity in censorship"—against conservative audiences that might otherwise raise a fuss and force controversial films out of cinemas and off the air. He has a point: in recent years, what has brought trouble on those pushing the boundaries of public sexual expression is community backlash first, law second. It's not the state but a collective state of mind that is setting the borders of acceptability.

Such rules apply not just to domestic films and series but to foreign imports as well. Hollywood sex scenes are easy to cut, which means that movies with the occasional racy interlude can still slip into cinemas, and onto TVs, with discreet deletions. But there's more than one way to police a foreign film or TV show. When the action is clean but the talk is dirty, euphemism is a censor's best friend. Historically, subtitling has been the rule for most foreign films and sitcoms playing in the Arab region, and plenty gets lost in translation. In the early 1960s, my father saw *The Sun Also Rises,* with Tyrone Power and Ava Gardner, at the Cairo Palace Cinema, which, with its crimson curtain, plush seating, and CinemaScope, was the last word in movie house glamour in those days. Set against the backdrop of the Roaring Twenties, the film's star-crossed love story hinges on the nature of its hero's wartime injury. In a pivotal scene, a doctor breaks the bad news: Power's wound has rendered him impotent. The force of this disclosure was lost, however, on the Egyptian audience because the subtitles translated Power's condition as *'inniin*—a classical Arabic word that even my father, a young medical school graduate, couldn't understand. Most of the other cinemagoers were in the dark on this vital point until someone piped up from the shadows, "*Ya'ni markhi, ya gama'a,*" roughly equivalent to "You know, guys, 'can't get it up.'"

Fast-forward fifty years and Arabic subtitles are as genteel as ever, creating just as much confusion.[15] During one of my taxi rides in Cairo, I chatted with a young driver whose excellent English was entirely due, he said, to hours of watching American movies and back-translating from the subtitles. "Yes, I learn a lot of English this way. Like 'fuck you,'" he said. I asked him the Arabic word he had seen in the corresponding subtitles: *tubban laka,* which is actually closer to "damn you" in English. I explained the difference, but it didn't seem to bother him. "What about 'son of bitch'?" he asked brightly.[16]

Subtitlers are aware they have a lot to answer for. "Once I was in a shop and the guy asked me, 'What do you do?' I said I work at a subtitling company, and he said, 'You do a lot of mistakes—you never do anything right.' Oh my God! They think we are stupid," said Sara, one of a dozen young women glued to their flat-screen monitors at Image Production House, a media company in Beirut. Sara and her colleagues are in demand: in addition to dubbing and editing, IPH churns out subtitling for TV channels across the Arab region: movies, sitcoms, talk shows—mainly prime-time American fare.

IPH gets its marching orders from local film distributors and broadcasters, who are in turn influenced by a mix of official and self-imposed censorship. Some subscription-based satellite channels demand few cuts and little glossing over in translation; indeed, this is their unique selling point. But free-to-air channels, terrestrial or satellite, can be quite explicit in their requirements: "[The show] should be edited according to Dubai spec, bearing in mind the below," instructed one Cairo-based company. "F-words are not acceptable. Too-passionate kissing is not acceptable. Sexual jokes and talks are not acceptable. Bikinis are okay."

There is a trend on Arabic TV channels to dub, rather than subtitle, foreign movies and serials; this used to be common for Mexican or Brazilian, and more recently, Turkish soap operas but is now extending to blockbuster American productions as well. Egyptian Arabic dominated the airwaves when Cairo was the heart of film and TV production, but times are changing and new media centers have emerged. Most of these dubbed series use Syrian or Lebanese actors, which means their Arabic is getting a wider hearing and may well have a profound effect on the lingua franca of a new generation of viewers. But it also makes censorship easier, since the original sound track is translated. With subtitles, however euphemistic, at least the original language remains on record—though even that can be scrubbed by bleeping out expletives in English sound tracks, which a younger generation of viewers, my taxi driver among them, has come to recognize.

At IPH there are no written guidelines on how to edify sexual language. "We don't have fixed rules, but it's evident," says Claude Karam, head of the subtitling division. "When you translate, you have to use the pattern in your own language. If we don't know a word in English, we research it, and once we find it in Arabic, we judge if we can use it." He gave me a few examples: "You can't say, 'I'm going to get laid tonight'; you can say, 'I'm going to have fun.'" In the subtitlers' lexicon, sex becomes "relations," an erection is "excited," a penis becomes a "member," semen is "liquid," and—my favorite—"that deviant practice" for fellatio. "These people [col-leagues] are not stupid," says Karam. "They know the word. But they don't want to be blamed for these words and putting them on-screen."

Back in Cairo, Fawzi reckons the next few years will be tough for filmmakers inclined to push sexual boundaries. Financing is scarce, and some performers, wary of public opinion, are cagey about tak-ing on risqué roles. Marwa, for example, who found herself banned from performing in the country after the uprising by the Egyptian Music Syndicate because of her saucy style, blamed Fawzi for lur-ing her into compromising positions on-screen; "double-faced" is his verdict on the current state of affairs. From his initial optimism that a new era of freedom of expression was dawning as the sun set on the Mubarak regime, Fawzi now welcomes censorship for as long as Islamism holds sway. Better scenes fall on the cutting room floor, he says, than audiences start burning down cinemas.

## CLASS ACTION

Whether the next generation of Egyptians will have the freedom to express themselves, and will allow others to do so, critically depends on education, at home and at school. As the country rebuilds its political foundations, all institutions are coming under scrutiny. Egypt has an opportunity to adopt creative new curri-cula across the board—including the facts of life. But its ability to actually deliver this sorely needed information is another matter altogether.

"You can't have sex education here as in the West. There, there is freedom. Teenagers can decide to have sex, no problem," declared one Ministry of Education official, overestimating, as I've found many Egyptians do, the extent of sexual freedom in the West. His preference, he told me, was to see sex education as an elec-tive course at university, taught around the time young people are starting to think about getting married. But what about youth who are sexually active before then? "Here we have no practice [sexual relations] before marriage," he said. At my look of frank disbelief, he revised his opinion. "Well, yes, there is. But we will not condone it, because it is rejected. If I regularize it and put rules around it, the world will collapse on me. Society will refuse this. Nobody likes this talk."

But it all depends on what you're saying and how you're saying it. As the official suggested, the least controversial form of sexual education in the Arab region is a just-in-time delivery of the essential facts to engaged couples before their wedding night. When my father was a young man, this "education" was, at best, a quiet word in the ear of the bride by an older relative; grooms were left to pick up details, factual and fantastical, as they went along. Today, however, things can get a little more elaborate.

"We have to understand erection." I was sitting in a classroom with sixty or so young women, draped in black abayas, when a detailed anatomical drawing of the male reproductive system flashed up on the screen, larger than life. *Shayla*-covered heads, bowed as the women pored over mobile phones or chatted with their neighbors, suddenly snapped to attention. An outburst of giggling followed, but the instructor was undeterred. "There is no need for laughter," she continued in a firm but pleasant voice. "We are discussing a scientific and religious topic, which is serious and not funny. We are trying to change your way of thinking about this subject."

For Sahar Talaat, this is all in a day's work. Since 2002, she's been helping young Arabs come to grips with sex in an age of uncertainty. A pathologist by training, Talaat got her start as a confidante and counselor to female friends back in Cairo. It was her husband, she said, who encouraged her to take it up as a profession: "He said, 'You are talented in managing marital life, and so you should exchange this experience with others.'" Talaat made her professional debut as a counselor on the health and social pages of Islam Online, a pioneering website offering information, advice, and fatwas on every conceivable aspect of modern life.

The giggling girls and I were in Doha, Qatar, where Talaat was a guest speaker at a course sponsored by Project Chaste, a Qatari initiative, like its Emirati counterpart we saw earlier, to help get young people married. In the Doha classroom, Talaat was keen to get the young women talking about sex—in an Islamic context. "Always I said that Islam is not closed regarding this issue. The prohibited thing is to speak about the intimate relationship between these particular men and these particular women for no reason. But we can speak openly about the issue in general; we can learn."

Aside from covering basic reproductive anatomy and physiology, much of the class was devoted to dispelling age-old fears. "You girls think that the pain on the day when [a woman] delivers a baby is the same as the pain on the first day of marriage. Please do not be afraid; it is different," Talaat gently explained. Her key message is to get women to enjoy, not fear, sex as an integral part of marriage. "In this picture"—she pointed to an anatomical drawing on the screen—"we can see that this part of women below [the clitoris] is the source of enjoyment and so men should focus on that area and be patient with his wife until she is ready and relaxed. This part which woman delivers a baby from, you should know in order to help a man in the marriage and to avoid making any pain to you if he enters a wrong or haram place [anal sex]."

Male and female sexual response curves ebbed and flowed across the classroom blackboard as Talaat explained how to get the most out of sexual life. She is big on communication and feedback. "It is important to know how his performance was good or not; this advice makes the next relationship [interaction] more successful," she counseled the students. "Sex includes practice and dialogue, so in the first day of marriage, do not expect that you will be so happy, because you need experience, which will happen after spending more time with your husband."

The students were, on the whole, unflustered by the content. "Yeah, yeah, this information is important," said Amal, a prospective bride in her early twenties. "We have some information before, but some mistakes. Our family tell us this is a very difficult process when you get married. And you get afraid you will get a lot of blood and very pain. And now it [sounds] very comfortable." Alongside her was Basma, a university student newly married to her cousin;

she had missed the class before her own nuptials and was making up for lost time. "I think it's very useful for girls. Yes, *dukhla* [defloration] is less scary. Very easy if we have this information before." She, however, learned the hard way. "I am reading a lot from sites from [the] Internet, in English and Arabic. But the information is confusion," she told me. "For the first days of the relationship with my husband, I have pain and get tired easily and I think I am pregnant. I am thinking, Oh my God, what's happen[ing]? I am going to websites and they say maybe you have this disease or you have this one; you don't get the right answer."

In Egypt, Islamic conservatives prefer to see such questions, and answers, kept within the family, and they promote the idea of parent training programs to teach mothers and fathers how to broach these topics. Yet there is growing evidence that at least some Egyptian parents are open to having others help teach their kids the facts of life.[17] As one middle-class, middle-aged mother of three in Cairo confided to me, "I married at eighteen, and my husband and I knew nothing. He bought a book on the day of our wedding, and was reading it until our marriage [ceremony], but he didn't know what to do. We read it together, and it took us ten days to get it done. I don't want my daughter to have this, so yes, in schools, it is a good idea when she is older; of course, only with other girls in the class." Egypt already has a number of pilot projects to communicate adolescent "life skills," among them sexual and reproductive health in after-school sessions across the country.[18] But research from around the world shows that the most effective means of getting this information to young people in schools is to incorporate it into comprehensive curricula over a number of years.[19] When Egypt's new order is ready to travel down this road, it should consider the trail blazed in the one place it is least likely to look: Israel.

Safa Tamish is a Palestinian who divides her time between Haifa, in Israel, and Ramallah, in the West Bank. She's the founder of Muntada Jensaneya, known in English as the Arab Forum for Sexuality, Education and Health.[20] In the Arab world, it's a bold stroke to put "sexuality" on your letterhead, especially if you're a woman. But Tamish is not easily fazed by convention. "I speak loudly about sexual topics in a very open way that is really not used to the Arab ears," she told me. "I am too much direct. Too much talking about things in their [rightful] name."

The name of the game for Muntada is sexuality education—not just cut-and-dried reproduction but the messiness of love and intimacy, pleasure and protection, sexual diversity and development. "We're not hiding and we're not saying that it's family education. It's sex education. For the first time [people] can really discuss sexuality in a respect[ful], open manner. We are putting everything on the table," says Tamish.[21]

Muntada's approach to communication is as unconventional as its subject matter. Case in point is one of its main initiatives—getting sexuality education into Arab schools in Israel. Tamish, who has a degree in sexuality education from the United States, is skeptical that in her part of the world a standardized curriculum can work—and certainly not if it's imported or directly modeled on one from the West. "What the Arab schools in Israel have is a translated version of the things they do for Israeli schools, for the Jewish schools, which are not sensitive to the Arab culture. For example, to make a choice to have sex or not to have sex. There is a whole unit on this issue. . . . I cannot put it in a curriculum, because no principal [of an Arab-Israeli school] will accept it: 'What, are you giving them the choice to have sex or not? [In] grade nine or ten?'"

Muntada's approach gets to the point, but in an indirect fashion. Two of the biggest hurdles to discussing sexuality in the classroom are parents and teachers. To deal with the first, Tamish and her colleagues go into schools with anonymous questionnaires to elicit students' most pressing concerns. Their questions are carefully worded, without a hint of sex about them—"kosher" is how she describes them. The same, however, cannot be said of kids' responses. "We say [in the questionnaire], for example, 'What are the topics related to puberty that you would like to know more?' All what you can dream of that is related to sexuality will be written to those questions—everything, everything. Contraceptives, masturbation, love, intercourse, pregnancy, changes among girls in puberty, boys kissing, French kissing—everything you can imagine, they could write. We are not opening their minds; they know and they put these things."

The next step is to help schools prepare for meeting the parents. When authorities mention that they are planning to introduce sexuality education, the parental response is predictable: if you open kids' eyes to this subject, the next thing you know, they'll be fornicating wildly. At this point, Tamish and her team intervene: "'Well, we just wanted to share with you the information we collected from the kids,'" they say to parents. "And we put everything in a PowerPoint [presentation], and they get shocked. 'What? Our kids, they wrote this?' They make this shift from yes-no to 'How are we going to do it?' This is amazing." In Tamish's experience, the power of this homegrown evidence is so strong that parents actually want to pitch in. "This is not something I imported from the U.S.," she says, "it is something happening in the Palestinian society, and it makes them feel responsible. And then they start to participate in the discussion. In most of the schools, the parents ask for at least four to five [training] sessions; they want to learn: 'When the kids come back home and they ask us a question, we don't want to be idiots.'"

While parents are being primed, school staff members are also being groomed to develop their own curriculum and make them more comfortable with the subject matter, which in turn makes students less embarrassed. Nor are sexual matters confined to biology class; Tamish recalls how one literature teacher in a school in East Jerusalem used a lesson on *ghazal*—classical Arabic love poetry—to broach the phenomenon of *'urfi* marriage between female students and sweet-talking taxi drivers looking for sex. "What is important is not the [classroom] activity," says Tamish. "What is important is the attitude of the teacher when he or she goes into the class. . . . I believe from my experience the song does not really matter; it is the singer who matters."

A decade ago, Muntada had difficulty convincing Arab schools in Israel to take on sexuality education; now there's a waiting list of institutions wanting its assistance. This is a long way from where Tamish started. Her first job, as a nurse in a village school in Galilee, in northern Israel, was a sudden plunge into the deep end of what would become her calling. "There was a girl who was twelve years old . . . and she was found pregnant in her eighth month. And from the investigation they found out that six kids from the same school raped her and convinced her they were playing and she shouldn't say anything about it to anybody. That was in the year 1990. The whole village was in total shock," she recalled. "I came to the school one or two days after this story came out. The principal did not allow any of the teachers to talk about the issue in the school. I opposed, and he said we are a conservative society. And I said, 'A conservative society who have pregnant girls and rapists?'"

Tamish convinced school officials to meet with parents, and from this traumatic start came her approach to talking through tough sexual issues. Life is far from easy for Arabs living in Israel, but Tamish readily admits Muntada could not have started without the country's institutional framework, which mandates sex education, among other sexual rights. "I don't say it in a shy way. I left the West Bank because it was not institutionalized and priorities were different back then; on the other hand, there was a lot to do. In the West Bank when I trained counselors and the rates of reported sexual abuse among students were raised, they stopped the program. They said, 'She [Tamish] is opening doors we cannot close,' and they finished the whole project. In Israel, if you are a counselor and you are faced with a sexual abuse case and you don't report it, you will be in prison. This [system] is something I use to the extreme."

For many Muntada participants, the program is a life-changing experience. Parents describe their delight at getting closer to their kids as a result of their newfound ease with personal matters, and participants talk about how home life has been transformed by husbands and wives feeling comfortable enough to hug each other in front of the family. Simple information is itself powerful: for those brought up in the shadows of sex, a clear presentation of the facts of life is a real eye-opener. And not just for women either; although men have more freedom to talk about sex, they rarely do so in mixed company, which leaves them largely in the dark about female sexuality. Muntada's training sessions, which put men and women in the same room, are a revelation, according to male participants.

Language also makes a difference. Tamish insists that Muntada's work be conducted in Arabic. For some Israeli Arabs, Hebrew or English is a much more comfortable language for discussing sexual matters. For example, new participants will use *min orali* (Hebrew for "oral sex") and *orgazma* instead of the respective Arabic terms, *jins fammii* and *nashwa jinsiyya.* "When you say the word, to be able to say the word freely, it's fifty percent of the work," says one woman, a social worker from Haifa. "Why [do] I choose to speak about a dick in Hebrew not in Arabic? It must show something about my attitude toward things."[22]

Some participants lack even this choice, because they simply do not know the Arabic for many of the topics under discussion. Part of Muntada's name—Jensaneya, which translates to "sexuality"—is a relatively new coinage that is not widely used, or even understood, by Arabic speakers. Even more basic terminology is problematic; until attending Muntada's training courses, some participants were simply unaware that there are, indeed, Arabic words for female genitalia, having been taught to consider such subjects shameful beyond discussion. Even for those who do know some terms in Arabic, it is often in language so crude as to be unusable off the street.

This is a far cry from the days of the *Encyclopedia of Pleasure* and the golden age of Arabic writing on sex. One tenth-century book, *The Language of Fucking,* for example, mentions more than a thousand verbs for having sex.[23] Then there are the seemingly endless lexicons for sexual positions, responses, and organs of every size, shape, and distinguishing feature. That linguistic wealth is long gone. Part of Muntada's mission is to give participants a new vocabulary with which to discuss sexuality openly, overcoming the double whammy of unease about the subject and embarrassment at the language. The fact that it's Arabic is a boost to the cultural—and, some would argue, political—identity of what is a minority population in Israel.

Times are changing, and Muntada is now reaching out to neighboring countries, where local groups are keen to learn from its experience, as well as working directly in the West Bank, providing sexuality education for social workers and other professionals. There, Tamish has seen a dramatic change in Muntada's participants since the Arab uprisings, their reticence on sexuality suddenly melting away. "It's as if each Arab person has so many layers of limitation and barriers that when you start to get rid of the external layers like the political, you feel the ventilation touches your deep soul," she notes. "The political thing gave them the urge to talk about their sexual liberation." And that, in turn, has reinforced their drive to tackle political concerns. "My sexual freedom begins with my family," Tamish observes. "But if I don't win the battle with my father, I cannot win it with Abu Mazen [Palestinian president Mahmoud Abbas] and with the occupation."

It's this connection between the personal and the political that makes sexuality education more than just a sideshow to Egypt's change in the coming decade. Suppressing facts and opinions in the classroom is a form of censorship, which the upheavals of 2011 vowed to fight in the political sphere to bring an end to secrecy and the control of information—although it is clear, in the ensuing order, that this change will be some time in coming. Freedom requires thinking, and that will take a different sort of teacher—one who is not afraid to share knowledge and answer tough questions. It also demands a different kind of student. Sexuality education that conveys accurate information, encourages personal responsibility, teaches reciprocity, promotes equality, respects diversity, and rewards the free expression of ideas is as good a training ground as any for both teachers and students alike.

There is nothing un-Islamic about teaching people about sex, including its pleasures; quite the contrary, in fact. Beyond questions of morality and hygiene, sexuality education is about trust—trusting young people with information, trusting them to make responsible decisions for themselves, trusting them to respect the rights and needs of others. If youth across the Arab world are mature enough to lead their societies into political revolt, and gain their elders' admiration for it, then surely they are ready for the unvarnished facts of life.

## MISSED CONCEPTIONS

Information isn't the only item in short supply. For youth who gravitate into the darker social orbits of sex outside marriage, protection is also a problem. Take contraception, for example. Like most medications in Egypt, the Pill is easy to buy—if you're a young person bold enough to face down disapproving pharmacists. No doctor's prescription required: just hand over the cash (around EGP 15, or USD 2.50) and walk away with a month's worth of pills. One of my unmarried Egyptian friends gets her supply delivered to the door, like pizza, no questions asked. Unfortunately, easy availability is not matched by ready knowledge: my friend was ill the first time she took the Pill because she had no idea what kind to buy or how to use it.[24]

Questions of *zina* aside, contraception per se is not forbidden in Islam. The Qur'an makes no mention of it, so it was left to Islamic scholars to come up with the rules, based in large part on hadiths. Some of these dealt with *'azl,* or coitus interruptus, a common method at the time of the Prophet and one he is said to have permitted. Some devout Muslims eschew contraception on the advice of their local shaykh, who might quote the following hadith: "Reproduce for I am going to boast about you among other nations on the Day of Judgment." But plenty of religious scholars through the ages have questioned the authenticity of this particular hadith and of other sayings of the Prophet invoked to prohibit birth control, and have argued the contrary.[25] And so contraception came to be permitted in the four main schools of Sunni Islamic jurisprudence that emerged in the eighth and ninth centuries as well as the principal schools of Shi'i legal thought.[26] Sterilization of healthy individuals, on the other hand, is a contentious issue in Islam. Some authorities allow it; others forbid it as a violation of shari'a, which enjoins believers to preserve the self, religion, reason, property, and procreation. The upshot is that sterilization is extremely unpopular in Egypt: scarcely 1 percent of married women opt for it, and it is vanishingly rare among men.[27]

Although Islamic debates on contraception sprang up around the singularly male technique of withdrawal, the vast majority of lotions, potions, and other contraceptive methods developed through the ages, and discussed in such exhaustive detail in the likes of the *Encyclopedia of Pleasure,* are for women. Today, birth control is seen as a female responsibility, which is problematic for single women. Such is the stigma associated with women taking the plunge before marriage, let alone planning for it with adequate contraception, that few unmarried women use protection.[28] While men have more scope for sex before tying the knot, this license does not translate into a greater willingness to step into the breach on contraception. Condoms (*al waqi al thakari,* literally "the male protective," or *tops,* as they are called in Egypt) are spectacularly unpopular. Like their counterparts the world over, Egyptian men complain that condoms are uncomfortable and reduce sexual pleasure.

The bigger problem, though, is that condoms are associated with *zina* across the Arab world. In Egypt, for example, only 2 percent of married couples use them—and not so much for family planning, in my experience, as to deal with some of the complications associated with intercourse. [29] Among them is a fear of coming into contact with menstrual blood, and the Islamic requirement that both partners wash after intercourse, making them popular with women who have spent hours at the beauty salon and don't want to muss their hair and makeup with a postcoital shower.[30]

Conventional wisdom holds that if you're buying condoms, you must be having sex outside of marriage, and that is haram—a further deterrent to purchasers. "Please, God, split the earth in two and drop me in and close it up right away," one twenty-something Egyptian condom marketer laughed, recalling the first time he bought condoms in a Cairo pharmacy and met with the pharmacist's withering glance. Ironically, most men don't appear to be using condoms for *zina* either. Anywhere the question has been asked—Egypt, Morocco, Tunisia, Syria, Lebanon, Yemen, for example—survey findings are much the same: Arab men (and presumably women too, despite their reticence) are having sex outside of marriage, and when they do, condoms are generally not part of the program.[31] The results can be seen in clinics across the Arab world. Sexually transmitted infections are a concern to public health experts in the region, and are in all likelihood more common than available statistics reflect, since few countries have systematic, nationwide surveillance. STIs and HIV are thought to be the second-leading cause of death from infectious disease in adults aged fifteen to forty-four in the region.[32] And while the prevalence of HIV is still low in the general population, the Middle East and North Africa is among the few regions in the world where new infections, and deaths from AIDS-related causes, are still rising. Upward of half of HIV infections reported in the majority of Arab countries are the result of sexual transmission, a route which hits unsuspecting wives hard.[33]

In Egypt, there have been creative, albeit discreet, attempts to boost condom use. Some of the most innovative have come from DKT International, a leading supplier of subsidized family planning and HIV prevention tools in the developing world. DKT, which has been using social marketing to promote condoms in Egypt, sells brightly colored, sprightly flavored "luxury" sheaths at rock-bottom prices. It has also launched clever campaigns to decouple condoms from *zina* by pitching them to married folk, trying to shift responsibility for family planning from wives to husbands as part of the revolutionary we're-all-one-Egypt zeitgeist, and to link condoms to notions of what it is to be a "real man."

But it's a tough sell. Egypt's condom consumption is less than a third of the market potential, according to some estimates. DKT saw its sales plummet along with the rest of the economy in the post-uprising doldrums, and the company has little hope of them bouncing back anytime soon, given restrictions on condom advertising and new regulatory requirements that would limit new brands coming to the market. Although population control remains a pressing concern for Egypt, with the rise of Islamism some experts notice a subtle shift in official talk away from contraception and toward the less controversial notion of "birth spacing," which does not bode well for condoms. "The government doesn't like to encourage pleasure," one DKT executive sighed.

Elsewhere in the Arab world, groups have been reaching out more directly to young people, condoms in hand. In Tunis, the capital of Tunisia—whose Jasmine Revolution catalyzed Egypt's own uprising and subsequent political convulsions across the region—I caught up with some enthusiastic promoters on the back lot of a technical college. Four attractive young women in stylish black coats, formfitting jeans, and high-heeled boots were surrounded by a crowd of young men. One of the women tore open a packet and carefully removed a condom, holding it up for all to see. "We are going to begin with a demonstration of condoms," another woman said into a microphone, her voice booming across campus. "It goes on top of the penis in erection. The reservoir goes on top. After relations, ejaculation, take it off carefully and then put it immediately in the bin." A third woman was passing out condoms to the crowd.

In Egypt, a young woman with a condom in her hand is generally assumed to be holding a tool of her trade. But these women in Tunisia were professionals of a different sort: all medical students and volunteers associated with Y-Peer, an international program under the umbrella of the United Nations Population Fund to promote reproductive and sexual health for youth by youth. The surprising sight of four young women—angels, as they're called—showing men how to use a condom (indeed, women showing men how to do *anything* in the Arab world is notable in its own right) was rendered all the more remarkable by the subsequent "condom race," in which the women divided the men into two teams, lined them up, and had each open the condom he had been given, place it on the raised index and middle fingers of his neighbor, and then remove it without tearing it, in sequence all down the line.

The game is intended to both familiarize youth with condoms and get them to associate the product less with shady dealings and more with fun and games. I asked Meryam Guedouar, one of the angels, if embarrassment was ever an issue. "Yeah, a little," she said. She herself was uncomfortable when she started with the project, but her confidence grew with time, as did that of her audience. "It takes charm. They learn better when it's a woman. They imagine . . . but they learn." She laughed.

Guedouar and her colleagues fielded questions from the audience. "Superficial relations? No, they don't protect at all [against HIV and STIs]. Even without penetration," she responded to one student's query. Further advice included where to go for free and confidential HIV testing, what types of condoms were available and how much they cost, and how to read the expiration date on the packet. And they deftly handled what seemed to be one of the students' most pressing concerns. "As for size, let us show you how big a condom can take," said one of the angels, sticking her arm into a sheath. "XXL!"

While the college itself is mixed, the condom crowd was almost entirely male. A few female students, all *muhajjabat,* were hanging around the fringes but seemed reluctant to take part. "They didn't dare approach us," said an angel, who runs information sessions with young women. "It's a pity, because they have questions you cannot imagine," she continued. "The other time, one thought she could get pregnant by going to the public toilet, because there's a risk that there was a man there before and he did, I don't know what, ejaculate. In the family, they say, you could become pregnant, be careful." Her colleague chimed in: "Yes, we do the [condom] contest with the girls, but the girls alone. Obviously, they need to know as well. But the problem is that they don't dare to ask a boy to put on a condom. So we have to make her learn that this is her right to protect herself."

That need is all the more pressing, said the angels, because there is a lot of premarital sex going down. "Ah, the men, yes, all of them," one angel answered when I asked if relations before marriage were common. "No, not all of them," her colleague piped up. "Some have entered into religion—you can't forget them." "But eighty percent or more," the friend replied. There were no disagreements, however, when it came to women's premarital activity. "The men, they brag; they are proud when they have sexual relations.

But the woman can't say it," they said. "Young women, there are some who dare, but we never know because there is always the way society looks at you. You can't just say, 'I had relations.' Even if she did, she wouldn't say."

This is at odds with Tunisia's long-standing reputation as light on religion and loose on sexual morality. This stereotype has a history. After Tunisia gained independence from France in 1956, its president, Habib Bourguiba, was bent on developing the country—and that included women. Tunisia was an early mover in outlawing polygamy and wife repudiation, giving women access to divorce, among other rights. In the 1980s, the country banned hijabs in public offices and educational establishments, as President Zine El Abidine Ben Ali consolidated power in what would be his two decades plus rule by circumscribing the scope of political Islam. Hence Tunisia's free-and-easy reputation in the Arab region.

The reality is rather different. Even before the rise to political power of Ennahda, its "moderate" Islamic party, and the more visible presence of their Salafi cousins, Tunisia is still, by and large, a patriarchal society where women grapple with legal, economic, and social obstacles precisely because they are women—a persistent challenge as the country struggles to reshape itself. Tunisia's open approach to reproductive health, for example, had more to do with a postindependence strategy of controlling fertility on the road to economic development than with sexual liberation: premarital sex, extramarital relations, and homosexuality were all illegal in Tunisia under Ben Ali, just as they are in its more ostensibly conservative Arab neighbors.

And so, in Tunisia, the region's rules on female sexuality still apply. "The men don't easily accept that women are not virgin. A minority is different, not very educated but open-minded. It's not a question of education. The man, he has all the right to a sexual life, but the woman, she has to be a virgin. That's why a lot of them resort to the [hymen repair] operation," one angel remarked. There are alternative strategies too. "There is a lot, a lot of anal sex. Frankly, because the girls say it is another way to control virginity. The men want her to be a virgin, so she finds another solution. That's why we raise awareness; when we talk about sexual relations, it includes anal as well," her colleague observed.

I asked the angels if they thought exposure to Europe, and its sexual culture, accounted for Tunisia's substantial rate of pre-marital sexual activity. "That's the song of the religious people," Guedouar scoffed. "They always say the same thing. Me, I think it's more because the age of marriage has grown. Women, they are more educated than before. She goes to university, she finishes her studies at twenty-four years old. She has to work. So she's marrying at thirty years old. She has the right to a sexual life [before marriage]."

For all their feistiness, the angels were skeptical of a wholesale change in the current sexual landscape. "The generation that is liberated, that's the minority, not the majority. It's not the same in the north or the south; it's not the mentality. It's not going to change everywhere. It will change in certain families, in certain types of people," one of the angels observed. "The women are becoming more and more open, but the men are not changing." Guedouar nodded her head in agreement. "He's still at the prehistoric stage."

## THREE MONTHS' NOTICE

If male evolution is taking too long, women in Tunisia have alternatives. Theirs is the only country in the Arab region to provide abortion (*ighad*) on request, meaning that a woman eighteen years or older, married or single, can have her pregnancy terminated, up to the end of the first trimester, on a variety of grounds, spousal consent not required. Tunisia started down this road more than four decades ago, when it first legalized abortion under limited conditions as part of Bourguiba's wide-ranging plans for national development.[34]

Two generations later, the fruits of this approach were clear during my tour of a youth clinic in Bardo, a suburb of Tunis. As the condom angels attest, Tunisian authorities have taken a comparatively bold approach to the delicate matter of providing sexual and reproductive health services to young, mainly single people—an

approach many hope will survive any attempts by Islamic conservatives to retrench. Since 2000, the National Office of Family and
Population (ONFP), the government's department on reproductive
matters, has set up centers across the country to help young people
steer a smoother course through the early years of their sexual life.

The day I visited, the clinic was buzzing with clients, mostly
young women in their twenties. One group was clustered around
a television, watching a video on breast cancer; others were in and
out of consulting rooms, meeting with gynecologists or midwives
or psychologists for advice and care on everything from acne to
diet to contraception, all free at the point of delivery. This diver-
sification beyond straight reproductive and sexual health makes
more than just good clinical sense, especially for centers in rural
areas, where young women are under closer surveillance and need
some cover to explain away a visit that might be noticed by friends
or family. Even in the capital, the Bardo youth center is discreetly
tucked behind the main clinic, which caters to married women,
with a separate entrance.

Youth-focused clinics are springing up in Egypt and a number
of other countries in the Arab region—often on rocky ground.[35]
Although they face many of the same social and cultural obstacles,
Tunisia's public clinics are unique in one key respect: the abortion wing. The facility I toured was spotless; a gynecologist and
two nurses in surgical greens were finishing up a procedure in the
small operating theater, and in a couple of darkened rooms to the
side, I saw the blanketed forms of three or four women. The wing
has a capacity for nine, but it's rarely full, I was told; surgical abortions are rare these days, in part because women are turning up for
terminations much earlier. And the procedure itself has become
safer thanks to the introduction of "medical abortion," which
uses a combination of synthetic hormones rather than mechanical means. It's not just that medical abortion has replaced surgical
procedures in Tunisia; the overall abortion rate has fallen dramatically since the late 1970s, confounding fears that widespread availability would lead to an abortion free-for-all, particularly among
unmarried women. The number of abortions in Tunisia's public

health system has fallen from twenty thousand a year in the late 1970s to an estimated fifteen thousand today, although the eligible population has grown by almost a third in that time. Unmarried clients are thought to account for roughly 15 percent of procedures, according to some estimates.[36]

Despite Tunisia's successful track record with legal abortion, there is trouble brewing, says Selma Hajri, a Tunis-based gynecologist and a leading researcher on abortion trends in her country. "There is not a big pushback against abortion, not yet, [but] there might be. We can't stop [abortion]; it is in the practice and it's a law. But you can make it more difficult," she explained. "For example, in the hospitals and family planning clinics, all women have access to abortion. But only to eight weeks [of pregnancy]. After that, you have to go to the hospital. And at that point, there is a stricter control. If a woman is single, they ask for her papers. The welcome is more difficult; barriers go up."

Hajri is typical of many educated women I met in Tunis—so stylishly dressed and perfectly accessorized and speaking such flawless French that I sometimes lost my bearings in conversation and forgot that I was in Tunis, not Paris. She's clear on where these new objections are coming from. "This is linked to the impact of religion. Midwives, even doctors, no longer want to be implicated in abortion. They are fine on contraception, but not on abortion. They think it is haram."

On the subject of abortion, Islam offers a certain degree of flexibility. While the Qur'an warns believers against infanticide—particularly the killing of baby girls, which was a custom in pre-Islamic Arabia—it doesn't touch on abortion per se.[37] The cornerstone of Muslim thinking on the issue comes from verses in the Qur'an on the origins of human life and the timing of "ensoulment" of the fetus.[38] All schools of Islamic jurisprudence forbid abortion after 120 days of pregnancy, except if a mother's life is in danger; before then, however, positions vary not only between schools but within them as well, from the strictest stance, which prohibits abortion altogether, to the most liberal of positions, which allows it on a wide range of grounds.[39] Today, however, there is plenty of fire and brimstone from local religious leaders, particularly with the rise in recent decades of Islamism, which condemns abortion outright. The upshot is that many women are firmly convinced that abortion is haram no matter what.

Hajri gets a lot of visitors from sub-Saharan Africa eager to learn from Tunisia, but delegations from other parts of the Arab region have been rare. "We tried to bring people from Arab countries," she remarked. "They also say, 'It is very good, it is very interesting, but we couldn't bring this experience to our countries. We don't have the law; we don't have the structure.' It's like visiting something completely new. They always have this feeling, Tunisia, it's not a real Arabic country, it's not a real Muslim country." While Tunisia has proved an inspiration to countries across the region on the political front in the "Arab Awakening," its laws and policies on gender and reproductive rights, the product of a particular history, have been harder to emulate. But the ascendance of Tunisia's Islamic conservatives has brought the country a little closer to its more religiously inclined neighbors, who now might be more willing to take a look at its experiences—good news if Tunisia's progressive policies and practices continue. Hajri readily acknowledges the difficulty of taking her country's show on the road. "One of the most important things is the will of the power, the government," she said. "If there is no real will, if they didn't want to bring to women the choice of abortion, it would be very difficult to make it happen."

For women across the Arab world, that will cannot come too soon. In Egypt, almost every married woman I know—and several of my unmarried friends—has had at least one abortion. What this means in terms of national numbers is a matter of speculation, since there are few official statistics. One calculation from the mid-1990s put the number of induced abortions in Egypt at 15 percent of pregnancies, roughly on par with rates in Western Europe.[40] Such numbers are hard to come by because abortion is against the law in Egypt, although legal wiggle room allows it in limited cases of "necessity"—notably, where a woman's life is in danger. And the penalties, on paper at any rate, are stiff: imprisonment for the patient and practitioner.[41]

This means, at the very least, that thousands of Egyptian women, and their doctors, are breaking the law every year; how they go about it depends on their social standing. Wealthy women can pay a private gynecologist around EGP 3,000 (USD 500) for a safe procedure, usually dilatation and curettage, or D and C, a tidy medical term for scraping out the uterus. Medical abortion, as we saw in Tunisia, is slowly gaining ground; although not quite as profitable for practitioners as surgery, it does have the advantage of plausible deniability, since the drugs needed for the procedure are used in other treatments as well and, in any case, can be procured without a prescription. For the less fortunate, there are doctors who will do a *tandiif* (cleaning) for around EGP 200. It is an unsurprisingly unpleasant experience: of dubious hygiene, offering inadequate pain relief, and perfunctory treatment mainly by male practitioners who, at best, just want to push patients out the door as quickly as possible or, at worst, refuse to treat unmarried women or actively condemn their morals while taking their money all the same; blackmail and sexual harassment can also be part of the service.

Meanwhile, poor women rely mainly on do-it-yourself techniques, including drinking boiled onion tea or soft drinks mixed with black pepper, or inserting the stem of a *mulukhiyya*, a tall weed whose leaves are commonly used to make soup, into the uterus—an organic version of the proverbial coat hanger. Some of these traditional approaches are being replaced by higher-tech versions. So instead of using a plant stalk, a woman who suspects she's pregnant might go to a clinic and get an IUD, which will stop implantation of the fertilized egg. And rather than taking an herbal concoction, women can improvise by swallowing a couple of packs of contraceptive pills to induce bleeding—a homemade attempt at emergency contraception that is, in fact, available in Egypt but little used by women or medical practitioners there. Much more grisly is the prick-and-stick approach, in which the woman is knocked out with an injection and then hit about the back and abdomen until she starts to abort. In many cases, these rough-and-ready approaches—either at private clinics or DIY—are not expected to finish the job. Rather they are meant to induce bleeding, which means a woman can then turn up at a public hospital and legitimately seek attention for a "spontaneous" miscarriage or hemorrhage.[42]

While the law makes getting an abortion a complicated and costly process, it doesn't appear to do much to deter either women or practitioners. It's only when a patient dies, or some other scandal erupts, that authorities step in; otherwise, a conspiracy of silence keeps the clandestine abortion business ticking along. It wasn't always like this. Egypt's current law dates from the late 1930s, but when my grandmother was a young married woman in the 1940s, abortion was an open part of life. The *daya,* traditional midwife, would come to my family's apartment, in a lower-middle-class part of Cairo, where there would be coffee and gossip as on any other social occasion; my father, then a young boy, remembers being sent outdoors to play, returning to find the *daya* throwing out an aborted fetus with the other remains of the day.

This laissez-faire approach to abortion reflected a long tradition in Egypt. Like everything else to do with sex, abortion wasn't something you shouted about, but you didn't go to great lengths to hide it either; hence the extensive advice on abortion in the books of Arabic erotica through the ages.[43] Today, abortion is a trickier affair. Single women, in particular, are caught in a double bind: the taboo of premarital sex not only makes abortion, already a secretive matter, even more furtive for them but, as we've seen, also increases their likelihood of having to resort to it in the first place, because of inadequate contraception. And as research shows, the burden of religious guilt weighs heavily on many.[44]

Most countries in the Arab region have more or less the same position as Egypt when it comes to abortion: technical illegality, tacit practice under most circumstances. All countries in the region permit abortion when a mother's life is endangered. Half a dozen, including Saudi Arabia, allow it in the case of a threat to a woman's physical health; Algeria adds the risk to mental health. Kuwait and Qatar also consider fetal impairment adequate grounds. Legislation in many of these countries is based on that of former colonial occupiers and so tends to reflect Western attitudes of the day rather than local tradition.[45] But whereas the United Kingdom, France, and Italy liberalized their abortion laws in the 1960s and '70s, legislative changes have been far less dramatic in most Arab states. The result is that 80 percent of the region's women live in countries where abortion is restricted in one way or another.[46] Every so often, police swoop down and arrest abortionists, and religious figures inveigh against the practice, then it's back to business as usual.

If, as in Egypt, women manage to get the job done anyway, does it really matter whether abortion is largely against the law? Of course it does, say health experts and reproductive rights advocates. Aside from arguments on the right to bodily autonomy, there is plenty of practical fallout from criminalizing abortion, safety being one of the main casualties. The burden of unsafe abortion hits poor women hard; according to some estimates, up to 10 percent of maternal deaths in Egypt are due to abortion, both natural and induced.[47] And then there is the cost to the health service of mopping up after so many crude terminations. This is not a uniquely Egyptian situation: across the Middle East and North Africa, the World Health Organization estimates, there are around 1.7 million unsafe abortions performed a year.[48]

Given that so many women are running so many risks, why is there so little public debate about abortion in Egypt and neighboring countries? The heavy hand of patriarchy, strengthened by the rise in recent years of Islamic fundamentalism, hardly encourages free and frank discussion of women's sexuality. Many women's organizations in the region have yet to engage on questions of sexual and reproductive rights, abortion among them, in part because they are busy fighting other battles and in part because of the "patriarchal bargain" some of them strike, trading off gains in certain areas for concessions in others, like sexuality.[49] And then there is the vested interest of a powerful medical profession reluctant to lose a steady source of income from a clandestine, and therefore lucrative, practice.

If Egypt is to change its laws on abortion as part of a broader platform of political and social reform, one country marking that trail is Morocco. The law on the books allows only for terminations in the case of danger to a woman's health or life and requires a husband's consent or, failing that, approval from a provincial medical authority. As in Egypt, the penalties for infractions can be severe. And as in Egypt, illegal abortions are commonplace—at least six hundred a day, according to some sources.[50]

One man out to change all that is Chafik Chraibi. As head of gynecology and obstetrics at a major maternity hospital in Rabat, he's seen enough complications from botched abortions to last a lifetime. "You cannot imagine how many women are doing abortions," he told me. "Here, every day, every day, I receive women, married or not, they are four to five months pregnant, they have ruptured their uterus, they are in a mess and they don't know what to do. Yet they don't want to admit it. But we know . . . they took something."

In 2007, Chraibi decided to shift course, from mopping up to leading the charge. He is president and founder of AMLAC, the Moroccan Association for the Fight Against Clandestine Abortion. Its name speaks volumes about how social change happens in the Arab region. "It would be shocking [for society] if I said the name of the association was for the liberalization of abortion," says Chraibi. "Maybe [in] the future generation, not mine."

Today's goal is already ambitious: a "softening" of Morocco's laws on abortion to allow terminations up to eight or ten weeks in certain cases: rape, incest, minors, fetal malformation, for women with psychiatric disturbances or caught in "dramatic" social situations (a housemaid seduced in her employer's family and thrown out on the street, for example). But Chraibi is also advocating for sexual education in schools and easier access to contraception, not only out of principle—this will reduce the need for abortion in the first place—but also out of pragmatism: it makes the association more socially acceptable if it's seen as promoting prevention rather than just abortion.

Chraibi's group isn't the only one pushing for change; Morocco has an active civil society and several organizations with an interest in these issues. But it's Chraibi who has become the identifiable face of this particular battle—and the man journalists at home and abroad call when they want to talk abortion. It's easy to see why. Chraibi is charming, confident, and urbane, with a dramatic voice and a lively manner. This is not a man who takes life lying down. When we met, he was juggling a uterine cancer surgery, staff meetings, a briefing for politicians, and a couple of media interviews with the local press and French and Italian TV.

Chraibi has been touring the country to raise awareness and stir public support. As far as he's concerned, the main obstacle to change isn't religion but politics. "Every month, I go to one or two towns in Morocco where I am invited by an association [of] doctors, women, etc. There are always two or three people who speak: a religious leader, a lawyer—the local magistrate—and me. I start, I pose the problem, and then we discuss. The religious guy is always flexible. He says until forty days, the fetus doesn't have a soul so abortion is authorized in the case of need. He distinguishes between forty days and four months in the case of necessity. The majority of religious leaders are in the same direction. But the lawyer, the local magistrate, he only talks about the law. Religion is a lot more supple than the law."

Unlike many others in the region, Morocco has been able to galvanize a public debate around abortion. This is, in part, because its greater freedoms of expression and civil society not only push such issues forward but also create a climate in which research on sexuality is at least possible; this research, in turn, generates facts and figures, however rough, on the scale of the problem, which allow for more informed argument. Thanks to Chraibi and others, there is visible progress on abortion: the more liberal-minded media, which loves to talk about sex in any case, is largely on board; major religious figures agree; there have been debates in Parliament, and national conferences, and a former government minister has gone on record supporting legal reform as advocated by Chraibi and his allies.

The winds which blew the "Arab Spring" touched Morocco too, with the result that its "moderate" Islamist party, Justice and

Development (also known as PJD, after its name in French), was elected to power in the wake of the 2011 uprisings. Although some of its members are opposed to Chraibi, he is confident that there is enough social and political momentum to push forward abortion reform, especially if King Muhammad VI, Morocco's highest political and religious authority, signals his approval. "Now we are all governed by Islamists," Chraibi told me. "If we succeed [with abortion reform] in Morocco, then there will be success in Algeria, in Egypt, in other countries in the region." Even with legal changes, though, there will be years of hard work ahead, making women aware of their new options and peeling away layers of religious and social compunction.

Back in Egypt, assembling those basic building blocks on abortion is tough work. Research on the subject has all but dried up since the late 1990s, and in recent years those tackling abortion have faced enormous personal and professional obstacles. "The problem with abortion is that there are not statistics to present to policymakers," one reproductive health expert in Cairo told me. "Authorities say the abortion rate is very low; if you want to have change, you need to bring the numbers, and we have no numbers." She sighed. "Authorities don't want to talk about abortion; they don't want confrontation with religious leaders, who clearly say it is forbidden and never talk about the [options allowed by] other sects. Religious figures say women die all the time. Why is abortion different?"

There have been periodic attempts in the past to ease Egypt's laws on abortion in the case of rape (a move backed by rulings from some religious authorities) and on other social or medical grounds (which have met with fierce religious resistance). All such efforts have faltered somewhere on the road to legislation, and for as long as Egypt's brand of Islamic conservatism influences policymaking, progress on abortion is unlikely. Whether subsequent governments will have the stomach to tackle abortion, a problem touching millions of its citizens, will be an important measure of Egypt's commitment to women's rights in the years to come.

Meanwhile, the consequence of paltry information, haphazard contraception, and illegal abortion is clear to see at the House of Muslim Girls, a towering apartment building in one of Cairo's more affluent suburbs. It's a *dar al-aytam* (house of orphans), one of hundreds of such facilities in the capital. There are just over a hundred girls at the orphanage (boys go to a different facility). They stay until they're eighteen, living four to a room and a dozen to a floor, sharing a kitchen, dining room, and bathroom. It's a cheerful place—the younger children's rooms are spotless, light, and airy, with brightly colored bedspreads and a menagerie of stuffed animals.

"Most of the kids here come because of an illegitimate relationship between a man and a woman. It happens because one of the two parties wants to get rid of the kid, who is evidence for what occurred," said Mona Sayed Mohamed, director of the orphanage, who's been working there for more than two decades. She's a stately woman, dressed in attire as sober as her tone: a long black skirt suit and matching *isdal,* a headscarf that covers her upper body as well. The children at the orphanage are mainly foundlings (*laqiit,* in Arabic) left in the street, abandoned in hospitals, or dumped in front of mosques. From the police reports she receives when the children are dropped off, Mohamed is fairly certain that most of them are the offspring of unmarried mothers.[51] There are so many of them now, she says, that the orphanage has stopped taking in new arrivals—there's just no more room.

There are no official statistics on illegitimate births in Egypt, since having a child out of legally recognized wedlock is something most people go to great lengths to conceal. The very word in Egyptian Arabic for an illegitimate child—*ibn haram* or *ibn zina* (son of fornication)—gives you some idea why. As we've seen, sex outside of marriage is off-limits in Islam and the Christian churches of the Arab region; in many countries consensual premarital sex is also punishable by law, on paper if not in regular practice. According to recent World Values Surveys, an overwhelming 98 percent of the Egyptians questioned disapproved of women as single parents.[52]

Legal strictures aside, Egyptian society takes a very dim view of unmarried mothers, including those who have gone through one of the many forms of unofficial marriage, like *'urfi;* research has shown that condemnation even leads some to condone the killing of women who conceive out of wedlock.[53]

As far as Mohamed is concerned, orphanages are a growth industry in Egypt. "When I see couples in streets without marriage, I immediately realize that the situation will get worse, and that's why orphanages are increased." In her opinion, it's a combination of poor education, loose morals, and financial need that is pushing girls into relations before matrimony. Mohamed regards modern technology as an enabler to this decline and fall: "I see that any girl can do bad things. If I have a mobile in my room and Internet, I can do anything I want."

The orphanage keeps a close eye on its charges: no mobiles or Internet, and TV viewing is strictly monitored for content. That's not to say there isn't fun: the kids can visit friends, they have parties in the orphanage, and people often come to take them out for the day—a form of fostering, or *kafala,* since adoption is forbidden in Islam.[54] The orphanage gives them names, registers them for birth certificates, enrolls them in school, and tries to integrate them into regular society, for all the social baggage they're carrying. "A lot of kids ask about their parents, and we tell them that they died in accidents," Mohamed said. "But some kids do not believe us."

I asked Mohamed if growing up in an orphanage, with the lingering suspicion of illegitimacy, hampers the girls' chances in later life. Quite the contrary, she said, at least when it comes to marriage; plenty of men come to seek their hands. "These grooms are from poor families and come to get a wife from here because we are not asking for *mahr* [groom's payment to the bride] and *shabka* [jewelry and gifts]." As for their mothers, though, she sees little hope of social integration: "The problem we have in the society is how to accept pregnant women without marriage. I know a girl in a university, and she had a baby from this relationship, and she didn't want the kid because she didn't want to remind her family of her mistake."

## GOING SOLO

It doesn't have to be this way. Faiza, a young woman I met in Morocco, is living proof that things can be different for unmarried mothers. Our paths crossed in Casablanca, where I fetched up after almost two years on the road. I had been shuttling across the Arab region with a giant duffel full of books and papers picked up along the way, and had the aching shoulders to prove it. When I reached Morocco, I took myself off to a hammam, that apex of Orientalist fantasy, for a little relief. The idea of so much naked female flesh, bathed, buffed, and perfumed, has famously turned on generations of Western authors and artists. I, however, was more interested in finding an osteopath than an odalisque, unless she also happened to be a qualified masseuse. What I really needed was someone who could turn my lumpen muscles back into long, sinuous fibers, from the anatomical equivalent of *basbousa,* a dense semolina cake my grandmother used to make, into golden strands of *kunafa,* another of her syrupy specialties. I was in luck, and after an hour's massage, restored to far better form.

A few weeks later, I returned to talk with Faiza, who was working on the till. She's in her early twenties, and a real head-turner: feline green eyes in a pale, heart-shaped face, set against a tumble of coppery curls. Her rare beauty comes from her unusual origins; she's *amazigh,* or Berber, one of Morocco's indigenous population. Faiza is bubbly and talkative, no more so than when she's describing her son: "We fell in love with the first contact. . . . You know, my baby, we speak with the eyes." She told me about the delivery—sixteen hours of undiluted pain, she said. Then she added, "I am a virgin. I have two papers [medical certificates] to prove my virginity."

Welcome to the modern Middle East, where, two millennia on, virgin births are still a fact of life. Faiza's announcement was not just a piece of wishful thinking. She met the father of her son, a man twenty years her senior, while he was working for a water company connecting houses to the main in her small town in the south. They were introduced through a mutual acquaintance: "I always thought of him as a friend. But one day he invited me [to where he was staying]; he said he was sick. [I said] I will go and see him, he's alone there. I went, then he asked me to sleep with him. I said yes, but only [come] between my legs."

A month later, Faiza missed her period, but thought little of it. Two more months and her mother—alarmed at her daughter's dizziness, sleepiness, and headaches—sent her to a doctor in Agadir, 250 kilometers away. "The doctor told me I was pregnant. I didn't believe it. I cried a lot; I didn't know what to do," she said. "It was the first time I was pregnant, so he thought I would want an abortion, because he saw me crying. But I was crying because I knew my situation. . . . I was still a virgin and I became pregnant. It was the biggest blow of my life."

When she came home with the news, only her mother and sister were let in on the secret. Faiza managed to stay with her family for four months until her condition was impossible to conceal, at which point her mother gave her money to go to Casablanca to find the father of her child. She crept out early one morning, leaving the men of the family in the dark, literally and figuratively. "My father didn't know; I was afraid he would hurt me. He could beat me, he could kill me . . . my brothers too [could do this]," she said.

Faiza failed to find the father of her child, but she did hear about a hospital that could put her in touch with INSAF (National Institution for Solidarity with Women in Distress), an NGO that helps unmarried mothers during pregnancy, delivery, and early motherhood. But getting to INSAF turned out to be an ordeal in itself. "The moment I got to the hospital, there was a man at security. He said, 'I know the number for INSAF.' He took my bag and I followed him [to a building around the corner from the hospital]. I wasn't feeling right. I was a little scared, and at that moment he pushed me in a room and closed the door," Faiza told me, in a surprisingly steady voice, given what followed. "For an hour, he tried to rape me. . . . He gave me nude photos of him; he gave me pictures—girls of Agadir who were having sex.[55] All this to sleep with me. I was dumbstruck; I was afraid for my baby. He kissed me. I hit him, really I hit him, so he hit my face. Never touch me, because I still have my virginity. He hit me with a belt. . . . He said, 'I'm going to kill you. I'm going to stick you in a bin,'" she recalled. "The day I delivered, it was he who was in my head. I could never forget him—a fear that I had never had before."

Fortunately, Faiza managed to escape with her prized virginity intact. From there it was relatively smooth sailing. She made contact with INSAF, which looked after her for the remainder of her otherwise uncomplicated pregnancy and delivery; a few months later she found a place at Solidarité Féminine, or SolFem, a Moroccan NGO whose mission is to knit unmarried mothers and their children together and weave them back into society.

SolFem has just around fifty women and their children under its wing at any one time, in a three-year program spread over three sites in Casablanca. For many of SolFem's beneficiaries, this program begins behind whitewashed walls in an industrial quarter called Ain Sebaa. Outside is roaring traffic and lines of weather-beaten men looking for work; through the gate lies a lovely courtyard with palm trees and flower beds exploding with color. There's a nursery on one side of this sanctuary, where a dozen or so toddlers are playing and infants lie dozing in cots; on the other is a kitchen, where young women are cooking up a storm, chopping mounds of vegetables and fanning small charcoal braziers on which are simmering earthenware tagines. By noon, the garden and dining room start filling up with young business types in shirtsleeves and ties and middle-aged women, their heads neatly covered in hijabs, with kids in tow. They've come for the food, and no wonder: my lamb and carrot stew, with a side dish of spicy eggplant, was delicious.

The Ain Sebaa facility is both a restaurant and a rehabilitation center. The idea behind it is to teach unmarried mothers a set of marketable skills they can use to build a new life. There is a lot of work to be done. The women who start here are the most fragile of SolFem's beneficiaries. They are young, mainly in their early to late teens, and come from poor rural families. Many are illiterate and have been working as housemaids, or *bonnes*, farmed out to wealthier families as child labor. Their shy, almost wounded demeanors come from a life of hard knocks, the hardest of which is their children's sometimes violent conceptions—through sexual abuse, either in their own families or at the hands of their employers.[56]

The facility at Ain Sebaa is calm and quiet, a world away from the life most of these young mothers have known. While they live in groups of two or three with their kids in nearby apartments, organized by SolFem, they spend their days at the facility. Aside from vocational skills, they are taught how to read and write; there is also a social worker, psychologist, doctor, and lawyer on staff, as well as child care professionals to teach them how to look after their kids, which is no easy task. When I visited the nursery, my best efforts to entertain half a dozen curly-haired toddlers set off an explosion of crying. "Don't worry," one of the attendants reassured me. "The children are not good with strangers. The mothers, they are anxious, and they transmit this insecurity to the kids. We try to help them over this."

After a year, mothers who are more at ease graduate with their children to another facility in the center of Casablanca that is a restaurant, patisserie, and a sewing workshop. A couple of years ago, the organization also opened the hammam where I met Faiza; it turns out beauticians and manicurists from a different sort of unmarried mother increasingly appearing at SolFem's door: a student or graduate who, more often than not, has slept with the man she thought she would marry, only to find herself pregnant and deserted.

For all their efforts, SolFem, INSAF, and other NGOs are reaching only a fraction of the upward of twenty-five thousand single women a year who become mothers in Morocco.[57] Those who don't come under the protection of one of these organizations have a much harder time of things. Not only do they go without medical attention during their pregnancy, but this neglect can turn into bigger problems come delivery. Those under the umbrella of NGOs have an easier time in the hospital than women on their own, who are on the receiving end of staff contempt, even abuse.

The trouble keeps coming, especially for those unmarried mothers toughing it out alone. Under Moroccan law, sex outside of marriage is punishable by imprisonment of up to one year, a point of considerable debate in recent years. But police tend to turn a blind eye to women who are in the care of one of the NGOs. INSAF, SolFem, and their counterparts are also indispensable when it comes to registering newborns with the state, as vital in Morocco as it is in Egypt. Legal reform means single mothers are now allowed to obtain birth certificates for their children.[58] While the law has changed on paper, cutting through the Gordian knot of red tape can be an overwhelming task, one compounded by the obstructive attitude of civil servants who disapprove of unwed mothers, a situation so dire that it drove one single mother to self-immolation in the wake of the Arab uprisings.[59]

Having overcome these hurdles, Faiza faced yet another set of obstacles. Although she informed the father of his son's birth, he at first refused to recognize the child, a common enough situation, even with the intervention of experts from SolFem. Reconciliation with her family, however, went more smoothly, much to Faiza's relief: "A girl in this problem, she never forgets her parents. That's the great curse. The father of the baby has taken off; a girl in this time, she thinks a lot about her family." According to social workers at SolFem, family reintegration is one of the biggest changes in the situation of unmarried mothers over the past decade; where once there was blanket rejection by families, there is now growing rapprochement.

Faiza even took her son home for a visit. There was some initial awkwardness, particularly with her father, but he has not only come around, she says, but is even impressed with her new sense of purpose. "I found a lot had changed. [Before] I was not responsible; I didn't know what responsibility was. I didn't know what it was to be strong," she told me. "You have a problem, but this problem gives you strength. I fell, and I fell, and I fell, but it taught me a lot of lessons."

Although surveys show that many unmarried mothers feel they have been given the cold shoulder by society, Faiza is proud of her new obligations. "People respect me, and why, from the young to the old? [Because] I look after my baby well: I dress him well, I take responsibility. That is why they respect me. They never say, 'You are an unmarried mother.'" As far as Faiza is concerned, times are changing. "Now is not like before. Now they understand what is a single mother. It is a problem in Morocco, but really, people know if you want to live with your baby, you can." This she attributes to the intervention of groups like SolFem and INSAF. "The associations are a point of contact with the people. Because through the newspapers, even the television, they speak directly with the people. Unwed mothers are not something bizarre in Morocco. They were always there, but it was a taboo. But now we are opening, we are talking."

This new candor is in large part due to Aicha Ech-Chenna, a larger-than-life grandmother and founder of SolFem. A quarter of a century ago, when she started the organization, getting unmarried mothers to talk in public was a struggle, so ashamed were they of their condition. "Listen, you haven't committed a crime, my girls," is her message. "You are the victim of an error, you are the victim of a promise of marriage, or a rape—I don't know what. If someone should tip the hat, it is society that dumped you at its feet, because you have the courage to keep your kids."

Ech-Chenna's passion for the plight of single mothers comes, in part, from her own background. Her mother was divorced and raised her daughter as a single parent. Ech-Chenna herself trained as a nurse and then became a social worker, where she met unwed mothers in desperate straits, handing off their children to orphanages. "I believe I am the first woman to talk about all these taboos on television, radio. I dropped the first bomb," she told me. She started speaking out in the 1990s; today she's a bona fide celebrity. King Muhammad VI is a fan, and high society has opened its doors, and wallets, to her cause. I met Ech-Chenna on her return from a tour of America, where she had won a million-dollar prize for "faith-based entrepreneurship." Her phone was ringing off the hook, and we squeezed in our discussion between radio and TV interviews.

For all this success, the going has not been smooth. In 2004,

Morocco introduced significant reforms to its *Mudawwana,* the legal code governing personal status, that tempered a number of traditional male privileges. Among other changes, the reformed law requires men to secure the explicit permission of current wives before taking on any others (and allows existing wives to rule out this option altogether as a condition of their own marriage contract); it restricts the practice of wife repudiation and brings divorce under court jurisdiction; and states that male guardianship expires once a woman comes of age. These changes were bitterly opposed by the PJD, but with the backing of the king, the law passed, establishing a trend toward greater rights for women—on paper, at any rate. At the time, though, Ech-Chenna came under fierce attack from Islamists, who considered her support of such female-friendly reforms as the slippery slope to *zina.* But as with most things in her way, Ech-Chenna has a ready response for Islamic opponents: "I am the granddaughter of a religious scholar. He used to say to my aunt, 'You must never say, "child of sin."'' Someone who does sin is an adult, sin of the spirit and the body, someone who does ill to another person. Me, as a practicing Muslim, I love God and I respect Him. Bringing moral judgments, that's not up to me. Only God can judge."

Ech-Chenna is old enough to remember how such matters used to be arranged, in Morocco as in Egypt: illegitimate children seamlessly absorbed into the extended family or quietly left on a neighbor's doorstep to be taken in as a gift from God. "Our grandmothers, a long time ago, like all enclosed women, they developed an intelligence. Because they could not go out, they developed an internal intelligence to deal with their problems in a discreet way." But all this changed with Morocco's independence in 1956, what Ech-Chenna calls the "social explosion": rapid urbanization, economic turmoil, breakdown of the family. Sex, once a natural part of life, got swept under the carpet. "No shame in [discussing any topic in] religion, they would say in Qur'an school. Even in the family, at least they would talk about menstruation—the mother, the aunt, or a female cousin," Ech-Chenna recalls. "With the explosion, clients who come to the association don't even know what sexuality is.

Even when they have their first period, they don't know what is going on—things that were totally ordinary in our societies a long time ago."

Ech-Chenna is convinced that the model she created in SolFem can work elsewhere in the region, including Egypt. Her advice is simple: start small, stay discreet, and steer clear of politics. Most important, though, is choosing the right leaders; in her opinion, ego is definitely not an asset: "It's work that takes a lot of patience and self-abnegation. If you want to be a star, go sing [on a TV talent show]. Civil society is the only field where you shouldn't be a star; if you become a star, if people recognize you, it should be because of the work you do."

That work is far from over. While there may be a little more appreciation of the plight of single mothers in Morocco, that doesn't mean widespread social acceptance. SolFem is careful to publicly present its beneficiaries as unwitting victims of sexual "accidents"; generally speaking, Moroccan society is, as yet, reluctant to recognize a woman's right to sexual and reproductive autonomy—to have sex, and children, however she chooses.[60] "We have not responded to all the problems of single mothers," Ech-Chenna told me. "There are lots of abandoned children everywhere. If the society had completely evolved, there would be no abandoned children. It is the work of two or three generations, working transparently and humbly." She compares the pace of social and legal change in Morocco since independence to water in the desert. "What the West did in two centuries, we did in fifty years. It's like a really dry land that hasn't benefited from human rights. If you pour a lot of water on it, what is going to happen? There will be floods; you have to give time for society to absorb the changes."

Back in Egypt, Ech-Chenna's words ring true in a time of transition. After the fast-track removal of Mubarak has come the much slower process of changing decades—centuries, really—of political culture. Social transformation, at the level of everyday life, is an even longer-term proposition. But I now hear a few voices in Egypt daring to imagine, after generations of disappointment and resignation, a country in which at least some on the margins—unmarried mothers among them—might one day find a place on the inside. "With time, the shame will change. We are getting better every day, I am sure," one unmarried mother in Cairo told me. "We are all becoming one world. . . . Otherwise, we will be extinct; we will not be there. The whole world is changing: North Africa is changing, even Saudi [Arabia] is changing. . . . You're telling me we will stay the same?"

## ٢
# Sex for Sale

*I am not a prostitute, and my husband isn't giving me money, so where am I supposed to find the cash?*
—My grandmother, on a woman's limited options

When my father was a teenager in the late 1940s, he and his best friend used to take a tram across Cairo on Fridays to pray at Al-Azhar, the historic heart of learning in the Muslim world. Today, Al-Azhar's great mosque, built like a fortress on the edge of Khan al-Khalili, Cairo's famous souk, is besieged by modern life, hemmed in by roaring traffic. But in my father's day, it dominated the landscape, both physically and spiritually; in an age before satellite preachers and online fatwas, Al-Azhar was the final word on Islam for Egyptians and much of the Muslim world beyond.

When prayers were over, my father and his friend were warned by the latter's father, a mosque official, not to wander too far beyond its precincts, and especially not to the nearby neighborhood of al-Batniyya, whose skein of dark alleys was a famous tangle of vice. This included prostitution (*da'ara* in colloquial Egyptian; *bagha'* in classical Arabic). In al-Batniyya, *sharamiit*—which means "rags" in Egyptian Arabic, but is also slang for prostitutes—were ready to cater to their clients' needs; this included easing the conscience in the case of Al-Azhar students known to frequent the area. "*Mallaktuka nafsi,*" the women would say, on starting proceedings with their more religious-minded customers. "I give you the right to own me."[1]

This formula has a long tradition. For all Egypt's current sexual hang-ups, the country's history is not one of denying the flesh, and conversion to Islam, which began in the seventh century, did little to change that. Islam, in its essence, acknowledges the power of sex—particularly women's desire—so much so that it established rules and regulations to channel its force, albeit with male satisfaction foremost in mind. One of these institutions was concubinage, essentially, sexual slavery—a feature of pre-Islamic life retained by the new religious order.[2] The Qur'an is clear on its acceptability. "The successful true believers are those who perform their prayers, avoid frivolous talk, render their alms and protect their genitals except with their wives and what their right hands possess [what they own], where there is no blame. Those who seek beyond those limits are the transgressors," exhorts one of several verses on the subject. While polygyny is limited to four wives at any one time, concubinage is an open-ended proposition, hence the great harems of Arab history, a bottomless source of fascination for Western observers.

Institutionalized concubinage is long gone in Egypt; slavery was formally abolished in the late nineteenth century, and by the time my father was a boy in the 1930s, slave-owning families like ours had long since released their right-hand men and women. But even if the letter of the law changed in Egypt's official statutes, the spirit of concubinage lived on in the working girls of al-Batniyya, who used an Islamic provision to get the job done, allowing themselves to be temporarily possessed by their clients—in more ways than one.

Today, certain forms of matrimony serve much the same purpose, lending religious respectability to what is nakedly commercial intercourse. A case-in-point is Samia, a soft-spoken woman in her early twenties. She comes from a town south of Cairo and had just spent a couple of weeks in the big city over the summer. "We stayed in Zamalek in a high-class area. I sat at home mostly; I didn't go shopping or to the movies," she told me. This might sound like a pretty dull family vacation, but Samia wasn't on holiday, nor was she with her parents, although she did spend time with a man old enough to be her grandfather.

"He was around sixty or seventy years old. He came with the broker. I saw him and the next day he came and married me," she said. "I knew that he was married in Saudi Arabia and has a wife. Every day we would have breakfast together, and then practice [have sex]. I didn't want to go outside with him because I didn't want anyone to see me. I asked him some questions [about his life], but he never answered, and I didn't really care because I just wanted to finish the relationship. After two weeks, I went back to my family."

Tourists from the Gulf pour into Cairo to escape the summer heat and humidity of home. In recent years, Egypt has sold itself as a holiday destination for well-heeled Arab visitors, working wonders for the local economy. But some of that business is of a sexual nature. There is a well-established network of brokers and lawyers in Egypt procuring young women for these visitors, who enter into *zawaj misyaf,* a summer vacationer's marriage, or a "deal marriage," as locals call it. These unions, lasting from a few days to a couple of weeks, usually include a written contract and witnesses, which makes them *shar'i,* or Islamically sound. However, they remain unofficial because they are not registered with the government. Although the intent is to keep these unions temporary, the actual term is rarely written down, which means they sidestep the issue of *zawaj mut'a,* pleasure marriage permitted in Shi'i Islam but prohibited for Sunni Muslims. Aside from the veneer of religious propriety, these contracts also give couples some cover in the rare event that police ask questions of wealthy visitors. Commercial sex work is illegal in Egypt, with penalties of up to three years in prison and a fine of EGP 300 (USD 50) for "any person who habitually practices debauchery or prostitution," as well as penalties for those who aid or abet the practice, though clients slip through this net.[3]

Many of the women engaged in such summer marriages come from a particular governorate, Giza, next to Cairo. Samia lives in a town called Hawamdiyya, one of three famous for supplying women for summer marriage. Hawamdiyya used to be known for its sugar refinery; in recent years it has become a major destination for sugar daddies. I asked Samia if her town is so popular because its daughters are so attractive. She looked at me, her pretty face framed by a chic red-and-black-spotted silver hijab, as if I were an idiot. "No." She frowned. "It's because we're so poor."

Samia is one of five children—two boys and three girls. The

family lives down a scrappy alley in Hawamdiyya in a three-room apartment along with her grandparents. Her father is a caretaker, but well-paid work in the town, like almost everywhere else in Egypt, is hard to get. Their monthly income is around EGP 700, between her father's salary, their vegetable patch, and a few chickens. So a couple of years ago, when a man turned up at their door with a "groom" for the nineteen-year-old Samia, and EGP 20,000, her father took the money; Samia got EGP 500 to buy some new clothes. "I was afraid because it was my first time. I did not know what to expect," she said. "It lasted for a week and he lived with me in Cairo, [in an area called] Mohandeseen. He was interested in sex most of the time. After a week I returned to my family and he left. When I was back, I was sad because something had changed in me, [but also] I was happy because my family had money to spend the whole year. I talked with my mother about what happened, but I did not talk with my sister because I want to avoid her doing that. [In any case], the subject is so sensitive, we do not talk a lot or frankly about it."

Mahmoud, on the other hand, has no such compunction. He's a *simsar,* which translates to "broker" in English. In reality, Mahmoud is a pimp. He works with Amir, who's a lawyer in a run-down office on a rubbish-laden, dirt-packed side street in Cairo. They look as if they've just come from central casting: both in their forties, Mahmoud is slick, with a gold chain and thicket of chest hair peeking out from an open-necked sports shirt; Amir is buttoned up in a crisp gray shirt and smart green tie, surrounded by his legal certificates and a giant gilded list of the ninety-nine names of God above his desk.

When I first met them, before the uprising, the global recession had yet to touch Mahmoud and Amir. Mahmoud and his broker friends—both men and women—were arranging at least two thousand "marriages" a year. For the legal paperwork, Amir receives EGP 1,000 per union; Mahmoud, who finds the girls, arranges the apartments, and generally smooths things along, gets EGP 2,000–3,000 in exchange. Such marriages were uncommon in the 1960s, says Mahmoud, but major changes since the 1970s—the Gulf oil

boom, Egypt's *infitah* (open-door economic policy), and a growing consumerism, along with the rise of Islamic conservatism—
ushered in this sex tourism with a religious twist. And prices have
more than doubled since then, he says.

Mahmoud is ideally placed for his profession, with a foot in both
worlds: he was born in Hawamdiyya and knows the families there,
but now works as a driver in one of the big five-star hotels in Cairo,
famous for its view and, so rumor has it, *hafalat khassa*—private
parties hosted by wealthy Gulf guests where wine and women flow
freely. Mahmoud walked me through how his side of the business
works. "I know a lot of Saudi men in the hotel, and they want to get
married to Egyptian girls . . . sometimes for ten days and sometimes
for two weeks. It [usually] starts when I pick up a Saudi from the
airport and he asks me to get him a wife, a 'young' girl; occasionally, he asks me for a virgin, but it's more expensive," Mahmoud
recounted. "I know the girls from their parents, who tell me that
they want to marry their daughters. For example, I know [a family
with] two girls in university, and their mother is a widow and they
need money. They came to meet the groom, and the mother told me
that the girls need money to spend on what they need. The mother
told me that the groom could marry both of them, but he refused.
He said, 'I am old and I cannot do that.'"

These arrangements are along the same lines as some of the
"informal" marriages discussed in chapter 2, but in contrast to the
secrecy that often surrounds those unions, a summer marriage is
a family affair. Parents come to the "ceremony," though it's a no-
frills occasion compared with the hoopla that accompanies a real
Egyptian wedding. Key to proceedings is the signing of a marriage
contract—"in the name of God and in the tradition of the Prophet,
peace be upon him"—in which both parties promise to fulfill their
marital obligations, including financial support from the husband
and obedience and conjugal access from the woman. Unlike an official marriage, which is presided over by a *ma'dhun* and registered
with the government, in these arrangements both parties and the
lawyer keep a copy of the contract, which is torn up when the couple go their separate ways. These unions dissolve without strings;

all the woman walks away with is the money she was promised up front by her partner.

Over the course of two years, Samia had three summer marriages. That's slow by Hawamdiyya standards; Mahmoud knows young women who go through five or six of these unions a year, which means that they are technically in violation of their marriage contract because they have not observed '*idda*—that is, the period of three months prescribed by the Qur'an that women have to wait between marriages, so as to assure their previous husbands that they are not pregnant. In any case, for women like Samia, more fundamental rights are at stake. The contract clearly stipulates that she enters into the union of her own free will, but Samia feels she has little choice: "My father forced me to marry because he wanted to get rid of me."

It's not just poverty that is driving families to this, but growing consumerism as well. "Seventy percent of the girls I know in the village, they do this marriage; I have two close friends who did that," says Samia. "Most of the girls, when they talk about this marriage, they talk from the money side. As for me, I wanted my sister to continue her studies in school; that's why I accept to marry. I do not want my sister to have the same problem." That money comes at a price, however. Samia drops her eyes, along with her voice, as she describes her husbands: "Most of them do anal sex with me and they took medicines [Viagra]. One of them was watching videos and sex scenes, and after that he practiced sex with me. One of them wanted to practice sex with me the whole time, but another one was lazy and quiet in asking for sex. The third one, he beat me once." It's rare that girls become pregnant from these relationships, says Samia, because they are all using some form of contraception. Condoms, however, are not on the cards, leaving these young women open to sexually transmitted infections; Samia herself was "sick in sex" after one of her marriages.

Mahmoud describes his work frankly as prostitution. "I know it is haram, but it's not my problem." He keeps his real job quiet from his family; Mahmoud's wife thinks he's in the travel business. Ever the lawyer, however, Amir insists that these unions are aboveboard. "I do not consider this marriage prostitution," he says, "because it is legal and *shar'i*." Technically, he has a point: Samia's marriage ticks all the right boxes in terms of Islamic formalities, dubious intent aside. But she herself is unconvinced. "I used to go to the mosque when I was little. I am a religious girl, but I know I am doing something haram by accepting this marriage." It's a problem for her family too. Although summer marriages are common in Hawamdiyya, they're also a source of shame. Samia's mother says she has no friends in the town, an isolation she ascribes to the coming and going of people to Cairo in search of work. But Mahmoud reckons this has more to do with ostracism than migration: "[Some] families cut their relationship with families who are in the business; they are conservative and religious. . . . They do not interact with these families so as to avoid a bad reputation."

When asked about her future, Samia says getting out of the business is top on her list. There's a light in her intelligent eyes when she describes her ambitions: having left school at twelve, she'd like to continue her studies and learn English. As for marriage, she's not hopeful. There is a young man in town she likes, but she avoids him now. "I cut the relationship with him because he will know what I do and he will be sad," she says, with a regret far beyond her years. Samia is torn between hating men and wanting to find someone who will take her out of all this. "I see, maybe I will make this operation to be virgin again if the man who wants to get married to me wants to do that. My dream in future is to find a good man."

In recent years, there have been attempts to clamp down on summer marriages by linking them to Egypt's broader push against underage unions, since research shows a majority of these holiday matches involve girls under sixteen.[4] Irrespective of coercion or prostitution, such unions are illegal, thanks to a 2008 amendment to Egypt's Child Law that raised the legal age of marriage of both men and women to eighteen. The change was fiercely opposed in Parliament by members representing the Muslim Brotherhood, who assert, among other points, that Islamic jurisprudence puts the age of self-responsibility, and therefore consent to marriage, around puberty. Indeed, one of the first legal reforms proposed by their ultraconservative cousins, the Salafis, come to Parliament was to again lower the age of marriage. Embedded in these arguments is the same reasoning that perpetuates female genital cutting: that girls could go off the sexual rails at any moment, all the more so with the temptations of modern life, and the sooner such libidinous energy is channeled into marriage, the better.

But when Egyptians talk about underage marriage, it is not a question of two love-struck teenagers tying the knot. Today, the vast majority of marriages of those under thirty are between older grooms and younger brides, with an average age difference of five or so years.[5] However, the marriages causing consternation for those with an interest in human rights are the ones with half a century, not half a decade, between husband and wife. Such spring-thaw/dead-of-winter unions are also a rising source of controversy in the Gulf; in recent years high-profile cases of child brides seeking to escape their middle-aged or elderly grooms have hit the headlines in Saudi Arabia and in Yemen, where more than half of women are wed by age eighteen and recent efforts to raise the age of marriage have also met with fierce resistance from Islamic conservatives.[6] Egypt's second-highest religious authority, the Grand Mufti, also came out against underage summer marriages.[7] However, proponents argue that such marriages are entirely permissible because they follow the example of the Prophet Muhammad and his favorite wife, Aisha, who, it is said, was six when they married and nine when the union was consummated—though this is a point of debate among some religious scholars today.

The Mubarak regime's assault on the summer marriage industry was also wed to the global campaign against human trafficking. For years, Egypt has been on the receiving end of international criticism as a major highway for the modern-day slave trade; it has spent much of this century flagged by the U.S. State Department as "a source, transit, and destination country for women and children who are subjected to trafficking in persons, specifically forced labor and sex trafficking"—not just the summer marriage business, but also sex tourism involving the country's legions of street kids, sexual exploitation of African migrants on their way to Israel via the Sinai, as well as further variations on the abuse of domestic and other workers.[8]

Suzanne Mubarak, then first lady and the driving force behind a number of national councils on women and children, took a highly public stand against human trafficking, at home and abroad. The Mubarak government set up a special anti-trafficking unit and passed several laws prohibiting the practice, including one directed against the exploitation of children, with penalties of up to life imprisonment. The government trumpeted its progress: training judges, police, and Ministry of Tourism and other officials on how to identify and handle trafficking cases; hotlines and shelters for victims; and high-profile arrests of marriage registrars for facilitating child marriages. (In one case the whole chain of summer marriage—parents, broker, lawyer, and the Saudi client—was arrested, the client sentenced in absentia to ten years in prison.)

For all the official fanfare, such measures did little to dent business for Mahmoud and Amir. Raising the age of marriage has proved a minor obstacle for determined parents, says Amir; all it takes to satisfy marriage registrars is a quick trip to the local clinic and some money under the table for a doctor to check a girl's wisdom teeth (considered a sign of physical maturity) and issue a certificate that she is of age. Indeed, this pervasive deception leads even some liberal activists to quietly endorse lowering the age of marriage, their argument being that families are doing it anyway, in some cases marrying their daughters through informal 'urfi unions, then switching them over to registered marriage when they turn eighteen. In the meantime, though, these young women have more often than not become young mothers, but without the rights accorded official wives. Better to have a law that recognizes this reality, one human rights lawyer from Alexandria told me, than to think the law will change people's behavior.

As for arrests, they have done little to deter clients either. "It's just propaganda," Amir sniffed. "Maybe there were a few [men charged], but that does not affect the numbers." Nor were anti-trafficking measures proving any more effective, one former employee of the government's anti-trafficking unit told me, dismissing most of the projects as hype. She laughed at the idea of anti-trafficking legisla-tion bringing an end to summer marriage. "When we talk about trafficking in [village] outreach, they all say in the community that none of us make this for our girls. To them it's not a problem, it's a way of life," she noted. "Egyptians are very clever to find gaps in the law."

Local NGOs, though, have had a little more success working inside communities, raising awareness of the medical and psycho-logical risks associated with these sorts of marriages, and encour-aging girls' education as one step on the long path to empowerment. The key to getting families out of the trade is economics: there are projects to create community savings pools that women can dip into in times of trouble, as well as vocational training and other income-generating alternatives—though it's hard to imagine hand-icrafts proving quite as lucrative as hand jobs. The best those work-ing to eliminate summer marriage are hoping for, in the uncertainty of the new order, is to hold on to the few gains that were made in recent years.

The uprising did have an immediate, if unintentional, impact on the summer marriage trade, largely because the stream of Gulf visitors dried to a trickle amid stories of lawlessness on the streets of Cairo; Amir had scarcely a dozen clients the summer follow-ing the upheaval, less than a third of his regular clientele. But he was optimistic that recent events would, ultimately, prove some-thing of a boon. "Summer marriage will take some time to recover. When the security [situation] is solved, a lot of marriages will take place. Because after the revolution, and being a democracy, a lot of Arabs will want to come and see what happened, so there is a better chance for more customers, more clients. Even if Egypt is a democracy, even if there is economic improvement, this business will continue," Amir confidently concluded.

None of this bodes well for Samia and her peers, who are looking for a different sort of life. Even if the laws were watertight, they'd offer them little relief: since Samia is over eighteen, restrictions on child marriage are not relevant. Nor are the laws on prostitu-tion applicable, since her relationship is covered by an Islamically accepted marriage contract. And though, according to the letter of the law, she is being trafficked—by her own father, no less— the chances of her coming forward as a victim, or bringing a case against her father, are slim. It's the same for any family shame, be it wife beating, incest, rape, or any of the countless other personal tragedies: the vast majority of women suffer in silence, as the director of one drop-in center for battered women in downtown Cairo told me, and will continue to do so until the price of speaking out no longer outweighs the costs of endurance. The ties that bind Samia to her summer job—financial need, family duty, and an Islamically grounded resignation to her lot—are hard to loosen, and for as long as Egypt welcomes a steady stream of Gulf visitors and their spending sprees, demand for her services is likely to continue.

### "THE WHOLE COUNTRY IS IN PROSTITUTION"

Summer marriage is only one face of prostitution in Egypt. Sex work is arguably a success story of Egypt's *infitah,* a triumph of private enterprise offering an array of services to suit all tastes and budgets—albeit with a heavy human price. Sex work is one of the clearest reflections of the ongoing power of patriarchy in Egypt and the wider Arab world, and a measure of just how conflicted individuals and their societies are over sex, proclaiming their Islamic credentials while ignoring, or indeed perpetrating, the exploitation and abuse of those who are in the business, by consent or coercion. In the Arab region, female sex workers carry a triple burden: as women who not only have sex outside of marriage but trade in it as well. This stigma, reinforced in law, leads them to keep quiet. As a consequence, sex work is both the most obvious and the most hidden aspect of sexual life in Egypt and the wider Arab world, and this makes these women getting their fair share of the prospective political, social, and economic gains of the region's uprisings all the more difficult.

Just how many sex workers there are in Cairo, let alone in Egypt as a whole, is a matter of guesswork. But a quick trawl through the International Sex Guide, "the Internet's largest sex travel website," where men looking for action swap tips, reveals a united nations of sex workers: Russian and Central European escorts, Chinese masseuses offering something on the side, Sudanese refugees and Moroccan migrants working the dance floor, Egyptian women available to pick up off the street or to order up by mobile phone in a playground stretching from the infamous bars and clubs of the main drag to the pyramids, and rented apartments in Mohandeseen to massage parlors in the leafy expat haven of Maadi to a landmark five-star hotel on the Nile where commercial sex workers—male and female—are not only tolerated by management but discreetly offered to guests as off-menu room service. According to one estimate, there are at least eight hundred hot spots for female sex work in Cairo alone.[9]

"The whole country is in prostitution," laughed Jihane, a chubby, bubbly woman in her midtwenties. She should know; Jihane sells sex to pay for her drug habit. We met at a private drug rehabilitation center in Cairo—one of the few to cater specifically to the swollen ranks of female addicts, who face even more stigma than their male counterparts. Jihane is on the more privileged side of Cairo's social spectrum: she comes from an educated, middle-class family, her Arabic peppered with French. In her early teens, Jihane started taking drugs with school friends—first *bangu* (a form of hashish), then pills, and on to heroin. This graduation was prompted in part by economics; in recent years, the street price of heroin has fallen, all the faster after the uprising, to the point where it's possible to pick up an eighth of a gram for around EGP 60—one of the few goods whose price has not skyrocketed in the years of double-digit inflation.

It was through her friends at school that Jihane got hooked on drugs; at first she used pocket money from her unsuspecting parents, who, like many middle-class Egyptian couples, were too busy working to stop the family from falling down the economic ladder to keep a close eye on the kids. Eventually, Jihane dropped out of school, left home, and moved in with her dealers. Direct bartering—sex for drugs—was how she managed to maintain her habit for a while, but then she drifted into the cash-only business, along with her friends.

Jihane's crowd charges a client EGP 100 on up for full vaginal intercourse. According to Jihane, her more successful colleagues are making as much as EGP 4,000 a day, and virgins—some of whom are born into a family business—command even more at their debut. Most, women, however, come to sex work after losing their virginity through marriage, a failed love affair, or sexual abuse. Many in Jihane's circle are working for pimps—*mi'arrasiin*, in colloquial Egyptian—husbands or boyfriends, but often other women too, themselves former sex workers, whose retirement plan consists of an apartment and a client roster passed on to younger women who use the flat as their workplace. It's a well-established pattern of succession: "If the prostitute repented, she would go pimping," so the Egyptian saying goes, referring to those—post–Mubarak era politicians, for instance—whose promises of change amount to nothing more than business as usual.

Because of all the obstacles to sex before marriage, I assumed that most of her clientele were single men, but Jihane set me straight. For her, at least, they're mainly married men looking for sexual excitement lacking in their conjugal relations. "In America, a girl before getting married can watch a sex film and she will get experience; she may have sex with a boy, so she is not a girl [virgin] now. But the girl in Egypt goes to her husband's house and she is virgin. And she does not watch sex films. When she gets married, she does not know how to do anything. The girls who work in prostitution, they have got more ideas and more experience. But if the wife has got this experience, the husband will doubt her behavior. And even if he tries to teach her, she will tell him it's *'ayb* [shameful]."

I asked Jihane what she and her friends could offer that a wife might not. She reflected for a moment: "A girl [sex worker] can go into different positions, but his wife may be overweight and she cannot go into these. She doesn't know how to move with him." Anal sex—which, as we've seen, is a bone of contention between spouses—is also on the cards: EGP 300 a shot, according to Jihane's price list. And that's not the only extra. "The girls working in prostitution have means [techniques] like sucking [fellatio]. There is no sucking with the wife. There are some men who try to be friendly with their wives and do this, but it will be a very strange thing if the man asks his wife to do this. Even if the wife does sucking for her husband, she does not have the experience of one who is doing it all day." The bottom line, says Jihane, is expertise and enthusiasm, feigned or not. "If she [the sex worker] is not enjoying it," Jihane reasoned, "she is like the one [the wife] at home, so she is not going to get the money."

As do many tourist attractions in Egypt, Jihane's circle practices tiered pricing—one rate for Egyptians, and a higher rate for foreigners. The big money comes from Gulf tourists, but unlike Samia and her peers, Jihane's clique also offers a rather more specialized service: same-sex intercourse. "Some girls know that some Saudi women like this matter and they go to the hotels and meet the Saudi women and they pay more than the men," Jihane observed. "I know a friend of mine, she has got a Saudi client woman, she goes to her place, and she gets paid three thousand dollars for two hours." According to Jihane, some of her colleagues owe their professional development in this particular department to the Mubarak regime. "Here in Egypt, when there is a girl sitting in a café, the morals police may arrest her when she is overexposed [revealingly dressed]. In the first case, if she's arrested, she will be discharged, but if it is a repeat, the second time she may get three years in prison. When she goes to the prison, the women have sex together. And then when they come outside again, they use this ability to have sex with women. So when they are arrested, after they have contact with the police, they work in the lesbian field."

Same-sex–inclined Saudis aren't the only female visitors in Egypt looking for action. Commercial sex work is one of the few equal opportunity employers in the country and across the Arab region; even heterosexual men have their corner of the business, or *bezness,* as it's called in Tunisia. From Agadir to Aqaba, where there are Western women on vacation, you will find local men at their service. With soaring unemployment, young men from around

Egypt have been making their way to Dahab, a resort town on the Sinai Peninsula, and other tourist destinations along the Red Sea in search of a decent wage to support themselves and their families—and some of the best money in town comes from female visitors looking for a little attention and adventure. While the stereotype is that of a fifty-plus woman on the prowl for a much younger man, women in their twenties and thirties are increasingly flocking too. The attraction is more than just physical. "In a romantic desert setting . . . most women prefer romance to sex," noted Anne Cumming, an aptly named English housewife who slept her way across the Arab region in the 1950s. "They want ambience and all the little attentions. They like the by-products of sex rather than its stark reality."[10]

For men, the by-products of sex are equally appealing: gifts ranging from mobile phones to houses, money enough to buy a motorcycle or start a new business. For some, who officially marry their foreign lovers, it is quite literally a ticket to another world; marriages between Egyptian men and foreign women have almost quadrupled in Egypt since 2005.[11] In a separate line of business, Summer Marriage Mahmoud is also approached by female Arab visitors looking to marry Egyptian men. The women are in it for a passport, so the marriages have to be official and registered with the government. And they don't come cheap: these women pay up to EGP 60,000 to buy a husband. For all the money changing hands, however, Mahmoud considers it tough work. "To find a groom is more difficult than finding a woman." He sighed.

For men who take the plunge, there are other benefits too. With the rising cost, and therefore age, of marriage, along with the taboo of premarital sex, libidinous outlets are hard to come by for some young Egyptian men. Sex with a foreigner allows them to assert a key element of their masculinity—sexual potency—in a context outside of social norms. Part of this is place: beach resorts in the Arab region are largely new creations where the "locals"—hotel staff, tour guides, shopkeepers, dive instructors—are mainly men from other parts of the country working far from home. "In Dahab, I enjoy the freedom which I missed when I used to live 'down there' [in the south]. . . . When everybody is having sex outside of marriage, I can also do the same," one waiter from Upper Egypt observed. "There are not family restrictions, and the society here is different. We have our own culture here."[12]

Western women are themselves another country when it comes to sex, with practices (oral sex), personal habits (depilation and ablution after intercourse, obligatory for Muslim women, are seemingly optional for foreigners), and sexual behavior considered so different from Egyptian women's that the normal rules of engagement do not apply. As one man from Lower Egypt, with a long history of foreign relations, explained: "Once you watch a video you can never go back and listen to the radio. . . . You cannot compare Egyptian women (radio) with foreign ones (video). There is a big difference. Egyptian women do not express their sexuality; they do not need long sexual intercourse. Maybe it is because of circumcision. While foreign women require longer time and ask even for more."[13] Further suspending reality is the inversion of conventional gender roles in these relations; while men still do the initial running, once a liaison is established, it's the women who call the shots when it comes to finances.

To be sure, some of these relations end happily ever after. But a quick glance across women's magazines and websites, with their travelers' tales of broken hearts and emptied purses, shows that plenty do not: "My dream of great happiness broke into a thousand pieces," "After the wedding he dropped his mask," and "Was it all just a lie?" are not exactly the stuff of Harlequin Romance.[14] Women, however, have been striking back: the Web is full of blacklists offering names, numbers, addresses, and other personal details of Egyptian men who have screwed female tourists in more ways than one. These individual outpourings have also crystallized into organized campaigns. The Community of Interests Against Bezness, for example, was set up in 2003 by Evelyn Kern, a German journalist who was herself swept up, and let down, by a holiday romance in Tunisia (an experience she later wrote up in an autobiographical novel, *Sand in der Seele* [*Sand in the Soul*]). The group has been offering information and support to women in trouble, as well as media outreach to raise awareness, and lobbying German authorities to help women who have lost their savings to the *bezness*.[15]

The suffering is not entirely one-sided; men can have their hearts broken too. Ghassan is a hotel employee from Luxor, a tall, dignified man in his midfifties. "We have a saying in Egypt," he told me one morning as I was breakfasting at his hotel. "All you need for happiness is water, some land, and a beautiful face. So I am happy." He sighed, fixing me with a glance while sweeping his arm toward the river. With such a flair for flattery, it didn't surprise me to learn that Ghassan had been married four times, once to Linda, a Scottish divorcée ten years his senior, whom he met while working on a cruise boat in Upper Egypt. It was a real romance, he said, and they had an unofficial, though *shar'i* (that is, Islamically sound), marriage. While Ghassan's mother and sister were in the know, he preferred not to inform his Egyptian wife. "I didn't want to scratch her feelings, because this not for [financial] benefit. This for love."

Ghassan and Linda used to meet a couple of times a year when he had time off and she could fly in to visit. He told me the secret of his success: "Egyptian men are emotional. They say nice things to a woman, they are open, they make her blood move. Western men are very rough, direct, always working." He and Linda got along swimmingly, especially in bed. "She [was] happy. Egyptian man [is] very strong sexually, she told me this. She [was] married [before], but not feeling like that. I treat her like a baby, hold her on my heart. In my experience, I make her love me by emotion; she take[s] everything, she enjoyed everything, and then dealing with her [was] excellent. In London, her first husband, just . . ." Ghassan pulled a long face, the sudden sagging of his features a telling commentary on Linda's ex-husband's sexual prowess, in keeping with his peers' widely held views on the weakness of Western men. "Maybe because the weather is cold," he suggested charitably.

Ghassan's romance lasted three years, but then Linda went back to the United Kingdom, never to return. Ghassan called and wrote, but no reply. "I don't know what happened. Maybe she [is] dead but nobody told me." He sighed. Ghassan married twice again but still pines for his foreign wife. "I love her, and until now I love her. I am dreaming to catch my Linda anywhere. For me, a lady foreigner [is] good. I would do it again."

Clamping down on intercultural summer-winter unions has the support of prominent religious leaders. Yusuf al-Qaradawi, the famous Islamic preacher, reckons that such marriages should be banned, even though the Qur'an allows Muslim men to marry (or take as concubines) Christian and Jewish women. Al-Qaradawi argues this provision is invalidated by the social corruption these marriages cause—namely, that by draining the pool of available men, they decrease the chances of marriage for local women, thereby raising the likelihood of them going astray. And some locals in coastal resorts are starting to grumble that foreign women, who, thanks to rising unemployment, find it increasingly hard to get jobs back home, are stealing not only their precious men but also coveted jobs in hotels and restaurants once they marry Egyptians and secure work permits.

Not everyone is against these unions, however: some Egyptian families—even wives, who might otherwise lose their men to long stretches of work in the Gulf—are willing to accept an older foreign partner as a local moneymaking alternative.[16] At the end of the day, when it comes to sex work, double standards still apply. When Egyptian women, like Samia, take money for sex in tourist marriages, it is seen as exploitation and authorities are, belatedly, up in arms. When men do the same (albeit under economic pressure, rather than direct family coercion), society largely turns a blind eye to what is considered just another day's work.

## RULES AND REGULATIONS

On the broader question of the future of sex work in Egypt, there are a few urging an alternative to denial or denunciation. One of the most outspoken is Inas al-Degheidy, a director famous for her films on love and sex beyond the borders of conventional morality. In 2008, al-Degheidy raised hackles by giving her fellow Egyptians a quick history lesson. "Prostitution is everywhere in the world. It was a recognized profession in Egypt before the [1952] revolution, and the neighborhoods where it was practiced were well known," she observed on a TV talk show, to the fury of conservatives. "But today it is a secret, at a time when these girls may be carrying serious diseases they could pass on to others." Her solution: state licensing of sex workers. "When I called for licensing the profession of prostitution in Egypt, and annual renewal of licenses, I'm not saying there are a lot of women engaged in this profession. But at the same time, it's not a small number either. We have to face reality rather than escape from it, and the first step is to protect society, regardless of how satisfied or dissatisfied it is with the existence of this profession." [17]

For centuries prostitution in Egypt was a regulated affair, for one simple reason: taxation. In early Islamic Cairo, from the tenth to thirteenth centuries, for example, there were established areas of the city where women plied their trade, sitting outside storefronts in shifts and trademark red pantaloons, all under the watchful eye of a supervisor, who recorded their business and collected taxes from them on behalf of the regime. In the early sixteenth century, following the annexation of Egypt by the Ottoman Empire, the regulation of prostitution became part of the imperial bureaucratic machine, and so working women (along with dancers, snake charmers, hashish sellers, and other public purveyors of pleasure) fell under the empire's rapacious taxation system.

As in much of North Africa, it was colonization that kicked organized prostitution in Egypt into high gear. Shortly after marching into the country in 1882, British authorities issued regulations requiring all prostitutes to register with police and present themselves for weekly medical exams to check for venereal disease, the results of which were noted in certificates the women were obliged to carry on them. Such medical attention was not primarily intended for their benefit but to protect, first and foremost, the legions of British soldiers pouring into the country.

By the early twentieth century, registered prostitution in Cairo was officially confined to particular neighborhoods, while the unregistered (and therefore illegal) variety knew no bounds. The most famous of these state-sanctioned precincts was an area called Clot Bey. In the early 1940s, my father and his friends used to sneak onto a tram to a less spiritual spot than Al-Azhar, one that took them downtown along the district's main artery, Clot Bey Street. In those days, it was a wide avenue bordered by trees, lined on either side by whitewashed two-story buildings in the colonial style, with shady arcades of shops and cafés on the ground floor and, above, French windows that opened onto balconies.

It was here, and in the tiny, twisty lanes that snake off the main avenue, that many of Cairo's thousand or so registered prostitutes went to work, for up to fifteen piastres a pop. "A stroll through its narrow and crowded lanes reminded one of a zoo, with its painted harlots sitting like beasts of prey behind the iron grilles of their ground-floor brothels" was the unsentimental view of Thomas Russell, better known as Russell Pasha, head of the Cairo police and the man in charge of keeping order in the brothel districts for much of the first half of the twentieth century.[18]

As a nine-year-old clinging to the side of a tram, my father had a boy's-eye view of the action on Clot Bey Street. He knew, more or less, what was going on there, from snippets of conversations between my grandparents. Then as now, prostitution wasn't exactly polite conversation for Egyptian couples, but it was a matter of professional interest for my grandfather. He was a civil servant, an administrator in the Office for the Protection of Morals, and Russell Pasha was his boss. I knew my father's father only briefly—he died when I was a child—but I do remember a kind, soft-spoken old man who seemed very much in the shadow of my larger-than-life grandmother. So it's hard for me to imagine him in the business of routing rowdy servicemen out of brothels and reading the riot act to their residents—but it was all in a day's work liaising with the British military police.

By the time my father was on that tram, however, the days of legalized prostitution in Egypt were numbered. From the early 1940s, orders went out to start closing down brothels, and by the end of the decade, state-licensed establishments were shuttered.

Successive laws in the 1950s and 1960s prohibited all prostitution—to little effect. There had been crackdowns on prostitution before; century after century, whenever plague or famine struck and men of religion started blaming widespread debauchery for God's wrath and the country's misfortunes, Egypt's rulers tightened up on public pleasures, only to let the good times roll once the trouble blew over.[19] This time, however, calls to stamp out brothels were linked to the drive to free Egypt from British occupation. Like today's rejection of homosexuality as a Western import, the fact that organized sex work had been a feature of Egyptian life long before the coming of the British was conveniently overlooked.

If Egyptians want to know what regulated sex work might look like, they don't have to turn back the clock half a century; they can just take a three-hour flight to Tunisia. While Tunisia's legal code takes as hard a line on commercial sex work as Egypt's—up to two years in prison and a fine of TND 200 (around USD 120) for both sex worker and client—there is one notable exception. To find it, take a walk down Avenue Habib Bourguiba, which runs like a backbone through central Tunis. Although named after Tunisia's freedom-fighting, postindependence president, this boulevard is an unmistakably French creation, its central promenade punctuated by onion-domed kiosks and wrought-iron lampposts and lined with clipped box trees that stack up like vertebrae along an urban spine. On either side, smaller streets curve out like ribs, and in between, a connective tissue of zinc-topped tables, wicker chairs, and broad umbrellas at the Café de Paris and a dozen others pulses with life.

This avenue became a familiar sight to millions around the world when clashes between protesters, fighting for the removal of long-time autocrat Ben Ali, and the army replaced café society in the winter of 2011. Today, Avenue Bourguiba is back in business, and it is, once again, easy to forget, as you stroll past the art nouveau Théâtre Municipal on your left and the Cathedral of St. Vincent de Paul on your right, that you're in Tunis, not Toulouse—until, that is, the avenue ends in a massive freestanding archway. It looks like a mini Arc de Triomphe, which the French called Porte de France, but it is actually a remnant of Tunis's medieval city walls—a gate better known, in Arabic, as Bab el Bhar (Gateway to the Sea).

Beyond the gate lies the medina, the old city that sits at the head of the avenue like a brain atop a spinal column, its alleyways twisting off in all directions, folding deep into its interior like cerebral fissures. Compared with the ramrod order of the avenue, with its international hotels and its Zara and MAC stores, the medina is a riot of unexpected commerce—filigree birdcages, multicolored shisha pipes, frothy tulle wedding decorations—buying and selling that fires from tiny shop to makeshift stall like a storm of nerve impulses.

Follow one of the side alleys from Bab el Bhar, through covered passages and past bright blue keyhole-shaped doors, and you'll come across trade of a different sort. Rue Sidi Abdallah Guech is Tunis's official red-light district—well, street. The two dozen brothels here and on an adjacent alley are sanctioned by the government, their residents registered as sex workers on municipal rolls. Now, the medina can seem a forbidding place—its massive studded doors, high whitewashed walls, and tiny windows are designed to keep the public out of private life. Not in Rue Sidi Abdallah Guech, however, where invitation is the order of the day. Doors are wide open to reveal neat foyers lined in blue faience tiles, with a couple of rooms on the ground floor and steep stairs leading to the same above. Even on the brisk winter's day I visited, women were sitting on stoops or standing in doorways—in G-strings or spandex leggings, breasts bared or braless in clinging tops, with dyed hair and brightly colored eye makeup—chatting with each other and chatting up passersby, the whole affair bathed in Day-Glo pink from lamps inside.

Rue Guech is all that remains of Tunis's once-extensive network of official prostitution. As in Egypt, what began as a source of public finance ended as a system for public health. During the Ottoman period in Tunisia, officials collected from prostitutes taxes that were calculated on what can best be described as a "cosmetically progressive" scale: the better-looking the woman, the more she had to pay, although the exact aesthetic criteria used are unclear.[20] When Tunisia fell under French "protection" in 1881, taxation was replaced by sanitation: prostitutes were required to have biweekly medical exams in an effort to keep syphilis at bay. As the twentieth century wore on, state-registered prostitutes were subject to increasing regulation as to where they could work. It was a system the French rolled out across their colonial interests in North Africa, one that reached its apogee in the reserved quarters of Casablanca and Algiers: vast prostitution ghettos under tight police supervision—what one French historian has described as "sexual Taylorism," the science of libido management.[21] Tunisia was fortunately spared this sort of industrial park prostitution; under pressure from abolitionists, plans for a giant brothel-city were scrapped in the 1930s. Nonetheless, the state did introduce French-style *maisons closes* (brothels) and in 1942 issued a decree setting down the rules for legal prostitution.[22] Such state-sanctioned activity survived calls to outlaw prostitution in Tunisia, resulting in today's two-track system, in which "clandestine" pimping and soliciting are illegal, while the "public" (that is, state-registered) activities of Rue Guech are permitted.[23]

Today, legal sex work occupies something of a gray area in Tunisia; ironically, it's more hidden than the "clandestine" activity flourishing around the corner on Avenue Bourguiba. "It's not a secret, but it's not widely admitted either," says Abdelmajid Zahaf, a small, grizzled physician who specializes in public health in Sfax, Tunisia's second city. Zahaf knows his way around a brothel, professionally speaking—his profession, not theirs—and gave me an insider's view of how the system is managed. Before the recent uprising, there were almost three hundred legal sex workers in a dozen or so sites across Tunisia, tucked away in the twisty lanes of Sousse, Sfax, Gabès, and even Kairouan, the "holy city" of Tunisia and birthplace of North African Islam.[24] Well over a hundred women were working in Tunis alone; a third of them freelancers who rent rooms on the street, and the rest organized into brothels, with two to five women per house. The women are mainly in their twenties and thirties; at fifty they are obliged to retire from active duty. Many stay on, however, as a *badrona,* or madam, renting (or, in some cases, buying) a house on the street.

One *badrona*—who, unlike her three employees, was seasonably dressed in a woolly blue burnoose—explained the system to me. A client pays the *badrona* TND 7–10 which she splits with the sex worker; in exchange, the sex worker gets room and board. This might not sound much like a road to riches, but as one of the working women explained, in the privacy of her room, those who agree to a little extra, like anal sex, can make double the base rate in tips, which stay in their own pocket. The clients are a mix of mainly young, single, working-class Tunisians, with the occasional white-collar professional and assorted visitors according to location: Tunis, for example, welcomes an international selection, including sub-Saharan African clients; while Sfax, farther down the coast and famous for its hospitals and doctors, sees Libyans crossing over for a spot of medical and sex tourism—a flow that continued even as their country plunged into civil war. As for daily traffic through the house? The madam whistled. "Oh a lot, a lot." A young, attractive woman can have up to a mind-boggling hundred clients a day, several of the sex workers told me, but the average is around a quarter of that. Sex here is a strictly in-and-out affair, ten minutes tops; nothing as time-consuming as kissing or fondling is on the program.

Rue Guech is not a place for lingering discussions. Time is money, and with rents above TND 3,000 a month, madams are keen to keep the customers flowing. The women themselves are equally bent on work. Many of those in Rue Guech are divorced, with families to support. Some women start out in clandestine sex work but switch to the legal trade when financial pressures mount. While you can find the occasional university graduate in Tunisia's legal brothels, the majority of women on Rue Guech have made it only through primary school. The financial attraction is clear: in a country with around 30 percent unemployment in the under-twenty-fives—one of the key triggers of Tunisia's Jasmine Revolution—there's a guaranteed income if you quite literally work your ass off.

While Rue Guech is largely staffed by locals, elsewhere in the country women have tended to travel to other cities to work in legal brothels; their families think they're doing something else, and no one wants to be recognized by a friend or relative on the job, or vice versa. It doesn't take much to register with local authorities to get a position: one must be unmarried, be age twenty or older, freely consent, and have a clean bill of health. Women usually stay three to five years in one house before moving on when clients get bored and business drops off. There are no fixed contracts, but the rules on the job are clear: women are allowed sick leave with a doctor's note, including a week's rest when they're menstruating. Aside from that, there's a day off a week to go to the hairdresser or hammam. These are strictly holidays; if legal sex workers are caught by police turning tricks on their days off, the consequences can be severe.

"Sincerely, in my experience, I believe the legal system is the best alternative for these people—for clients and women," says Zahaf. The women receive biweekly medical exams—a quick peek with a bright light and a speculum to check for symptoms of sexually transmitted infections—and monthly HIV testing. While the majority of women say they use condoms, sheaths are often more honored in the breach than the observance.[25] Towns provide free supplies and encourage legal sex workers to use them, but if clients are willing to pay a premium for condom-free sex, it's hard to refuse.

Zahaf points to other benefits of the system: the women are at least guaranteed payment and a roof over their heads and have less chance of being beaten up than out on the streets.[26] Nonetheless, life is tough. "There are lots of mental problems. Almost eighty percent of them are on tranquilizers—they take them to sleep, they take them to calm themselves. They drink a lot, they smoke a lot," says Zahaf. "They all end badly. I don't know one, up until now, who was left unscathed—either the *badrona* or the prostitutes."[27]

Zahaf is not hopeful for the future of the legal trade; the number of legal sex workers has dropped by more than half over the past few decades. "In my opinion, in five to ten years' time, there will be no more legal prostitution," he predicts. It's the same old story across the economy: when it comes to customer service, free enterprise wins every time. Clients prefer clandestine sex workers, Zahaf says; although they're more expensive, there's more freedom to do what you like, how you like it. Meanwhile, social and economic changes mean the number of willing providers has risen sharply, in his opinion. And there's no shortage of takers: according to one study of more than twelve hundred Tunisians under twenty-five, roughly a third of the sexually active men had exchanged money for sex in the preceding year.[28] "It's like a market: there is the law of supply and demand. Now there is the legal, it is recognized by the state, but more and more people are going to the other. We can't exactly advertise."

But Zahaf has other ideas: "If we could make it like Holland, with windows, with welcoming conditions, it would be like promoting legalized prostitution." He wants to see brand-new houses, built by the municipality, which would not only improve working conditions but might also bring down rents, thereby allowing more money to flow to the workers themselves. Other improvements include more time off, documents entitling the women to free medical and psychological treatment, and social security, as well as loans to start their own tiny businesses and job training. "They want to get out [of this life], but there is no money. What's the point of offering them a job for a hundred dinars a week when they can make four hundred to five hundred doing this?" Zahaf is not optimistic about change. "No one wants to talk about it." He sighs. "I'm always depressed when I think about this situation."

Life became a lot more difficult for Tunisia's official working girls after the Jasmine Revolution. When the regime of Ben Ali fell in 2011, decades of political suppression went with it, and as in Egypt, this included lifting the lid on the country's Islamists. Given the vast array of problems to contend with in rebuilding Tunisia, legalized sex work might seem low down on the list of national priorities, but some Islamic conservatives have the country's state-sanctioned brothels squarely in their sights. Street protests against, and attacks on, legal brothels put employees everywhere on high alert and shut down operations in provincial cities. The immediate upshot was an extra day off a week for the women still in the business—Fridays are no longer part of the working week on Rue Guech. "No to prostitution in a Muslim country" was the protesters' slogan, mustering religious arguments with a feminist twist against the commodification of women's bodies. Other voices, however, have defended the system, pushing back against what they consider creeping Islamism.

The women themselves are fearful of the future. Business had fallen off in the wake of the uprising, since money was tight and the Islamist pressure was on. "What if they close us down?" one *badrona* asked me. "Then what will we do? We don't know how to do anything else." Rising violence was adding to their anxiety. One independent operator, who kindly gave me a guided tour of her tiny, tidy room, showed me the iron gate she had newly installed to protect her from the men outside. "It was better in the period of Ben Ali," she said. "The police were here. But yesterday the men from outside, seventeen to eighteen years old, they broke things, they made a mess. That is why I no longer spend the night here. Now there is no security."

## STREETS AHEAD

Whether Tunisia's legal brothels will survive the coming waves of constitutional and legal reform remains to be seen. On the ground, though, it is clear that the old-school colonial approach to regulating sex work in the name of disease prevention has run its course. In the twenty-first century, however, public health continues to provide an opportunity—that is, money, tacit social acceptance, and a political blind eye—to reach out to sex workers, albeit in less of an assembly-line fashion.

In the name of HIV prevention, researchers are now able to take a closer look at the lives of those in the sex trade across the Arab world. In Egypt, for example, studies show that Jihane's experience of drug use, violence, and other occupational hazards is all too common.[29] So far, HIV levels among female sex workers in Egypt, and in most other parts of the Arab region where there have been surveys, are significantly lower than those of their peers elsewhere in the world.[30] But given the risky nature of their business—including sex with others also on the front lines of infection, among them injecting drug users and men who also have sex with men—the spread of HIV among sex workers in Egypt, and, by extension, to their clients (and their clients' wives), is likely. All the more so since it's an uphill battle on condom use: in one recent study, only a quarter of Cairo sex workers said they used protection the last time they traded sex.[31] While condoms can safeguard against infection, they can also leave Jihane and her friends open to a different sort of trouble: grounds for arrest. "If a girl is walking on the street and stopped with condoms in her purse," Jihane explained, "[she will be taken to the police station, where] there will be a report and [if her rap sheet is clean] the public prosecutor will discharge her next day. But if she has got a record, she is prosecuted for prostitution; she will get a prison sentence."

Egyptians trying to improve the lives of sex workers, including reducing their risk of HIV, look westward, to Morocco. And with good reason: Morocco is a regional leader in dealing with HIV, with an extensive network of free, confidential HIV testing and a distribution system for free antiretroviral medicines.[32] Although HIV infection is stigmatized across the Arab world, there is more openness to talking about it in Morocco, for all the touchy issues it raises: while Egyptians have shown themselves more than capable of taking to, and over, the streets in recent years, I can't think of too many who would turn out, as they did when I was in Casablanca, for a public march to raise awareness and promote tolerance of HIV, carrying placards announcing I AM HIV-POSITIVE.

But it's not just Morocco's proactive stance on HIV that offers lessons to countries in the region. As I mentioned earlier, the Arab world abounds in sexual stereotypes, and one of the most pervasive is that Moroccan women are a little light on sexual morals. Or, as a leading Moroccan newsmagazine put it rather more bluntly on its cover: "Moroccan Women as Seen by the Arabs. In Two Words:

Witches and Prostitutes"—sorcery being just another instrument of seduction in the sex worker's tool kit, so the thinking goes.[33] Moroccan women will tell you that wherever they travel in the Arab region, they are generally assumed to be sex workers until proven otherwise. "Moroccan . . . isn't a nationality, it's a profession," the magazine observed. This reputation is not helped by such high-profile incidents as the indictment of former Italian prime minister Silvio Berlusconi on charges of having paid for sex with an underage Moroccan "dancer" in Milan. Such impressions translate into concrete discrimination; in 2010, for example, the Saudi government refused to issue unmarried Moroccan women between the ages of eighteen and twenty-two visas to visit the holy cities of Mecca and Medina, their justification being that these women were more likely to be turning tricks than circumambulating the Ka'ba. Moroccans were predictably furious at this slur on their nation's womanhood.

Nonetheless, sex work is big business in Morocco. According to one rough estimate, there are hundreds of thousands of women engaged in sex work of some description in the country. It's such a popular calling that some observers talk about the country's "prostitution economy," illegal on paper (as a sop to Islamic conservatives) but tacitly permitted (to relieve unemployment, encourage local spending, and keep the minds of disgruntled young people on sex rather than politics, so critics argue).[34]

Rima and Najma are on the front lines of this particular trade. They work for ALCS (Association for the Fight Against AIDS), a leading NGO grappling with HIV, and their job is to get the message of safe sex out to the legions of Casablanca sex workers, one of more than twenty such programs across the country.[35] By day, they do the rounds of the city's markets, where "occasionals"— women looking to pick up day work as cleaners but agreeable to being picked up themselves for a quickie and some cash—gather. At night, the duo—one with platinum-dyed dreadlocks and the other in a hijab—takes to the streets downtown, handing out free condoms and hugely popular sachets of lubricant. ("By the end of the evening, the women get so dry from so many clients," Rima explained.) The two have their work cut out for them: a map of the city, posted at local headquarters, is a rash of red dots marking the hot spots for sex work in the city.[36]

I joined them for a night on the town, and we walked the streets for hours. It was a slow evening in Casablanca, just after Eid al-Adha, one of the most important feasts in the Islamic calendar, and most of the women had gone back to their towns and villages to see their families. "You should have seen it just before," Rima said. "We had seventy beneficiaries [of our outreach] a night, working to get money for presents, the sheep to slaughter." As we turned one corner, a middle-aged woman, dressed in a dumpy beige burnoose, ambled up to us and started exchanging pleasantries. I thought she was just a friend of the team until I watched her walk away and pause to talk to a young man. "She's an old hand," Najma explained. It took me a moment to grasp exactly where her expertise lay. "The young men, they like older women," said Rima, trying to talk away my bewildered expression. "They like them after menopause. You don't have the problem with the period, and they're less demanding." Najma laughed. "Yes, especially when the men can't do the business." Younger men are certainly good for business: according to one survey of Moroccans under twenty-five, almost 40 percent of young men make their sexual debut with a sex worker, and close to two-thirds frequent them off and on.[37]

Next we headed down a side street and into a neon-lit basement. Two girls, dressed identically in skintight jeans, short puffy jackets with fur-trimmed hoods, and pink headbands, sat in a corner, nursing a drink as some young men stared from the bar and pool table. The girls looked a little nervous as Najma and Rima approached, but the women soon put them at ease. "We're from ALCS, an organization that looks after women's health," they explained, and quickly managed to gain the girls' confidence. Their story was brief and blunt: both in their early twenties, the women were studying hairdressing but came from poor families and so could not afford to keep up with their more fashionable classmates. To earn a little pocket money, they took themselves off to Casablanca's Atlantic Corniche and were picked up by men cruising in cars, offering sex at MAD 300 (USD 30) on up, six times what the woman we had just passed working her corner was asking.

The team gently probed the girls' knowledge of how HIV is transmitted and how they could protect themselves. No, they never used condoms, they said, for one simple reason: they specialized in anal and oral relations, so it never struck them as necessary since pregnancy was not considered a likely prospect. Vaginal intercourse was out of the question, as far as they were concerned, because both had their eyes on marriage, and virginity—that is, an intact hymen—was essential; if they broke that seal and their husbands got angry, their apparently unsuspecting families would start asking awkward questions. Najma gave them a lesson on condoms and urged them to visit the ALCS office for free HIV testing and other services. She handed over some business cards to remind them, and on our way out, the owner of the café asked for a few as well. "Some owners, they welcome us; they know we are trying to keep the girls safe and sound," Najma said. "But others, they don't want us; they say we cause problems with the police, we encourage prostitution."

Gaining the women's trust isn't easy. Their life histories are full of hard knocks, and what with the violence, the sporadic police harassment, the financial insecurity, and the general stigma associated with their work, they are inclined to be initially suspicious of any outstretched hand, which, in the past, would have been much more likely to beat them down than to pull them up. "I tell the women they are young, they are beautiful, they need to protect themselves," said Rima. "It's a question of developing their self-esteem." Among the many services offered by ALCS are legal advice, information sessions on sexual and reproductive health, discussion circles, as well as the occasional hair and makeup class, to help the women take pride in themselves, and parties, organized by the women themselves, to give them a sense of community and a break from an unrelenting routine. "Eighty percent of the women in the work, they want to get out," Najma told me, but the means to do so, like financial and other assistance to open their own tiny businesses, is hard to come by.

Elsewhere, ALCS's condom message had clearly hit home. Our next stop was a café full of men watching a football game on TV. Clustered in the back corner, completely ignored by the patrons, were half a dozen women in velour burnooses, drinking tea and smoking. It looked like a coffee morning of housewives, but the reality was a little different: all the women present, from eighteen to forty-five years old, were sex workers, on a break between clients. They eagerly took the condoms offered by the team and told me they insisted that clients use them. Money is tight for these women, who have little education and few other options; most were divorcées who took up sex work to make ends meet and support their children when their husbands left them high and dry. If a client refused to use protection, I asked, could they really afford to say no? "'Go to your mother!' we tell them." The women laughed. So long as the group holds the line on condoms, those clients who refuse will find it hard to get laid anywhere in the vicinity. Although significantly higher than in Egypt, condom use is far from systemic in Morocco's sex trade. Many women would prefer to use female condoms, but these are more expensive and hard to come by. Although most sex workers are aware of the benefits of male condoms and where to find them, they have plenty of reasons not to use them, including client objections and the fear that the mere suggestion of protection implies that they themselves are infected, which would be bad for business.[38]

While direct outreach to clients remains tricky, teaching the women how to negotiate condom use is key. "The woman, when she has confidence in herself, she wants to protect herself and to save her health. In this case, she can transmit the message to her clients," Rima explained. There are other techniques of persuasion as well. Back at base I was shown an array of brightly colored plastic penises that sex workers use to practice putting on condoms with their mouths—one way to encourage clients to comply. But such advanced skills can fall foul of conservatives: when one ALCS instructor—in a hijab, no less—was broadcast on French satellite TV demonstrating oral delivery of condoms, outrage erupted at home and she was temporarily run out of her neighborhood. The resulting publicity, however, raised public awareness, and, says ALCS, there has been a slight uptick in condom sales ever since.

Quiet efforts are being made to transplant the Moroccan experience elsewhere in the region, including Cairo. More than sixty years after my father took that tram down Clot Bey Street, I found myself in the very same spot, watching Cairo's working girls go about their business. In a café up a narrow flight of stairs, a couple of women seated on divans were wrapped in close conversation; across the room, a pair of clients whiled away the time, smoking shisha and playing backgammon. It was a classic scene—one of Cairo through the ages—but for the ring of mobile phones and the subject of conversation: how the women could protect themselves against HIV and other occupational hazards.

This outreach program, sending "peers" (that is, former sex workers) to spread the good word, is even harder in Cairo than it is in Casablanca. There are scarcely a handful of NGOs in Cairo and Alexandria reaching out to female sex workers, and funding is forever tight. Most of the work is done behind closed doors, in drop-in centers offering legal, medical, and psychological support. For a time, the uprising made their job even tougher than usual. Before the events of 2011, Egypt's vast security apparatus was a major headache for NGOs working with groups on the margins of society. Not only were sex workers regularly apprehended, and sexually exploited, by police, but the arrests often included outreach workers as well, whom government ministries were willing to have do the work in the shadows, but reluctant to publicly acknowledge with written authorization. "The police were dealing in a very rough way with all the people—sex workers, ordinary citizens, anyone," one of the outreach workers told me, describing her various arrests. "I was supposed to be afraid and weep and beg 'Please forgive me,' but I didn't do anything wrong, so I didn't do this. He [the policeman] was upset and provoked and so I spent a horrible night at the police station." This, however, was kid-glove treatment compared with other tales of police brutality, behavior that put Egypt's law enforcement personnel in front of the firing line when the uprising broke out.

The result, in the months that followed, was a far more passive approach to policing Cairo, which in turn brought new problems for outreach workers. "Before [the revolt], the girls would sit in a place and wait one or two hours for a client, so we would have time to work," another member of the outreach team explained. "[But afterward] in public places, they sit freely and take clients, many clients, right away; the clients feel freer too. There is no police, no security. It is much easier for the women, but for us it is harder because they have no time for us." Fewer police raids also meant sex workers could more easily move their operations into private apartments, where *baltagiyya* (thugs) and pimps make outreach a risky proposition.

Further complicating matters is the rising voice of Islamists. Some of the sex workers who turned up at the drop-in center in the months following the uprising were clearly targets of their more overtly religious neighbors. "One of the beneficiaries came one day wearing niqab, because they are having pressure on them from the wives of Salafis. They say, 'Unless you believe in your religion, the Christians will be rulers, they will catch the authority in Egypt.' So they try to convince them on the religious side, but the real target is politics." There was considerable anxiety among NGOs as to how far this pressure might go and how their work might be affected by the political ascendance of Islamic conservatives. In the months following the uprising, one drop-in center was besieged by both Salafis looking to shut down what they considered an immoral operation and by a group of thugs looking to pick up girls; the result was a punch-up between the two opposing factions—a scene that pretty well sums up the state of post-Mubarak Egypt.

Despite the current climate, some reformers dream of change. "Decriminalization—I do have hope. Because the revolution was based on two pillars—social justice and human rights—this is a very supportive environment for change," one young lawyer working at an NGO told me. "We can use the cause of HIV, especially if criminalization is affecting outreach." In global debates on the future of sex work, decriminalization—that is, repealing criminal laws around all aspects of commercial sex and replacing them with regulation under civil codes, like in any other business, with separate criminal penalties to deal with trafficking, coercive sex, and sex with minors—is emerging as the preferred option of those with an interest in the health, safety, and human rights of sex workers. Legalization, in which the state plays a key role in regulating sex work, as it does in Tunisia and a handful of other countries in the Global South, creates as many problems as it solves—even with the refinements Zahaf envisages. In any case, given the rise of Islamic conservatism in Egypt in recent years, neither option is realistically in the cards—and it will take time for the pragmatism that characterized the faith of my forefathers, and that found a way to reconcile the needs of the flesh with the exigencies of the faith, to find its place again.

In the meantime, the most expedient measure would be a de facto decriminalization, in which authorities turn a blind eye to the practice, halting arrests of sex workers and allowing the slow expansion of efforts to provide these women with medical, legal, and social services. For example, a couple of NGOs in Cairo have been trying to soften the law's impact in practice, training sex workers on their legal rights and what to do if they're arrested. The hope is to expand such services to other parts of Egypt and to strengthen their voice by bringing in other NGOs—those working on women's rights, for example—which currently steer clear of such controversial beneficiaries.

There's nothing exceptional about the situation facing sex workers in Egypt and their colleagues across the Arab region. As a member of the Global Commission on HIV and the Law, I heard testimonies from sex workers from around the world, and there is a sobering consistency to their stories: economic insecurity, stigma, discrimination, violence, police harassment and brutality, poor access to health and legal services, and medical and psychological problems are just some of the daily challenges in this line of work. One difference, though, between sex workers in Cairo and, say, Kolkata is that while the latter are organized into vocal groups to fight for members' rights, sex workers in Egypt, and indeed across the Arab world, are still in the shadows. Of course, before the uprising, it was hard to establish an NGO in Egypt around any rights-based issue, let alone sex work. But now that possibilities for change, however long-term, are in the air, the ability of sex workers to organize, mobilize, and connect to the wider world of sex work activism will be key to them getting a piece of the promised gains of the new order—employment, education, and prosperity among them.

In Egypt, however, all this seems a distant prospect. "You can't change the culture of a whole nation in five to ten years," one outreach worker told me as we sat on Clot Bey Street. "It's the upbringing, how we are raised. [For example], the girl who is not covered is not a good girl, but it's all about appearance." At that very moment, a sex worker in a Saudi-style black hijab and abaya got up and walked past us to the door, with a much younger client in tow. The outreach worker looked to her, then straight at me when I asked if he expected any improvement in the situation of sex workers in the new scheme of things. "Not [in] five years, not fifty years," he said matter-of-factly. "All this work will stay under the table."

# 6

## Dare to Be Different

*So long as it's away from my ass, I don't mind.*[1]
—My grandmother, on the importance
of minding your own business

This is a tale of two cities, in as many city blocks. About a year
before the uprising, I made my way through the streets around
Tahrir Square to a party at a private club. My host was Nasim, an
immensely charming and cultured man in his forties and a teacher
at an elite foreign language school. The place was heaving that
night, rickety tables jammed with artists, writers, doctors, lawyers,
and other professionals—Muslims and Coptic Christians, like
Nasim, united in leisure. Alcohol was flowing freely, and conversations switched seamlessly between Arabic, English, and French. It
was a lively and sophisticated scene—and unmistakably, unabash-
edly gay.

I don't use that word lightly, since "gay" carries some hefty baggage outside the West. A few years ago, Joseph Massad, a Palestinian academic based in America, raised a storm by suggesting that
the "Gay International"—an alliance of Western NGOs promoting
the interests of lesbian, gay, bisexual, and transgender people—was
foisting a Western gameplan on the Arab world and perverting its
natural sexual order, in which men have sex with men, and women
with women, without considering themselves "homosexual" or
"gay."[2] In Massad's book, this form of sexual imperialism puts the
lives of those whose inclinations and activities transgress the heterosexual norm at risk by linking such desires to a despised Western agenda of gay rights, as well as limiting the sexual sphere of
Arabs by freezing them into rigid sexual categories with specific

labels, while their own tastes freely flow from one sex to another. As Massad put it:

> When the Gay International incites discourse on homosexuality in the non-Western world, it claims that the "liberation" of those it defends lies in the balance. In espousing this liberation project, however, the Gay International is destroying social and sexual configurations of desire in the interest of reproducing a world in its own image, one wherein its sexual categories and desires are safe from being questioned.[3]

Back at the club, these "configurations of desire" were busy getting down on the parquet dance floor, well-honed bodies in tight T-shirts and snug jeans, gyrating to the sounds of Dalida, a gay icon. Around the room, clusters of men, arms draped over each other's shoulders, were head to head in conversation. At first glance, there was nothing out of the ordinary in this. Intense homosociality, including close physical contact and strong emotional attachments among people of the same sex, is perfectly acceptable in Egypt without necessarily signaling sexual attraction. These interactions can be confusing to those brought up in the West, where the one is generally assumed to follow the other. I remember as a child having to be restrained by my mother when one of my father's friends took his hand while we were walking in Luxor. This wasn't early-onset homophobia, mind you, but pure and simple jealousy that someone other than my mother and I should claim such intimacy. Today, even after years of working in the Arab region, I still do a double take when I get messages like "My darling Shereen, how I miss you and count the days until I see you again, God willing. Much love and kisses"—this from a happily married, straight-as-an-arrow female friend.

But even before being introduced to Nasim's friends, I could tell from the look of frank disgust on the waiters' faces that this was something else entirely. "And you?" I swiveled around to answer what I thought was a question directed at me, because it used a feminine pronoun in Arabic; it turned out to be one man talking to another. Nasim shook his head, in clear disapproval of this sort of grammatical gender-bending. "It's to joke, but I hate this. Some of the guys get quite camp. The important thing is how you appear. Enjoy yourselves, just don't make a scandal."

A few weeks later, and a couple of blocks away, another face of Cairo came to light. I joined Munir and his friends at an *ahwa,* a traditional coffee shop, where men gathered around tables, talking and laughing between sips of strong coffee and syrupy tea. A football match was blaring on a tiny TV mounted high in the corner, and the only women in sight were myself, a colleague, and some female sex workers in the back trying to sweet-talk a few of the men. The *ahwa* is an intensely masculine space—you'd swear they put testosterone in the shisha—where Munir and his friends were clearly in their element, although all of them happen to have sex with other men. It was a world apart from Nasim's smart set. Munir and his friends are all working-class—when they can get the work, that is. Some of them turn tricks with men to make ends meet.[4]

Like heterosexuals in Cairo, Nasim and Munir rarely mingle socially. "We're all educated, wealthy," Nasim remarked, looking around the club. "The problem is that the gay community is very segregated, classwise. The idea that a minority will lose its social differences because it is a minority? This is not so." Nasim is no snob, but he is wary of those outside his circle. "The rich lead their own lives, and the poor lead their lives and there are real dangers in mixing. You cannot imagine what a relief it is when I find a man and he doesn't want to rob me, beat me, or rape me. When you find such a man, you grab him."

The tie that binds these disparate classes is distrust. Nasim is extremely wary of the places and parties he frequents, and if the scene gets "too gay," in his words, he steers clear. His caution comes from a defining moment, the aptly named Queen Boat incident of 2001, in which a lively party on the Nile was raided by police, triggering a roundup of more than fifty homosexual men, who were charged, convicted, named, and shamed in the media.[5] Even men who were children at the time, too young to understand the nature of the incident, today find their attitudes and activities colored by it. While Nasim exercises caution, prison is not his main concern.

"When [the police] see me, they see my social identity, so they don't do it [arrest me]. It's about power," he explained. From the other side of the tracks, Munir confirmed this great divide. "If [a man] is arrested and he knows someone important, he calls him and [the police] let him go. In the high-class gay places, the police cannot go. So expensive places, nobody cares whether they are gay or not." Outside this shiny bubble, however, people do very much care; what most concerns Nasim is the specter of public exposure to family and neighbors should there be any sort of run-in with officialdom.

Over at the *ahwa,* Munir and his friends are also careful of the company they keep. "Some people are afraid and apprehensive. They do not speak freely with anyone," Munir explained. "We are not safe. We are afraid to go this place, or that place. I will never linger in any place where there are many gays. It is very dangerous. Most of the gays, they are young, they are still hyper, they are not very safe." The danger here is the police. For Munir, jail is not some abstract threat. There is a complex array of laws in countries across the Arab region criminalizing same-sex activity. None specifically mention "homosexuality" per se, though they manage to embrace it all the same through the criminalization of sodomy, vaguely defined "homosexual acts," and other loosely interpreted infractions.[6]

Egypt, along with Jordan and the West Bank, does not actually have a law against sodomy or same-sex acts, but it does have long-standing laws on public indecency and prostitution, including the charge of "habitual debauchery." This has been thrown at Munir twice, as well as some trumped-up drug charges. "The police can take you just sitting here . . . just for gathering. If they hear about us, or someone tells him that I have HIV, you can be arrested."[7] The night we met, Munir and his friends were distinctly on edge. There had just been a murder in the neighborhood, and the group was resigned to the prospect of being rounded up among the usual suspects.

Why authorities should prove so keen to arrest men who have sex with men when there is, in fact, no specific article criminalizing such consensual acts is an interesting question, one I put to several lawyers and their clients. The consensus was that police activity was less a matter of moral objections, closeted homosexual desire, or even blackmail and more to do with the exercise of power, be it a coordinated campaign from on high or individual initiative, in an authoritarian system that encourages the subjugation of those next down the line. But when I presented such theories to one former Cairo police chief, he was simply baffled. "But there is a law criminalizing sodomy and the homosexual," he insisted. "Not prostitution—specifically sodomy. This law is written down, taught in police college." He was clear on its value. "They punish these people, because it is in the law. We criminalize things against our religion and it causes AIDS. The best thing is to put them in prison. Yes, I believe it will reduce the number of these incidents and it conforms with shari'a." His chilling confidence was proof positive of what the lawyers had told me: for those in power, the law is whatever you want it to be. Such impunity was made all the easier by three decades of Emergency Law imposed in 1981, giving authorities the right to arrest, detain, and try with minimal accountability, thereby allowing police to pick up Munir and his friends whenever, wherever, and for whatever reason it suited them.

Munir is a small and gentle man, with Nefertiti cheekbones, large, liquid eyes, and the sort of eyelashes mascara marketers dream of. He told me of his experiences in a soft, good-humored voice, which makes such violence all the more horrifying. On one occasion, Munir was arrested in an apartment he was sharing with six friends; they had been betrayed by a roommate who, in a familiar story, had turned police informant to get off the hook. "When they arrested us, they took us to the doctor to see if we were practicing [sodomy]," Munir explained. "Yes, anal testing," he replied to my quizzical look, referring to a popular forensic technique. Anal exams are apparently a big hit with "CSI Cairo," which looks for certain deformities of the anus, among other signs, as proof of sodomy. Foreign experts, however, are singularly unimpressed with such methods, as was Munir, whose objections lay less in the gross human rights violation they represent and more in what he considers their general uselessness.[8] Munir said he tested negative, but no matter: he was sentenced to six months in prison for habitual debauchery all the same.

As the men drew on their shisha and we drank our way through bottles of 7Up, the terrible tales kept on coming: electrocution, beatings, rape, and forced confession in police custody, witnesses and competent legal representation apparently optional extras. Stretches in prison, followed by months of monitoring, again often in police custody, were even worse. "To break his eye" is the Egyptian expression for humiliating someone, and forced sodomy has been a tool of choice for those in power in the Arab region throughout the ages. Munir shook his head at the absurdity of the situation. "Sometimes when we sleep in the station, the police, they do it [have sex with us]. Why do they arrest us for homosexuality and then put us in prison, where it happens again? Are we just entertainment, pleasure for another person?"[9]

## A MAN'S WORLD

In sharing these intimacies, Munir and Nasim regularly referred to themselves as "gay" or *homo*—words borrowed from English and French. There are alternatives in Arabic, but none of them quite hit the mark. Historically, there was no shortage of Arabic words to describe men and women getting it on with their own sex, but these were, as some scholars maintain, related to actions, not orientation—having intercourse with the same or opposite sex, they argue, being more a question of activity than identity. This distinction is reflected in the classical terms *luti* (a man who penetrates a younger male) and *suhaqiyya* (a woman who "grinds against" another woman).

Over the past century, the words people use to talk about same-sex relations have shifted, reflecting changing times—a transformation I have seen in my own family. When my father talks about homosexuality, he uses *khawal* and *'ilq*, words that refer to the active and passive male partner, often used in insult or jest; a generation later, my cousins talk about *shadh* (pronounced *shaz*), a term meaning "deviant" that entered use around the middle of the twentieth century.[10] I, on the other hand, because of my work with civil society and the United Nations, use the Arabic equivalent of international HIV/AIDS-speak—"men who have sex with men," for example, which is just as much of a mouthful in Arabic as it is in English. This is part of a terminology developed over the past decade or so that borrows from the international LGBT movement: *mithli* and *mithliyya,* masculine and feminine derivatives of the word for "same," referring to men and women who have relations with their own sex; *ghairi* and *ghairiyya,* from the word for "different," for heterosexual men and women; *thuna'i* and *thuna'iyya,* from the word for "double," for male and female bisexuals; *mutahawwil* and *mutahawwila,* from the word for "to change," for transsexual or transgendered people. In Egypt, these terms are still mainly restricted to specialized circles, and in my experience, words other than *shadh* elicit perplexed looks or bursts of laughter.

But "gay" is not for everyone. At the club, Anwar, who's an artist, was describing his busy career, dashing between performances and projects in Cairo, Paris, and Amsterdam. I naively assumed that life as a homosexual man must be easier for him in Europe, but that was not his experience. "I find it more liberating here. I'm out—my parents know, my colleagues know I like men. In Europe, my art is seen as 'gay art.' But here, I'm a performer who happens to like men. I'm not pigeonholed in the same way."

Over at the *ahwa,* Hisham, one of Munir's friends, felt similarly constrained by the term "gay." At first glance, Hisham is a model of middle-class propriety—married for fifteen years, with a couple of kids and a steady job in the ever-popular air-conditioning business. But he also has sex with men, long-term relationships lasting months or years—in one instance with someone who went on to marry one of his cousins. To Hisham, "gay" implies a full-time occupation, with sex at the center of things, whereas he sees his relations with other men as "a small corner of our lives, something we can go to or not go to, but it is not obsessing." He keeps his social worlds distinct. "My wife doesn't know; the neighbors don't know. My character at work or at home is different from my character with my [male] friends," he told me, adding proudly, "Look at me—I have a mustache, I'm masculine." Terms like "gay" or "bisexual" simply do not resonate with him. It's not that Hisham doesn't understand—through Munir, for example, he is well aware of what the "gay scene" looks like, at home and abroad—it's just that such labels don't apply. Yes, he leads a double life, but he finds that perfectly normal, no matter which sex you bed; for him, these are useful compartments, not unwanted closets.

Nasim, Munir, and their friends represent a tiny cosmopolitan fragment of same-sex desire in the vastness of Egypt. But the way they see themselves, and their sexuality, gives a glimpse of the sheer complexity of what it is to break the heterosexual mold in the twenty-first-century Arab world. Part of that complexity comes from history. For all their modern mien, when these men talk about their sex lives, it sometimes sounds like a page out of the great books of Arabic erotica, among them *A Promenade of the Hearts, in What Does Not Exist in a Book*.[11] Its author, Ahmad ibn Yusuf al-Tifashi, was a Tunisian scholar who lived and died just across town from us nine centuries before.

Nasim is, in many ways, reminiscent of the *la'ita* (practitioners of sodomy) of al-Tifashi's description—a man of some wealth and great refinement, who loves boys with a passionate longing, sometimes for their youth and beauty and sometimes for their intellectual companionship, sometimes unconsummated and sometimes paying for the pleasure. Munir, with his lithe gait and fluttering eyelashes, is the essence of the beardless young men who flit across al-Tifashi's pages. Hisham's pride in his vigorous masculinity is an echo of attitudes toward active and passive homosexual activity through the ages, also reflected in Nasim's father's response to his son's disclosure. "I said, 'Dad, I will never marry. I love men,'" Nasim recalled. "My father, who's a professor, said, 'Okay, but you must never tell your mother.' And then he started asking me questions. 'How do you have sex?' At that point, I was never negative [passive], so I told him. And he said, 'Ah, so you are not *homo*!'"[12]

It's not all glitter and gold in al-Tifashi's book. For all its amusing anecdotes, there is a dark side to his account of men who have sex with men. Nasim's less privileged predecessors were said to need thick skins to survive a lashing should they be hauled in front of a tribunal for their activities, and were at risk of being robbed blind and beaten by pickups—the very same fears expressed by Nasim. At the same time, some of their own activities were less than desirable by today's standards of human rights, including the practice of "creeping," essentially raping boys by stealth.

This history of homosexuality in the Arab world is largely forgotten. For example, Nasim, who is extremely well-read, was unaware of al-Tifashi and the vast body of homegrown musings on same-sex relations through the ages.[13] "What, there is more than Abu Nuwas?" he asked me, referring to the famous poet of eighth- and ninth-century Baghdad who celebrated sex in all its forms. In the rewriting of Arab sexual history over the past century or so, homosexuality has been buried—to the point that today's intolerance is now seen as the authentic voice of tradition when it is (as in so many other parts of the Global South) arguably more of an echo of the region's European colonial masters and is certainly less forgiving, in practice, than at other times in its history.

Going to bed with someone of your own sex seems a lot more complicated these days than in al-Tifashi's time, as much a matter of geopolitics now as personal pleasure. Attitudes toward homosexual men and women have long been a litmus test, distinguishing the "civilized" from the "backward," though where you place tolerance or rejection of same-sex relations has shifted East and West over the centuries. The status of same-sex relations has become a hallmark of liberal democracy in recent years—and so the question of how Egypt and its tumultuous neighbors will handle the rights of citizens who depart from the heterosexual norm is politically charged. Long a feature of the fissure between Europe and America, and the Arab world, homosexuality has even been sucked into the conflict between Palestine and Israel.[14]

Because of such international interest, there is more research on the intimate lives of men who have sex with men in Egypt, and in many of its Arab neighbors, than on almost any other group in society. Official surveys, NGO reports, academic dissertations, and popular books are laying bare these lives: in numbers (including population estimates), and the nitty-gritty of sexual behavior (how often, with whom, in which positions, and for how much), and the nuances of how these men see themselves and their relations in society beyond the bedroom. Some extremely rough estimates put the proportion of men having sex with each other in the Middle East and North Africa at a few percentage points of the male population, on a par with global figures, though these rates are considerably higher in certain groups, among them street children or prisoners or students, where relations with the opposite sex can be harder to come by.[15]

As with other aspects of sexuality in the Arab region, HIV is easing the way to information, opening access and funding in the name of public health. The results, however, are unsettling. In Egypt, for example, surveys of men who have sex with men in Cairo, Alexandria, and Luxor have shown HIV infection rates running around 6 percent, giving them a top spot on the country's infection charts; elsewhere in the Arab region, rates can be substantially higher.[16] Meanwhile, condoms and HIV testing are about as unpopular with men who have sex with men in Egypt and many of its Arab neighbors as they are with anyone else. This information is a boon, in that it has persuaded authorities to allow some outreach by NGOs in the name of HIV prevention (as we saw in the previous chapter with female sex workers), but it is also something of a bane, in that knowing so much about the sex lives of one particular population, without similarly valuable insight into the rest, runs the risk of further marginalizing men who have sex with men and cementing their popular image as a sexed-up, disease-ridden social menace.

Such stereotypes die hard. In Egypt, homosexuality is widely seen as the result of some childhood trauma—sexual abuse or a gross lapse in parenting, for instance. Trying to convince stolidly heterosexual Egyptians otherwise is a tough sell. Nasim, for example, was aware from an early age that his preference lay with men. "I knew I was gay from age six or seven," he said. "We were living in Iraq. It was in the seventies; men had sideburns and tight trousers. I always admired their trousers." He dismisses popular notions of the origins of homosexuality. "I have many friends and they all say they knew from when they were children. None of us were abused as children."

Munir, on the other hand, discovered his love of men a little later in life. "I was twenty-three years old when I was gay. I was having relations with women before, many." But life changed after one close encounter with a relative with whom he used to cruise for girls. "Suddenly he is in my home one night, and I was taking a shower. He knocked, so I said welcome. He told me, 'It is too hot. I want to take a shower as well.' And then he was turned on. I told him, 'What's going on?'" Munir recalled. "I hated what happened, but from inside me, I liked it. I enjoyed it because it was a weird pleasure, all the feelings were weird, but I wanted to go back to him and check what are these feelings."

Munir continued his story, a smile dawning. "We stayed together for two years. I didn't have anyone in my life except for him. We had relations everywhere you can imagine. On the roof, under the stairs, at my place, at his place, at the cinema," he said. "We loved each other, not as friends or relatives but as men. I have never felt guilty for being gay. For one reason: I made it with love."

It's a rare parent who buys such arguments, however. For many a family, discovering a relative's same-sex activity prompts an immediate visit to the doctor to see if something can be done. Given that medical schools in Egypt largely gloss over basic sexuality, let alone more complex aspects of sexual orientation, the average physician is out of his or her depth on this one. The usual medical response is a round of antidepressants, accompanied by a stern lecture on the evils of homosexuality.

While religious conversion is a matter of life and death in Egypt, sexual conversion—gay to straight, that is—is generally viewed as not just acceptable but strongly advisable. Indeed, Cairo is home to the Arab world's best-known practitioner of "reorientation" therapy. Awsam Wasfy, a psychiatrist, believes that homosexuality is a developmental disorder. "Homosexuality is not a natural choice in life. It's not the sin which will not be forgiven, nor is it the stain which cannot be mentioned. But it is a disturbance in the sexual development of children which can be avoided in children and adolescents and can be treated later on, but with serious difficulty," he argues.[17] According to Wasfy, boys who fail to bond with their fathers, and girls with their mothers, in early childhood will later lack identification with their own sex and thus a sense of their own masculinity or femininity.

Children naturally long for same-sex love, Wasfy says, but by puberty this usually changes into an attraction to the opposite sex—a transformation made more difficult in some Arab societies, in his opinion, by a strict segregation of boys and girls. He points to studies that homosexual men suffer higher rates of depression, suicide, drug abuse, and other psychological disturbances than their heterosexual peers. "Is it because homosexuality is a pathology of disconnection with self or is it the persecution of society?" he asks. "My view is that it is a pathology, though societal persecution certainly does not help. You can still have these findings in San Francisco, in any place that has reached a higher degree of tolerance of homosexuality."

Wasfy uses group therapy, in which he mixes homosexual clients with heterosexual ones. His aim is to help men connect with each other on an emotional, yet nonsexual, level, a link that he says homosexual clients find difficult to forge because of their early childhood experiences. The goal is to reach the "healing moment," as Wasfy puts it, "when a homosexual talks to a straight guy about his homosexuality and the straight guy would love and accept him."

These ideas and techniques will sound familiar to many in the West, particularly in the United States, where so-called sexual orientation change efforts find their most enthusiastic proponents. Among them are conservative Christian movements, which promise "freedom from homosexuality through the power of Jesus Christ."[18] Indeed, Wasfy, who's an evangelical Christian, came to reorientation therapy through his religious connections.

Reparative therapy, as it is also known, is highly controversial in the West. Efforts to treat homosexuality—as opposed to the psy-

chiatric problems homosexual men and women may experience—
were commonplace before the 1970s. But in 1973, the American
Psychiatric Association voted to remove homosexuality as a disorder from its bible, the *Diagnostic and Statistical Manual of Mental Disorders (DSM)*. After languishing in the 1970s and 1980s, the
treatment of homosexuality made a comeback in the 1990s in the
guise of "reorientation therapy," embraced by psychiatrists who
argued that homosexual men and women who want to change their
orientation should be helped to do so.

Whether such a thing is possible, however, is another question.
Mainstream mental health professionals are highly skeptical. After
wading through the peer-reviewed research on reparative therapy,
the American Psychological Association recently concluded that
"efforts to change sexual orientation are unlikely to be successful
and involve some risk of harm"; the American Psychiatric Association is similarly unconvinced.[19] Wasfy is well aware of these
debates. While sexual rights advocates maintain that reparative
therapy can thrive only in a culture of intolerance to homosexuality, he argues the contrary—that it is cultural intolerance in
the form of Western political correctness that prevents reparative
therapy from getting the resources needed to do the sorts of large-
scale, long-term studies that could validate its approach. He also
disagrees with the declassification of homosexuality as a disorder
and is clear on where the pressure is coming from: "The gay rights
movement is prosecuting [denying] the notion of disorder and
change. They are practicing a double standard. They want freedom,
but they don't give a say to others."

Although inspired by his faith, Wasfy is quick to point out that
the therapy he practices is not overtly Christian and that more than
three-quarters of his clients are Muslim. He does, however, think
it's easier for Christians to succeed with this approach. "I see that
Christian theology has much room for change and miracles, the
healing. They believe in change more, and a stronger notion of
grace and unconditional acceptance. So I think this helps Christians more," he told me. "This in the culture of Christianity makes

it easier for Christians to speak out about their problems and find acceptance without being judgmental."

Wasfy claims some success with his approach. I met his star patient at Wasfy's office in an apartment building in a bustling part of Cairo called Madinat Nasr, kitty-corner to a gigantic mosque, whose booming call to prayer punctuated our conversation. Rashad is a tall, good-looking man in his thirties, with an open, engaging manner and a lively sense of humor. You'd never guess that he was troubled by his sexuality. But Rashad had a rough start in life. He was abandoned by his father and grew up in an orphanage, where he was sexually abused by some of the other boys.

For the next couple of years, Rashad had sex with men every few days; he was mainly the passive partner. Finding a man was never a problem, but the insults and the jokes were troubling: "They insult me, *abu shakha* [son of a shit], *multi* [sodomizer]. All these insults were stamps of shame put inside me. When somebody tells me I'm good, I thought they wanted sex."

At twenty, Rashad says, he began to question his way of life. "I started to feel I need to stop it [sex with men]. At first, I started to look at the people around that they are normal, and I am not normal. I asked myself, Was I created like this and God wanted me like this, or there is a situation where I am between the two?" At first he consulted a string of hostile doctors. Nor did the church offer much relief: "In church I met someone and I told him that I have a problem. He asked me, 'What is it?' I wanted to tell him, but I was afraid. He told me that this was coming from Satan and you shouldn't do that. Next time I met him, it was different. He gave me a bad look, and when he sees me near a small boy, he says, 'Get away from him!'"

Through friends, Rashad reached Wasfy. He was extremely wary of the group sessions at first but eventually found the confidence to talk about his sexual desires. "I started to discover there was something called unconditional love—somebody can accept me as I am. That's not present in the Egyptian society generally. When they hear somebody is a thief, he is branded as a thief for the rest of his life. When somebody is branded as an adulterer, he is an adulterer. When he is branded as a homosexual, he is a homosexual for life and nobody will come near him," he told me.

After building his confidence within the group, Rashad shared his story with friends outside, some homosexual, some heterosexual. They are the family he never had, he says, their bond including simple things like watching TV together to the complex intertwining that comes from sharing secrets. "Some of them said, 'If you want to have a home meal, my home is always open.'" He smiled. "This built a bridge for me and I crossed over it. This is the love I was looking for. That showed me that there is love of a different way apart from same-sex." Rashad found that these different sorts of interactions with men built up his sense of masculinity, and he says he gradually stopped thinking of men in a sexual way. Critics of reparative therapy argue that those who change their orientation most likely had some heterosexual inclination in the first place, but Rashad denies this outright: "I wasn't sexually in-between. Before that, I was never interested in girls. But after that, there were girls!"

Rashad was in therapy for more than a decade. He is married to a woman who knows about his past but fought her family to marry him all the same. Rashad admits it wasn't easy to get used to sex with women, beginning with some basic mechanics: "I never knew you practiced sex with a woman from the front [vaginal intercourse]. In my mind, I thought you take a woman from the back [anal sex]. I didn't have anybody to correct this information. The only one who corrected me was a doctor, but that was years later. It took some time to get pleasure. I tried several times with women before my wife; I didn't like it as I liked homosexual sex. I felt that homosexual sex is more pleasurable than heterosexual sex. I'm sure of that." Today, however, he says he has a good sexual relationship with his wife, and they have a son and a daughter.

While Rashad appears to have found happiness through reparative therapy—so much so that he is now reaching out to men in similar straits as a lay therapist—Wasfy admits that it doesn't work for everyone, nor do all homosexual men need it. His work attracts fans, but also plenty of critics—from all sides. Muslim conservatives accuse Wasfy of providing a covert cruising ground for homosexuals at his clinic. On the other hand, I once heard gay men from Tunisia and Lebanon lambast him as an "agent of [President] Bush" before storming out of a presentation in protest at his suggestion that homosexuality is a disorder.

There are professionals in the region who are equally dismissive. Dorra Ben Alaya, a professor of social psychology at the University of Tunis El Manar, has studied the social representation of homosexuality and how its characterization may contribute to the spread of HIV. She is frankly appalled at the idea of trying to convert homosexuals to heterosexuality: "Reparative therapy is an absurdity. In *DSM*, it's no longer considered a disease. If a doctor says I can change your orientation, that must mean that your orientation is not normal. My problem with all this is that every time someone doesn't fit with society, we are going to repair them; then the world will not advance. We will be like the men of prehistory. We will all look alike, dress alike, behave alike. If nature created something, it has a function."

Ben Alaya earned her doctorate in France, and it shows, from her chic attire to the way she talks about sexual orientation. She is a proponent of so-called gay affirmative therapy, in which homosexual men and women are helped to feel more comfortable with their orientation. "If these people are depressed, it's not because they are homosexual, it's because they don't accept that they are homosexual. The work of a psychiatrist is to integrate this into their identity. For example, someone who lacks a hand is depressed, and people stare at him in the street. Is it better that you replace the hand with a plastic one or to integrate it into his head that it doesn't matter what people think? It is not about changing a person in response to a constraining situation, but to better help them deal with the constraining situation."

There are psychiatrists in Egypt who practice affirmative therapy. Unlike Wasfy, they tend to keep a low profile because their approach is very much against the grain of society. "I am condemned for this by my colleagues," says Nabil Elkot, who works with homosexual clients in Cairo. " 'They [homosexual men] don't

deserve your time, how can you stand for this?' or 'They are homosexuals, so don't believe them, they are trying to abuse you,'" is how
he characterizes prevailing medical attitudes. Elkot got into affirmative therapy by accident when he started working on drug addiction in private practice in the late 1990s. A high proportion of his
clients were homosexual, which prompted him to learn more about
the subject. Today, he has a handful of patients in regular therapy,
and his single biggest challenge is convincing them that they are
indeed attracted to other men: "Most of them, they say they do
this because they don't have a chance with women or because they
are with friends and they cannot say no. They cannot believe that
they desire men; the first step is to convince them that they have
this desire." Without this acknowledgment, says Elkot, it is difficult for clients to overcome their problems, and they remain bur-
dened by anxiety, self-loathing, and intense fear, particularly of an
almighty scandal should their activities be discovered by friends
or family.

Many clients come to Elkot after trying, and failing, to self-
medicate with religious healing. He takes a different approach,
one grounded in months of psychotherapy and supplemented by
medication, to help patients manage their anxiety, depression, or
paranoia. The idea, he says, is not to tell a patient he is homosexual
but to "come to the conclusion together." This realization and its
consequences—that patients are not like everyone else and will
have to learn to live as a minority—come as a relief to some but hit
others hard and necessitate even more therapy to get them to accept
the situation. Borrowing a leaf from his work on drug addiction,
Elkot says, "It is difficult to control the [homosexual] desire, so the
solution is to control the harm"—which means reducing the risks
associated with keeping homosexuality under wraps, among them
unhappy wives used as cover for their husbands' homosexuality or
furtive, urgent, and generally unsafe sex whenever and wherever
one can get it. Elkot urges his clients to accept their desires and to
manage them: "I am telling him if you have to do it, do it safely, do
it at your home, do it with someone you know, for a long time and

not in the street. . . . Eventually, I try to get them to move into more stable relationships."

But that's not easy in a society that openly acknowledges only one sexual context: man, woman, marriage, children. As we've seen, the pressure on single Egyptians to wed is unremitting—all the more so if your family is in a position to afford it. The fact that the age of marriage has risen in recent years, particularly for men, has not brought breathing space to men and women who prefer their own sex—it just means more years of parental nagging. My grandmother, as usual, had a saying that summed up conventional wisdom on this subject, used to write off anyone who failed to live up to the mark: "If there was any good in the 'ilq [faggot], he would have had children."

Nasim, now in his midforties, has been living under this gun for decades. "The pressure to marry is the most difficult part." He sighed. "Until now, I have this pressure from my mom. Every day she sees me; every day she talks about marriage." Although Nasim disclosed his sexuality to his father, failure to have a family of his own drove a wedge between them. "Every time the family talked about marriage, my father would become sad and would not say anything. I told myself I had increased my father's unhappiness. He had hoped, until he died, that I would marry. I told him [about my sexual relations] and it made me feel good, but it did not do any good for him." With his mother, Nasim eventually took a different tack. "Look Mama, I will never marry. I cannot make a woman happy sexually and this will just end in divorce," he explained, citing phantom visits to the doctor and medical grounds for his alleged impotence. "I couldn't tell her the reality. She doesn't want to believe. I was scared about her having a heart attack," he told me. "If something happens to her, I will never forgive myself. I have to say it, but in a light way."

Although Nasim is a successful professional with a place of his own, setting up house with another man has proved difficult. While neighbors pry, it's orders of magnitude less intrusive than if he were living with a woman and, as Nasim points out, so long as you're discreet, living arrangements can be talked away. But that wasn't enough to convince Walid, his lover of four years, to move in. "Often, I remember, I asked Walid, 'Come live with me.' But he could not. His parents would not understand. When he stayed with me one night a week, already that was not easy."

Nasim talked about Walid in the past tense because he had just been dumped. His lover had decided to marry a young woman he had met a few months earlier, catching Nasim completely off guard. "'I am getting engaged, and I want you to be there. You are so important in my life. I can't imagine my life without you, [but] I want her differently,'" Nasim recalled Walid's bombshell of an announcement, shaking his head incredulously. It's a common enough story—I've seen a trail of broken hearts from Casablanca to Beirut, men losing their male lovers to heterosexual marriage, some partners moving on because they want to, some under family pressure, and some to prove to themselves and the outside world that they are not homosexual after all.

Whatever the reason for his lover's decision, it got Nasim thinking. "I will tell you something, *ya* Shereen, Walid has just left me. I don't have any hope of another, he was the only love of my life," he said miserably. "I see that it is very hard to live with a man, to have a stable life with a man," Nasim continued, his midlife crisis unfolding: "I am fed up. I am afraid of getting old alone. This morning I took my mobile and asked myself, Nasim, who are your gay friends? Who are the ones who call you? I only found two. And when I go out, there are forty, but it's me who calls them, who invites them out. I am the driver. If I didn't make that effort, the day when I don't have the energy, I will find myself alone."

## CONDEMN OR CONDONE?

Nasim's predicament is not helped by religion. When Egyptians and their Arab neighbors come down hard on homosexuality, they bring the full weight of scripture with them. The Qur'an refers on several occasions to the "people of Lot," annihilated by God for their infamy. Lot, who also features in the Book of Genesis, was a righteous man visited by divine messengers on a seek-and-destroy mission:

> And when Our messengers came to Lot, he was anxious for them, feeling powerless to protect them, and said, "This is a truly terrible day!" His people came rushing towards him; they used to commit foul deeds. He said, "My people, here are my daughters. They are cleaner for you, so have some fear of God and do not disgrace me with my guests. Is there not a single right-minded man among you?" They said, "You know very well that we have no claim whatever to your daughters. You know very well what we want."[20]

According to the Qur'an, those scheduled for annihilation were duly warned to mend their ways. Lot tried time and again: "How can you practise this outrage? No other people has done so before. You lust after men rather than women! You transgress all bounds."[21] This "outrage"—the word in Arabic is *fahisha*—is conventionally interpreted in this context as homosexual anal intercourse. In fact, the classical Arabic words for male sodomy (*liwat*) and the man who commits such an act (*luti*) are derived from Lot's Arabic name. Other Qur'anic verses that talk about *fahisha*—which can cover a multitude of sins—are also often read as specifically condemning same-sex relations among both men and women:

> If any of your women commit a lewd act [*fahisha*], call four witnesses from among you, then, if they testify to their guilt, keep the women at home until death comes to them or until God shows them another way. If two men commit a lewd act, punish them both; if they repent and mend their ways, leave them alone—God is always ready to accept repentance, He is full of mercy.[22]

In addition to the Qur'an, those condemning homosexuality also turn to hadiths. There are plenty of reports of the sayings and doings of the Prophet that take a dim view of same-sex relations, variously invoking God's curse, execution in this life, and punishment in the hereafter. Among them is this uncompromising statement, attributed to the Prophet:

When the male mounts another male the angels are alarmed and raise a cry to their Lord. The wrath of the mighty One comes down upon those [men], the curse covers over them, and the tempters surround them. The earth asks its Lord for permission to swallow them up and the divine throne grows heavy upon those who bear it up, while the angels declare God's greatness and hellfire rears up high.[23]

Plenty of grist, then, for the homophobic mill. Even less strident voices—including the well-known scholar Yusuf al-Qaradawi, who is prepared to cut Muslims a little slack on other controversial practices like fellatio and masturbation—are unyielding when it comes to the question of homosexual intercourse. "The spread of this depraved practice in a society disrupts its natural life pattern and makes those who practice it slaves to their lusts, depriving them of decent taste, decent morals, and a decent manner of living," al-Qaradawi opined in his user's guide to the faith.[24] "The jurists of Islam have held differing opinions concerning the punishment for this abominable practice. Should it be the same as the punishment for fornication, or should both the active and passive participants be put to death? While such punishments may seem cruel, they have been suggested to maintain the purity of the Islamic society and to keep it clean of perverted elements."[25]

With this burden of scriptural proof, it would appear that Islam and homosexuality are fundamentally incompatible. There are, however, those who question these seemingly irreconcilable differences. Some of the most outspoken voices come from outside the Arab world, but a few are piping up from within the region. Among them is Olfa Youssef, a professor of linguistics and psychoanalysis, and former director of Tunisia's National Library. In 2008, Youssef published a slim volume called *Hayrat Muslima (A Muslim Woman's Confusion)*. In it, she asked a series of hard-hitting questions: "What happened to Muslims these days? Why is Islam equivalent to closed-mindedness and rigidity? Why are we damaging this brilliant Islam, the Islam of freedom of faith and belief, love and forgiveness, and replacing it with an Islam that is alien and terrifying? Why do we present [the face of] Islam to the West as a Muslim in a secret society, thinking only of martyrdom, killing himself and other people, which is forbidden by God, and justifying it on a difference of opinion or faith?"[26]

Youssef and I met at a café in Sidi Bou Said, a picture-perfect seaside village just outside Tunis, once home to Michel Foucault, the famous philosopher and thinker on sexuality—a pleasing, though unintended, bit of historical symmetry, given our subject. With her black corkscrew curls and animated manner, Youssef is like a human spring, coiled with mental energy. She pins the blame for today's sorry state of affairs on contemporary *fuqaha'*—that is, interpreters of Islamic jurisprudence—who present their views as inviolate truth and on those who follow them blindly. As a Muslim, Youssef isn't questioning the Qur'an; rather, she has its narrow-minded interpreters in her sights. "The Qur'an alone is the only thing perfect for every time and place, but the human reading is relative and depends on the nature of who's doing the reading, and their historical situation and their psychological complexes," she observed.[27] Those who argue that it's their way or the highway are, in her opinion, on dangerous ground: "Anyone who says that he owns the only correct meaning for the Qur'an is talking in the name of God almighty and putting himself in the position of one who knows everything in infinite knowledge."[28]

To illustrate her point, Youssef tackles a number of topics that appear black and white to many Muslims, based on conventional interpretations of the Qur'an, but perplex her because of her own and others' alternative readings through the ages. Among them is homosexuality. Youssef questions the reading of Qur'anic verses used to condemn sodomy, among them "And Lot said to his people: you are committing the outrage which no one from the two worlds has done before. You are getting at men, and cutting the road and committing evil at your gatherings."[29] Is this outrage sodomy ("cutting the road," being a metaphor for blocking the path to reproduction), she asks, or actual highway robbery (literally cutting the road off to wayfarers) and other violent practices for which the people of Lot were famous? In another instance, the Qur'an presents Lot's neighbors as they are about to sexually assault the visiting angels. And so, Youssef asks, "What was the sin of the people of Lot? Having sex with men, or forcing men to have sex without their consent," thereby violating one of their key codes of conduct—hospitality— and dishonoring Lot?[30]

According to Youssef, the patriarchal nature of Islamic society over the ages has encouraged readings of the Qur'an that condemn sodomy, which, by putting men in a position of giving pleasure to other men, reduces passive partners to the status of women, "against the rules of nature and contradicting God's wisdom," as such interpreters would have it.[31] This also explains the enduring popularity of hadiths in which the Prophet is said to condemn sodomy and its practitioners, hadiths that have been known for centuries to be of dubious authenticity.

Since the Qur'an does not specify a punishment for *liwat,* Sunni jurisprudence has relied on a variety of ways and means, among them analogy to *zina* (sex outside marriage) to derive a penalty for male sodomy. The upshot is death by stoning, or lashing, according to three of its four main schools. This *hadd* punishment, as it is known in Islam, translates into laws on the books in a handful of Arab countries—among them Sudan, Yemen, and Saudi Arabia— that directly apply shari'a. However, there is a debate among legal experts as to whether such punishments are, indeed, based on reliable evidence and sound reasoning, doubts that Youssef also raises.

Homosexuality isn't the only hot topic she tackles—child marriage, masturbation, polygamy (for men and women), heterosexual anal intercourse, *mut'a* unions, and less sexy subjects like *mahr* and inheritance are also on Youssef's list. But it's her arguments on homosexuality that have provoked the most vitriolic response. "The papers said that I said homosexuality is licit, that homosexual marriage is not forbidden. . . . I didn't say that, though I do think it," Youssef explained. For her, homosexuality and sexuality in general are entry points to a deeper understanding of Islam's holy book and a fertile ground for *ijtihad,* which she aptly describes as "a perpetual adventure in search of the real meaning of the Qur'an, which is known only to God."[32] Unfortunately, much of the public response to her book, particularly on Islamist websites, has focused more on the sex and less on that deeper purpose. "I understand [why], because sex is sacred and religion is sacred." Youssef laughed. "Together it's a Molotov cocktail, and especially when it's a woman [involved] as well."

She was quick to point out that her arguments draw on more than a millennium of Qur'anic interpretation—although the earlier thinkers she cites were unlikely to have been branded sluts for their intellectual pains, as Youssef has been. "Why is the new 'ulama' [community of Islamic scholars] so much more closed and rigid toward sexuality than the ancient ones?" she asked rhetorically. "It is extraordinary. The old ones talked in detail about homosexuality, no problem." Then, ever the teacher, she offered an answer. "There are [several] reasons why we went from an open to closed interpretation. The first is that Muslims were colonized by a Christian point of view. In Christianity, sex is not just taboo, it is locked up," she opined. "Another reason is the Wahhabism. [The Wahhabis] are people who show Islam in a completely different way to its real essence. To have power, you need to subjugate people. What is the thing that is freest and most shared by human beings? It's sexuality. So it's the best way to block all desire to be individual, to be different. We are all the same; therefore there is control." The final straw, in Youssef's opinion, is the general decline in religious education. "The other reason is ignorance," she said, her eyes alight with frustration. "People don't read anymore—they watch television; they listen to al-Qaradawi, Amr Khaled [television preachers]; they don't read what al-Tabari, al-Razi [two early Islamic scholars] said. They don't even read the life of Muhammad." Her indignation suddenly turned to a smile at the name of the Prophet. "I like that man. He never had a problem with the sexual."

This winding down of individual religious thinking—a sort of spiritual and intellectual malaise—may seem at odds with the rise of Islamic fundamentalism and religiosity over the past few decades. But, as Youssef and others argue, religious form has come to replace spiritual substance for many. "In Islamic countries, if you stop someone in the street and ask them, 'What is haram?' they will say fornication and alcohol, things on the surface. But everything else, we don't talk about it: love your neighbor, honor—forget it. We throw rubbish in the road, no problem; we say bad things about our neighbor, no problem. Religion, it's [now about] sex. But this is the institution of religion, not religion [itself]." Questioning Islamic interpretations on homosexuality and other issues is Youssef's way of trying to kick-start that thinking, even if the process begins with an angry riposte. "I would like to make people think there are other ways of reflecting. It's too boastful to say a book will change things directly. But already, it has touched people, it has set off something. And that's a good thing, because it's time to speak. We cannot change on the sexual level without speaking. Talk doesn't change things directly, but it's with talk that things will change."

But it's going to take a lot of talk to get even the most open-minded religious leaders in the region on board. "No, no, no, [with] God Almighty [as my witness]." Shaykh Ahmad, imam of one of the largest mosques in Damascus, shook his head and laughed when I discussed these alternative interpretations with him. "The Lot people, why did they want to rape the angels? Because the angels came like boys, and they wanted to make sex with the boys. This is settled. To my mind, there is no debate."

If anyone might consider taking a second look, it's Shaykh Ahmad. He's been a leading light in a network of religious leaders and faith-based organizations established by the United Nations Development Program. The initiative was started by Khadija Moalla, a human rights lawyer from Tunisia, who spent almost a decade trying to improve the status of people living with HIV in the Arab region—against terrific odds. Too often, religion was used as an excuse for inaction, especially by politicians, because the groups at highest risk of infection—men who have sex with men, female sex workers, injecting drug users—were also the ones roundly condemned by prevailing religious discourse. So in 2004, Moalla set out to engage Muslim and Christian religious leaders, male and female, to break through the fear, ignorance, and stigma that characterized their attitude toward HIV and those living with the infection.

Under these auspices, religious leaders have had a chance to sit down with men who have sex with men at workshops across the Arab region, including a series of annual meetings in Cairo. If it were not for HIV, Shaykh Ahmad and his peers could not have come to the table in the first place, but the focus on public health and protection gives them a socially respectable cover. For Shaykh Ahmed and some of his more open-minded peers it has been a real eye-opener. "The word 'homosexual' is connected in our minds with lots of dirty things. Like molesting children and raping girls. That they are dirty people, they are hypersexed, they are living a wrong life," he freely admits. Years of working together, however, have changed his outlook. "They are like the religious leaders: some of them are nice and not nice. There is a singer with a good voice and a singer with a bad voice. In them, there are all sorts of people."

Shaykh Ahmad is a deeply religious man, and his conviction compels him to do whatever he can to reach all corners of his community. "The function of the religious leader is not to say this guy is going to hell or going to heaven. No. That's not my mission. My mission is to try and say to these people, 'Come, come, my friends, let's try to solve your problems.'" I asked him if that "solution" and those "problems" included trying to turn homosexual men straight, given the current fashion, among some religious leaders, of talking about treatment where they once spoke of punishment. Not at all, he said, with feeling. "If he wants to repent, God willing, I am going to help. If he does not want to repent, at least he shouldn't harm other people." By that, Shaykh Ahmad means unsafe sex and the spread of HIV; although he himself does not openly endorse condoms, he discreetly recommends those in need to seek medical advice, knowing full well that condoms will be part of the package.

In talking to Shaykh Ahmad over the years, I have the impression of a man who is walking a thin line. On the one hand, he is genuinely interested in helping men whose sexuality crosses the heterosexual norm to find inner peace. This dialogue cuts both ways, as he is also acutely aware of the dangers of falling out of touch with his community. "We need new, innovative ways of thinking. Otherwise, we will be like the Christians: 'Bye-bye,' and they put religion to their back," he remarked. "For Islam to stay alive, it has to live with the problems of society. It's not essential that I agree with your way of life, but I have got to deal with you. There is a difference in dealing with you when I am frustrated and angry with you, since I should be dealing with you when I am happy. It's possible that I find open doors between me and him, and [as a result] I'll be more responsive to him."

Yet, in light of his own religious beliefs, Shaykh Ahmad can go only so far in making those who come to him feel at ease. "I tell them, 'I love you. You are my brother, and you are welcome at the mosque.' But I cannot tell him it is not haram." And so Shaykh Ahmad falls back on a long-standing distinction in Islam: acknowledging the inclination to love men while condemning the sexual act itself—a "hate the sin, love the sinner" approach. It's the best he can do under the circumstances. And it's compromise that he has tried to communicate to his students and the broader community. "We started telling the people that sexual orientation is one thing and doing [it] is something else. And that raping the children is not homosexuality. The person who rapes is not a homosexual, so we are now limiting the definition of the homosexual. Maybe he could be influenced by his environment, his surroundings. This might not be his own free will a hundred percent. And that the people who move in that world did not leave God's path after all; they are still our brothers and we can still live and coexist with them."

Many men and women I know across the region whose lives depart from the heterosexual norm are deeply suspicious of religious leaders. Duplicity is high on their list of indictments: imams and priests who are happy to talk tolerance and compassion when there's an all-expenses-paid trip to a workshop or international funding in the offing but who quickly take a hard line at Friday or Sunday prayers or when talking to the media. And in some cases, the hypocrisy goes beyond words. Munir described one visit to an imam. "I wanted to have an answer if gay is bad or not; ultimately, I wanted to know am I going to hell or not," he said. The result was a four-hour lecture on the evils of *liwat* and *zina*. "He talked to me, and then he tried to do it. He was telling me it was haram, and then he had sex with me." Munir laughed.

By his own admission, Munir is "not a religious man," but he does believe in God, and this belief has helped him find a peace that eludes many of his peers. "I have a brother. He is straight; he is married and has children. We are coming from the same womb. So why are the feelings inside me and everything different to him? What are the reasons?" he asked. "Maybe it's something from God, it is the order of God: You gave me this, and You know my areas of weakness, and You know the places inside me, the dark areas I cannot enter. Maybe it is a test. He wants to see if I will tolerate this load, because I am helpless, I didn't choose these feelings. So if they are wrong, and it's made by You, God, how can You judge me?"

Such views are echoed by Nasim, who sees a central role for religious figures in the search for sexual tolerance in Egypt, and the wider Arab world, should they take such lessons to heart. "They have not well studied their religion. God is love, and all religions say that. From this base, since God is love, he loves us as we are. Like a father, who can pardon his son even when he makes mistakes, he will never take a knife and kill his son," he observed. Nasim's advice comes from his own struggle to reconcile his faith with his sexual life. "If they transmit the image of a God who makes laws and punishes on the basis of them, we are very far from the heart of religion. The heart of all religion is the love of God for man. I consider myself religious. I felt, at the beginning, guilt, but when I understood this, [that feeling was] finished."

Like Nasim, Munir dismisses suggestions that religion, and religious leaders, must take a backseat in order for homosexual men and women to find acceptance in Egyptian society. "The shaykhs can change everything; they can do everything. Because what's focusing the whole world, what's affecting the whole world, are religious leaders, shaykhs and priests." Munir wants a spirit of tolerance. He is not looking for approval, nor is he asking for more slack than he himself is willing to cut religious leaders. For all his close encounters with men of God, Munir appreciates that they are in a tight spot: "Shaykhs are afraid to say they are supporting the gays. He is afraid of the people; they will kill him or they will think that he himself is gay."

The long-term solution, in Munir's view, lies in the sorts of interactions that these workshops have fostered, opportunities for dialogue that have changed Munir's view of religion and the pos-sibility of accommodation. "When I spoke with [the imam of one of Cairo's largest mosques], he didn't know what I was suffering, what are my feelings. When I spoke to him and told him all the stories, he was about to weep. He said, 'I can't imagine that these groups of you are suffering this much. I thought you were just doing pleasure and sleeping together, but you are being tortured. Yes, I do have reservations about this, and I don't approve of what you are doing, and it is haram. But I feel that you are subject to many injustices.'" Munir clearly sees a role for himself and his peers in shifting atti-tudes. "Even the scientists or the shaykhs need us to point out the picture for them because they see in the movies this ugly picture, so they take this idea. I feel the problem, so I am the one who can speak about it. So [when] I tell you what I feel, this will touch you inside."

## PUBLIC DISPLAYS OF AFFECTION

"This ugly picture," as Munir puts it, is the stereotype of homosexual men and women in Egyptian cinema and television: camp, comic, conflicted, or corrupted—take your pick. One study of Egyptian movies made between 1979 and 2009 that touch, however briefly, on homosexuality found that less than a tenth presented homo-sexual characters in anything close to a sympathetic light.[33] Few mainstream filmmakers are willing to risk alienating audiences, or financial backers, by cracking old chestnuts, like homosexual men and women driven to their appetites by childhood sexual abuse or homosexual men as indiscriminate sexual predators.[34] Even such superficial and unflattering portrayals raise the ire of conserva-tives, who accuse filmmakers—under the influence of America or Israel—of tempting young people into perdition merely by depict-ing such behavior. And there's rarely a happy ending for homosex-ual characters on-screen. The film adaptation of 'Imarat Ya'qubian (Yacoubian Building) by Alaa Al Aswany, Egypt's best-known liv-ing novelist, is a good example. A central character in the movie is a homosexual newspaper editor who (warning: spoiler) is murdered by one of his lovers, much to the delight of audiences. "I went to see *Yacoubian Building* four times. Every time, people cheered [at the murder scene]; I felt like they were stabbing me," Nasim recalled. "Once, I was watching it, when the gay character was being killed, someone said, '*Ahsan, ahsan* [Great, great].' I turned around and saw it was a woman, a distant relative whose husband had once made advances to me and I fooled around with him." He laughed.

Just the idea of presenting homosexuality in a less glaring light is enough to set off a firestorm. *Tul Omri* (*All My Life*), directed by Maher Sabry, an Egyptian filmmaker based in San Francisco, is a low-budget, DIY production and one of the few films in recent years to offer a more rounded portrayal of homosexual life in Egypt— with stories and characters echoing the experiences of Nasim and Munir. It is unlikely to show at a Cairo multiplex anytime soon, but that hasn't stopped the fatwa*s* from flying, sight unseen. "Burn it immediately," was the verdict of one former Grand Mufti of Egypt. "These films are the gateway to debauchery, to committing that forbidden by Allah and propagate deviant social behaviors."[35] And it's not just religious authorities in a twist; one high-ranking U.N. official in Egypt suggested that the movie might even encourage the spread of HIV by promoting illicit behavior.

Egyptian cinema has yet to have its *Brokeback Mountain* breakthrough on homosexuality; what with the rise of Islamic conservatives, this looks to be some time in coming. That being said, the growth of independent filmmaking and the new possibilities of alternative distribution (including private screenings and Internet streaming), as well as the longer-term possibility of lighter censorship once Egypt has shaken off its post-Mubarak spasms, make this a less fantastic prospect than it was under the heavy hand of dictatorship. Already, there are a number of other art-house movies and documentaries on homosexual life in the Arab world that give a more nuanced view, though these have not had mainstream distribution in the region.[36]

It's a similar situation with Arabic literature. Long gone are the days of al-Tifashi and his playful treatment of same-sex relations. The past half century has seen the publication of some truly bleak portrayals of homosexuality, which have come to symbolize a sense of emasculation of Arab society at the hands of colonial occupiers, Israel, their own governments, and a global consumer culture—the "fucked-over" school of writing, in which sodomy represents just one of the many ways people of the region have been oppressed in recent decades.[37] There are, of course, exceptions—books, and in particular novels, that do justice to the complexity of homosexual life in the region without having it carry all the woes of the Arab world. One to emerge from Egypt in recent years is *The World of Boys,* written by Mostafa Fathi, an Egyptian journalist, and put out by a small indie publisher. It's the tale of Essam, one of Fathi's friends, a rare coming-of-age story in which the lives of middle-class homosexual men are fleshed out in some detail. It is also a plea for tolerance of diversity—sexual, ethnic, and religious. At the end of the book, Essam makes peace with himself by taking the plunge and baring his soul on the bridge over the Nile leading into Tahrir Square, wearing a sign reading I AM GAY. I AM A HUMAN BEING.[38]

This is not something Nasim and Munir would recommend. Thanks to the Internet, however, there are easier ways to make a stand. Nasim, for example, took a step out, ever so discreetly, online. "I wrote on my Facebook, 'I like women and men.' My kids [students] are not stupid—they read this. They started to talk about it, and I started to talk about it also, and now we speak openly about it." The news soon spread through the school. "The directors know, the priests know, all the teachers know; we even joke about it. Of course there are some who are a bit uptight . . . but if they attack me, I know how to defend myself. My private life is my own. I don't ask you if you fuck your wife from up or down or right or left."

Not every online entry takes as feisty a tone. "To be homosexual is to live a miserable life, to get used to those disdainful looks, to hear hurtful and mocking words . . . without being able to defend yourself," writes a young Moroccan man on his blog, *A Forgotten Life.* The misery goes on: "You are looking for the relationship of your dreams in a society that refuses to recognize you or your existence and does not want to accept these relationships in spite of their nobility and sincerity. To be homosexual means that you live with a thousand and one faces to show what you do not feel and cover your true feelings. To be homosexual means to think on your own . . . to express yourself on your own . . . to feel happy on your own . . . to cry on your own . . . to be angry on your own . . . sleep on your own . . . on your own . . . on your own."[39]

For some young men and women, access to the Internet brings the stunning realization that they are, in fact, not alone in their desires. Some young men describe gay porn as life changing, revealing a world of same-sex relations that they thought was unique to them. Online mating and dating sites can have a similarly transformative effect, as well as offer a concrete chance to hook up. Manjam, for example, has more than a hundred thousand listings from across the Middle East (including Iran and Turkey)—tops, bottoms, and versatiles looking for action, complete with discreetly cropped photos of their vital assets. Indeed, such sites are so popular that NGOs working on HIV prevention use them to reach one of their key populations: men who have sex with men. Women find the Internet an especially valuable tool to meet potential partners because their opportunities to do so in the real world are more constrained than men's. And a growing number of websites in Arabic offering news, views, and accurate information about homosexuality—from social, psychological, medical, legal, and cultural perspectives— are working wonders in bringing men and women to terms with their divergent sexuality.

Such online exchanges are all the more vital in places where physical gatherings are risky. In the summer before the uprising, a real-world discussion group tried to launch in Cairo, with unnerving consequences for participants, when its foreign host was suddenly deported, and they were left in the lurch, wondering if they might be next in line for the attentions of state security. This sobering tale highlights one of the chief risks of online communication— rapid exposure, with potentially damaging consequences—should confidentiality be compromised. I know several men and women who have been inadvertently outed when they forgot to activate their screen saver and family members came across their profiles on Facebook or GayRomeo. Or worse, given a police penchant for Internet entrapment.[40] Nonetheless, the fall of the Mubarak regime triggered a flourish of online activity, but how far, and how fast, to translate this into offline action was the question facing Nasim and his friends in the shifting new order.

## WOMEN IN LOVE

To understand where the Internet, determination, and a conducive climate might one day take Nasim and company, I took a front-row seat at a theater in downtown Beirut. It was a full house, hundreds of men and women cheering the performance onstage, where two young women were reading from a hot new book, *Bareed Mista3jil (Express Mail)*. An anthology drawn from the lives of more than forty young Lebanese, its stories covered the usual rites of passage—problems with parents, tensions with friends, pressures to marry, struggles with self-image, trouble at school, thoughts about religion, dreams and disappointments of emigration, and that age-old favorite, falling in and out of love. "I get really shy and nervous when I have a crush on someone. I even get shy when I fantasize about someone. I get clumsy when I go out on dates and I never make the first move," one of the testimonies unfolded, with a final twist in the tale: "I am a lesbian."[41]

The crowd went wild. I, meanwhile, was looking around nervously, having brought my Cairo anxieties with me, and half expecting the police to burst in at any moment. But I needn't have worried. Beirut enjoys a freedom of expression and assembly lacking in Cairo and other capitals before the upheavals of 2011, freedoms that are still more aspirational than actual in the wake of the "Arab Spring." All the same, the evening was remarkable, even by local standards, not for the sex talk per se, but for its focus on one of sexuality's largely neglected facets: same-sex relations between women.

While homosexual men in the Arab region are often in the line of fire, their female counterparts are all but off the radar screen. Time and again, I've heard female friends living on their own (moving out, for those with means to do so, being slightly less fraught in Beirut than Cairo) remark on how having male friends or colleagues stay over elicits stern lectures from neighbors, but female lovers can come and go without comment. Generally speaking, people— even in worldly Beirut—just don't get same-sex relations between women: with Clinton-like logic, if it doesn't involve a penis and penetration, then it really doesn't count as sex.

Same-sex relations between women were not always this obscure. In the golden age of Arabic erotica, love and sex between women were well understood: analyzed, anatomized, and very often appreciated.[42] Elaborate medical explanations were advanced to explain the phenomenon of "grinding," and there were debates as to whether it was inborn or acquired. While medieval explanations of vaginal shape or labial irritation are a little out-of-date, the social justifications invoked for same-sex relations are as true for some women today as they were a thousand years ago: preservation of virginity and an avoidance of adultery and illegitimacy.

Al-Tifashi was one of the more sympathetic commentators; although he referred to grinding as a disorder in *A Promenade of the Hearts,* his admiring tone belies his vocabulary. "[These women] love each other as passionately as men do, but with even more intensity," he wrote. "They seek out the best and most beautiful furniture, food and objects they can afford, no matter the place and time of origin."[43] The women in al-Tifashi's book appear to have enjoyed considerable economic and social freedom—they are bold, beautiful, independent, and a lot smarter than the men around them, who are generally disdainful of ladies who can get along without their precious "tool." Warda, one of the famous "grinders" quoted by al-Tifashi, felt sorry for men as she described in arousing detail the journey to mind-blowing orgasm one woman can make with another. "If philosophers could observe our pleasure, they would be baffled. And the people who like fun and music would fly [sky-high]," she observed.[44]

Warda's twenty-first-century sisters are a lot less cocky. They are in a double bind—being both homosexual *and* female, with all the trouble that brings. As we've seen, it is a problem for women in the Arab region to admit to any sort of sexual activity before marriage, let alone same-sex relations. And regardless of their sexual preference, women who do not conform to the wife-mother mold cast by patriarchal society are also in a tight spot. Then there is the loneliness of the long-distance lesbian, the sheer difficulty that many women I know face in finding partners because of their social isolation. "It's more difficult to be a lesbian than a gay man. A gay man can go and come anytime. They can walk at night, they can move out anytime. They can be bachelors when they're sixty and still be eligible. They can travel. They have a better chance of finding jobs. It's [being a] man that tips the scale."

Nadine M. took me through the trials and tribulations of loving women. She should know, having founded Meem, a support group for queer women, in Lebanon in 2007. I've struggled throughout this chapter to find the right words in English to describe men and women who do not hold the heterosexual line—sometimes "gay" and "lesbian" cut it, sometimes not. But with Nadine, it's easy: "queer" fits the bill nicely. "As queer women, we have the part that is gay, and that's that. But we look at other things that affect us, like our gender expression, including what we wear and how we look and what we look like; the pressure to get married; sexual harassment, including rape; heteronormativity and the family structures; and sectarianism and religions and fundamentalism. Even the politics of this country, even environmentalism affects us," she explained. "We started realizing this is not about lesbians. This is about something bigger. If we're going to be queer, we're going to be politically queer. It's not enough to be queer in myself or in my friends; I stand against all of these systems that are oppressive."

Nadine is acutely aware of the difficulty of balancing a sexual identity with all the other affiliations Lebanese carry, including religion, ethnicity, and class. And there is the more fundamental difficulty of reconciling one's individual sexuality with the demands of, and obligations to, the family. "Our bonds with our families are so much stronger [than in the West]. It's not because we love our family more than some American guy loves his family, but because our family are our providers, not the state. The state will not give me money if I don't have a job; the state will not protect me if someone beats me up on the street. The police, you call them and then they come, like, two hours late," she said. "We don't have the sort of protection someone would feel in Britain, for example, that the state protects me. Or in France, if you're not working for a few months, the state is there for me—I exist as an individual in the state. We don't have that here because we exist as daughters and sons and wives and husbands of people. This is how we exist. I don't have a record in the Lebanese government that's Nadine as an individual. I'm in the record with my father. When I get married, they move me to the record of my husband. What does it mean for me to exist in this country and depend on the state to go against my family?" Nadine's point is well-taken: it's hard to hold fast to a sexual identity, of any description, if you don't have an individual identity in the first place. What this means, in very practical terms, is that your family largely calls the shots, which makes going against their norms all the more difficult.

In dealing with this complexity, the four hundred or so members of Meem can get a helping hand at Womyn House, a cozy apartment in the trendy Gemayze district of Beirut, where fellow travelers from all over Lebanon go to find a room of their own—a place where they can talk about their problems (as detailed in *Bareed Mista3jil*), support each other, and come to terms with their sexuality. It is also a place to simply socialize with other women and overcome their isolation. "I think that a lot of women come into activism not because they want to be activists but because it's the only way they can see other visible lesbians. I believe that that's the case because it's also been my experience," Shahira, a queer activist in her thirties, told me. The Meems, as members are called, are also extremely well connected online, given the group's origins as an Internet discussion forum. They tweet, they blog, they post on Facebook and YouTube, and they campaign, organize, and inform online—including the weekly publication of *Bekhsoos* (*With Reference To*), one of the most informative magazines on sexual diversity in Lebanon and the wider Arab world.[45]

Meem is one of half a dozen or so organizations that have sprung up over the past decade to offer support to people across the Arab region who identify as LGBTQ (lesbian, gay, bisexual, transgender/transsexual, queer). Among those out, if only on the Internet, are Kifkif (focused on Morocco), Abu Nawas (Algeria), Bedayaa (Sudan and Egypt), Iraqi LGBT (based in London), and Aswat and Al Qaws (working with Palestinians). And then there are the dozens of NGOs dedicated to HIV, a handful of which also reach out to men who have sex with men, with an emphasis on public health rather than sexual rights per se. Like most of these groups, Meem is not registered as an NGO with the government. In much of the Arab region, official registration of an LGBT group is a long shot, given the current cultural and political climate; although the possibility exists in Lebanon, Meem doesn't see the point in going the official route, in any case—"using the master's tools to dismantle the master's house," as Nadine puts it.

Meem's way of getting its message across is a subtle process of "infiltrating" organizations working on other social issues, such as violence against women or drug addiction. Meem can afford to take a softly-softly approach because women whose sexuality crosses the heterosexual line lack the visibility of, and therefore pressure on, their male counterparts. That pressure is enshrined in law. Lebanon (along with Syria, Bahrain, and Morocco) penalizes "sexual intercourse against nature," which can result in imprisonment of up to one year; other laws, such as those against loitering or "offending public morals," can also be invoked. What exactly constitutes a sexual act, let alone an "unnatural" one, and the evidence needed to prove this, is largely in the eye of the beholder: according to one study of the Lebanese law, while homosexual men are picked up and prosecuted, other potential infractions, among them same-sex relations between women and heterosexual sodomy, essentially slip under police radar.[46]

Repealing this law—Article 534, to be exact—is one of the targets of Helem, the granddaddy of all LGBT support groups in the Arab world.[47] Helem began as a group of people connected by e-mail; it morphed into a social club, then an informal group focused on personal freedoms, from which Helem emerged in 2004 (and from which Meem subsequently budded). Helem is the most visible LGBT group in the region—there aren't many other organizations there that run public events to mark International Day Against Homophobia—and is involved in a wide array of projects, including advocacy, research on LGBT issues, information and education for LGBT men and women and their families, HIV outreach (in collaboration with the government), weekly discussion groups, and a hotline. Although it aims to serve both men and women, and to reach out beyond the capital, Helem's core constituency is gay men in Beirut.

Meem and Helem offer an interesting contrast in styles. While it has a strong presence on the Internet, Meem is low-key in the offline world; membership is confidential, and you need to be in the know to visit the meeting place. (The *Bareed Mista3jil* performance was fronted by Meem's more public feminist sister organization, Nasawiya.) Helem, on the other hand, is right out there, its voice loud and clear—in part a reflection of general sexual norms, where men can strut and women are expected to keep silent. Helem's meeting place is Zico House, a rambling old building in central Beirut with butterscotch-colored walls, red shutters, and lush greenery. It welcomes all comers, including officials from Hizbullah, who visited to thank Helem in person for participating in a coalition to support refugees from southern Lebanon during the 2006 conflict with Israel. ("They saw pictures like this one," a Helem volunteer told me, pointing to a sketch above a doorway of two men kissing. "They were like, 'What is this place?' " He laughed. "We explained about the whole thing, and they were okay.")

Helem has worked to raise public awareness of Article 534, plastering downtown Beirut with posters and discussing the issue in the media—which, thanks in large part to Helem's efforts, is now more politically correct and these days talks, more often than not, about "homosexuality" rather than "deviance." Some journalists have come out in support of repealing Article 534, various celebrities have made encouraging noises, and a couple of government officials, including one former minister of health, have said they think the law should be scrapped.[48] But in the complex social and political mosaic of Lebanon, change takes time. In the meanwhile, people are taking the law into their own hands. In 2009, a judge in Batroun, a coastal town in the north of the country, threw out a case against a homosexual man charged under Article 534, not only because the evidence presented was flimsy but also on the grounds that "unnatural" is a social construct not applicable in this context. "Man is part of nature and one of its elements and one of its cells and no one can say that any act of his acts or behavior is contradicting nature, even if the act is criminal or offending simply because these are the rules of nature," the judge philosophically observed. "If the sky is raining during summer time or if we have a hot weather during winter or if a tree is giving unusual fruits, all these can be according to and with harmony to nature and are part of its rules themselves."[49]

Quite aside from the admirable poetry of the verdict, this is the sort of judicial common sense that LGBT activists across the region would like to encourage—through informal dialogue with, and formal training of, judges and lawyers—as an effective way to mitigate the impact of repressive laws where full-scale legal reform is not yet a realistic prospect. For its part, Helem is running workshops where its beneficiaries can learn their legal rights and how to respond, politely but firmly, to police intervention; it also arranges legal representation for those arrested and informally interacts with police to try to keep arrests to a minimum.

Legal reform is a useful rallying point, but no one is kidding themselves that repealing Article 534 will transform the lives of homosexual men and women without much more work on many more fronts. Nadine shook her head when I asked her if abolishing the law was a priority for her. "Let's say [the prime minister] gives us gay rights tomorrow, abolishes Law 534. What's going to happen? Absolutely nothing. Is it going to help my mother accept me?

Is it going to help people not harass me because of the way I look? If [the prime minster] stands up and says, 'I give you gay marriage, men can marry men and women can marry women,' then I will have to marry someone of my own sect, right? What does it mean to talk about these things? What does it mean to say there's a protective law for gay people in this country when women don't have a protective law?"

These deeper fractures in Lebanese society belie Beirut's shiny, seemingly tolerant surface. Lebanon's capital has long had a reputation for glamour and sexiness and is widely regarded—more often with envy than genuine disapproval—as the fleshpot of the Arab world. The city, famous as a "Paris of the East" before its fifteen-year civil war, is today back with a perfectly manicured vengeance. In Solidere, its chichi downtown district, I found myself gawking at designer boutiques with the latest flesh-baring, figure-hugging fashions and transfixed by women tottering past in twin-tower stilettos and the shortest skirts I've seen this side of the Bosporus. Beirut's entertainment industries—talk shows, soap operas, magazines, and music videos—project an image of a society at ease in its sexual skin. But when you look at what research says about sexual lives in this hugely diverse city, you come away with the sense that all this is like a shot of Botox to the public face of sexuality, smoothing out appearances without actually curing the contractions that are furrowing society. In Beirut, and Lebanon more widely, there are wives who are just as sexually trammeled, unmarried women as concerned about virginity, and young people as ill informed about sex as anywhere else in the region.

With Beirut actively marketing itself as the Arab world's playground, and having become something of a gay tourist destination, it is easy to be seduced by its sparkling nightlife into thinking that homosexuality is no big deal in the wicked city.[50] But as residents quickly point out, these spots are largely out of reach for all but moneyed folk, whatever their sexual inclination, and life is tough for homosexual men and women outside this gilded circle. "It's not all roses and peaches. Homophobia is still available. People still get kicked out of their homes once their parents find out, get kicked out of their jobs. There's oppression, and there are people in prison. It's not a safe place," Shahira reminded me.

The real measure of Beirut's willingness to make space for sexual diversity is not Bardo, one of its famous "gay-friendly" venues, but an office two floors above it. This is Marsa, Lebanon's first sexual health center for those on the far side of socially sanctioned sexuality. Marsa spun out of a project at Helem to offer health-care services to men who have sex with men, a population with plenty of experience with prejudice from the medical profession across the Arab region.[51] One study of physicians in Lebanon found that scarcely a tenth considered homosexuality an "acceptable" behavior, the vast majority classifying it as a disease that requires either medical or psychological treatment; half said they'd refuse to treat a homosexual patient.[52] Such attitudes hardly attract clients for testing and treatment—more's the pity, since research shows men who have sex with men at high risk for a number of health problems beyond HIV.

*Marsa* means "harbor," and the center aims to live up to its name by creating a safe space for patients. It has proved popular—and not just because its services are subsidized and therefore a fraction of the cost at other private facilities. The young staff members bubble with enthusiasm as they go through the list, including HIV testing, genital wart treatment, hepatitis C management, psychological counseling, and the other nitty-gritty of sexual health. They showed me around their sparkling facilities, which included a tidy setup for gynecological services—not exactly a pressing need for homosexual men, I thought. But Marsa is casting its net widely, aiming to attract not just men who have sex with men, but also women, no matter their sexual preference. "We are offering a gay-friendly and sex-friendly place so that women can talk about their sexuality," one of the clinic's counselors told me. Doing so is not easy for any woman, even those who fall within the magic circle of marriage. "I remember just yesterday [a woman] saying, 'I never imagined myself talking about sex to a man. . . . I never imagined myself doing it, and now I can . . . no discrimination, no judgment.'"

Marsa is a concrete example of a wider strategy advocated by many LGBT activists in Lebanon, and across the Arab region, who are couching their needs in the broader struggle for basic human rights. One woman who sees the big picture is Rasha Moumneh, a soft-spoken but fiercely articulate analyst of the emerging LGBT movement in the Arab region. For several years Moumneh looked at these issues for Human Rights Watch, an NGO headquartered in New York. Her position has given her a unique view not only of what is happening at home but of how outside eyes see the situation.

Like many of her peers, Moumneh is a staunch opponent of "identity politics," in this case rallying around the rainbow flag and pushing for specific LGBT rights. As she points out, the situation facing sexually diverse groups in Lebanon and its Arab neighbors is just part of a spectrum of exclusion, albeit at the far end of the rainbow: "I'm not comfortable with this whole gay double life thing. It really extends beyond that. Even if you're heterosexual, in most places you're going to have to live some kind of double life. And so to separate the gay angle and say people have to live a double life is really not looking at the big picture, at the social fabric as a whole and what people in general have to deal with when navigating between personal desire and tradition and family commitments. This is not a gay issue; this is a social issue. And I'm sure you've seen it among straight young [unmarried] people in Egypt. Everybody has to deal with this."

Thanks to the efforts of Helem and Meem, there's no question in Moumneh's mind that constraints on same-sex relations have loosened in Beirut. "I remember what the situation was ten years ago, and I can see what the situation is now. And it's a sea change. The LGBT issues have gone mainstream; things are talked about in various corners of civil society, positively or negatively," she noted. "Because there is an increasing number of spaces that are open and accepting of homosexuality, whether it's in the social sphere or wherever it is, people feel more emboldened to—not really to come out to their families, but to carve some space for themselves. There is more space for them to live gay or whatever they want to do. This is, of course, inside Beirut; nowhere outside of Beirut has this dynamic. The increasing visibility of gay people, the space in Beirut, has had a tremendous effect. Not necessarily a sense of acceptance, but a sort of live-and-let-live atmosphere."

There are blind spots to this tolerance, however. Lamia is a Lebanese student who grew up in Saudi Arabia and is now studying in Beirut. She realized her sexual attraction to women while a teenager in Riyadh. Unlike many of the other women I've met, Lamia did not find loneliness to be a problem—at least not while she was living in Saudi Arabia. "They are lots of gays and lesbians in Riyadh, you know. Some people because they really are lesbians, and some because they can't sit with men and interact with them openly. There's a lot of it, a lot, a lot, a lot of it." And the living is relatively easy, in Lamia's experience. "They don't have a problem. They don't feel discriminated. They're living normally. Some get married, some don't," she went on. "No one would, like, tell you are gay or not because they all pass through that stage. I never felt that I am different there."[53]

Far from finding her faith an obstacle, Lamia feels Islam has helped her come to terms with her sexuality. "In the Qur'an, there is a passage about hypocrites. I can simply tell everybody that I'm straight. I can go, get married, have kids, have a happy life. But I would be lying to my husband, I would be lying to my children, I would be lying to God," she explained. "I would be an awful hypocrite. And I don't want to do that." It has also helped her parents to accept her, despite their fears for her future without a husband and children. "My mother is a devout Muslim woman. Her belief in God is so powerful that she surrenders everything to His will. Anything that happens is because God wills it. And so she didn't question or challenge my homosexuality," Lamia recalled. "Shortly after, I told my father, and he had the same reaction: 'We cannot change what is God's will. If it is meant for you to change, you will change on your own.'"

For Lamia, the problems started when she came back to Beirut— because she wears a hijab. "When I'm walking in the street, no one questions me about my sexuality, but they do question me about my dress. I thought Lebanon is more open-minded than this." She sighed. "Everything is very underground [in Saudi Arabia]. But here it is open. I'm a human being. I like to party. But people, they don't understand; all they can see is a veiled person at a party place. They don't understand you—they just judge you."

## GENDER-BENDING

Randa, an Algerian migrant whom I met in Beirut, knows all about the importance of summary judgments and first appearances. She's a tall, slim, and attractive thirtysomething, with just a hint of makeup and silky straight black hair loosely brushing her shoulders. Compared with the hyperfemininity and supermasculinity of Beirut's beautiful people, Randa was decidedly low-key, dressed in a plain black tank top, a demure cardigan, and sensibly scaled brown heels. Randa was trying very hard to fit in because she is, in fact, on the outer edge of the sexual margins of Arab society.

Randa was born a man but is on her way to becoming a woman. Of all the sexual diversity in the Arab region, those who visibly cross the great gender divide—transvestite, transgendered, and transsexual individuals—are in for the roughest ride of all. "The state of transsexuals is worse than homosexuals," Randa told me, her voice shaking. "Really, it's serious; really, it's lamentable."

Her own story is proof enough. Growing up in a middle-class family in Annaba, on the Algerian coast, Randa appeared to follow much the same path as any young man: army, marriage, children. However, Randa knew from an early age that she was not the same as other kids, and the army proved fertile ground for her to explore that difference, through sexual relationships with other personnel. Algeria's bloody civil war of the 1990s raised her political awareness, and a decade later she cofounded the country's first LGBT support network, appropriately named Abu Nawas.[54]

Along the way, Randa decided she was easier in her skin as a woman. "My transsexuality was open because I started my hormonotherapy when I was in Algeria and the changes happened fast." Randa, who trained as a nurse, was lucky enough to begin that transition under medical supervision, but she knows scores of men and women who resort to a DIY approach. "Ninety-nine percent of the [male-to-female] transsexuals I speak with started savage hormonotherapy, without any medical supervision. They don't know what hormones to take; they latch onto the Pill, which is very toxic for their health." Randa took me through the consequences in frightening detail: diabetes, heart complications, liver failure, and breast cancer, among them.

Between her political militancy and her sexual nonconformism, Randa had no shortage of enemies at home. She received plenty of hate mail, falling into two broad categories: "official" threats from those claiming to have a police file on her activities and promising to put her away in prison for good, and religious intimidation by those who called her a menace to Muslim morals and promised to slit her throat. Throughout her troubles, Randa got little support from her family; it was, in fact, an ultimatum from her relatives that prompted her flight from Algeria. "Someone came to talk to my brother-in-law who said, '[Randa] did this, this, this. You have to tell him to leave the country in ten days; if not, it will be bad for you and your family,'" she recalled. "My brother-in-law added his own threat: 'It's best you leave. If the scandal bursts because you were militant LGBT or a trans, certainly me and [Randa's other brother-in-law] will repudiate your sisters.' Repudiate a woman in Algeria, in the region, it's the drama—she's no longer a human being. For my security, for the security of my sisters, for their happiness, I had to leave."

Randa was fortunate; thanks to Meem, she was able to take refuge in Beirut. But life is far from easy in the Arab region if you don't toe the gender line. "Transsexuality here and in the Arab world is seen as an extreme case of homosexuality by the society, by everyone. They can't make the difference between homosexuality and transsexuality. But homosexuality is an issue of sexual behavior, and transsexuality is an issue of gender identity," Randa explained. This confusion extends to trans people themselves. "They say, 'I am a girl in the body of a young man.' They give you the definition of a transsexual in their own words. But they also say they are gay bottom [passive homosexual partner]. But they are not. They are women. They just don't know any better."

There was a time when people did. Gender-bending has a long history in the Arab world; in seventh-century Medina, for example, the Prophet Muhammad regularly interacted with men who crossed the gender divide. These were the *mukhannathun:* people who were anatomically male and raised as boys but behaved like women. Today, we would consider them transvestite or possibly transgendered. Although they talked, walked, and looked female, the *mukhannathun* were not assumed to be sexually attracted to men; it was, however, generally believed that they were not interested in women either, which is why, for example, they were allowed access to the Prophet's wives and played a recognized social role as matchmakers, as well as entertainers.

Those who consider cross-dressing un-Islamic draw on what they see as the clear-cut duality of creation as specified in the Qur'an: "By the enshrouding night, by the radiant day, by His creation of male and female, the ways you take differ greatly."[55] And they invoke the many hadiths in which the Prophet Muhammad is said to have condemned *mukhannathun:* "The Prophet cursed effeminate men and mannish women" is just one of the variations on this theme.[56] But there is some debate as to exactly why the Prophet took this line with particular *mukhannathun* in the first place, and whether this indictment can be generalized to all such individuals. Some scholars argue that it is not the cross-dressing per se that landed the *mukhannathun* in trouble, but rather that the Prophet may have suspected that one particular individual's lack of interest in women was less than ironclad or that another may have been arranging illicit trysts between men and women—an individual injunction that came to be applied to all such people.[57] Over time, the line on the *mukhannathun* hardened and their gender behavior came to be associated with passive sodomy—something that earlier generations of Arabs had been able to differentiate—resulting in a widely held confusion that continues to this day.

To be sure, homosexual men and women in today's Arab world

are carrying a lot of baggage. But, as Randa sees it, they at least have a closet to put it in should they choose. Coming out as a transsexual, however, is not particularly good for your health— self-administered sex change aside. And it's even worse, in a patri- archal society, for men who think of themselves as women. "They usually leave school young because of discrimination, problems in the family, in society. If they haven't gone through hormonother- apy, they can live in the day as boys and nights in the clubs as girls. Or they have suddenly started on hormones, and they are thrown out by their families. They are obliged to prostitute themselves and to become a creature of the night," was Randa's grim assessment. "The ones who come from the upper classes, if they have their own business, their own projects, property in their own name, they can live peacefully even if they are thrown out of the family and their society. They can live with dignity."

That dignity is in particularly short supply in parts of the Gulf where gender differences are color-coded—women in black and men in white—and cross-dressing is a source of rising social anxi- ety. In 2007, for example, Kuwait passed an amendment to its crimi- nal code specifying that "imitating the opposite sex in any way is to be punished with up to one year in prison and a fine of 1,000 Kuwaiti dinars [approximately USD 3,600] or with one of these two punishments."[58] Since then, scores of male-to-female trans- gendered or transsexual people have been arrested, often on the basis of just looking a little different, since the law doesn't actually define what constitutes such imitation; even a medical certificate of gender identity disorder, authorized by the government, doesn't save them from arrest. As Munir found out back in Cairo, time in police custody can include torture, sexual abuse, and blackmail by officers; the law also acts as a license for men in general to prey on them.

The question is why the Kuwaiti government should have decided to clamp down on cross-dressing in the first place. As one Arab commentator put it, it's not as if the country doesn't have more pressing problems: "Who are the perverts, anyway? Is delinquency such as the growth and spread of bribery, political corruption in the House of Representatives, rampant corruption in government institutions, and the collapse of morals in the Kuwaiti society . . . more or less of a danger to society than the so-called phenomenon of . . . the third sex [male-to-female trans people]?"[59]

Kuwait, like many of the smaller Gulf states, is on the sharp end of globalization: foreign nationals make up around two-thirds of its population. In recent years, the country has seen women rise to prominence in government and business, over the vociferous objections of Islamic conservatives.[52] Anxieties about preserving national identity and local culture often fix on what appears to be the most visible symbol of Western depredation: those who are seen to violate traditional sexual or gender roles—be they empowered women, homosexuals, or cross-dressers. The fact that, "traditionally"-speaking, women have occupied significant roles in Islamic society and that alternative sexualities have long been a feature of Arab life is glossed over. Taking a hard line on as vulnerable a group as the "third sex," is a convenient way to prove your Islamic street cred, and they make a far easier target than the country's well-connected women's movement.

It's not just nonconforming men who are raising the temperature in the Gulf. *Boyat* is the Arabic term that's been coined to describe women who look and behave like young men. *Boyat* are also causing something of a panic in some Gulf societies: in the UAE, for example, police squads scan malls and other public places in organized campaigns targeting suspicious-looking girls: those arrested for the first time are released into parental custody, but repeat offenders can find themselves in court for "violating public moral norms."[60] *Boyat* have been variously accused of mental illness, defying God's creation, and sowing moral corruption through predatory homosexuality and same-sex marriage, not to mention Satan worship and *jinn* possession.[61]

Although *boyat* are today characterized as a dangerous foreign import, there is, in fact, nothing new about women cross-dressing in the Arab region. In ninth-century Baghdad, the hottest girls on the streets looked like boys. These were the *ghulamiyyat*—a feminine derivative of the Arabic word for a young man. These women were a curious combination of male and female. The *ghulamiyyat* dressed like men, yet wore makeup. While they plucked their eyebrows and painted their lips, they also drew on mustaches in musk. In an age of strict segregation, they hung out with men at dogfights, hunts, horse races, and chess matches, all the while eschewing such feminine niceties as wearing jewelry and braiding their hair. They even took male names. Yet they made no attempt to bind their breasts and were decidedly heterosexual, often painting their male lovers' names on their cheeks.[62]

The *ghulamiyyat* fashion reached its height during the Abbasid caliphate in Baghdad. According to some accounts, there were up to four thousand of them in the court of its most famous sultan, Harun al-Rashid. The fashion gained momentum during the reign of his son, al-Amin, thanks to Zubayda, al-Rashid's wife. Same-sex relations flourished in the Abbasid court and al-Amin was famous for his taste in boys. Zubayda was so concerned about her son's dwindling prospects of producing an heir that she hatched a plan: she dressed slave girls as boys and cut their hair, in the hope that they would attract her son. It seems to have worked, at least in part. Al-Amin took to the *ghulamiyyat,* and some rose to considerable prominence: his favorite, 'Arib, was famous not only for her beauty but for her talent as a singer, poet, chess player, and daredevil horsewoman as well.

Today's attitudes toward cross-dressing women are rather less tolerant, ranging from outright condemnation to attempted conversion. Qatar has one of the most public and organized efforts on the latter front; in 2007 the government set up a special "social rehabilitation" center to treat youth problems including addiction, aggression, and "sexual deviance," into which the *boyat* are bundled. When I visited the facility, on the sandy outskirts of Doha, no one was quite sure just how common the phenomenon was, what was really driving it, and whether girls would outgrow it.

Many people I met in Doha spoke of seeing *boyat* in shopping malls in the same astonished tones usually reserved for UFO sightings. But according to one psychologist dealing with *boyat,* such public displays are rare: girls tend to keep their cross-dressing quiet and under their abayas, unwrapping as boys only at school or among friends in private. Discretion is the rule, so I was told, since family ties are strong in Qatar and news travels fast. "The percentage of Qatari people are maybe 16 percent or 18 percent only [of the total population]. And they are families; it's a lot of families with the same name, maybe fifty families with the same name. So doing something wrong, that's it—stigma for the whole family," the psychologist said.

Most of the teenage girls brought in for consultation don't consider themselves troubled: "Women do not feel it's a problem. They feel it's their freedom; they don't feel it's wrong." From observation, the psychologist divided the *boyat* into at least three groups: those whose gender identity is male; those who think of themselves as women but are actually attracted to their own sex; and those who behave like boys to be cool, fashionable, and popular with the beautiful people at school. The practitioner described one patient, a sixteen-year-old who felt uncomfortable as a girl and was disguising her blossoming body through dress, dieting, and battening down her breasts. "She was treated as a boy at home, playing with other boys with a ball," the psychologist told me, ascribing the girl's gender confusion to her upbringing. "[Her parents] did not try to make her play with dolls and in the kitchen. That family has no friends with young female kids, but they did not try to think or find other female friends for her."

After psychotherapy, the young woman started to change outwardly. "She began to decrease the hours of seeing football, knowing everything about the issue. She began to accept wearing makeup and trying to have different dress. She began to think about her future . . . 'At the end, I have to be married in this society, so I have to accept to think about this issue.'" But are such alterations merely skin-deep? If a *boya* were content with her situation, would the psychologist try to change her? "No," was the reply, but this particular expert was doubtful of a happy ending in such cases. "If you are something in between men and women, you will not find your freedom. The same pressures are still there; it is not a solution."

For some transgendered people, that solution lies in changing sex altogether. It's an expensive process: USD 30,000 to 40,000, says Randa, for the full course of hormones, hours of plastic and reconstructive surgery, and years of psychotherapy. Those who take the plunge often travel outside the Arab region—Thailand and Singapore are popular destinations for those who can afford it. It is possible to surgically change your sex in the Arab region, but the procedure is laden with restrictions.[63] Hard-liners who oppose all sex change operations lean on a phrase in the Qur'an: "There is no altering God's creation."[64] However, a fatwa issued by a former Grand Mufti of Egypt, the late Shaykh Sayed al-Tantawi, opened up a little space for those who have clinically defined gender identity disorder.[65] Some Shi'a religious scholars take a more flexible stance, most prominently Ayatollah Khomeini, who, in the 1980s, issued a fatwa permitting sex change operations (including for transgendered people) on the grounds that these procedures are not explicitly forbidden in the Qur'an and that such operations reconcile the disharmony between the soul and the body and prevent the transgendered person from falling into sinful acts—that is, same-sex relations.[66]

In the Arab region, though, changing your sex can be as hard on paper as it is in the flesh. In the Gulf states, for example, getting government permission to have sex reassignment surgery and altering your sex on identity documents—a procedure with profound implications for matters like inheritance that vary according sex—can involve years of legal challenges. In Lebanon, things are a little less formal, says Randa. "For Lebanese, it's very complicated, but it's possible. It costs money, time, but it can be done." Not for her, though. Randa was a foreign national in Lebanon, so changing her papers there was not an option, and given her history in Algeria, the prospects are equally slim back home. In the end, Randa headed to Europe for a new life, one she could lead as a full-fledged woman.

On the personal front, Randa was lucky and rarely lacked for male companionship. Professionally, though, times were a lot tougher. She was denied employment at a private Beirut hospital, even though her experience as a health administrator in Algeria more than qualified her for the post; no matter how convincing she is as a woman, without the sex to match her official ID, which prospective employers ask to see, bias against transgenders and transsexuals can put regular employment out of reach. Those who do get work can find themselves exploited by employers, facing longer hours, lower wages, and fewer benefits than other employees, with the possibility of sexual abuse thrown into the bargain.[67]

Trans people in the Arab region have been largely overlooked by organizations supporting other sexually diverse groups, although there are a few initiatives now springing up to better understand and to address their needs. But it's not easy to bring many of them into the fold. "The transsexuals are so despairing of society, tired of everything, they don't want any more," Randa told me. " 'What are you saying? You want to bring us here, you want to give us rights?' They don't believe that." But she also appreciates why society is reluctant to engage with them. "That is partially the responsibility of some transsexuals themselves. When you go overboard into extreme vulgarity, extravagance, and all that, what are you expecting in the way of respect? It is the question of the chicken and the egg. If you treat me as a slut, okay, I will be a slut, a slut to the extreme. You only have to dig a little to see the suffering that has engendered this extravagance."

## FUTURE TENSE

Experiences like these underscore calls by LGBT activists in the region to fight their fight in a broader context. This strategy is prompted in part by fears of a conservative backlash if the focus is on the bogeyman of "gay rights" but more so by an understanding that nonconformism and diversity in general—ethnic, religious, racial, and sexual—make people uneasy, and not just in Beirut, a city built, broken, and reborn along sectarian lines. Moumneh is very much in the broader-is-better camp. "I think the best-case scenario for LGBT individuals in our region is [to] stop thinking in terms of LGBT. I think it just limits so much. I think it would be better if people looked at the underlying causes of the problems that we're facing, and looked at connections between these problems and the wider problems in society. Because if not, we are going to end up with a situation that any progress that we do achieve will be progress for a privileged few."

She continued in this vein: "I find it very difficult to see how far an LGBT rights discourse would go in a culture that places so much emphasis on the family, for example. I don't see how far that could go without work on women's bodily autonomy and women's bodily integrity. And LGBT organizations have historically never worked on these issues because they are primarily headed by gay men. I generally don't think this is an appropriate model for the region. No one is going to decriminalize homosexuality while women are still being punished for adultery. It's absurd; it's not going to happen. Without tackling the issue of sexual autonomy as a whole, nothing is going to move forward."

Shahira echoed these sentiments. "As a starting point to rally communities, we have to find something other than 'We're all gay,' and that's partly my issue with identity politics. Just looking at the realities of the region, LGBT individuals are not as visible as we think they are. But everyone in the region is suffering from the repression of morality—whether it comes from the state, from religion, from society—everybody. So why would I work on liberating a subgroup, for just a very small subset, when I can invest in doing the real work which needs to get done, which is a very long-term strategy?" she asked me, with quiet determination. "When I was younger, I didn't identify with L or B or G or T. . . . I was just someone who was repressed because I was a woman. Injustice was on me not because I'm queer, but because I'm a woman—an Arab woman, a single woman." For Shahira, the grand plan of social justice, at the end of the day, comes down to the personal. "I want to go and be able to rent an apartment without being called a whore. I want to be able to walk down the street without my ass being touched. It doesn't matter what I do in my bed—because I can close my door."

In many ways, Lebanon is an outlier in the Arab region. I asked Moumneh what lessons might be drawn, if any, from the experi-

ence of Meem and Helem in carving out space for sexual diversity. Without skipping a beat, she gave me her prescription. "I think
the key issue to look at here is freedom of association. In countries
where you have a more relaxed freedom of association law, you
will have more space for people to organize over whatever issue,
including sexuality or LGBT issues. So that was why Lebanon was
in the vanguard, because, however flawed it is, it has the institutions of a democratic state. So you have multiple political parties,
you have an active civil society, and you have a very, very liberal
law of association that basically does not require the consent of the
state—it just requires that you inform the state. Without those factors, you would not have what you have today in Lebanon in terms
of work on sexuality and sexual rights. And I think that's the key
factor to look at in other countries." Her advice to Nasim, Munir,
and their peers is to go slow. "Now is not the time to say in Egypt,
'I want to establish an LGBT organization.' There are foundational
things that need to be laid first. You're talking about a society in a
huge sway of transition, and the building blocks of a more open and
democratic society need to be laid down first."

Just as the uprisings, and their aftermaths, are playing out differently from country to country, the strategies of the region's LGBT
groups are also diverging—some advocating full-throttle legal reform to seize a moment of change, and others taking a slower approach. None of this strategizing is occurring in isolation, however;
compared with the fragmentation of, and competition among, civil
society groups that I've seen in other domains—old school women's
rights organizations, for example—the region's LGBT activists are
remarkably well organized and well connected, both online and
off. A steady stream of workshops and conferences on HIV across
the Arab region, like the one described earlier, are bringing them
together on a regular basis to swap stories and compare strategies.
Turkey, in particular, has proved a handy incubator for budding
sexual rights activists across the Arab region, hosting workshops
and networks to help them hone their skills and learn from its particular model of social and sexual change in an Islamic context.[68]
The most prominent activists in the region are booked months in

advance with invitations to international meetings on sexuality, and the rising tide of conferences on the "Arab Spring," in which the status of homosexual men and women in the new order increasingly features, means the air miles are adding up.

These men and women, mostly under forty, are impressive—educated, thoughtful, and articulate. They're not into hierarchies, and their networks and organizations are run on refreshingly meritocratic grounds. Their numbers are still small—a minority within a minority—but not their ambitions. They know exactly how the world turns and can tell you with devastating precision what they think has worked abroad and what will work back home. "The Global South has numerous examples to learn from, whether it's from Africa and the religious fundamentalists or from Latin America and the trans [transsexual] movement there, what's happened in India and the decriminalization of the [sodomy] law. The Global South is extremely rich in examples, successful ones and not successful ones," said Shahira, giving me a wide-ranging view of international developments in sexual rights. "To say that the West has these perfect solutions, it's extremely imperialist and extremely condescending, and it's just another form of colonization, and it's problematic." She went on: "If we want help, we have voices, we have computers, we have brains, we know how to ask the questions. If the solutions are not local, they are not going to work. If we need help, we know where and how to ask for it. There are enough of us who have studied, learned, and been in the field for so long."

One of the most interesting opportunities for the region's LGBT activists to network, and a measure of their progress in recent years, is Mantiqitna Qamb (Our Region's Camp).[69] Since 2010, LGBT individuals from across the region have been meeting once a year in a "secret" location for workshops on sexuality, gender, and activism, as well training on life skills and advice on the personal front. As Shahira, a regular at the event, pointed out, the key to Mantiqitna is connecting "not just through our gay identity, but through our Arab identity."

It is already yielding results. Hassan, an LGBT activist from Tunisia, was there from the beginning. "It's an initiative I really appreciate. I got experience and I learned how to coordinate and create a small regional network [called Khomsa]. It was the 2010 camp, on the last day, we had a meeting of LGBT activist groups from Greater Maghreb—Morocco, Tunisia, Algeria. We have experience, but we don't know each other. It was the moment when we saw we have common objectives. We work together, exchange experience, conference-call by Skype."

This solidarity is invaluable for Hassan as an activist and as a gay man. "What is really important for us as LGBT? We are not safe. We lived like this for years, being discriminated against, stigmatized, ignored and no one wants to talk to you, refused by the family, isolated, excluded," he said. "The fact of having a network that supports you, that you are not alone in this world, it's moral support. Plus technical support, to have experience, to have had activities which achieved their objectives and others that did not work, so we can learn from these failures."

Hassan is clear on his goals: for starters, a repeal of Tunisia's article in the penal code criminalizing same-sex relations (with up to three years in prison) and the creation of a new NGO to advance the rights of minorities and marginalized groups, across the board. Like Meem's, the strategy of his nascent group is to join other organizations working on women's rights, children's welfare—any human rights issue, really—to mainstream its interests and subtly introduce its message into the broader debate on social justice. "We try, wherever there is a chance, to raise the issue of LGBT, so [the other groups] sympathize. If you find a heterosexual woman, married, who speaks openly against the stigmatization, or [putting] men in prison simply because they had [same-sex] relations, or punished, that is less of a risk [of a backlash] than if you came out directly [and said], 'I'm gay and proud of it.' We don't do that—it's provoking. Our work is to advocate, do meetings, unite with others who can carry the torch to convince others."

Like his counterparts in many other parts of the region, Hassan also knows exactly what he doesn't want. "I know Tunisian society. We will never ask for gay marriage, that's for sure, because most don't want the classic frame of relationship, marriage; we don't think of that. No, not having children, no, no, no. Most [of the men] are young; they want to live their lives normally, correct, without stigmatization or discrimination. That's our objective for the next five years, and even after."

Hassan sounds cautiously confident that the uprising will eventually pave the way for change. "The revolution lets us open discussions of sexual liberty, but we could make a walk back of five years too. It's a difficult moment," he said. "And we have to be very vigilant. We watch 24/24 and 7/7—in a second, everything could change. There are many Tunisians who are pleading for liberty of expression, sexuality, et cetera, and others who want us to return to society ruled by shari'a and Islam. There are two forces, and a balance between them," he continued. "As LGBT, we know exactly what we want: to create a democratic life. I'm not against the Islamists; I am not against anyone. I want to create a real debate, respecting each other's views, not to change one another. We live in one country—Tunisia for you, for me, for us all."

Over in Cairo, calculated steps have succeeded the revolutionary rush. For Munir, who camped out in Tahrir Square from start to finish, those eighteen days were transformative. "I could not imagine Egyptians would be so brave. It was beautiful, beautiful," he says, his voice warming at the memory. And for a time, divisions were forgotten—along all lines. "There were many gays in the revolution, but nobody was focusing on this. Honestly, I forgot I was gay. I was an Egyptian only. People were wounded, were dying, were only Egyptians, nothing else. No difference between gays and straights; nobody was feeling any difference."

The immediate wake of the uprising was for Munir a "paradise," in part because of newfound respect from friends and neighbors; though he was once despised for his effeminacy, a stretch on the square proved his manhood to detractors. More dramatic, however, was the melting away of police and security forces, turning downtown Cairo into something of a playground. Private parties were flourishing, creating a pink pound economy in certain bars and clubs. "Gay men feel a little freer now," Munir remarked as we sat at a packed sidewalk café in Borsa, humming with life. As if on cue, two impeccably groomed, sexily dressed twentysomething men walked by hand in hand, whispering in each other's ears. "If I go among these people"—Munir swept his hand down the length of the café—"they are all gay."

The question is how to sustain, and diffuse, this fleeting sense of freedom. It's an issue that preoccupies Hossam Bahgat, whose NGO, the Egyptian Initiative for Personal Rights, has been fighting for legal recognition of personal freedoms in all domains—including the bedroom—for years. EIPR is one of the few NGOs in Egypt to go to bat for sexuality, arranging legal counsel for homosexual men caught up in police sweeps, for instance, or taking the government to task on forced virginity testing.

For Bahgat, Tahrir Square was a realization of all that EIPR has fought for. "It was a moment when it seemed so matter-of-fact that we are a diverse society and people are entitled to do what makes them happy so long as they are not assaulting, invading others' spaces," he told me. "[But] it's not as if this was the true essence of Egyptians that was uncovered," he cautioned. "No, this was a moment, a good moment—we just need to keep it alive."

Human rights are a hot topic in Egypt these days, and Bahgat's phone is ringing off the hook with groups from Europe and America looking to work with him. While foreign interest, and funding, are potentially welcome, Bahgat is worried that "gay rights"—a preoccupation of Western groups—may undermine the bigger prize of building a society that recognizes and respects personal freedoms across the board. "There is a global fight for gay equality. That global movement is extremely interested in the Arab world. They are much more powerful and well resourced than the small group of activists that believe we should work for respect for personal autonomy and social diversity," he noted. "I am increasingly convinced that the more they spend, the more they allocate resources and execute interventions here, the less space we have for the discussion on sexual rights as part of personal autonomy and diversity in a pluralistic society."

If you want proof, says Bahgat, just look at the emerging landscape of sexual activism in the Arab world. "If we do a mapping of who is working on these issues in the region, you will find maybe seven or eight projects looking at MSM [men who have sex with men]/LGBT, and maybe one or two actors working on sexuality broadly defined," Bahgat noted. "Give me the name of the organization that works on the sexuality of heterosexual women, adolescent sexuality, or sexual education. . . . You will find very few compared with budgets allocated for LGBT."

When it comes to change, Bahgat is firmly in the camp arguing that now is not the time to open a public debate on the rights of those who cross the heterosexual line. Bahgat fears that will only feed what he calls an "artificial identity battle," in which defending or denying "gay rights" becomes part of making a claim for Egypt as an Islamic or a secular state, when what's really at stake transcends these divisions. For all his liberal credentials, Bahgat is not asking to put religion aside. He envisages a constitution that rests on many pillars: the "principles of Islam" as well as the personal freedoms he advocates.

Key to this balance is enforcing the right to privacy—a core principle in Islam. The Qur'an reminds Muslims, time and again, to mind their own business. "Believers, avoid making too many assumptions—some assumptions are sinful—and do not spy on one another or speak ill of people behind their backs" is a recurrent theme.[70] My grandmother exhorted the family to do the same, ramming home her wisdom with pointed sayings like the one that starts this chapter. These rules worked their way into a famous story about one of the Prophet's companions, 'Umar bin al-Khattab, who became caliph, or leader, of the expanding Muslim community after the Prophet's death. 'Umar was walking through Medina one night, so the story goes, when he heard a noise. He peered over a wall and saw a forbidden act—drinking or some other dark deed, depending on the account. 'Umar started to upbraid the man in question, admonishing him with God's wrath. But the man gave as good as he got, noting that if he sinned once, 'Umar trebled the offense, God having forbidden him to spy, skip into people's homes through the back door, and approach someone without greeting them first.[71]

Generally speaking—and there are of course exceptions, as Munir can clearly attest—sexually diverse populations in Egypt and across the region are getting on with their lives, with the understanding that they keep their sexual behavior quiet; when their lives spill into the public domain, then authorities swoop. What's at stake here is not so much "coming out"—which holds little appeal for most of the men and women I know living in the region—but rather the freedom to stay in and do as they choose. This drive to keep private matters private is not unique to homosexual men and women; it covers all sexual behavior—and presents a delicate balancing act for democratic freedoms of expression, association, and assembly.

The right to privacy was enshrined in the old (that is, pre–2011 uprising) constitution and Egyptian law—but it is enforcement that's the problem. The primacy of privacy, as well as protection from violence, stigma, and discrimination, is emerging as a point of agreement in discussions between activists and religious leaders. There are moves afoot in Egypt to realize these rights on an individual basis—small-scale efforts to train lawyers to defend those who are arrested and self-help circles, modeled on the movement in Beirut, to help men and women to talk through their issues and to understand their rights, such as they are. Many of the men and women I know working at the socially acceptable coalface of sexual rights in Egypt—youth sexual education and sexual harassment, for example—as well as those staffing feminist groups, human rights organizations, and new political movements, are themselves LGBT; when the time is right, they will be well-placed to weave their message into the broader tapestry of social and political change.

For all these welcome steps, neither Munir nor Nasim is optimistic about his short-term prospects. For Munir, personal security is a prime concern. "We are afraid of each other now, not just of the government. For instance, I am afraid to walk at two a.m. in the street; someone can show his weapon. This is not just about me being gay, it is about me being Egyptian." As one of millions who is in and out of work, Munir sees the problem as mainly economic, splitting men and women into classes and putting them at odds, another tension in a society full of fractures. "In the revolution, rich and poor [were] together, more than you can imagine," he recalled. "Now there is a gap, when I find someone in the streets for twenty-four hours selling himself to eat and drink, whereas another gay is living the life of a king. So when social and economic circumstances improve, there will be no problem, there will be no people going with a rich man to kill him and take his money. When I find to eat and drink and have a productive life, why should I kill? Why should I steal?"

As a double minority—gay and Christian—Nasim is focused on the rising voice, and political power, of Islamic conservatives. "Before [the revolution] was a bad time . . . the reign of stealing and corruption. It was awful for LGBT; it was awful for everyone," he said. Right after the uprising, there was room to breathe, but Nasim was steeling himself for a crackdown once Islamists settled into power. Ever the optimist, though, he reckons this will be a passing phase of reactionary politics. "It will be [for] five, ten, twenty years, we will have Muslim rule, Islamic power. And when people live under this rule and feel they are fucked of their rights, there will be another revolution to reach a moderate Islam and secular state."

In the longer term, both are confident of better times. Nasim, who once thought of emigrating, has decided to stay put. His contact with students gives him hope that a younger generation, with better education and opportunities, will one day help to realize his aspirations for change: "First, that people are not frightened to come out. That your private life is your private life, not a selection criterion in relationships of friendship or professional relationships. Attacking someone on the basis of their private life would be a criminal offense. [And] religion would come to build bridges between people, to establish peace for those who are homosexual. To give this image, 'Okay, you are like that—we love you anyway.'"

But this is the work of decades. "I don't look at history in my short life. Maybe I won't live to see that [change]." Nasim sighed. Munir is similarly banking on the long haul. Given all that he has suffered, he has every reason to want a break with the past. But for Munir, that change means walking away from a Western path of gay liberation. "I want my rights, but only within the framework of Egyptian and Eastern society and Islam. The limits are that I should not understand democracy or freedom in a wrong way. Go and kiss a man in the street? No, this is an Islamic country," he stressed. "I, as a gay, I don't want to see this. I want change but only within the limits of being Muslims and Egyptians and conservatives. If I go for this gay pride, what will I really ask for?"

Munir spoke for many now working toward an equal footing for sexual minorities in Egypt and beyond. "I want respect—that's all I ask for. Respect for me as a human, not because I am a gay." But in that one small word—respect—lies a long wish list: the right to privacy; freedom from arbitrary arrest, detention, and torture; the right to a fair trial; freedom of expression, association, and assembly; and freedom from discrimination. If Munir and his peers can play a part in achieving such change—for everyone—then we really are talking about a revolution.

# 7
## Come the Revolution

*Safety is in slowness; regret is in haste.*
—My grandmother, on evolution over revolution

"Citadel! Citadel!" my taxi driver shouted in Arabic, our eyes locking in the rearview mirror. "Take off your clothes!"

I was on my way to one of Cairo's famous landmarks: the Citadel, a massive fortress built by Salah al-Din, the famous crusader-crusher, almost a millennium ago. We were traveling in a tin-pot Panda, one of Cairo's aging fleet of black-and-white taxis, an endangered species now that sleek white sedans with all mod cons (including working meters and windows that slide, rather than fall, down) roam the land. Given my experience of sexual harassment in the city, I should have been outraged by my driver's suggestion, or at the very least relieved that he didn't reach over with a helping hand. But I was, in fact, grateful. "You are right." I laughed. "A thousands thanks," I added, for what was less a proposition and more a lesson in pronunciation.

"Citadel" is what we call this bastion in English; in Arabic, however, the word is Qal'a, something of a mouthful the way Egyptians say it. I kept stumbling over the letters until my driver, in exasperation, tried to help by drawing my attention to a familiar word with a similar pronunciation—Egyptian Arabic for "undressing." As the day was heating up, and sweat poured down my back, I was inclined to put this lesson into practice. By then, however, we had reached our destination.

The Citadel sits on a promontory to the east of Cairo. Until TV towers and concrete apartment blocks started sprouting in the 1960s and '70s, it dominated the city's skyline, crowned by the

Mosque of Muhammad Ali, built by the ruler who set Egypt on its path to industrialization in the nineteenth century and founded a dynasty that lasted until the revolution of 1952. Beyond the mosque's vast domes and soaring minarets is a terrace with commanding views. On a clear day—admittedly rare, what with Cairo's pollution—you can see right across the city: straight down, along the twisting alleys of Khan al-Khalili, the souk that was once the trading heart of the city, to gleaming skyscrapers in the north, its twenty-first-century successors; across the Nile, to pyramids in the distance, ringed by luxury housing compounds with names like Dreamland and Beverly Hills; to a glance over the shoulder at a tumbledown, off-the-grid 'ashwa'iyya, Cairo's answer to the favela. From the Citadel, you begin to appreciate how difficult it is to ever really know a culture at its most intimate: so many people, so much diversity, such a tumultuous time. No wonder the great writers of Arabic erotica called on God's blessing before embarking on their labors.

When it comes to sexuality, the Arab world can seem like a citadel, an impregnable fortress whose outer face repels any perceived assault on the bastion of heterosexual marriage and family. But the reality, as I have found through my travels, is that there are plenty of openings—not just innovators who are working for change on a larger political, social, and cultural canvas but ordinary people trying to find happiness in the miniature of their own lives. Not once, in all my travels, was I ever rebuffed when I broached questions of sex; in fact, the poorer and less educated the people, the more open I found them to a frank, and often very funny, exchange of views.

This was especially true of wives, who were generally more articulate on these matters than their husbands, partly because of their greater ease at talking with someone of the same sex and partly because of the heavier burden they carry; when among female friends, they were happy to let their hair down, in all respects. People opened up to me in remarkable ways, even men I knew would never bring up such issues with their wives or sisters, mothers or daughters. Such candor came, in part, I think, from a relief in finding someone from a place where sex was something that could be discussed without judgment or censure but who also had a grounding in their own culture. I was both an insider and an outsider, which could have been the worst but turned out to be the best of both worlds.

This willingness to talk, and to listen, to those who don't necessarily share your point of view will be crucial for Egypt moving forward. The drive to conformity and consensus is a feature of authoritarian regimes; democracy needs a respect for disagreement and competition. The uprising, and subsequent political developments, have accentuated a split in Egyptian society—between a minority who espouse liberalism and a majority who adhere to conservative values. Such differences were steamrolled under the old regime, but are springing up in the new landscape. How these groups manage to coexist will be a huge challenge for Egypt's emerging political, social, economic, and cultural order.

When they had little political clout, Islamic conservatives frequently seized on sex as an easy way to attack the regime; less often did they criticize the immorality of torture, economic injustice, or corruption. It is to be hoped that new political powers, of all stripes, will devote more time to fixing these and other fundamental failings of the past sixty years than to arresting men who have sex with men, or banning movies and censoring the Internet, or repealing laws that empower women, the cornerstone of social change. Realistically, though, sex will continue to raise its tantalizing head in running battles between liberals and conservatives in the years to come.

How Egypt comes to terms with the sexual issues discussed in this book has implications beyond its borders. Although its society has been powerfully influenced by neighboring countries, notably those in the Gulf, Egypt in turn has tremendous soft power in the region; through media and migration of millions of workers, Egypt spreads its culture across the Arab world. Egypt is uniquely placed to adopt outside lessons, adapt them to a local context, and broadcast them to others in the region. Through the United Nations, its influence extends even farther. For almost two decades, civil society and governments around the world have struggled to get sexual rights enshrined in international agreements, a move that helps those on the ground fighting for change; but with almost every such push, Egypt has pushed right back. In these battles, Egypt and its Arab neighbors are not alone. Muslim-majority countries, collected under the umbrella of the Organization of Islamic Cooperation (OIC), hold the party line, joined by the Vatican, which has plenty of leverage to dissuade any move that the Holy See views as undermining its definition of family values. Conservative Christian NGOs from America and Europe have also tried get into bed with their Arab and Muslim counterparts, in what must be an uneasy arrangement, given the suspicion with which many right-wing ideologues view Islam. Further "unholy alliances," as sexual rights advocates describe them, have formed in recent years between governments in sub-Saharan Africa and those in the Arab region to take a stance against same-sex relations.

There are many recent examples of the ways in which Arab governments have resisted advancement in sexual rights on the international stage. In this pushback, Egypt plays a key role. I saw its powers of persuasion in action at a landmark meeting of the United Nations Human Rights Council in Geneva on discrimination and violence against people because of their sexual orientation and gender identity—a sore point for Arab states, among others, who do not wish to see such protections explicitly recognized in international human rights treaties. It was Egypt that rounded up the Arab delegates in the chamber and led them out in a protest against what they consider a slippery slope toward gay marriage, gay parenting, and the collapse of family values. One diplomat from an Arab state told me how its delegation had wanted to participate in the discussion but peer pressure from Egypt was too much to bear. "'Either you go out of the room, or you go to hell,'" the diplomat said, recalling Egypt's ultimatum. "I think they were joking." The Egyptian delegation, however, was taking its clout very seriously. "We are the chair of the Non-Aligned Movement, we are a member of the Arab group, the African group, and the OIC group," one of its representatives explained to me. "I'm not bragging, [but] we are influential in all the blocs. By virtue of being Egypt, still."

In the past, talking tough on "family values" in international forums allowed Egyptian officials to score points with Islamic conservatives back home without actually having to do anything domestically. And it allowed Egypt to stand tall among its Arab and Islamic peers as a bulwark against the perceived onslaught of "Western values"; practically speaking, such resistance is also a useful bargaining chip with those countries that have either taken the lead in advocating for sexual rights at the United Nations or are strongly opposed to such moves, trading off cooperation on this front for concessions on political or economic issues of more pressing interest to Egypt and its allies. Given the newfound political clout of Egypt's Islamists, this resistance may find even firmer ideological purchase and renewed strength. It looks unlikely that Egypt and its neighbors will be switching sides in the international battle on sexual rights anytime soon.

Back at home, change—on all fronts—will also take time. I have used many terms to describe the events that began this decade in Egypt and the wider Arab region—"revolt," "uprising," "upheaval," "Arab Spring," and "Arab Awakening"—but it's only others in these pages who call it a "revolution." That's because Egypt's scenic route to democracy—full of detours, U-turns, false starts, and emergency stops—is hardly a dramatic break with the past. Yes, the latest— and, Egyptians are hoping, the last—in a line of military dictators has been deposed, but the army remains a powerful force in political and economic life. Yes, Islamic conservatives, once persecuted, now have political power, but this is the public culmination of a long-standing private trend in which many Egyptians have moved toward religious and social conservatism in their personal lives.

Throughout their history, Egyptians have turned to religion in times of trouble and uncertainty, only to loosen up when prosperity and stability return. The Salafis, whose ideas are a foreign graft onto the body of Egyptian Islam, quickly felt the reaction of their host on coming to political prominence; their sudden turn under the bright light of public scrutiny has also revealed their weaknesses, and their attempts to reshape Egypt, and many of its Arab neighbors, in their own image of Islam are unlikely to succeed in the long term. Their more moderate counterparts across the region—including the Muslim Brotherhood—are a greater force to be reckoned with, but their ascent to power is also a gamble: solving their countries' formidable problems will demand significant shifts in their own policies and principles, transforming political Islam as we know it. If they fail in this endeavor, the resulting loss of public confidence could, conceivably, not only ruin their own prospects but shake faith in political Islam as well. No matter how the next few years play out, the rise of these groups in an emerging democratic system has already stimulated ordinary people (the so-called "party of the sofa") to question and debate the shape and role of Islam in society, vital public engagement that was absent in the old order. And it has galvanized those who oppose a mixing of religion and politics, shocking liberals out of decades of torpor to fight for their vision of the country.

Egypt is a pot that has been boiling with corruption, injustice, and incompetence ever since its last uprising, six decades ago; in 2011, a variety of circumstances served to turn up the heat and blow off the lid in protests that rocked the region. The steam is still rising and will continue to do so over the next decade, in shifting forms that make it hard to tell what shape society will take. This uncertainty is reflected in voices throughout this book, some of which look to the future with optimism, others of which fear that little will change, or if so, not for the better. Personally, I am hopeful that when the tumult has simmered down, Egypt will be left with a stronger, richer base for future generations.

What this means for the country's sexual culture depends on a complex interplay of law, economics, religion, and tradition. Generations of Egyptians have spent enough of their lives being told by those in power, at home and abroad, what they should or should not do; thanks to their own courage, it is up to them to decide the way forward. When the time comes that Egyptians are ready to tackle these questions—and I believe it will—then a number of changes will be needed in order for sexual culture to head in a different direction.

Since the upheaval, all eyes have been on the balance of political power, and on constitutional and legal reform. When it comes to gender and sexuality, Egypt's legislation has been positively liberal compared with that of other countries in the region. As we've seen, premarital sex or same-sex relations, for example, are not technically illegal; and as activists have rightly argued in these pages, a number of foundation stones need to be laid first, before directly addressing the legal aspects of these more charged issues. On paper, Egyptian women are accorded many more rights than their counterparts elsewhere in the region—rights that women from seemingly open Lebanon to seemingly closeted Saudi Arabia are now struggling to achieve. In practice, though, these rights remain hard for Egyptian women to realize—because of poverty, because of prejudice, because of patriarchy.

On so many issues—be it abortion or domestic violence or other political, economic, and social rights—there is plenty of room for improvement in Egypt's criminal code and personal status laws. The real problem isn't the law on the books so much, but how it is, or is not, implemented and enforced. During the long decades of dictatorship, Emergency Law and the power of the State Security apparatus, which allowed arbitrary arrest, detention, and torture, had a chilling effect on all aspects of society, including sexuality. The entire system needs reform for any chance of breathing room, though as the immediate post-Mubarak period has shown, autocratic tendencies die hard. Reining in the long arm of the law—which includes a retooling of law enforcement and the judiciary—will be a welcome step. Encouraging and equipping lawyers to defend all corners, irrespective of who they are or how they live, is also important.

But the biggest challenge lies in changing the way ordinary people think about the law. For generations, Egyptians have come to see the law as a tool of control, not protection, something to get around rather than uphold, for the good of the elite, not the man on the street. This applies to legislation related to sexuality as well, be it female genital mutilation or abortion. A law—good or bad—is only as powerful as the respect people accord it; when people trust their government, they are more likely to trust the legislation it passes. So it's not just laws that need changing, but a culture of law as well. Achieving that, in Egypt and its neighbors, is going to take wide-sweeping changes beyond the halls of government.

Education is the point of departure. The task is daunting—a complete overhaul of a system as sclerotic, unimaginative, and corrupt as the government in charge of it. Education is so dysfunctional in Egypt that it often seems to make students less creative and more closed-minded than their less-learned peers. And it's not just the schoolyard either. Medical schools, law schools, religious institutes—they all require a reboot. Among the many, many reforms needed is a shift to a system that inculcates and rewards creative thinking, not conformity, in all domains—in particular religion, and specifically Islam. When young people have the tools to think critically about religion for themselves, they may be better able to appreciate the inherent flexibilities in their faith and see choices where they once found only absolutes.

It's not just God, but money that will also make a difference. So much of the sexual trouble Egyptians have experienced in recent years relates, in one way or another, to the economy. It's not that Egypt's economy drastically declined under Mubarak. Quite the contrary, in fact: economic growth was a much-vaunted success of his regime, and arguably kept it in power for as long as it did, as the elite were bought off with moneymaking opportunities. As for everyone else, if they didn't actually become poorer during these years, they certainly felt like it, economic liberalization and global media dangling a shiny new consumer culture beyond their grasp. Millions continue to be hobbled by underemployment, which has soared in recent decades with Egypt's demographic boom and the failure of the public sector—the traditional sponge of the workforce—to absorb a flood of increasingly educated youth. Unfortunately their training has not prepared them for a place in a globalized, competitive economy, leaving those lucky enough to get jobs with employment unequal to their talents.

Economic reform is a massive undertaking for the new and improved Egypt—cutting red tape, cleaning up corruption, and fostering the institutions, skills, and attitudes needed for an entrepreneurial, job-creating culture. There is no shortage of grand plans and clever schemes, proposed by international advisers and home-grown reformers, but this is a project of years, if not decades. In the meantime, though, even the earliest shoots of economic revival might be enough to change everyday lives. Less economic uncertainty might well temper the appeal of some of the more stringent forms of Islam that have offered material and spiritual comfort to millions in the past decades. This influence might also wane with more job opportunities at home, meaning fewer Egyptians migrating to the Gulf, which could also ease some of the stress on families. Commercial sex work thrives in even the most vibrant economies, but offering men and women a fair chance at gainful employment will at least give them the choice of whether or not to engage in such trade. And it will be interesting to watch the impact of job creation on marriage. As we've seen, people have blamed the so-called marriage crisis in Egypt—and indeed the entire region—on economics, and more specifically on unemployment among young men, which makes family formation unaffordable. When jobs are more plentiful, will the age of marriage drop?

Better job prospects could also go some way to giving women more choices through economic empowerment. But they could also help ease male insecurities, meaning that attitudes toward women—at home, on the job, and in the streets—might become less fractious, and that could mean greater scope for sexual expression within marriage, particularly for women, and less sexual harassment in public places. In the wake of the uprising, and the side-by-side struggle of both sexes, surveys show that Egyptians endorse the principle of equal rights for men and women. But this view is still shaped by Islam, and seen through this lens, equal rights does not mean identical roles or expectations. Women will be flexing their muscles in the boardroom, I think, long before they have an equal chance in the bedroom or will be willing to openly demand it.

So many of the efforts for women's empowerment in Egypt and the wider Arab world have, naturally enough, been focused on women—their voice, their opportunities, their problems. But for change to really take hold, it is time for men, and particularly boys, to be brought into this program—to understand how they feel about shifting women's roles and to help them not just to accept but to advance these social changes. Again, education will be key, in the living room as well as the classroom. How a new generation of parents raises their kids—whether girls and boys are taught to communicate openly and respectfully with one another—will shape gender expectations, and marriages, in the years to come.

All of which raises questions about the future of patriarchy. Just because Egyptians, and their neighbors, have risen up against the head of state does not necessarily mean that they will rebel against the head of the family. For all the talk of the youth-led revolution in Egypt, when children took to the streets, they often did so with the blessing, and indeed in the company, of their parents. Telling the father of the nation to get lost was very much a family affair. At the end of the day, the nation's young people may find that it's more difficult to move away from home than it was to get Mubarak out of office. And for as long as religion remains central to people's lives, with God, the ultimate father figure, in charge, the patriarchy is unlikely to totter.

Yet the uprising was a real coming-of-age for Egyptian youth, and the older generation knows it; for a brief, brilliant moment, young people went from layabouts to leaders in their elders' eyes. Parents may one day be prepared to cede a little more autonomy to their children, and this, combined with more economic independence, will give young people more leeway in personal decision making, including how they lead their sexual lives. But until individuals have confidence in the evolving state to not only recognize but defend their political, social, and economic rights, they will seek protection in the collective, and so the family will remain a powerful force in people's lives—especially for women. Men on top—fathers and husbands, in particular—is unlikely to change much in the immediate future.

Eventually, though, these uprisings may catalyze greater democratization of personal relationships—what one British sociologist famously called the "transformation of intimacy."[1] Free and equal relations among individuals are not only key to sexual rights but are also the cornerstone of political democracy; by leveling hierarchies, accepting differences, and respecting individual choices in the one, you help to foster the same in the other.

Media—new and old—is one tool of this transformation. Much has been made of its power in catalyzing the Arab uprisings. As we've seen, long before the upheavals took place, the culture of disclosure and the discussion it fostered on sexual taboos—premarital sex, same-sex relations, sexual violence—became a comparatively safe space (safer, that is, than politics) for some to tilt against received wisdom and bring hidden lives to light. When mass revolt finally took hold, the Internet, satellite TV, and mobile telephones challenged—and eventually undermined—regimes' attempts to keep a lock on information.

Today, as writers, filmmakers, and artists negotiate the possibilities of greater political freedom, including freedom of expression, they too are asking how far they can go in breaking taboos. Certainly people, myself included, feel much freer to speak their minds after the uprisings. The limits of such expression are not just a matter of what new laws may or may not allow but of what society will accept in the new climate—and of how fast years of self-censorship will fall away. How close can artists now hold the mirror to their country's sexual life, and how might this public reflection influence private behaviors? This is more than a question of artistic freedom: it has real implications for the health and welfare of Arab societies. When it comes to sexually transmitted infections, or abortion, or sexual violence, finding a comfortable way to talk about sex—its problems and its pleasures—transcends popular notions of propriety or morality.

Traditionally, religion and culture have encouraged people in the region to keep private matters under wraps. "All my nation will be forgiven except those who boast about theirs sins," the Prophet Muhammad observed in a well-known hadith. For those a little vague on this point, he offered clarification: "Included among the boasters is the man who does something at night, and in the morning, although he has been covered by God [from exposure] he says,

'Hey, man, last night I did such and such.' Although he slept, veiled by God, in the morning, he unveils God's protection from himself."[2]

Across the Arab world, there remains a sizable gulf between appearance and reality, between what is practiced in private and what is admitted to in public. Homes mirror lives: immaculate salons to impress the visitors, but far-from-sightly backrooms concealed from general view. There's a word for this, doing one thing in private and another in public: "hypocrisy." Men free to have sex before marriage, but women expected to be intact; virginity defined by anatomy, not chastity; sex tourism masquerading as marriage; travelers who make a great show of their piety at home, but who waste no time in breaking every rule once abroad and far from the eyes of their fellow countrymen; and many more instances of the gap between public appearance and private reality.

In the West, there is—and I am, of course, generalizing here—a greater overlap between the public and private faces of sexual life than in Egypt and its neighbors. Indeed, you only have to watch reality TV, poke around on Facebook, or scan your incoming tweets to wonder if the distinction exists at all. There seems to be, in many quarters, a compulsion to broadcast one's sexual self: far better to come out than be caught out. As Michel Foucault wrote in his famous history of Western sexuality: "Among its many emblems, our society wears that of the talking sex . . . an insatiable desire to hear it speak and be spoken about."[3]

Foucault theorized that sex, far from being repressed in the nineteenth century, was actually alive and kicking, channeled and proliferated in a medical and scientific discourse he called *scientia sexualis*. Central to the emergence of this new way of thinking and talking about sex, in his opinion, was an age-old institution: the confessional. Christian confession, an obligation of faith, always had a high sexual content, but around the sixteenth century, so Foucault argued, it gradually detached itself from the sacred and migrated into secular fields, like medicine and psychiatry. Foucault didn't live to see *Oprah* or YouPorn, but it's clear that the spirit of confession lives on in our world of 24/7 media.

Islam, however, lacks a culture of confession. Both the Qur'an and hadiths enjoin believers to mind their own business and keep quiet. Enshrining and enforcing the right to privacy is key to progress on human rights, particularly for those whose behaviors, including commercial sex work and same-sex relations, do not conform to social norms. As we've seen, Islam—with its emphasis on privacy—can provide a helping hand, and any future government that looks to Islam as a foundation of its constitutions and laws needs to be firmly reminded of this fact.

A respect for privacy, and an Islamic duty to protect the community from "wrong," however defined, needs to be balanced with freedom of expression. As we've seen throughout these pages, there are certainly those across the region who are forging a path between silence and exposure. They have found what Abdelwahab Bouhdiba, whom we met in chapter 1, called a way of speaking about sex "in the propriety of the Qur'an"—or rather, rediscovered it. The long history of Arabic writing is a master class in the ease with which Arab culture once treated its sexual life.

Part of that comfort was the generation and communication of sexual knowledge. As we've seen, the study of sexuality—and sociology in general—has been hampered in Egypt and in much of the Arab region by both official and self-censorship. A clearer view of the sexual lives of Egyptians would ultimately benefit Egyptians themselves: those trying to understand and halt the spread of HIV or stem the tide of sexual violence; those advocating sexual education or a more liberal stance on abortion; those arguing for tolerance of same-sex relations. The precedent of the power of sexual information lies in the West: the landmark Kinsey reports on male and female sexuality in 1940s and '50s, whose authority even the Islamic arch-conservative Sayyid Qutb scathingly acknowledged. These studies opened a statistical window on the very private lives of Americans in a way that transformed public understanding of sexual behavior. People could no longer argue that premarital sex, same-sex relations, and masturbation were deviations tucked away at the margins of society after Kinsey's studies of thousands of their fellow citizens showed these to be mainstream pursuits.

Kinsey passionately believed that knowledge would liberate people from the guilt and unhappiness induced by what one of his contemporaries called the "hush and pretend" culture of American society. For all their methodological flaws, his studies allowed the public discussion of sexuality to move to different ground, away from salaciousness and sermonizing to a sober discussion of scientific facts. Kinsey made talking about sex respectable. Although his findings and conclusions met with considerable resistance, his research paved the way for an eventual shift in attitudes. As one of his colleagues remarked, "The times were changing anyway, but I think he helped to change the times."[4]

In Egypt today, there are plenty of researchers willing to catalyze such a shift. But it has been hard for them to find formal training and to get approval from universities or government departments to undertake large-scale studies; and even when they have the green light, results have often been hidden away. This culture of concealment—and not just on sexual matters—has been compounded by a reluctance of individuals and organizations to cooperate and collaborate, arguably a by-product of the general climate of suspicion and distrust and the every-family-for-itself mentality engendered by decades of political repression. As a result, researchers and activists are busy reinventing the wheel, unaware of the excellent work being done across the region, or even across town.

Promoting research, and the open exchange of information, is key to new thinking. It begins with words—reclaiming Arabic as a language of sexuality, as many of the writers and educators in this book are trying to do. It is not enough for Egypt and its Arab neighbors to walk out of U.N. meetings, or to rail against Western values or deny their problems back home. "Just say no" is not the way forward. What is desperately needed in the Arab region is a coherent, positive intellectual framework for sexuality. Arab thinkers once had a worldview of sex that accommodated both religion and science and that fit their age, but there is no going back; their twenty-first-century successors urgently need to develop their own, one that makes sense for our time.

Such a framework would allow a more systematic approach to addressing sexuality. At the moment, the only time sex gets a public hearing is when tragedy strikes or scandal unfolds. The medicalization of sex, through disease or dysfunction, is providing a respectable cover for public discussion, but it is also limiting, leaving out a vast range of issues and groups that a broader conception of sexuality would allow. The challenge here is to turn sex from a problem that needs to be solved to a source of pleasure and creativity.

Key to changing attitudes on gender and sexuality on the ground is a vibrant and independent civil society, with both the freedom to act and the support of government and communities. There are plenty of pioneering initiatives across the Arab region, a few of which are highlighted in these pages. The trouble is in scaling up these projects so they can have the impact they deserve. While better networking is important, steady and substantial funding is key. Times are tough, however: Western governments and philanthropic bodies are cutting back on funding in many fields—HIV and family planning, for instance—putting many excellent projects in the region at risk.

Matters have not been helped by aspects of so-called "aid conditionality," in which donors, such as America and Britain, link their funding to domestic reform on policies or practices toward LGBT populations, and other sexual rights. Unfortunately, such a stance serves to reinforce the prejudice that these initiatives are foreign implants. New local sources of funding are desperately needed to sustain and expand the excellent work already under way. Wealthy Gulf states certainly have deep pockets, but they also have their own agendas. Getting them and others to fund programs in, say, sexuality may seem a little optimistic, but it is not inconceivable; as we've seen in the cases of sexual harassment and sexual education, for example, it is possible to package even the most awkward issue with a label that makes it look like a gift, not a burden.

This is, I admit, a rosy view from a liberal Muslim woman's perspective of how sexual life might develop in Egypt and the wider Arab region in the coming decades. There are those, I know, who fear that the unexpected upheaval in the political order and attendant rise of Islamism will move countries further away from freedom, accountability, openness, and equality and toward religiously sanctioned reaction, and that the socially imposed restrictions of recent decades—particularly on women and youth—will gain greater force as the formal law of the land. My sense, however, is that Egyptians, when given a free hand, will eventually make their way back to a more pragmatic, forgiving, and frankly joyful interpretation of their religion—be they Muslim or Christian. This homecoming was clear in the 2011 protests, where personal piety was clearly on display in the millions of protesters who bowed down in public prayer but whose uprising was essentially political, not religious.

As the West urges Egypt and its neighbors toward democracy, it is tempting to project its own past onto the future of the Arab region and to see organized religion as an obstacle to sexual rights; after all, the rise of the sexual revolution in the West came as the sun set on the power of the church. This is not the situation in the Arab world. Even if the power of political Islam wanes, as it well may, after the coming trials and tribulations of trying to govern as complex a country as Egypt, faith will remain as strong—but more a matter of personal belief than public policy, I hope, and more about substance than appearance. Despite the concerns of sexual rights advocates who want to see religion out of the bedroom, I don't believe that religious adherence is a form of regression. As I have argued, sexual rights can be realized, and exercised, in an Islamic framework, so long as individuals have the freedom to think, and act, for themselves.

There are still plenty who strongly oppose these views, who say that to talk openly about sex, to frankly face its problems and extol its pleasures, to consider the inherent flexibility of marriage in Islam, to advocate a live-and-let-live approach to sexual diversity, is to sell out to the West. I disagree. For more than two centuries, from Napoleon's invasion of Egypt to the 1967 defeat by Israel to the war in Iraq, Egypt has been carrying a hefty grudge–cum–inferiority complex, which has allowed conservative forces to reject so-called Western social mores as a form of resistance. The irony is that so much of what they brand as dangerous foreign ideas were features of the Arab-Islamic world long before they were embraced by Western liberalism.

I am hopeful that the uprisings that began this decade will eventually knock that chip off the Arab world's shoulder. Those who rose up in the days of rage, whether or not they have yet succeeded in removing or reforming their sclerotic regimes, are rightly proud of their actions. The postupheaval paranoia and knee-jerk tendency to blame "suspicious foreign elements" for subsequent turmoil notwithstanding, this confidence will, in the long run, help to dispel some of that fear and suspicion of the West and allow people to appraise other ways of life with less prejudice. Young Egyptians, and their peers throughout the region, are aware of how Westerners lead their intimate lives; there are aspects they admire and aspire to and those they can do without. In a world of instant access, their choices are based on information, not ignorance—and it behooves outsiders, with grand visions of social, cultural, and sexual reform in the Arab region, to respect the different directions its people may choose to take.

The world has turned since I set out, five years ago, to better understand the intimate lives of Egyptians, and in the process, better understand myself. My journey across the Arab region has certainly changed me. The overwhelming emotional generosity of Egyptians has worn down any reticence or reserve I once possessed, and I find myself a more impassioned, more open person for it. Having been brought up in a one-child household, far from my roots, I know now what it means to be part of an extended family, and the contentment this can bring, for all its constraints. I have far greater respect for my elders than I ever did growing up in a society that prizes youth above all. And I now have a better understanding of Islam, which has only served to increase my adherence to a faith that, I believe, gives me both freedom and direction in my life.

I also have not just affection and gratitude, but a deep admiration for people across the region who welcomed me so warmly into their lives—not just the customary hospitality extended to strangers, but an acceptance as one of their own. It isn't easy, on the face of it. There's nothing remotely Arab about my appearance (I have the fair features of my Welsh mother and a figure that's more arrow than Arabesque); my Arabic is far from perfect; and my upbringing is a world away from their own. But people were able to look beyond these differences, and we managed to connect through our shared sense of humor and an unexpected personal affinity. If they can make even *me* feel at home, then I am hopeful that societies in the region will find a way to accommodate diversity.

It takes a staggering lack of introspection to spend so much time probing other people's personal lives and to not occasionally question one's own. Until I met Azza, and Amany, and the many other women in this book, I never fully recognized the good fortune of my upbringing. My parents raised me to think I could do anything, be anything, and the men who later came into my life—friends, colleagues, mentors, and husband—have never treated me as anything less than equal, in all domains. My years in Egypt have given me a keen appreciation of the value of growing up in a liberal democracy, where I was taught a respect for diversity and a tolerance of others, however much their lives differed from my own.

I look forward to a day when these values are reflected not just in the politics of the Arab world, but in private lives as well. It took a revolt to shake up politics in Egypt, and even then, change is far from smooth and steady. I am skeptical of any seismic shift in sexual life. Sexual attitudes and behaviors anywhere in the world are tightly intertwined in myriad threads of past and present. Weaving a different tapestry needs a new pattern, and that will take decades to unfold. Change *is* coming to Egypt; not a sexual revolution, I think, but a sexual reevaluation, in which people will one day have the education, the inclination, and the freedom to take an unblinkered view of what they were, how they came to be what they are, and what they could be in the years to come. The confidence and creativity of Arab civilization was once reflected in its sexual life. For the first time in a long time, we have a chance to see this again—not by gazing at our past, but by looking to our future.

With the sun setting over Cairo, I left the Citadel through a massive gateway and walked down its steep drive. As I climbed into a taxi, my driver asked me where we were heading. I told him the address but explained I didn't know how to get there. "No problem," he said. "We'll find the way, God willing." And with that, we slipped into the fast-flowing traffic and plunged into the city below.

# Notes

### Introduction

1. See Bernard Lewis, a well-known historian of the Arab region, as quoted in Horovitz, "A Mass Expression of Outrage Against Injustice."
2. Foucault, *The History of Sexuality*, vol. 1, *The Will to Knowledge*, p. 103.
3. Ibn Hazm, *The Ring of the Dove*, p. 17.

### 1. Shifting Positions

1. For more on the scope of sexual rights, see World Health Organization, *Defining Sexual Health*; International Planned Parenthood Federation, *Sexual Rights*; and Miller, *Sexuality and Human Rights*.
2. Ronald Inglehart, personal communication, 2012.
3. Norris and Inglehart, *Islam and the West*, p. 2.
4. For an entertaining history of European views of Arab sexuality, and vice versa, see Hopwood, *Sexual Encounters in the Middle East.*
5. Steegmuller, *Gustave Flaubert*, p. 141.
6. Ibid., p. 41.
7. Ibid., p. 29.
8. Ibid., p. 44.
9. Ibid., p. 114.
10. Flaubert, *Voyage en Égypte*, p. 285.
11. Steegmuller, *Gustave Flaubert*, p. 38.
12. Ibid., p. 12.
13. Ibid., p. 84.
14. Ibid., pp. 83–85.
15. Said, *Orientalism*, p. 3.
16. Al-Tahtawi, *An Imam in Paris*, p. 221.
17. Ibid., p. 182.
18. Ibid., p. 184.
19. Ibid., pp. 181–82.
20. Ibid., p. 182.
21. Ibid., p. 181.
22. For a fascinating account of early-nineteenth-century Egypt, including its sexual practices, see the chronicles of 'Abd al-Rahman Jabarti, a famous Egyptian historian, in Jabarti, *'Aja'ib al-Athar* [Astonishing accounts].
23. Examples of this line of anti-Islamic argument can be found at www.sex andthecitadel.com.
24. For an insightful history of the sexual revolution, including more detail

on the sexual and social climate of Wales in my mother's day, see Weeks, *The World We Have Won*.

25. Al-Munajjid, *Al-Hayat al-Jinsiyya 'ind al-'Arab* [The sexual life of the Arabs], p. 10.
26. Bouhdiba, *Sexuality in Islam*, pp. 247–48.
27. Ibid., p. 231.
28. Ibid., p. 248.
29. For more on Arab intellectuals' tussles with their collective sexual history, see Massad, *Desiring Arabs*.
30. A detailed account of the parallel rise and fall of sexual openness in the Ottoman Empire, once overlord of the Arab region, is provided by Ze'evi, "Hiding Sexuality"; and Ze'evi, *Producing Desire*.
31. Al-Khalidi, *Amrika min al-Dakhil bi-Minzar Sayyid Qutb* [America from the inside, from the viewpoint of Sayyid Qutb], p. 49.
32. Ibid., p. 67.
33. Ibid., p. 113.
34. Calvert, " 'The World Is an Undutiful Boy,' " p. 97.
35. Al-Khalidi, *Amrika min al-Dakhil bi-Minzar Sayyid Qutb* [America from the inside, from the viewpoint of Sayyid Qutb], p. 143.
36. Dialmy, *Susyulujiyyat al-Jinsiyya al-'Arabiyya* [Sociology of Arab sexuality], p. 6.
37. Reich, "The Sexual Misery of the Working Masses," p. 98.
38. Reich, *The Mass Psychology of Fascism*, p. 38.
39. Ibid., p. 24.
40. Ibid., p. 211.
41. Bouhdiba, *Sexuality in Islam*, p. 248.

## 2. Desperate Housewives

1. El-Mahdi and Marfleet, introduction to *Egypt: Moment of Change*, ed. El-Mahdi and Marfleet, p. 5; Marfleet, "State and Society," p. 17.
2. Handoussa, *Egypt Human Development Report 2010*, p. 245, UNESCO Institute for Statistics (www.uis.unesco.org). Many of the statistics about Egyptian women in this book are taken from a periodic, nationally representative survey of those who are or who have ever been married (known as "ever-married") aged fifteen to forty-nine, indicated by El-Zanaty and Way, *Egypt: Demographic and Health Survey 2008*; as in this instance, p. 28.
3. While Egypt's penal code is largely based on Western statutes, laws on personal status such as marriage, divorce, and inheritance are derived from shari'a. For more on Egyptian laws regarding women and their relation to international legal conventions, see www.sexandthecitadel.com.
4. These results come from Pew Research Center surveys of more than twenty nations, which included Egypt, Jordan, Lebanon, and Tunisia: *Most Muslims Want Democracy*, p. 22; *Men's Lives Often Seen as Better*, p. 7.
5. For more on who decides what in Egyptian households, see El-Zanaty and Way, *Egypt: Demographic and Health Survey 2008*, pp. 37–41; Bashier, "Knowing the Ropes: Autonomy in the Everyday Life of Egyptian Married Women."
6. Egyptian Cabinet, Information and Decision Support Center (hereafter

IDSC), *Istitla' Ra'ii al-Muwatiniin hawla Makanat al-Mar'a* [Citizens' opinion poll on the status of women].

7. In the World Values Surveys conducted in the Arab region from 2000 to 2008, Egypt led the pack, closely followed by Algeria, Morocco, and Jordan, in rejecting the notion that "marriage is an outdated institution"; those polled in Saudi Arabia were only slightly less enthusiastic on marriage. See www.worldvaluessurvey.org.

8. Qur'an 24:32.

9. As mentioned by Abu Hamid al-Ghazali, one of the great figures of Islamic thought and author of the premier Islamic marriage guide through the ages, the eleventh- to twelfth-century *Book of Etiquette in Marriage* (Farah, *Marriage and Sexuality in Islam: A Translation of al-Ghazali's Book on the Etiquette of Marriage from the Ihya'*, p. 49).

10. Many of the statistics on Egyptian youth in this book come from a 2009 national survey of ten- to twenty-nine-year-olds, as detailed in chapter 3. Results calculated directly from the data are indicated by Population Council and IDSC, *Survey of Young People in Egypt*. Some of this data has been published already, as in this instance, in Sieverding and Elbadawy, "Marriage and Family Formation," p. 125.

11. Tradition aside, marrying a cousin makes economic sense; it reduces matrimonial costs by roughly a quarter and offers particular savings on housing, since around two-thirds of such couples set up house with their relatives (Singerman, *The Economic Imperatives of Marriage*, p. 23; Singerman, "Marriage and Divorce in Egypt").

12. Population Council and IDSC, *Survey of Young People in Egypt*. For more on what young Egyptians are looking for in the perfect mate, see www.sexandthecitadel.com.

13. Ibid.

14. More than 90 percent of Egyptian men under the age of thirty claim to have the final say in spousal choice, but less than half of the poorest young women in Egypt have similar scope; their fathers enjoy considerable say in whom their daughters marry (Population Council and IDSC, *Survey of Young People in Egypt*).

15. Osman et al., *Ta'khkhur Sinn al-Zawaj* [Delay in the age of marriage], p. 3.

16. The latest statistics on Egypt, including marriage and divorce, are available from the government's Central Agency for Public Mobilization and Statistics at www.capmas.gov.eg. For more on marriage in Egypt and across the Arab region, see Osman and Girgis, "Marriage Patterns in Egypt."

17. Osman et al., *Ta'khkhur Sinn al-Zawaj* [Delay in the age of marriage], p. 5.

18. Singerman, *The Economic Imperatives of Marriage*, p. 13.

19. Zaiem and Attafi, "Les Mariages en Tunisie, 1991–2007" [Marriages in Tunisia, 1991–2007].

20. Sieverding and Elbadawy, "Marriage and Family Formation," p. 122.

21. Kholoussy, *For Better, for Worse: The Marriage Crisis That Made Modern Egypt*, p. 27.

22. Qur'an 4:34.

23. Population Council and IDSC, *Survey of Young People in Egypt*.

24. Sabiq, *Fiqh al-Sunna* [Jurisprudence for Sunni Muslims], p. 219.

25. Sieverding and Elbadawy, "Marriage and Family Formation," p. 127.

26. Singerman, "The Negotiation of Waithood," p. 72.

27. For more on youthful suggestions to make marriage more affordable, see Sieverding and Elbadawy, "Marriage and Family Formation," pp. 128–29.

28. For more on concerted efforts elsewhere in the region to get young people into marriage, see www.sexandthecitadel.com.

29. The UAE Marriage Fund and its many criteria are detailed at www.zawaj.gov.ae/en.

30. Bristol-Rhys, *Emirati Women*, p. 80.

31. Bristol-Rhys, "Weddings, Marriage and Money," pp. 23–25.

32. Abdulla and Ridge, *Where Are All the Men? Gender Participation and Higher Education in the United Arab Emirates.*

33. Tadmouri et al., "Consanguinity and Reproductive Health Among Arabs."

34. United Arab Emirates National Bureau of Statistics, *Marriage Contracts and Divorce Certificates.*

35. For more on the tensions over foreign spouses, particularly foreign husbands, across the Arab region, see www.sexandthecitadel.com.

36. Differences between Sunni and Shi'i Muslims over *mut'a* marriage are discussed at www.sexandthecitadel.com.

37. For more on the practice of *mut'a* marriage in its Shi'i homeland of Iran, see Haeri, *Law of Desire: Temporary Marriage in Shi'i Iran*; and Mahdavi, *Passionate Uprisings: Iran's Sexual Revolution*. For Lebanon, see Drieskens, "Changing Perceptions of Marriage in Contemporary Beirut." For the UAE, see Hasso, *Consuming Desires: Family Crisis and the State in the Middle East.*

38. For more on *'urfi* marriage and its variations elsewhere in the Arab region, see www.sexandthecitadel.com.

39. El Tawila and Khadr, *Patterns of Marriage and Family Formation Among Youth in Egypt*, p. 88.

40. Al-Kordy, *Al-Zawaj al-'Urfi fi al-Sirr* [Secret *'urfi* marriage], p. 181.

41. M. A. S. Abdel Haleem, personal communication, 2012.

42. Hasso, *Consuming Desires*, pp. 1–2.

43. Al-Sayed, "Mufti of Egypt: Misyar legally permissible and not an affront to women." For more on *misyar* marriage in the Arab region, see Hasso, *Consuming Desires.*

44. Population Council and IDSC, *Survey of Young People in Egypt.*

45. The sexual problems of Moroccan wives, and their husbands, are discussed in Chabach, *Le Couple Arabe* [The Arab couple]. For more on emerging research on married women elsewhere in the Arab region, see www.sexandthecitadel.com.

46. Farah, *Marriage and Sexuality in Islam*, p. 106. For more on female sexual prerogative in the pre-Islamic period, the role of women in early Islamic society, and modern calls to revive some of these early features, see Al-Munajjid, *Al-Hayat al-Jinsiyya 'ind al-'Arab* [The sexual life of the Arabs], pp. 15–25; Mernissi, *Beyond the Veil*, pp. 77–98; Ahmed, *Women and Gender in Islam*, pp. 41–63; and www.sexandthecitadel.com.

47. Daniel, *Islam and the West*, p. 93. For modern-day successors to this early Christian condemnation of Islamic sexual mores, see www.sexandthecitadel.com.

48. Elnashar et al., "Female Sexual Dysfunction in Lower Egypt."

49. Hassanin et al., "Prevalence and Characteristics of Female Sexual Dysfunction in a Sample of Women from Upper Egypt."

50. For more on this line of argument, see El-Mouelhy, Fahmy, and Ragab, *Investigating Women's Sexuality in Relation to Female Genital Mutilation in Egypt*, as detailed in chapter 3.

51. Kotb, "Sexuality in Islam." For more on Egyptian law on adultery, including the differing burdens of proof and penalties for husbands and wives, see Abu Komsan, *Egypt Violence Against Women Study:Violence Against Women and the Law*; and www.sexandthecitadel.com.

52. 'Ali ibn Nasr al-Katib, *Encyclopedia of Pleasure*, p. 23. For an overview of the history of Arabic erotic literature, including a summary of the *Encyclopedia*, see Rowson, "Arabic: Middle Ages to Nineteenth Century."

53. Examples of such frank female advice can be found at www.sexand thecitadel.com.

54. Qur'an 12:23–34.

55. 'Ali ibn Nasr al-Katib, *Encyclopedia of Pleasure*, p. 245.

56. For more on Arab women writers and their approach to sexuality, see www.sexandthecitadel.com.

57. Al-Nafzawi, "Al-Rawd al-'Atir" [The perfumed garden], p. 19.

58. Haddad, *Invitation to a Secret Feast*, p. 13.

59. Haddad, *I Killed Scheherezade*, pp. 33–34

60. Ibid., pp. 73–74.

61. Ibid., p. 74.

62. Ibid., p. 88.

63. Haddad, *Superman Is an Arab*, pp. 163–66.

64. Haddad, *I Killed Scheherazade*, p. 43.

65. For more on the appearance of sex toys in the history of Arabic erotic writing, see www.sexandthecitadel.com.

66. For more on sex during Ramadan, see Berrada et al., "Sexuality in the Month of Ramadan."

67. Tampon use remains rare in Egypt beyond a Westernized elite; its increase would be an interesting measure of socioeconomic change, though the United Nations might not be quite ready to use it as one of their standard indicators of "human development." For more on tampons and menstrual hygiene in Egypt, see World Health Organization Task Force on Psychosocial Research on Family Planning, "A Cross-Cultural Study on Menstruation"; El-Gilany, Badawi, and El-Fedawy, "Menstrual Hygiene Among Adolescent Schoolgirls"; and Yosri, *Mother-Daughter Communication About Sexual and Reproductive Health Matters*.

68. These and other fanciful creations are given their artistic due in Halasa and Salam, *The Secret Life of Syrian Lingerie*. For more on lingerie battles in Saudi Arabia, see www.sexandthecitadel.com.

69. Hull, *The Sheik*, p. 59. For more on the history of the desert romance, see Teo, *Desert Passion: Orientalism and Romance Novels*.

70. Sellers, "Sheikh's Honour," p. 145.

71. Taylor, "And You Can Be My Sheikh: Gender, Race and Orientalism in Contemporary Romance Novels," pp. 1043–47.

72. Kendrick, *Promised to the Sheikh*, p. 41.

73. Sabiq, *Fiqh al-Sunna* [Jurisprudence for Sunni Muslims], p. 245. For more on the issue of anal sex at the time of the Prophet Muhammad, see www.sexandthecitadel.com.

74. 'Ali ibn Nasr al-Katib, *Encyclopedia of Pleasure*, p. 240.

75. Qur'an 2:223.
76. See Alami, "Le Comportement Sexuel de la Femme" [Female sexual behavior], p. 69; and Haffani and Troudi, *La Sexualité des Hommes Tunisiens* [Sexuality of Tunisian men].
77. Ayman Zohry, personal communication, 2012.
78. For more on tough times for foreign domestic workers across the Arab region, see Human Rights Watch, *Slow Reform: Protection of Migrant Domestic Workers*; and Jureidini, *Domestic Workers in the Middle East.*
79. Qur'an 2:222.
80. Ali, *Planning the Family in Egypt*, p. 130.
81. Kotb, "Sexuality in Islam."
82. Al-Magribi, *A Jaunt in the Art of Coition*, p. 129.
83. For two excellent examples of this emerging field, see Dialmy, *Vers une Nouvelle Masculinité au Maroc* [Toward a new masculinity in Morocco]; and Inhorn, *The New Arab Man.*
84. El-Sakka, "Erectile Dysfunction in Arab Countries, Part I," p. 1.
85. Sengers, *Women and Demons: Cult Healing in Islamic Egypt*, p. 261.
86. Badran et al., "Etiological Factors of Unconsummated Marriage"; and Shamloul, "Management of Honeymoon Impotence."
87. In the region, honeymoon impotence is not a uniquely Muslim phenomenon. For sexual stage fright among Orthodox Jews in Israel, see Shalev, Baum, and Itzhaki, " 'There's a Man in My Bed.' "
88. The Thursday night special is deeply rooted in Egyptian Islamic culture. According to sunna—the words and deeds of the Prophet Muhammad— believers should thoroughly cleanse their bodies after sex, a process called *tatahhur*. Sunna also obliges Muslims to perform *ghusl al-jumu'a*— a thorough wash before turning up to the mosque for Friday prayers. Ever-canny Egyptians developed the custom of having sex on a Thursday night, thereby combining two washes in one, a highly practical measure in places where bathing facilities are scarce. It is for this same reason that Thursday nights are a popular slot for weddings in Egypt.
89. Ibn Qayyim al-Jawziyah, *Medicine of the Prophet*. For more entertaining advice on how to maintain male prowess, see arguably the most famous book of Arabic erotica, al-Tifashi, *Ruju' al-Shaykh ila Sibah* [The old man's return to his youth].
90. Qur'an 16:69.
91. El-Zanaty and Way, *Egypt: Demographic and Health Survey 2008*, p. 68.
92. Population Council and IDSC, *Survey of Young People in Egypt*. For more on shifting fertility in Egypt and the wider Arab world, see www.sexand thecitadel.com.
93. Inhorn, "Middle Eastern Masculinities in the Age of New Reproductive Technologies," p. 166.
94. For more on *Noor*-mania, and how Turkish soap operas are shaping women's romantic expectations in the region, see Salamandra, "The Muhammad Effect: Media Panic, Melodrama, and the Arab Female Gaze."
95. Inhorn, "Masturbation, Semen Collection, and Men's IVF Experiences," p. 42.
96. Qur'an 23:5–8.
97. Musallam, *Sex and Society in Islam,* p. 33.

98. Inhorn, "Masturbation, Semen Collection, and Men's IVF Experiences," p. 41.
99. Chebel, *Encyclopédie de l'Amour en Islam* [Encyclopedia of love in Islam], vol. 2, p. 85.
100. For traditional methods of circumventing such restrictions, see www.sex andthecitadel.com.
101. The line taken by Shi'i authorities on assisted reproduction, and their own differences of opinion on this topic, are discussed in Inhorn, "Making Muslim Babies: IVF and Gamete Donation in Sunni versus Shi'a Islam"; and Clarke, "Kinship, Propriety and Assisted Reproduction in the Middle East."
102. For more facts and figures on domestic abuse, including sexual violence in Egypt and across the Arab region, see www.sexandthecitadel.com.
103. These figures fall dramatically with wealth and education; for more details, see El-Zanaty and Way, *Egypt: Demographic and Health Survey 2008*, p. 43.
104. Population Council and IDSC, *Survey of Young People in Egypt*.
105. Qur'an 4:34.
106. Alternative interpretations of this verse are discussed in Ammar, "Wife Battery in Islam."
107. For a thorough assessment of the strengths and weaknesses of Egypt's response to domestic violence, see Said et al., *Egypt Violence Against Women Study: Overview of Services on Violence Against Women.*
108. Such trade-offs are explored in Yount, "Women's Conformity as Resistance to Intimate Partner Violence."
109. In a number of countries across the Arab region, rape can be grounds for marriage, allowing assailants to escape criminal sanction if they marry their victims. In Morocco, the recent suicide of one such wife sparked a fierce debate around the practice, as well as raising broader questions about gender and sexuality in the country (Mamarbachi, "Moroccan Women Demand Reform After Rape Victim's Suicide").
110. For more on where divorce rates are rising—the Gulf—and what is driving them, see www.sexandthecitadel.com.
111. Osman and Girgis, "Marriage Patterns in Egypt," pp. 23–25; and www .capmas.gov.eg.
112. For more on historical trends in Egyptian divorce, and why they diverge from Western patterns, see Fargues, "Terminating Marriage"; and Cuno, "Divorce and the Fate of the Family in Modern Egypt."
113. For more on young Egyptians' attitudes toward divorce, see www.sexand thecitadel.com.
114. Divorce is highly restricted for Egypt's Coptic Christians, and a source of considerable debate within the church. These struggles are discussed in Bishay, "Till Death (or Conversion) Do Us Part."
115. For more on debates over the Islamic basis of *khul'*, see Sonneveld, *Khul' Divorce in Egypt.*
116. Sholkamy, "Women Are Also Part of This Revolution," p. 170.

### 3. Sex and the Single Arab

1. Dhillon and Yousef, *Generation in Waiting: The Unfulfilled Promise of Young People in the Middle East*, p. 11. The youth bulge in the Arab region

is set to slim down over the coming decades, thanks to falling fertility rates (Courbage, "The Demographic Youth Bulge and Social Rupture").

2. Qur'an 24:33.

3. "Kitab al-Nikah" [Book of marriage], Book 8, Number 3231.

4. For more on laws across the region that can, if applied, put a damper on premarital sex, see www.sexandthecitadel.com.

5. The hard-knock lives of Egyptian street kids are detailed in Nada, Suliman and Zibani, *Behavioral Survey Among Street Children*.

6. For details of these and other studies of youth sexual behavior across the Arab region, see www.sexandthecitadel.com.

7. Nationally, Internet use is low among Egypt youth: less than 10 percent of men, and 5 percent of women under twenty-nine are online. But these countrywide averages mask vast differences, access being dramatically higher among the wealthiest, most educated, and urban youth of both sexes (Population Council and IDSC, *Survey of Young People in Egypt*).

8. Rakha, *The Poison Tree: Planted and Grown in Egypt*, pp. 138–45.

9. Population Council and IDSC, *Survey of Young People in Egypt*.

10. For more on the etiquette of phone flirtation, and government efforts to clamp down on sexed-up calls and texts, see www.sexandthecitadel.com.

11. Those aged fifteen to twenty-nine account for 70 percent of Facebook users across the Arab region; this number has almost tripled since June 2010, before the Arab uprisings. (Salem and Mourtada, "Social Media in the Arab World," p. 7)

12. See "Nude Art," http://www.arebelsdiary.blogspot.co.uk/2011_10_01_archive.html.

13. Fahmy, "Egyptian Blogger Aliaa Elmahdy. Why I Posed Naked."

14. Kobeissi and Suleiman, "Egypt Youth Movement Denies Ties with Girl in Nude Self-Portrait."

15. "Citizen censorship" can take many forms in Egypt. For more on a legal provision called *hisba*, which allows ordinary citizens to bring cases in pursuit of their Islamic duty to "promote good and forbid evil," see www.sexandthecitadel.com.

16. Ammar, "Legal Action Taken Against Egypt 'Nude Revolutionary' Activist."

17. For more on this illuminating episode, see www.sexandthecitadel.com.

18. Bucking global trends, in the Arab region men outnumber women on Facebook by two to one (Salem et al., "The Role of Social Media in Women's Empowerment," p. 2).

19. For more on Morocco, see Axétudes, *Enquête Connaissances, Attitudes et Pratiques des Jeunes* [Study of the knowledge, attitudes and practices of youth], p. 49; for Algeria, see Toudeft, *Étude sur les Connaissances, Attitudes et Comportements des Jeunes Universitaires* [Study of the knowledge, attitudes and behaviors of university students], p. 25; and for Tunisia, see Ben Abdallah, *Enquête Nationale sur les Comportements à Risque Auprès des Jeunes Non-scolarisés en Tunisie* [National study of risk behaviors among out-of-school youth in Tunisia], pp. 66–67.

20. Other countries in the Arab region have their own rituals and customs to preserve virginity. For more on the tradition of *tasfih* in Tunisia, see Ben Dridi, *Le Tasfih en Tunisie* [*Tasfih* in Tunisia]. For a discussion of

*r'bit* in Algeria, see Ferhati, "Les Clôtures Symboliques des Algériennes" [Symbolic closures of Algerian women]; and Moussa, Masmoudi, and Barboucha, "Du Tabou de la Virginité au Mythe de l'Inviolabilité" [From the taboo of virginity to the myth of inviolability].

21. Cohen, "Why Aren't Jewish Women Circumcised?", pp. 138–39.

22. El-Zanaty and Way, *Egypt: Demographic and Health Survey 2008*, p. 197. For more on female circumcision elsewhere in the Arab region, see www.sexandthecitadel.com.

23. The various types of female circumcision are detailed in World Health Organization, Department of Reproductive Health and Research, *Eliminating Female Genital Mutilation.*

24. For more firsthand accounts of female circumcision across the generations in Egypt, see El-Mouelhy, Fahmy, and Ragab, *Investigating Women's Sexuality in Relation to Female Genital Mutilation in Egypt.*

25. El-Zanaty and Way, *Egypt: Demographic and Health Survey 2008*, p. 201.

26. For more on the fallout from the CNN broadcast, which raised hackles across Egypt, and its complex intersection with Arab-American geopolitics, see Malmström, "Just Like Couscous: Gender, Agency and the Politics of Female Circumcision in Cairo," pp. 33–66.

27. See Mostafa et al., "What Do Medical Students in Alexandria Know About Female Genital Mutilation?"; and Rasheed, Abd-Ellah, and Yousef, "Female Genital Mutilation in Upper Egypt."

28. In 1994 Gad al-Haq Ali, then head of Al-Azhar, issued a fatwa stating: "Female circumcision is a part of the legal body of Islam and is a laudable practice that does honor to the women." For more on this, and other religious pronouncements on FGM, see Gruenbaum, *The Female Circumcision Controversy*, pp. 62–66.

29. Moussa, "Coptic Religion and Female Genital Mutilation," p. 24. The differential success of efforts to eliminate FGM among Christians and Muslims are discussed in Yount, "Symbolic Gender Politics, Religious Group Identity, and the Decline in Female Genital Cutting."

30. Population Council and IDSC, *Survey of Young People in Egypt.*

31. The Grand Mufti's comments on FGM are available at www.aligomaa.net /initiatives.html.

32. Population Council and IDSC, *Survey of Young People in Egypt.* A revealing study of the challenges in convincing local Muslim religious leaders to change their private beliefs and public pronouncements on FGM can be found in El-Gibaly, Attar, and Fahmy, "Is Change in the Attitude of Rural Imams Toward FGC [Female Genital Cutting] Happening?"

33. United Nations Population Fund Cairo, personal communication, 2009.

34. El-Zanaty and Way, *Egypt: Demographic and Health Survey 2008*, pp. 204–06.

35. El-Mouelhy, Fahmy, and Ragab, *Investigating Women's Sexuality in Relation to Female Genital Mutilation in Egypt*, p. 15.

36. El Sayed, "Medical and Ethical Perspectives," p. 27.

37. Those interested in the nitty-gritty results of this research should visit www.sexandthecitadel.com for a full discussion.

38. El-Mouelhy, Fahmy, and Ragab, *Investigating Women's Sexuality in Relation to Female Genital Mutilation in Egypt*, p. 16.

39. Ibid., p. 21.

40. Fahmy, El-Mouelhy, and Ragab, "Female Genital Mutilation/Cutting," p. 184.
41. El-Mouelhy, Fahmy, and Ragab, *Investigating Women's Sexuality in Relation to Female Genital Mutilation in Egypt*, p. 23.
42. Ibid., p. 28.
43. Malmström, "Just Like Couscous."
44. El-Zanaty and Way, *Egypt: Demographic and Health Survey 2008*, p.197; Harbour and Barsoum, "Health," p. 44.
45. Population Council and IDSC, *Survey of Young People in Egypt*; and Tag-Eldin et al., "Prevalence of Female Genital Cutting Among Egyptian Girls."
46. El-Zanaty and Way, *Egypt: Demographic and Health Survey 2008*, pp. 202–04.
47. Ibid., p. 199.
48. "Egypt parliamentarians and advocates attacking the government because of the 'Chinese membrane' "; and Najjar, "China promotes synthetic hymens in Egypt."
49. "She guarded her chastity, so We breathed into her from Our spirit" (Qur'an 66:12).
50. Qur'an 55:56. For more on the age-old debate over sex in paradise, see www.sexandthecitadel.com.
51. Juynboll, *Encyclopedia of Canonical Hadith*, p. 496.
52. For more details on opinions toward premarital sex across the Arab region, see www.sexandthecitadel.com.
53. *Dukhla baladi* as a social compromise is discussed in further detail in El-Kholy, *Defiance and Compliance: Negotiating Gender in Low-Income Cairo*.
54. El-Mouelhy, Fahmy, and Ragab, *Investigating Women's Sexuality in Relation to Female Genital Mutilation in Egypt*.
55. My thanks to Hinda Poulin for sharing her preliminary findings on hymen repair in Egypt.
56. For more on religious arguments for and against hymen repair, see Rispler-Chaim "The Muslim Surgeon and Contemporary Ethical Dilemmas Surrounding the Restoration of Virginity."
57. Eich, "A Tiny Membrane Defending 'Us' Against 'Them' "; and Gomaa, "Fatwa Number 416: Hymen Restoration Surgery."
58. Hinda Poulin, personal communication, 2009.
59. For a rare pocket of resistance to premarital testing in the region, see Boutros and Bahgat, "Sexual Health and Human Rights: Middle East and North Africa."
60. Shalhoub-Kevorkian, "Imposition of Virginity Testing: A Life-Saver or a License to Kill?"
61. For more on how ideas about Arab sexuality became weapons in the war on terror, see Hersh, "The Gray Zone"; and Patai, *The Arab Mind*, pp. 126–51.
62. Amnesty International, "Egyptian Women Protesters Forced to Take 'Virginity Tests' "; and Human Rights Watch, *Egypt: Impunity for Violence Against Women*.
63. See www.marwarakha.com.
64. Population Council and IDSC, *Survey of Young People in Egypt*.

65. For more on youth and *wasta*, see Silatech and Gallup, *The Silatech Index*, 2009.

66. Qur'an 31:14.

67. See Harb, *Describing the Lebanese Youth: A National and Psycho-Social Survey*; Farhood, "Family, Culture and Decisions"; and Dwairy et al., "Adolescent-Family Connectedness Among Arabs." See also the World Values Survey at www.worldvaluessurvey.org.

68. Osman et al., *Ta'khkhur Sinn al-Zawaj* [Delay in the age of marriage], p. 8.

69. In contrast, just over a third of young women in rural areas reported being harassed. It is possible that rural settings, with stronger community ties and traditions, keep sexual harassment in check; it is also possible that rural women are less likely to report the phenomenon than are their urban counterparts (Population Council and IDSC, *Survey of Young People in Egypt*).

70. For a male perspective on sexual harassment, see Schielke, "Ambivalent Commitments: Troubles of Morality, Religiosity and Aspiration Among Young Egyptians."

71. U.S. Department of State, *Egypt: Country-Specific Information*.

72. Hassan, *Clouds in Egypt's Sky: Sexual Harassment from Verbal Harassment to Rape*.

73. El-Kogali, Krafft, and Sieverding, "Attitudes Toward Gender Roles," p. 167.

74. An overwhelming majority of young Egyptian women said that personal choice, rather than direct parental or peer pressure, motivated them to wear hijabs. However, they drew the line at niqabs, with only 5 percent opting for a full-face cover (El-Kogali and Krafft, "Social Issues, Values and Civic Engagement," p. 135).

75. Harbour and Barsoum, "Health," pp. 24–25.

76. Hassan, *Clouds in Egypt's Sky*.

77. For more on creative attempts to tackle sexual harassment, see www.harassmap.org and www.ecwr.org.

78. Amar, "Turning the Gendered Politics of the Security State Inside Out?"

79. For more on honor killings across the Arab region, see Kulczycki and Windle, "Honor Killings in the Middle East and North Africa." For weaknesses in the law covering honor crimes and related "crimes of passion" in Egypt, see Abu Komsan, *Egypt Violence Against Women Study: Violence Against Women and the Law*; and for the situation across the Arab region, see Welchman and Hossain, *"Honour": Crimes, Paradigms and Violence Against Women*.

### 4. Facts of Life

1. For more on masturbation across the Arab region, past and present, see www.sexandthecitadel.com.

2. Other innovative uses of technology to communicate the facts of life across the Arab region can be found at www.sexandthecitadel.com.

3. Krafft and El-Kogali, "Education"; and Silatech and Gallup, *The Silatech Index*, 2011.

4. For more on the high drama of teaching sex in the classroom, see www.sexandthecitadel.com.

5. On a countrywide level, less than 15 percent of boys and 5 percent of girls

in Egypt said they learned the facts of life from school (Harbour and Barsoum, "Health," p. 39). For more on where young people elsewhere in the Arab region are learning about sex, see www.sexandthecitadel.com.

6. International conventions and agreements covering sexuality education are discussed in UNESCO, *International Technical Guidance on Sexuality Education*, pp. 30–33.

7. For more on historical debates over sexual education in Egypt, see Jacob, "Overcoming 'Simply Being': Straight Sex, Masculinity and Physical Culture in Modern Egypt."

8. For more details on whom young people talk to about love and sex, see www.sexandthecitadel.com.

9. More information on tongue-tied parents and the facts of life is available at www.sexandthecitadel.com.

10. Population Council and IDSC, *Survey of Young People in Egypt*.

11. For more on the making, watching, and sharing of porn in Egypt, see Leonard, "Of Masculinity and Men: Exploring Ambivalence, Pornographic Consumption and Sexual Desire in Cairo."

12. The long view on Egyptian cinema and its treatment of women and their sexuality is presented in Shafik, *Popular Egyptian Cinema: Gender, Class, and Nation*, pp. 119–238.

13. For a discussion of the rise of "clean cinema," see Tartoussieh, "Pious Stardom: Cinema and the Religious Revival in Egypt."

14. Ezzat, Zain al-'Abidine, and Mubarak, *Taqriir Hurriyya al-Fikra wa-l-Ibda' fi Misr* [Report on freedom of thought and creativity in Egypt], pp. 20–25.

15. For some spectacular examples of censorship through subtitling, visit www.sexandthecitadel.com.

16. A few examples of Arabic's rich repertoire of sexual insult, past and present, can be found at www.sexandthecitadel.com.

17. Geel, "Improving Adolescents' and Youth Reproductive Health in Egypt."

18. Wahba and Roudi-Fahimi, *The Need for Reproductive Health Education in Schools in Egypt*.

19. UNESCO, *International Technical Guidance on Sexuality Education*. One country in the Arab region well on its way to a comprehensive sexuality curriculum is Lebanon; for more on the challenges of this lengthy and complex process, see Baydoun, "Sex Education in Lebanon"; and www.sexandthecitadel.com.

20. For more on Muntada Jensaneya, visit the forum's website at www.jensaneya.org.

21. Flaherty, "Reconstructing Sexuality and Identity Through Dialogue: The Muntada's Actions for Palestinian Arab Citizens of Israel," p. 165.

22. Ibid., p. 159.

23. In Arabic, this book is known as *Kitab al-Nikah fi al-Lugha*, by Ibn Al Qatta' (as detailed in Al-Munajjid, *Al-Hayat al-Jinsiyya 'ind al-'Arab* [The sexual life of the Arabs]), p. 142.

24. For some of the more remarkable misconceptions in Egypt regarding contraception, even after decades of widely publicized family planning campaigns, see www.sexandthecitadel.com.

25. Omran, *Family Planning in the Legacy of Islam*, pp. 85–112.

26. The grounds for contraception in Islam are discussed in detail in Musallam, *Sex and Society in Islam*.

27. El-Zanaty and Way, *Egypt: Demographic and Health Survey 2008*, p. 93.
28. There is little published research on how much unmarried Egyptians understand or use contraception; for more on use by young people elsewhere in the Arab region see www.sexandthecitadel.com.
29. El-Zanaty and Way, *Egypt: Demographic and Health Survey 2008*, p. 93.
30. There is a debate as to whether condom use abrogates the need for ablutions after sexual intercourse. Some religious authorities argue that if there is a barrier (such as a condom), the male and female "parts" do not technically come in contact, and therefore washing is not required; others maintain that condom or not, it's penetration all the same, and therefore ablutions are necessary. For more on these varying opinions, see "Islam QA," http://islamqa.info/en/ref/37031. Showers and hairdos aside, many Egyptian wives I know dislike condoms and complain (as do their husbands) that they reduce their own sexual pleasure.
31. For more on condom use and sex outside of marriage in Egypt and elsewhere in the Arab region, see www.sexandthecitadel.com.
32. For a comprehensive review of the epidemiology of sexually transmitted infections in the Arab region and what this says about sexual behavior, see Abu-Raddad et al., *Characterizing the HIV/AIDS Epidemic in the Middle East and North Africa*, pp. 151–69.
33. The predicament of HIV-positive women in the Arab region is explored in El Feki, *Standing Up, Speaking Out*.
34. Asman, "Abortion in Islamic Countries—Legal and Religious Aspects," pp. 85–87. Second-trimester abortion is also available in Tunisia, but on more restricted grounds, such as risk to the mother's health or fetal abnormalities, because of the greater clinical risks associated with a later-stage procedure.
35. For more on the difficulties faced by young people turning up at Egypt's three dozen or so public clinics for youth sexual and reproductive health, see El-Damanhoury, *Exploratory Study of Attitudes and Communication Behaviors of Providers in Youth Friendly Clinics in Egypt*.
36. Selma Hajri, personal communication, 2012; Blum et al., "The Medical Abortion Experience of Married and Unmarried Women in Tunis"; and Bouchlaka, Bouaziz, and Smida, "Profil des Femmes Célibataires Bénéficiaires d'IVG dans les Structures de l'ONFP" [Profile of unmarried women using ONFP abortion facilities].
37. "Do not kill your children for fear of poverty. We shall provide for them and for you—killing them is a great sin." Qur'an 17:31.
38. Qur'an 23:12–14.
39. The extensive Islamic discourse on abortion can be found in Bowen, "Contemporary Muslim Ethics of Abortion"; and Katz, "The Problem of Abortion in Classical Sunni *Fiqh*."
40. Huntington, "Abortion in Egypt: Official Constraints and Popular Practices," p. 180.
41. For more on Egypt's abortion laws, see Lane, Jok, and El-Mouelhy, "Buying Safety: The Economics of Reproductive Risk and Abortion in Egypt"; and Asman, "Abortion in Islamic Countries—Legal and Religious Aspects."
42. For more on medical work-arounds and restrictions on abortion, see www.sexandthecitadel.com.
43. A selection of prescriptions can be found at www.sexandthecitadel.com.

44. El-Damanhoury, *Why Do Women Abort? The Determinants of Induced Abortion in Egypt.*

45. A comprehensive discussion of abortion laws in the Arab region is available in Hessini, "Abortion and Islam: Policies and Practice in the Middle East and North Africa"; and Hessini, "Islam and Abortion: The Diversity of Discourses and Practices."

46. Dabash and Roudi-Fahimi, *Abortion in the Middle East and North Africa*, p. 2.

47. El-Mouelhy, "Maternal Mortality in the Last Two Decades in Egypt."

48. Because of the way UN agencies divide the world into regions, this figure includes several non-Arab states: Armenia, Azerbaijan, Cyprus, Georgia, Israel, and Turkey (World Health Organization, *Unsafe Abortion: Global and Regional Estimates*, p. 19).

49. For more on such trade-offs, see Kandiyoti, "Bargaining with Patriarchy."

50. See AMPF (Association Marocaine de Planification Familiale), *Étude Exploratoire de l'Avortement à Risque* [Exploratory study of risky abortion], for further details on the scale of abortion in Morocco.

51. For more on the legal process that applies to abandoned children in Egypt, see Thomason, "On the Steps of the Mosque."

52. See World Values Survey at www.worldvaluessurvey.org.

53. Loza and Social, Planning, Analysis, and Administration Consultants, "Experiences, Attitudes, and Practices: A New Survey of 4,408 Women, Men, and Female and Male Youth," p. 31.

54. For more on the Islamic stance on adoption, see www.sexandthecitadel.com.

55. For more on "Girls of Agadir," an infamous porn CD, visit www.sexandthecitadel.com.

56. Moving accounts of the lives of unmarried mothers, and the organizations that are trying to help them, can be found in Naamane Guessous and Guessous, *Grossesses de la Honte* [Shameful pregnancies].

57. According to a study by INSAF (Institution Nationale de Solidarité avec les Femmes en Détresse) and UN Women, unmarried mothers accounted for roughly 4 percent of all recorded deliveries in Morocco in 2009 (INSAF, *Le Maroc des Mères Célibataires* [Unmarried mothers in Morocco], pp. 109–19).

58. For more on the official obstacles facing unmarried mothers, see Willman Bordat and Kouzzi, "Legal Empowerment of Unwed Mothers: Experiences of Moroccan NGOs."

59. Karam, "Moroccan Single Burns Herself in Protest."

60. My thanks to Jamila Bargach for bringing this aspect of SolFem's public positioning to my attention.

## 5. Sex for Sale

1. For more on a recent attempt to revive this practice in Egypt, see Suleiman, "First case of 'what your right hand possesses' marriage."

2. Ali, *Sexual Ethics and Islam: Feminist Reflections on Qur'an, Hadith, and Jurisprudence*, pp. 56–74.

3. Laws covering sex work in Egypt are detailed in Al-Kardousi and Mag-

doub, *Darasa li-Shabakat al-Bagha' fi Misr* [Study of prostitution networks in Egypt].

4. Oyoun Center for Studies and Development, *Modern Slavery: Tourist Marriages in Egypt,* pp. 62–66.

5. Sieverding and Elbadawy, "Marriage and Family Formation," p. 119.

6. Human Rights Watch, *How Come You Allow Little Girls to Get Married? Child Marriage in Yemen.*

7. "Fatwa of the Grand Mufti of the Republic Dr Ali Gomaa with regard to child marriage."

8. *Trafficking in Persons Report 2012*, p. 146. For more on sex trafficking elsewhere in the Arab region, including such hot spots as Iraq, see www.sexandthecitadel.com.

9. Cairo outreach worker, personal communication, 2012.

10. Cumming, *The Love Quest: A Sexual Odyssey*, p. 144.

11. "355% increase in marriages between Egyptians and foreign women."

12. Abdalla, *Beach Politics: Gender and Sexuality in Dahab*, p. 140.

13. Ibid., pp. 61–62.

14. For these and other sad stories, see www.1001geschichte.de.

15. See www.cibev.de.

16. An interesting account of reactions to Western brides elsewhere in the Arab region can be found in Cauvin Verner, "De Tourisme Culturel au Tourisme Sexuel" [From cultural tourism to sexual tourism].

17. Madkur, "Inas al-Delgheidy talks about a campaign against her for asking for the legalization of prostitution in Egypt."

18. Russell, *Egyptian Service, 1902–1946*, p. 179.

19. The colorful history of prostitution in Cairo is detailed in Bakr, *Al-Mujtama' al-Qahira al-Sirri* [Secret Cairo society].

20. Larguèche and Larguèche, *Marginales en Terre d'Islam* [Women on the edge in the land of Islam], p. 31.

21. Taraud, *La Prostitution Coloniale* [Colonial prostitution], p. 321.

22. For more on this history, see Snoussi, "La Prostitution en Tunisie au Temps de la Colonisation" [Prostitution in Tunisia in the colonial period].

23. For more on the gray area of legal sex work in other Arab countries, among them Algeria and Lebanon, see www.sexandthecitadel.com.

24. Abid and Ghorbel, *Enquête sur l'Utilisation du Préservatif Auprès des Jeunes Clients des Professionelles du Sexe Declarées* [Study of condom use among young clients of registered sex workers], p. 11.

25. Znazen et al., "Sexually Transmitted Infections Among Female Sex Workers in Tunisia," p. 501.

26. The violence and other occupational hazards of Tunisia's clandestine sex workers are detailed in Ben Abdallah, *Enquête Comportementale sur les Travailleuses du Sexe Clandestines en Tunisie* [Behavioral study of illegal sex workers in Tunisia].

27. For a fascinating account of life as a legal sex worker in the 1940s and '50s, and how little conditions have changed since then, see Aziz, *Les Chambres Closes* [Brothel rooms].

28. Ben Abdallah, *Enquête Nationale sur les Comportements à Risque Auprès des Jeunes Non-scolarisés en Tunisie* [National study of risk behaviors among out-of-school youth in Tunisia], pp. 67–69.

29. For more details on the challenging lives of Cairo sex workers, see Al-Zahid, *Tijarat al-Jins* [Sex trade].

30. A 2010 survey in Cairo found no HIV in the two hundred female sex workers it tested, but experts note that because of limitations in testing, rates may well be higher (Family Health International and Ministry of Health Egypt, *HIV/AIDS Biological and Behavioral Surveillance Survey*, p. 31). Elsewhere in the Arab region, HIV infection rates among female sex workers are generally running between 1 and 5 percent, although these are much higher in particular regions in a number of countries (Abu-Raddad et al., *Characterizing the HIV/AIDS Epidemic in the Middle East and North Africa*). For the latest statistics, see www.sexandthecitadel.com.

31. Family Health International and Ministry of Health Egypt, *HIV/AIDS Biological and Behavioral Surveillance Survey*, p. 11. More details on condom use by, and risk behaviors among, sex workers in selected countries across the Arab region can be found in Abu-Raddad et al., *Characterizing the HIV/AIDS Epidemic in the Middle East and North Africa*; and at www.sexandthecitadel.com.

32. About 40 percent of Moroccans eligible for antiretroviral treatment are actually getting their medicine (Royaume du Maroc [Kingdom of Morocco], *Mise en Oeuvre de la Déclaration Politique sur le VIH/SIDA* [Implementation of the political declaration of commitment to HIV/AIDS], p. 12), compared to a regional average of about 13 percent (UNAIDS, *Together We Will End AIDS*, p. 23).

33. Akalay and Mrabet, "Investigation. Moroccan women as seen by the Arabs."

34. Dialmy, "Prostitution et Traite des Femmes au Maroc" [Prostitution and the trade in women in Morocco].

35. For a detailed survey of the many shades of sex work in Morocco, see Ettoussi and Jebbour, *Les Travailleuses du Sexe et les IST/SIDA* [Sex workers and STIs/AIDS]; and ALCS (Association pour la Lutte Contre le SIDA), *Surveillance des Comportements à Risque: Le Cas des Professionnelles du Sexe* [Surveillance of risk behaviors: The case of commercial sex workers].

36. For an excellent study of sex work in Morocco's commercial capital, see Benito, *La Prostitution dans les Rues de Casablanca* [Prostitution in the streets of Casablanca].

37. Axétudes, *Enquete Connaissances, Attitudes et Pratiques des Jeunes Concernant les IST et le SIDA* [Study of the knowledge, attitudes and behavior of youth in relation to STIs and AIDS], p. 60.

38. The upshot is that Morocco's sex workers have among the highest rates of HIV infection in the country, up to 6 percent in some regions compared with less than 0.2 percent for the general population (Royaume du Maroc, *Mise en Oeuvre de la Déclaration Politique sur le VIH/SIDA* [Implementation of the political declaration of commitment to HIV/AIDS], p. 15).

### 6. Dare to Be Different

1. For the story behind this proverb, which is the punch line to a famous tale in Egyptian folklore, see www.sexandthecitadel.com.

2. Massad, "Re-Orienting Desire: The Gay International and the Arab World," pp. 383–84.

3. Massad, *Desiring Arabs*, p. 189.

4. For an excellent and detailed study of male sex workers in Egypt, see Orhan, "Men Selling Sex in Cairo and Alexandria."

5. Human Rights Watch, *In a Time of Torture: The Assault on Justice in Egypt's Crackdown on Homosexual Conduct*.

6. Laws covering same-sex relations in the Arab region are discussed in detail in Al Farchichi and Saghiyeh, *Homosexual Relations in the Penal Codes*.

7. For more on the episode Munir is referring to, which raised an international outcry at the arrest, detention, forced medical testing, and conviction of HIV-positive men in Cairo, see Human Rights Watch, *Egypt: 117 NGOs Slam HIV-Based Arrests and Trials*.

8. Egypt's love affair with anal exams is detailed in Human Rights Watch, *In a Time of Torture*. On their dubious forensic value, see Al Farchichi and Saghiyeh, *Homosexual Relations in the Penal Codes*; and for pushback in Lebanon, see 'Ilwah, "Civil society wins: Abolition of 'tests of shame.' "

9. For more on state-sanctioned and community violence against men who fail to fit the heterosexual mold, including its murderous extremes in postwar Iraq, see www.sexandthecitadel.com.

10. El-Rouayheb, *Before Homosexuality in the Arab-Islamic World: 1500–1800*, pp. 158–59.

11. My thanks to Daniel Newman for sharing material from his forthcoming translation of Al-Tifashi, *Sensual Delights of the Heart*.

12. For more on young men's shifting attitudes toward active and passive sex roles, see www.sexandthecitadel.com.

13. The detail and tone of Arabic writing on same-sex relations from the ninth to thirteenth centuries are remarkable, and so vast and varied as to be beyond the scope of this book. But many others have covered the field in admirable detail. For Arabic readers, Al-Munajjid, *Al-Hayat al-Jinsiyya 'ind al-'Arab* [The sexual life of the Arabs]; and Mahmud, *Al-Mut'a al-Mahzura* [The forbidden pleasure], offer an excellent introduction. In French, the collected works of the Algerian historian Malek Chebel provide an impressive overview; see Chebel, *Encyclopédie de l'Amour en Islam* [Encyclopedia of love in Islam]; and Chebel, *Le Kama-Sutra Arabe* [Arab Kama-Sutra]. And there is a wealth of writing in English, including Amer, *Crossing Borders: Love Between Women in Medieval French and Arabic Literatures*; Babayan and Najmabadi, *Islamicate Sexualities: Translations Across Temporal Geographies of Desire*; El-Rouayheb, *Before Homosexuality in the Arab-Islamic World*; Murray and Roscoe, *Islamic Homosexualities: Culture, History, and Literature*; and Wright and Rowson, *Homoeroticism in Classical Arabic Literature*.

14. For more on "pinkwashing," a term used by activists to describe what is seen as Israel's self-promotion as an island of tolerance for homosexual men and women in a sea of Arab homophobia, and its political implications for an emerging Palestinian state, see www.sexandthecitadel.com.

15. Mumtaz et al., "Are HIV Epidemics Among Men Who Have Sex with Men Emerging in the Middle East and North Africa?" p. 3.

16. Family Health International and Ministry of Health Egypt, *HIV/AIDS Biological and Behavioral Surveillance Survey*, pp. 13–21. Biological-behavioral surveillance surveys, which probe the risk behaviors and HIV vulnerability of men who have sex with men, have been conducted in a number of other countries in the Arab region, among them Jordan, Lebanon, Morocco, Sudan, Tunisia, and Yemen. Details are available at www.sexandthecitadel.com.

17. Wasfy, *Shifa' al-Hubb* [The cure is love], p. 73.

18. An assessment of such attempts to "reorient" sexual minorities through faith-based therapy is detailed in Jones and Yarhouse, "A Longitudinal Study of Attempted Religiously Mediated Sexual Orientation Change."

19. APA Task Force, *Report of the Task Force on Appropriate Therapeutic Responses to Sexual Orientation*; and American Psychiatric Association, "Position Statement on Therapies Focused on Attempts to Change Sexual Orientation."

20. Qur'an 11:77–83.

21. Qur'an 7:80–81.

22. Qur'an 4:15–16. My thanks to Everett Rowson for sharing his unpublished paper, "Straight or Gay? The Curious Exegetical History of Qur'an 4:15–16," explaining alternative readings of this verse through the ages.

23. Kugle, *Homosexuality in Islam*, p. 85.

24. Al-Qaradawi, *The Lawful and the Prohibited in Islam*, p. 165.

25. Ibid., p. 165.

26. Youssef, *Hayrat Muslima* [A Muslim woman's confusion], p. 225.

27. Ibid., p. 226.

28. Ibid., p. 226.

29. Qur'an 29:28–29.

30. Youssef, *Hayrat Muslima* [A Muslim woman's confusion], p. 189.

31. Ibid., p. 184.

32. Ibid., p. 226.

33. Sayed, "Al-Mithliyyun wa-l-Mithliyya fi al-Sinima al-Misriyya" [Homosexuals and homosexuality in Egyptian cinema], pp. 89–105.

34. For a look at homosexuality in Egyptian movies, past and present, see Hassan, "Real Queer Arabs: The Tension Between Colonialism and Homosexuality in Egyptian Cinema"; and Menicucci, "Unlocking the Arab Celluloid Closet: Homosexuality in Egyptian Film."

35. Suleiman, "Egyptian film about the life of deviants takes part in 'queer' world festival."

36. For more on alternative presentations of same-sex relations on-screen, see www.sexandthecitadel.com.

37. This shift in tone on homosexuality in the Arabic novel, and how it reflects broader social concerns, is detailed in Massad *Desiring Arabs*, pp. 269–334; Al-Samman, "Out of the Closet: Representation of Homosexuals and Lesbians in Modern Arabic Literature"; and Whitaker, *Unspeakable Love: Gay and Lesbian Life in the Middle East*, pp. 77–113.

38. Fathi, *The World of Boys: A True Story of Youth*, p. 45.

39. "A Forgotten Life," http://karimblog-karim.blogspot.com.

40. The pitfalls of the Internet, including false representation in Syria and entrapment in Egypt, are discussed in detail at www.sexandthecitadel.com.

41. *Bareed Mista3jil. True Stories* [Express mail], p. 35.
42. An excellent overview of the history of same-sex relations between women in Arabic literature is provided by Habib, *Female Homosexuality in the Middle East.*
43. Al-Tifashi, *Sensual Delights of the Heart,* trans. Newman.
44. Ibid.
45. For a detailed account of Meem's origins, and the role of the Internet in LGBT activism in Lebanon and the wider Arab world, see Moawad and Qiblawi, "Lebanon: Who's Afraid of the Big Bad Internet?"
46. Al Farchichi and Saghiyeh, *Homosexual Relations in the Penal Codes,* pp. 31–59.
47. For more on Helem, see Dabaghi, Mack, and Jaalouk, *Helem: A Case Study of the First Legal, Above-Ground LGBT Organization.*
48. Mikdashi and Moumneh, "The Emerging Discourse on Same-Sex Sexualities and Rights in Lebanon."
49. Jernow, *Sexual Orientation, Gender Identity and Justice*, p. 43.
50. For an analysis of the business of gay tourism in Lebanon, see McCormick, "Hairy Chest, Will Travel: Tourism, Identity, and Sexuality in the Levant."
51. For more on a similar health clinic in Marrakech, see Harri et al., "Expérience d'un Centre de Santé Sexuelle Destiné aux Hommes ayant des Relations Sexuelles avec des Hommes au Maroc" [Experience of a sexual health center for men who have sex with men in Morocco].
52. Al-Kak, *Homophobia in Clinical Services in Lebanon*, pp. 19–20.
53. Same-sex relations among Saudi women are a source of breathless fascination for many foreign writers. For the inside track from a young Saudi woman, see al-Herz, *The Others.*
54. For more on Randa's life, see Saghieh, *Mudhakarat Randa al-Trans* [Memoirs of Randa Trans].
55. Qur'an 92:1–4.
56. Rowson, "The Effeminates of Early Medina," p. 673.
57. For a discussion of the status of trans people in Islam, including alternative readings of scripture, see Kugle, *Homosexuality in Islam*, pp. 235–68.
58. For more on the plight of trans Kuwaitis, and what is driving such persecution, see Human Rights Watch, *"They Hunt Us Down for Fun": Discrimination and Police Violence Against Transgender Women in Kuwait.*
59. Al-Baghdadi, "The perverts . . . who are they?"
60. Fikri, "When Things get Topsy-Turvey: Foreign Youth Cultures Invade UAE Society." In Kuwait, a 2006 survey by the Scientific Committee of the National Conference on Negative Trends, a government body, found that *boyat* were the number one social concern of the six thousand citizens polled. For more on this trend in Kuwait, see Abdel Khalek, *Mushkila Adatarrab al-Hayat al-Jinsiyya lada al-Banat* [Gender identity disorder in girls].
61. Nigst and Garcia, "Boyat in the Gulf: Identity, Contestation, and Social Control," pp. 18–19.
62. Al-Zayyat, "Al-mar'a al-ghulamiyya" [Woman as ghulamiyya].
63. Sex change surgery in the Arab region is fleshed out at www.sexand thecitadel.com.
64. Qur'an 30:30.

65. For more on this fatwa, and the famous case that prompted it, see www
.sexandthecitadel.com.
66. Najmabadi, "Transing and Transpassing across Sex-Gender Walls in
Iran," p. 26.
67. Ding, Jennings, and Pan, *Employment Discrimination Against the Transgender Community in Lebanon: A Needs Assessment Report for Helem*,
pp. 4–14.
68. For more on efforts to link sexual rights advocates across the Arab and
wider Islamic world, see the Coalition for Sexual and Bodily Rights in
Muslim Societies at www.csbronline.org.
69. For more on the camp, go to www.mantiqitna.org.
70. Qur'an 49:12.
71. Al-Banna, *Jawaz Imamat al-Mar'a al-Rijal* [The permissibility of a woman
leading men in prayer], p. 107.

### 7. Come the Revolution

1. Giddens, *The Transformation of Intimacy: Sexuality, Love and Eroticism
in Modern Societies*.
2. Al-Zubaidi, *Mukhtasar Sahih al-Bukhari* [A summary of authentic hadith
according to al-Bukhari], p. 523.
3. Foucault, *The History of Sexuality*, vol. 1, *The Will to Knowledge*, p. 77.
4. Jones, *Alfred C. Kinsey: A Life*, p. 772.

# Bibliography

Abdalla, Mustafa. 2007. *Beach Politics: Gender and Sexuality in Dahab*. Cairo Papers in Social Science, vol. 27, no. 4. Cairo: American University in Cairo Press.

Abdel Khalek, Ahmed. 2010. *Mushkila Adatarrab al-Hayat al-Jinsiyya lada al-Banat* [Gender identity disorder in girls]. Kuwait: Kuwait University.

Abdulla, Fatma, and Natasha Ridge. 2011. *Where Are All the Men? Gender Participation and Higher Education in the United Arab Emirates*. Dubai: Dubai School of Government.

Abid, Faouzi, and Chafik Ghorbel. 2009. *Enquête sur l'Utilisation du Préservatif Auprès des Jeunes Clients des Professionelles du Sexe Declarées* [Study of condom use by young clients of registered sex workers]. Tunis: Ministère de la Santé Publique, ONFP.

Abu Komsan, Nehad. 2009. *Egypt Violence Against Women Study: Violence Against Women and the Law, A De Jure and De Facto Review of the Legal and Regulatory Structure*. Cairo: USAID and National Council for Women.

Abu-Raddad, Laith, Francesca Avodeji Akala, Iris Semini, Gabriele Riedner, David Wilson, and Ousama Tawil. 2010. *Characterizing the HIV/AIDS Epidemic in the Middle East and North Africa: Time for Strategic Action*. Washington, D.C.: World Bank.

Ahmed, Leila. 1992. *Women and Gender in Islam: Historical Roots of a Modern Debate*. New Haven: Yale University Press.

Akalay, Aïcha, and Ayla Mrabet. "Investigation. Moroccan women as seen by the Arabs" [in French]. *TelQuel*, September 11, 2010, http://www.telquel-online.com/En-couverture/Enquete-Les-Marocaines-vues-par-les-Arabes/438.

Alami, Khadija Mchichi. 2000. "Le Comportement Sexuel de la Femme: Étude Épidémiologique sur un Échantillon Représentatif de la Population Générale de Casablanca" [Female sexual behavior: An epidemiological study of a representative sample of the general population of Casablanca]. PhD diss., University Hassan II, Faculté de Médicine et de Pharmacie de Casablanca.

ALCS (Association pour la Lutte Contre le SIDA). 2008. *Surveillance des Comportements à Risque: Le Cas des Professionnelles du Sexe* [Surveillance of risk behaviors: The case of sex workers]. Casablanca: ALCS.

Ali, Kamran Asdar. 2002. *Planning the Family in Egypt: New Bodies, New Selves*. Austin: University of Texas Press.

Ali, Kecia. 2006. *Sexual Ethics and Islam. Feminist Reflections on Qur'an, Hadith, and Jurisprudence*. Oxford, UK: Oneworld.

'Ali ibn Nasr al-Katib, Abul Hasan. 1977. *Encyclopedia of Pleasure* [Jawami' alladhdha]. Edited by Salah Addin Khawwam. Translated by 'Adnan Jarkas and Salah Addin Khawwam. Toronto: Aleppo Publishing.

Amar, Paul. 2011. "Turning the Gendered Politics of the Security State Inside Out? Charge the Police with Sexual Harassment in Egypt." *International Feminist Journal of Politics* 13 (3): 299–328.

Amer, Sahar. 2008. *Crossing Borders: Love Between Women in Medieval French and Arabic Literatures.* Philadelphia: University of Pennsylvania Press.

American Psychiatric Association. 2000. "Position Statement on Therapies Focused on Attempts to Change Sexual Orientation (Reparative or Conversion Therapies)." *American Journal of Psychiatry* 157: 1719–21.

Ammar, Manar. "Legal Action Taken Against Egypt 'Nude Revolutionary' Activist." *Bikya Masr*, November 17, 2011, http://bikyamasr.com/48732 /legal-action-against-egypt-nude-activist/.

Ammar, Nawal. 2007. "Wife Battery in Islam: A Comprehensive Understanding of Interpretations." *Violence Against Women* 13 (5): 516–26.

Amnesty International. "Egyptian Women Protesters Forced to Take 'Virginity Tests.' " March 23, 2011, http://www.amnesty.org/en/for-media/press -releases/egyptian-women-protesters-forced-take-'virginity-tests'-2011 -03-23.

AMPF (Association Marocaine de Planification Familiale). 2008. *Étude Exploratoire de l'Avortement à Risque* [Exploratory study of risky abortion]. Rabat: AMPF.

APA Task Force on Appropriate Therapeutic Responses to Sexual Orientation. 2009. *Report of the Task Force on Appropriate Therapeutic Responses to Sexual Orientation.* Washington, D.C.: American Psychological Association.

Asman, Oren. 2004. "Abortion in Islamic Countries—Legal and Religious Aspects." *Medicine and Law* 23: 73–89.

Axétudes. 2007. *Enquête Connaissances, Attitudes et Pratiques des Jeunes Concernant les IST et le SIDA* [Study of the knowledge, attitudes and practices of youth concerning STIs and AIDS]. Rabat: Ministère de la Santé, Royaume du Maroc, GTZ.

Aziz, Germaine. 2007. *Les Chambres Closes* [Brothel rooms]. Paris: Nouveau Monde.

Babayan, Kathryn, and Afsaneh Najmabadi, eds. 2008. *Islamicate Sexualities: Translations Across Temporal Geographies of Desire.* Cambridge, Mass.: Harvard Middle Eastern Monographs.

Badran, W., N. Moamen, I. Fahmy, A. El-Karaksy, T. M. Abdel-Nasser, and H. Ghanem. 2006. "Etiological Factors of Unconsummated Marriage." *International Journal of Impotence Research* 18: 458–63.

Al-Baghdadi, Ahmad. "The perverts . . . who are they?" [in Arabic]. *Al Arabiya*, March 3, 2009, http://www.alarabiya.net/views/2009/03/03/67604 .html.

Bakr, 'Abd al-Wahhab. 2001. *Al-Mujtama' al-Qahira al-Sirri 1900–1951* [Secret Cairo society, 1900–1951]. Cairo: Al-'Arabi al-Nashr.

Al-Banna, Gamal. 2011. *Jawaz Imamat al-Mar'a al-Rijal* [The permissibility of a woman leading men in prayer]. Cairo: Dar al-Shuruq.

*Bareed Mista3jil. True Stories.* [Express mail]. 2009. Beirut: Meem.

Bashier, Naveen. 2010. "Knowing the Ropes: Autonomy in the Everyday Life of Egyptian Married Women." MA diss., American University in Cairo.

Baydoun, Azzah Shararah. 2008. "Sex Education in Lebanon: Between Secular and Religious Discourses." In *Deconstructing Sexuality in the Middle East: Challenges and Discourses*, edited by Pinar Ilkkaracan, pp. 83–100. Aldershot, UK: Ashgate.

Ben Abdallah, Sénim. 2009a. *Enquête Comportementale sur les Travailleuses du Sexe Clandestines en Tunisie* [Behavioral study of illegal sex workers in Tunisia]. Tunis: ATUPRET.

———. 2009b. *Enquête Nationale sur les Comportements à Risque Auprès des Jeunes Non-scolarisés en Tunisie* [National study of risk behaviors among out-of-school youth in Tunisia]. Tunis: ONFP, Global Fund, UNFPA, and UNAIDS.

Ben Dridi, Ibtissem. 2004. *Le Tasfih en Tunisie: Un Rituel de Protection de la Virginité Féminine* [*Tasfih* in Tunisia: A protective ritual for female virginity]. Paris: L'Harmattan.

Benito, Sara Carmen. 2008. *La Prostitution dans les Rues de Casablanca* [Prostitution in the streets of Casablanca]. Translated by Abdelmouneim Bounou and Mohammed Abdelhamid. Casablanca: Les Éditions Toubkal.

Berrada, S., S. Dorhmi, L. Bouhaouli, and N. Kadri. 2008. "Sexuality in the Month of Ramadan." *Sexologies* 17: 83–89.

Bishay, Barbara Viktoria. 2010. "Till Death (or Conversion) Do Us Part: Coptic Divorces in Egyptian Courts and Their Implications." MA diss., American University in Cairo.

Blum, Jenna, Selma Hajri, Hela Chélli, Farouk Ben Mansour, Nabiha Gueddana, and Beverly Winikoff. 2004. "The Medical Abortion Experience of Married and Unmarried Women in Tunis, Tunisia." *Contraception* 69: 63–69.

Bouchlaka, Amel, Faouzi Bouaziz, and Sihem Smida. 2009. "Profil des Femmes Célibataires Bénéficiaires d'IVG dans les Structures de l'ONFP" [Profile of unmarried women using ONFP abortion facilities]. *Famille et Population* 6–7: 145–76.

Bouhdiba, Abdelwahab. 2012. *Sexuality in Islam*. Translated by Alan Sheridan. London: Saqi.

Boutros, Magda, and Hossam Bahgat. 2009. "Sexual Health and Human Rights: Middle East and North Africa." Unpublished paper.

Bowen, Donna Lee. 2003. "Contemporary Muslim Ethics of Abortion." In *Islamic Ethics of Life: Abortion, War and Euthanasia*, edited by Jonathan E. Brockoff, pp. 51–80. Columbia: University of South Carolina Press.

Bristol-Rhys, Jane. 2007. "Weddings, Marriage and Money in the United Arab Emirates." *Anthropology of the Middle East* 2 (1): 20–36.

———. 2010. *Emirati Women: Generations of Change*. New York: Columbia University Press.

Calvert, John. 2000. " 'The World Is an Undutiful Boy!': Sayyid Qutb's American Experience." *Islam and Christian-Muslim Relations* 11 (1): 87–103.

Cauvin Verner, Corinne. 2009. "Du Tourisme Culturel au Tourisme Sexuel: Les Logiques du Désir d'Enchantement" [From cultural tourism to sexual tourism: The logic of desire for enchantment]. *Cahiers d'Études Africaines* 49 (1–2): 123–45.

Chabach, Amal. 2011. *Le Couple Arabe au XXIe siècle: Les Secrets d'une Sexualité Plus Épanouie* [The Arab couple in the twenty-first century: Secrets of a more fulfilling sexual life]. Aubagne, France: Éditions Quintessence.

Chebel, Malek. 2003. *Encyclopédie de l'Amour en Islam* [Encyclopedia of love in Islam]. 2 vols. Paris: Payot et Rivages.

————. 2007. *Le Kama-Sutra Arabe* [Arab Kama-Sutra]. Paris: Fayard.

Clarke, Morgan. 2007. "Kinship, Propriety and Assisted Reproduction in the Middle East." *Anthropology of the Middle East* 2 (1): 70–88.

Cohen, Shaye J. D. 1998. "Why Aren't Jewish Women Circumcised?" in *Gender and the Body in the Ancient Mediterranean,* edited by Maria Wyke, pp. 136–154. London: Wiley-Blackwell.

Courbage, Youssef. 2011. "The Demographic Youth Bulge and Social Rupture." In *Arab Youth: Social Mobilization in Times of Risk,* edited by Samir Khalaf and Roseanne Saad Khalaf, pp. 79–88. London: Saqi.

Cumming, Anne. 1991. *The Love Quest: A Sexual Odyssey.* London: Peter Owen.

Cuno, Kenneth M. 2008. "Divorce and the Fate of the Family in Modern Egypt." In *Family in the Middle East: Ideational Change in Egypt, Iran, and Tunisia,* edited by Kathryn Yount and Hoda Rashad, pp. 196–216. New York: Routledge.

Dabaghi, Lara, Alena Mack, and Doris Jaalouk. 2008 *Helem: A Case Study of the First Legal, Above-Ground LGBT Organization in the MENA Region.* Beirut: Helem.

Dabash, Rasha, and Farzaneh Roudi-Fahimi. 2008. *Abortion in the Middle East and North Africa.* Washington, D.C.: Population Reference Bureau.

El-Damanhoury, Hala. 2009. *Why Do Women Abort? The Determinants of Induced Abortion in Egypt.* Cairo: IPAS.

————. 2011. *Exploratory Study of Attitudes and Communication Behaviors of Providers in Youth Friendly Clinics in Egypt.* Cairo: Population Council.

Daniel, Norman. 1993. *Islam and the West: The Making of an Image.* Oxford, UK: Oneworld.

Dhillon, Navtej, and Tarik Yousef. 2009. *Generation in Waiting: The Unfulfilled Promise of Young People in the Middle East.* Washington D.C.: Brookings Institution Press.

Dialmy, A. 2005. "Prostitution et Traite des Femmes au Maroc" [Prostitution and the trade in women in Morocco]. In *Prostitution, la Mondialization Incarnée,* edited by Richard Poulin. *Alternatives Sud* XII (5): 97–215.

————. 2009a. *Susyulujiyyat al-Jinsiyya al-'Arabiyya* [Sociology of Arab sexuality]. Beirut: Dar al-Tali'a.

————. 2009b. *Vers une Nouvelle Masculinité au Maroc* [Toward a new masculinity in Morocco]. Dakar: CODESRIA.

Ding, Jeffrey, Frederic Jennings, and Susan Pan. 2010. *Employment Discrimination Against the Transgender Community in Lebanon: A Needs Assessment Report for Helem.* New York: Walter Leitner International Human Rights Clinic, Fordham Law School.

Drieskens, Barbara. 2009. "Changing Perceptions of Marriage in Contemporary Beirut." In *Les Métamorphoses du Mariage au Moyen-Orient,* edited by Barbara Drieskens, pp. 97–188. Beirut: IFPO.

Dwairy, Marwan, Mustafa Achoui, Reda Abouserie, and Adnan Farah. 2006. "Adolescent-Family Connectedness Among Arabs: A Second Cross-Regional Research Study." *Journal of Cross-Cultural Psychology* 37 (3): 1–14.

"Egypt parliamentarians and advocates attacking the government because of the 'Chinese membrane' " [in Arabic]. *Al Arabiya,* October 10, 2009, http://www.alarabiya.net/articles/2009/10/10/87557.html.

Egyptian Cabinet, Information and Decision Support Center (IDSC). 2009. *Istitla' Ra'ii al-Muwatiniin hawla Makanat al-Mar'a fi al-Mujtama' al-Misri:*

*Taqriir Muqaran* [Citizens' opinion poll on the status of women in Egyptian society: A comparative report]. Cairo: IDSC.

Eich, Thomas. 2010. "A Tiny Membrane Defending 'Us' Against 'Them': Arabic Internet Debate About Hymenorraphy in Sunni Islamic Law." *Culture, Health and Sexuality* 12 (7): 755–69.

Elnashar, A. M., M. El-Dien Ibrahim, M. M. El-Desoky, O. M. Ali, and M. El-Sayd Mohamed Hassan. 2007. "Female Sexual Dysfunction in Lower Egypt." *BJOG* 114: 201–6.

Ettoussi, Azzouz, and Mohamed Jebbour. 2008. *Les Travailleuses du Sexe et les IST/SIDA: Enquête dans les Régions du Souss, du Moyen Atlas et Rabat* [Sex workers and STIs/AIDS: A study in the regions of Souss, Middle Atlas and Rabat]. Rabat: OPALS and Global Fund.

Ezzat, Ahmed, Riham Zain al-'Abidine, and Emad Mubarak. 2009. *Taqriir Hurriyya al-Fikra wa-l-Ibda' fi Misr* [Report on freedom of thought and creativity in Egypt January–June 2009]. Cairo: Association for Freedom of Thought and Expression.

Fahmy, Amel, Mawaheb T. El-Mouelhy, and Ahmed R. Ragab. 2010. "Female Genital Mutilation/Cutting and Issues of Sexuality in Egypt." *Reproductive Health Matters* 18 (36): 181–90.

Fahmy, Mohamed Fadel. "Egyptian Blogger Aliaa Elmahdy. Why I Posed Naked." CNN, November 20, 2011, http://edition.cnn.com/2011/11/19/world/meast/nude-blogger-aliaa-magda-elmahdy/.

Family Health International and Ministry of Health Egypt. 2010. *HIV/AIDS Biological and Behavioral Surveillance Survey: Round Two Summary Report.* Cairo: FHI and Ministry of Health Egypt.

Farah, Madelain. 1984. *Marriage and Sexuality in Islam: A Translation of al-Ghazali's Book on the Etiquette of Marriage from the Ihya'.* Salt Lake City: University of Utah Press.

Al Farchichi, Wahid. 2011. *Law and Homosexuality. Survey and Analysis of Legislation Across the Arab World.* New York: Global Commission on HIV and the Law.

Al Farchichi, Wahid, and Nizar Saghiyeh. 2009. *Homosexual Relations in the Penal Codes: General Study Regarding the Laws in Arab Countries with a Report on Lebanon and Tunisia.* Beirut: Helem.

Fargues, Philippe. 2001. "Terminating Marriage." In *The New Arab Family*, edited by Nicholas S. Hopkins. *Cairo Papers in Social Science,* vol. 24, no. 1/2, pp. 247–73. Cairo: American University in Cairo Press.

Farhood, Diana Nicole. 2009. "Family, Culture and Decisions: A Look into the Experiences of University Students in Lebanon." MA diss., American University of Beirut.

Fathi, Mostafa. 2009. *The World of Boys: A True Story of Youth.* Translated by W. Scott Chahanovich. Cairo: Shebab Books.

"Fatwa of the Grand Mufti of the Republic Dr Ali Gomaa with regard to child marriage" [in Arabic]. February 13, 2010. http://www.child-trafficking.info/upload/Files/13375926122.pdf.

El Feki, Shereen. 2012. *Standing Up, Speaking Out: Women and HIV in the Middle East and North Africa.* Cairo: UNAIDS MENA Regional Office.

Ferhati, Barkahoum. 2007. "Les Clôtures Symboliques des Algériennes: La Virginité ou l'Honneur Social en Question" [Symbolic closures of Algerian women: Virginity or social honor in question]. *Clio* 26 (2): 169–80.

Fikri, Rasha. 2010. "When Things Get Topsy-Turvey: Foreign Youth Cultures Invade UAE Society." *999 Society and Security Monthly* (May): 20–21.

Flaherty, Elizabeth. 2008. "Reconstructing Sexuality and Identity Through Dialogue: The Muntada's Actions for Palestinian Arab Citizens of Israel." PhD diss., Ohio University, Scripps College of Communication.

Flaubert, Gustave. 1991. *Voyage en Égypte* [Travels in Egypt]. Paris: Bernard Grasset.

Foucault, Michael. 1998. *The History of Sexuality.* Vol. 1, *The Will to Knowledge.* London: Penguin.

Geel, Fatma. 2011. "Improving Adolescents' and Youth Reproductive Health in Egypt: Lesson Learned from Europe." PhD diss., Cairo University.

El-Gibaly, Omaima, Ghada Attar, and Amel Fahmy. 2010. "Is Change in the Attitude of Rural Muslim Imams Toward FGC [Female Genital Cutting] Happening?" Unpublished paper.

Giddens, Anthony. 1992. *The Transformation of Intimacy: Sexuality, Love and Eroticism in Modern Societies.* Stanford, Calif.: Stanford University Press.

El-Gilany, Abdel-Hady, Karina Badawi, and Sanaa El-Fedawy. 2005. "Menstrual Hygiene Among Adolescent Schoolgirls in Mansoura, Egypt." *Reproductive Health Matters* 13 (6): 147–52.

Gomaa, Ali. "Fatwa Number 416: Hymen Restoration Surgery." Dar al-Ifta, June 3, 2007, http://www.dar-alifta.org/ViewFatwa.aspx?ID=416&text=hymen&Home=1&LangID=2.

Gruenbaum, Ellen. 2000. *The Female Circumcision Controversy: An Anthropological Perspective.* Philadelphia: University of Pennsylvania Press.

Habib, Samar. 2007. *Female Homosexuality in the Middle East: Histories and Representations.* London: Routledge.

Haddad, Joumana. 2008. *Invitation to a Secret Feast: Selected Poems.* Edited by Khaled Mattawa. Dorset, UK: Tupelo Press.

———. 2010. *I Killed Scheherezade: Confessions of an Angry Arab Woman.* London: Saqi.

———. 2012. *Superman Is an Arab: On God, Marriage, Macho Men and Other Disastrous Inventions.* London: Westbourne Press.

Haeri, Shahla. 1989. *Law of Desire: Temporary Marriage in Shi'i Iran.* Syracuse, NY: Syracuse University Press.

Haffani, Mohammed Fakkreddine, and Hichem Troudi. 2005. *La Sexualité des Hommes Tunisiens* [Sexuality of Tunisian men], http://haffani.blogspot.co.uk/.

Halasa, Malu, and Rana Salam. 2008. *The Secret Life of Syrian Lingerie: Intimacy and Design.* San Francisco: Chronicle Books.

Handoussa, Heba. 2010. *Egypt Human Development Report 2010. Youth in Egypt: Building Our Future.* Cairo: Institute of National Planning, Egypt and UNDP.

Harb, Charles. 2010. *Describing the Lebanese Youth: A National and Psycho-Social Survey.* Beirut: Issam Fares Institute for Public Policy and International Affairs, American University of Beirut, and UNICEF.

Harbour, Catherine, and Ghada Barsoum. 2010. "Health." In *Survey of Young People in Egypt. Final Report,* pp. 12–33. Cairo: Population Council.

Harri, M., O. Mellouk, Y. Yatine, N. Rafif, N. Amine, and M. Zagloul. "Expérience d'un Centre de Santé Sexuelle Destiné aux Hommes ayant des Relations

Sexuelles avec des Hommes au Maroc" [Experience of a sexual health center for men who have sex with men in Morocco]. Paper presented at Sixième Conférence Francophone sur le VIH/SIDA, Geneva, March 25–28, 2012.

Hassan, Omar. 2010. "Real Queer Arabs: The Tension Between Colonialism and Homosexuality in Egyptian Cinema." *Film International* 43: 18–24.

Hassan, Rasha Mohammad. 2008. *Clouds in Egypt's Sky: Sexual Harassment from Verbal Harassment to Rape. A Sociological Study.* Cairo: Egyptian Center for Women's Rights.

Hassanin, Ibrahim M., Yasser A. Helmy, Mohamed M. F. Fathalla, and Ahmed Y. Shahin. 2010. "Prevalence and Characteristics of Female Sexual Dysfunction in a Sample of Women from Upper Egypt." *International Journal of Gynecology and Obstetrics* 108 (3): 219–23.

Hasso, Frances S. 2011. *Consuming Desires: Family Crisis and the State in the Middle East.* Stanford, Calif.: Stanford University Press.

Hersh, Seymour M. "The Gray Zone." *New Yorker*, May 4, 2004, http://www.newyorker.com/archive/2004/05/24/040524fa_fact?currentPage=all.

Al-Herz, Seba. 2009. *The Others.* New York: Seven Stories Press.

Hessini, Leila. 2007. "Abortion and Islam: Policies and Practice in the Middle East and North Africa." *Reproductive Health Matters* 15 (29): 75–84.

———. 2008. "Islam and Abortion: The Diversity of Discourses and Practices." *IDS Bulletin* 39 (3): 18–27.

Hirschfeld, Magnus. 1935. *Women East and West: Impressions of a Sex Expert.* London: William Heinemann.

Hopwood, Derek. 1999. *Sexual Encounters in the Middle East: The British, the French and the Arabs.* Reading, UK: Ithaca Press.

Horovitz, David. "A Mass Expression of Outrage Against Injustice." *Jerusalem Post,* February 25, 2011, http://www.jpost.com/Opinion/Columnists/Article.aspx?id=209770.

Hull, Edith Maude. 2001. *The Sheik.* Philadelphia: University of Pennsylvania Press.

Human Rights Watch. 2004. *In a Time of Torture: The Assault on Justice in Egypt's Crackdown on Homosexual Conduct.* New York: Human Rights Watch.

———. 2008. *Egypt: 117 NGOs Slam HIV-Based Arrests and Trials.* New York: Human Rights Watch.

———. 2010. *Slow Reform. Protection of Migrant Domestic Workers in Asia and the Middle East.* New York: Human Rights Watch.

———. 2011a. *How Come You Allow Little Girls to Get Married? Child Marriage in Yemen.* New York: Human Rights Watch.

———. 2011b. *"They Hunt Us Down for Fun": Discrimination and Police Violence Against Transgender Women in Kuwait.* New York: Human Rights Watch.

———. 2012. *Egypt: Impunity for Violence Against Women. Whitewash in Virginity Test Trial.* New York: Human Rights Watch.

Huntington, Dale. 2001. "Abortion in Egypt: Official Constraints and Popular Practices." In *Cultural Perspectives on Reproductive Health*, edited by Carla Makhlouf Obermeyer, pp. 175–92. Oxford, UK: Oxford University Press.

Ibn Hazm, 'Ali ibn Ahmad. 1994. *The Ring of the Dove: A Treatise on the Art and Practice of Arab Love.* Translated by Arthur John Arberry. London: Luzac Oriental.

Ibn Qayyim al-Jawziyah, Muhammad ibn Abi Bakr. 1998. *Medicine of the Prophet.* Translated by Penelope Johnstone. Cambridge, UK: Islamic Texts Society.

'Ilwah, Sa'ada. "Civil society wins: Abolition of 'tests of shame' " [in Arabic]. *As-Safir,* September 1, 2012, http://www.assafir.com/Article.aspx?ArticleId=57&EditionId=2244&ChannelId=53832.

Inhorn, Marcia C. 2004. "Middle Eastern Masculinities in the Age of New Reproductive Technologies: Male Infertility and Stigma in Egypt and Lebanon." *Medical Anthropology Quarterly* 18: 162–82.

———. 2006. "Making Muslim Babies: IVF and Gamete Donation in Sunni versus Shi'a Islam." *Culture, Medicine and Psychiatry* 30: 427–50.

———. 2007 "Masturbation, Semen Collection and Men's IVF Experiences: Anxieties in the Muslim World." *Body and Society* 13 (3): 37–53.

———. 2012. *The New Arab Man: Emergent Masculinities, Technologies, and Islam in the Middle East.* Princeton, N.J.: Princeton University Press.

INSAF (Institution Nationale de Solidarité avec les Femmes en Détresse). 2010. *Le Maroc des Mères Célibataires. Étude Diagnostique de la Situation. Ampleur et Réalités, Actions, Représentations, Itinéraires et Vécus* [Unmarried mothers in Morocco. Situation analysis, magnitude and realities, actions, representations, agendas and lives]. Casablanca: INSAF and UN Women.

International Planned Parenthood Federation. 2008. *Sexual Rights: An IPPF Declaration.* London: International Planned Parenthood Federation.

Jabarti, 'Abd al-Rahman. 1997. *'Aja'ib al-Athar fi al-Tarajim wa-l-Akhbar* [Astonishing accounts of biographies and news]. Vol. 2. Edited by A. A. El Din. Cairo: Madbuli.

Jacob, Wilson. 2010. "Overcoming 'Simply Being': Straight Sex, Masculinity and Physical Culture in Modern Egypt." *Gender and History* 22 (3): 658–76.

Jernow, Ali. 2011. *Sexual Orientation, Gender Identity and Justice: A Comparative Law Casebook.* Geneva: International Commission of Jurists.

Jones, James H. 1997. *Alfred C. Kinsey: A Life.* New York: W. W. Norton.

Jones, Stanton L., and Mark A. Yarhouse. 2011. "A Longitudinal Study of Attempted Religiously Mediated Sexual Orientation Change." *Journal of Sex and Marital Therapy* 37 (5): 404–27.

Jureidini, Ray. Forthcoming. *Domestic Workers in the Middle East: Status Enhancement and Degradation in Arab Households.* London: Routledge.

Juynboll, G. H. A. 2007. *Encyclopedia of Canonical Hadith.* Boston: Brill.

Al-Kak, Faysal. 2009. *Homophobia in Clinical Services in Lebanon: A Physician Survey.* Beirut: Helem.

Kandiyoti, Deniz. 1988. "Bargaining with Patriarchy." *Gender and Society* 2: 274–90.

Karam, Souhail. "Moroccan Single Burns Herself in Protest." Reuters, February 23, 2011, http://ca.reuters.com/article/topNews/idCATRE71M4ZF20110223.

Al-Kardousi, 'Adel, and Ahmad Magdoub. 2006. *Darasa li-Shabakat al-Bagha' fi Misr* [Study of prostitution networks in Egypt]. Cairo: Maktab al-Adab.

Katz, Marion Holmes. 2003. "The Problem of Abortion in Classical Sunni Fiqh." In *Islamic Ethics of Life: Abortion, War, and Euthanasia,* edited by J. E. Brockopp, pp. 25–50. Columbia: University of South Carolina.

Kendrick, Sharon. 2008. *Promised to the Sheikh.* London: Mills & Boon.

Al-Khalidi, Salah 'Abd al-Fattah, ed. 1986. *Amrika min al-Dakhil bi-Minzar*

*Sayyid Qutb* [America from the inside from the viewpoint of Sayyid Qutb]. Jeddah, Saudi Arabia: Dar al-Manarah.

Kholoussy, Hanan. 2010. *For Better, for Worse: The Marriage Crisis That Made Modern Egypt.* Stanford, Calif.: Stanford University Press.

El-Kholy, Heba Aziz. 2002. *Defiance and Compliance. Negotiating Gender in Low-Income Cairo.* New York: Berghahn Books.

"Kitab al-Nikah" [Book of marriage]. In *Translation of Sahih Muslim.* Translated by A. H. Siddiqui. Available at http://www.iium.edu.my/deed/hadith /muslim/008_smt.html.

Kobeissi, Kamal, and Mustafa Suleiman. "Egypt youth movement denies ties with girl in nude self-portrait." *Al Arabiya,* November 16, 2011, http://www .alarabiya.net/articles/2011/11/16/177555.html.

El-Kogali, Safaa, and Caroline Krafft. 2010. "Social Issues, Values and Civic Engagement." In *Survey of Young People in Egypt. Final Report,* pp. 133–47. Cairo: Population Council.

El-Kogali, Safaa, Caroline Krafft, and Maia Sieverding. 2010. "Attitudes Toward Gender Roles." In *Survey of Young People in Egypt. Final Report,* pp. 155–68. Cairo: Population Council.

Al-Kordy, Maha. 2008. *Al-Zawaj al-'Urfi fi al-Sirr bayn Tulabat al-Jami'at* [Secret marriage among university students]. Cairo: National Center for Social and Criminological Research.

Kotb, H. 2004. "Sexuality in Islam." PhD diss., Maimonides University.

Krafft, Caroline, and Safaa El-Kogali. "Education." In *Survey of Young People in Egypt. Final Report,* pp. 51–86. Cairo: Population Council.

Kugle, Scott Siraj al-Haqq. 2010. *Homosexuality in Islam.* Oxford, UK: Oneworld.

Kulczycki, Andrzej, and Sarah Windle. 2011. "Honor Killings in the Middle East and North Africa: A Systematic Review of the Literature." *Violence Against Women* 17 (11): 1442–64.

Lane, Sandra, D., Jok Madut Jok, and Mawaheb T. El-Mouelhy. 1998. "Buying Safety: The Economics of Reproductive Risk and Abortion in Egypt." *Social Science and Medicine* 47 (8): 1089–99.

Larguèche, Dalenda, and Abdelhamid Larguèche. 2000. *Marginales en Terre d'Islam* [Women on the edge in the land of Islam]. Tunis: Ceres Productions.

Leonard, Sarah. 2011. "Of Masculinity and Men: Exploring Ambivalence, Pornographic Consumption and Sexual Desire in Cairo." MA diss., American University in Cairo.

Loza, Sara, and Social, Planning, Analysis, and Administration Consultants. 2009. "Experiences, Attitudes, and Practices: A New Survey of 4,408 Women, Men, and Female and Male Youth." In *Egypt Violence Against Women Study: A Summary of Findings,* pp. 25–36. Cairo: USAID and National Council for Women.

Madkur, Mona. "Inas al-Delgheidy talks about a campaign against her for asking for the legalization of prostitution in Egypt" [in Arabic]. *Al Arabiya,* August 5, 2008, http://www.alarabiya.net/articles/2008/08/05/54309.html.

Al-Magribi, al-Samaw'al ibn Yahya. 1978. *A Jaunt in the Art of Coition.* Edited by Salah Addin Khawwam. Translated by 'Adnan Jarkas and Salah Addin Khawwam. Toronto: Aleppo Publishing.

Mahdavi, Pardis. 2009. *Passionate Uprisings: Iran's Sexual Revolution.* Stanford, Calif.: Stanford University Press.

El-Mahdi, Rabab, and Philip Marfleet. 2009. Introduction to *Egypt: Moment of*

*Change,* edited by Rabab El-Mahdi and Philip Marfleet, pp. 1–13. London: Zed Books.

Mahmud, Ibrahim. 2000. *Al-Muta' al-Mahzura, al-Shudhudh al-Jinsi fi Tarikh al-'Arab* [The forbidden pleasure: Homosexuality in Arab history]. Beirut: Riyad El Rayyes.

Malmström, Maria. 2009. "Just Like Couscous: Gender, Agency and the Politics of Female Circumcision in Cairo." PhD diss., University of Gothenburg.

Mamarbachi, Henri. "Moroccan Women Demand Reform After Rape Victim's Suicide." Agence France Presse, March 17, 2012.

Marfleet, Philip. 2009. "State and Society." In *Egypt: Moment of Change,* edited by Rabab El-Mahdi and Philip Marfleet, pp. 14–33. London: Zed Books.

Massad, Joseph A. 2002. "Re-Orienting Desire: The Gay International and the Arab World." *Public Culture* 14 (2): 361–85.

———. 2007. *Desiring Arabs.* Chicago: University of Chicago Press.

McCormick, Jared. 2011. "Hairy Chest, Will Travel: Tourism, Identity, and Sexuality in the Levant." *Journal of Middle East Women's Studies* 7: 71–97.

Menicucci, Garay. 1998. "Unlocking the Arab Celluloid Closet: Homosexuality in Egyptian Film." *Middle East Report* 206: 32–36.

*Men's Lives Often Seen as Better: Gender Equality Universally Embraced, but Inequalities Acknowledged.* 2010. Washington, D.C.: Pew Global Attitudes Project.

Mernissi, Fatema. 2011. *Beyond the Veil: Male-Female Dynamics in Muslim Society.* London: Saqi.

Mikdashi, Maya, and Rasha Moumneh. 2011. "The Emerging Discourse on Same-Sex Sexualities and Rights in Lebanon." Unpublished paper.

Miller, Alice M. 2009. *Sexuality and Human Rights: A Discussion Paper.* Versoix, Switzerland: International Council on Human Rights Policy.

Moawad, Nadine, and Tamara Qiblawi. 2011. "Lebanon: Who's Afraid of the Big Bad Internet?" :*//Erotics Sex, Rights and the Internet. An Exploratory Research Study,* edited by Jac sm Kee. pp. 109–134. Melville, South Africa: Association for Progressive Communications.

*Most Muslims Want Democracy, Personal Freedoms, and Islam in Political Life. Few Believe U.S. Backs Democracy.* 2012. Washington, D.C.: Pew Global Attitudes Project.

Mostafa, S., N. El Zeiny, S. Tayel, and E. Moubarak. 2006. "What Do Medical Students in Alexandria Know About Female Genital Mutilation?" *Eastern Mediterranean Health Journal* 12 (suppl. 2): S78–S92.

El-Mouelhy, Mawaheb. 1992. "Maternal Mortality in the Last Two Decades in Egypt." *Saudi Medical Journal* 13 (2): 132–36.

El-Mouelhy, Mawaheb, Amel Fahmy, and Ahmed Ragaa Abdel Hamid Ragab. 2009. *Investigating Women's Sexuality in Relation to Female Genital Mutilation in Egypt.* Cairo: Cairo Family Planning and Development Association and World Health Organization.

Moussa, Bishop. 2004. "Coptic Religion and Female Genital Mutilation." In *Afro-Arab Expert Consultation on Legal Tools for the Prevention of Female Genital Mutilation Cairo 21–23 June 2003,* pp. 24–26. Cairo: "Stop FGM" International Campaign.

Moussa, Fatima, Badia Masmoudi, and Rania Barboucha. 2009. "Du Tabou de la Virginité au Mythe de l'Inviolabilité: La Rite du R'bit chez la Fillette dans l'Est Algérien" [From the taboo of virginity to the myth of inviolability: The rite of *r'bit* among young girls in the east of Algeria"] *Dialogue* 185 (3): 91–102.

Mumtaz, Ghina, Nahia Hilmi, Willi McFarland, Rachel L. Kaplan, Francisca Ayodeji Akala, Iris Semini, Gabriele Riedner, Oussama Tawil, David Wilson, and Laith J. Abu-Raddad. 2011. "Are HIV Epidemics Among Men Who Have Sex with Men Emerging in the Middle East and North Africa? A Systematic Review and Data Synthesis." *PLoS Medicine* 8, http://www.plos medicine.org/article/info%3Adoi%2F10.1371%2Fjournal.pmed.1000444.

Al-Munajjid, Salah al-Din. 1975. *Al-Hayat al-Jinsiyya 'ind al-'Arab, min al-Jahiliyya ila Awakhir al-Qarn al- Rabi' al-Hijri* [The sexual life of the Arabs from jahiliyya to the end of the fourth century of the Muslim era]. Beirut: Dar al-Kitab al-Jadid.

Murray, Stephen O., and Will Roscoe. 1997. *Islamic Homosexualities: Culture, History, and Literature.* New York: New York University Press.

Musallam, Basim. 1983. *Sex and Society in Islam: Birth Control Before the Nineteenth Century.* Cambridge, UK: Cambridge University Press.

Naamane Guessous, Soumaya, and Chafik Guessous. 2011. *Grossesses de la Honte* [Shameful pregnancies]. Casablanca: Afrique Orient.

Nada, Khaled, ElDaw Suliman, and Nadia Zibani. 2008. *Behavioral Survey Among Street Children in Greater Cairo and Alexandria: Final Report.* Cairo: Population Council.

Al-Nafzawi, 'Umar ibn Muhammad. 1991. "Al-Rawd al-'Atir fi Nuzhat al-Khatir" [The perfumed garden of sensual delight]. In *Al-Jins 'inda al-'Arab: Nusus Mukhtarah.* Vol. 2. Cologne: Al-Kamel.

Najjar, Mostafa. "China promotes synthetic hymens in Egypt" [in Arabic]. *Youm 7*, September 13, 2009, http://www.youm7.com/News.asp?NewsID=136135.

Najmabadi, Afsaneh. 2008. "Transing and Transpassing Across Sex-Gender Walls in Iran." *Women's Studies Quarterly* 36 (3–4): 23–42.

Nigst, Lorenz, and Jose Sanchez Garcia. 2010. "Boyat in the Gulf: Identity, Contestation, and Social Control." *Middle East Critique* 19 (1): 5–34.

Norris, Pippa, and Ronald Inglehart. 2002. *Islam and the West: Testing the 'Clash of Civilizations' Thesis.* Cambridge, Mass.: John F. Kennedy School of Government at Harvard University.

Omran, Abdel Rahim. 1992. *Family Planning in the Legacy of Islam.* London: Routledge.

Orhan, Soad. 2008. "Men Selling Sex in Cairo and Alexandria: Perspective on Male Sex Work and AIDS in Egypt." MA diss., American University in Cairo.

Osman, Magued, and Hanan Girgis. "Marriage Patterns in Egypt." Paper presented at the Twenty-sixth IUSSP International Population Conference, Marrakech, September 27 to October 2, 2009.

Osman, Magued, Hussein Abdel Aziz, Mohammed Ramadan, and Fatma Geel. 2009. *Ta'khkhur Sinn al-Zawaj: Hal 'Asbah Mushkila Tabhath 'an Hal?* [Delay in the age of marriage: Is it a problem in search of a solution?]. Cairo: Egyptian Cabinet, Information and Decision Support Center.

Oyoun Center for Studies and Development. 2010. *Modern Slavery: Tourist Marriages in Egypt.* Cairo: Oyoun Center for Studies and Development.

Patai, Raphael. 1982. *The Arab Mind.* New York: Hatherleigh Press.

Population Council and Egyptian Cabinet, Information and Decision Support

Center (IDSC). 2009. *Survey of Young People in Egypt*. Cairo: Population Council and IDSC. www.popcouncil.org/projects/234_SurveyYoungPeople Egypt.asp.

Al-Qaradawi, Yusuf. 2001. *The Lawful and the Prohibited in Islam*. Cairo: Al-Falah Foundation.

*Qur'an*. 1985. Medina: Mujamma' al-Malik Fahd li-l-Tiba'at al-Mushaf al-Sharif.

*Qur'an*. 2005. Translated by M. A. S. Abdel Haleem. Oxford, UK: Oxford University Press.

Rakha, Marwa. 2007. *The Poison Tree: Planted and Grown in Egypt*. Cairo: Malamih Publishing House.

Rasheed, Salah M., Ahmed H. Abd-Ellah, and Fouad M. Yousef. 2011. "Female Genital Mutilation in Upper Egypt in the New Millennium." *International Journal of Gynecology and Obstetrics* 114: 47–50.

Reich, Wilhelm. 1946. *The Mass Psychology of Fascism*. Translated by T. P. Wolfe. New York: Orgone Institute Press.

———. 1973. "The Sexual Misery of the Working Masses and the Difficulties of Sexual Reform." *New German Critique* 1: 98–110.

Rispler-Chaim, Vardit. 2007. "The Muslim Surgeon and Contemporary Ethical Dilemmas Surrounding the Restoration of Virginity." *Hawwa* 5: 324–49.

El-Rouayheb, Khaled. 2005. *Before Homosexuality in the Arab-Islamic World, 1500–1800*. Chicago: University of Chicago Press.

Rowson, Everett K. 1991. "The Effeminates of Early Medina." *Journal of the American Oriental Society* 111 (4): 671–93.

———. 2006. "Arabic: Middle Ages to Nineteenth Century." In *Encyclopedia of Erotic Literature*, edited by Gaëtan Brulotte and John Phillips, pp. 43–61. New York: Routledge.

Royaume du Maroc (Kingdom of Morocco). 2012. *Mise en Oeuvre de la Déclaration Politique sur le VIH/SIDA: Rapport National 2012* [Implementation of the political declaration of commitment to HIV/AIDS: National report 2012]. Rabat: Royaume du Maroc.

Russell, Thomas Wentworth. 1949. *Egyptian Service, 1902–1946*. London: John Murray.

Sabiq, al-Sayyid. 1993. *Fiqh al-Sunna* [Jurisprudence for Sunni Muslims]. Vol. 2. Cairo: Dar al-Fatah li-l-'Alam al-'Arabi.

Saghieh, Hazem. 2011. *Mudhakarat Randa al-Trans* [Memoirs of Randa Trans]. Beirut: Saqi.

Said, Edward. 1995. *Orientalism: Western Conceptions of the Orient*. London: Penguin.

Said, Samar, Amal Zaki, Ashgan Abdel Hamid, Mozn Hassan, and Hala Abdel Kader. 2009. *Egypt Violence Against Women Study: Overview of Services on Violence Against Women*. Cairo: USAID and National Council for Women.

El-Sakka, Ahmed I. 2012. "Erectile Dysfunction in Arab Countries, Part I: Prevalence and Correlates." *Arab Journal of Urology* 10(2): 97–103.

Salamandra, Christa. 2012. "The Muhammad Effect: Media Panic, Melodrama, and the Arab Female Gaze." *Anthropological Quarterly* 85 (1): 45–77.

Salem, Fadi, and Racha Mourtada. 2012."Social Media in the Arab World: Influencing Cultural and Societal Change?" *Arab Social Media Report* 2 (1), July 2012. Dubai: Dubai School of Government.

Salem, Fadi, Racha Mourtada, May Al-Dabbagh, and Ghalia Gargani. 2011. "The Role of Social Media in Women's Empowerment." *Arab Social Media Report* 1 (3), November 2011. Dubai: Dubai School of Government.

Al-Samman, Hanadi. 2008. "Out of the Closet: Representation of Homosexuals and Lesbians in Modern Arabic Literature." *Journal of Arabic Literature* 39: 270–310.

Al-Sayed, Ahmed. "Mufti of Egypt: Misyar legally permissible and not an affront to women" [in Arabic]. *Al Arabiya*, July 22, 2009, http://www .alarabiya.net/articles/2009/04/16/70794.html.

El-Sayed, Hamdy. 2004. "Medical and Ethical Perspectives." In *Afro-Arab Expert Consultation on Legal Tools for the Prevention of Female Genital Mutilation, Cairo, 21–23 June 2003*, pp. 26–29. Cairo: "Stop FGM" International Campaign.

Sayed, Safaa. 2011. "Al-Mithliyyun wa-l-Mithliyya fi al-Sinima al-Misriyya" [Homosexuals and homosexuality in Egyptian cinema]. In *Al-Abhath al-Khassa bi-l-Ijtima'at al-Tashawuriyya hawla Afdal al-Subul li-l-Wusul li-l-fi'at al-Akhtar 'Urdah li-l-Isabah bi al-AIDS fi al-Duwal al-'Arabiyya.* 2:89–105. Cairo: HARPAS and UNDP.

Schielke, Samuli. 2009. "Ambivalent Commitments: Troubles of Morality, Religiosity and Aspiration Among Young Egyptians." *Journal of Religion in Africa* 39: 158–85.

Sellers, Alexandra. 2008. "Sheikh's Honour." In *The Desert Sheikh's Bride*. Richmond, UK: Harlequin Books.

Sengers, Gerda. 2003. *Women and Demons: Cult Healing in Islamic Egypt*. Boston: Brill.

Shafik, Viola. 2007. *Popular Egyptian Cinema: Gender, Class, and Nation*. Cairo: American University in Cairo.

Shalev, Ofra, Nahemi Baum, and Haya Itzhaki. 2013. " 'There's a Man in My Bed': The First Experience of Sex Among Modern Orthodox Newlyweds in Israel." *Journal of Sex and Marital Therapy* 39(1):40–55.

Shalhoub-Kevorkian, Nadera. 2005. "Imposition of Virginity Testing: A Life-Saver or a License to Kill?" *Social Science and Medicine* 60: 1187–96.

Shamloul, Rany. 2006. "Management of Honeymoon Impotence." *Journal of Sexual Medicine* 3: 361–66.

Sholkamy, Hania. 2012. "Women Are Also Part of This Revolution." In *Arab Spring in Egypt*, edited by Bahgat Korany and Rabab El-Mahdi, pp. 153–74. Cairo: American University in Cairo Press.

Sieverding, Maia, and Asmaa Elbadawy. 2010. "Marriage and Family Formation." In *Survey of Young People in Egypt. Final Report*, pp. 118–32. Cairo: Population Council.

Silatech and Gallup. 2009. *The Silatech Index: Voices of Young Arabs*. Doha, Qatar: Silatech and Gallup.

———. 2011. *The Silatech Index: Voices of Young Arabs*. Doha, Qatar: Silatech and Gallup.

Singerman, Diane. 2007. *The Economic Imperatives of Marriage: Emerging Practices and Identities Among Youth in the Middle East*. Dubai: Middle East Youth Initiative, Wolfensohn Center for Development, Dubai School of Government.

———. 2009. "Marriage and Divorce in Egypt: Financial Costs and Political

Struggles." In *Les Métamorphoses du Mariage au Moyen-Orient*, edited by Barbara Drieskens, pp. 75–96. Beirut: IFPO.

———. 2011. "The Negotiation of Waithood: The Political Economy of Delayed Marriage in Egypt." In *Arab Youth: Social Mobilization in Times of Risk*, edited by Samir Khalaf and Roseanne Saad Khalaf, pp. 67–78. London: Saqi.

Snoussi, Mohamed Larbi. 2000. "Prostitution en Tunisie au Temps de la Colonisation" [Prostitution in Tunisia in the colonial period"]. In *La Tunisie Mosaïque: Diasporas, Cosmopolitisme, Archéologies de l'Identité*, edited by J. Alexandropoulos and P. Cabanel, pp. 389–413. Toulouse, France: Presses Universitaires du Mirail.

Sonneveld, Nadia. 2012. *Khul' Divorce in Egypt: Public Debates, Judicial Practices, and Everyday Life*. Cairo: American University in Cairo Press.

Steegmuller, Francis, ed. and trans. 1987. *Gustave Flaubert: A Sensibility on Tour. A Narrative Drawn from Gustave Flaubert's Travel Notes and Letters*. Chicago: Academy Chicago Publishers.

Suleiman, Mustafa. "Egyptian film about the life of deviants takes part in 'queer' world festival" [in Arabic]. *Al Arabiya*, June 26, 2008, http://www.alarabiya.net/articles/2008/06/26/52151.html.

Suleiman, Mustafa. "First case of 'what your right hand possesses' marriage" [in Arabic]. *Al Arabiya*, July 3, 2012, http://www.alarabiya.net/articles/2012/07/03/224214.html.

Tadmouri, Ghazi O., Pratibha Nair, Tasneem Obeid, Mahmoud T. Al Ali, Najib Al Khaja, and Hanan A. Hamamy. 2009. "Consanguinity and Reproductive Health Among Arabs." *Reproductive Health* 6: 7–26.

Tag-Eldin, Mohammed A., Mohsen A. Gadallah, Mahmoud N. Al-Tayeb, Mostafa Abdel-Aty, Esmat Mansour, and Mona Sallem. 2008. "Prevalence of Female Genital Cutting Among Egyptian Girls." *Bulletin of the World Health Organization* 86: 269–74.

Al-Tahtawi, Rifa'a Rafi'. 2011. *An Imam in Paris: Account of a Stay in France by an Egyptian Cleric (1826–1831)*. Translated and introduced by Daniel Newman. London: Saqi.

Taraud, Christelle. 2003. *La Prostitution Coloniale: Algérie, Tunisie, Maroc (1830–1962)* [Colonial prostitution: Algeria, Tunisia, Morocco (1830–1962)]. Paris: Payot et Rivages.

Tartoussieh, Karim. 2011. "Pious Stardom: Cinema and the Religious Revival in Egypt." In *African Sexualities: A Reader*, edited by Sylvia Tamale, pp. 217–30. Oxford, UK: Pambazuka Press.

Taylor, J. 2007. "And You Can Be My Sheikh: Gender, Race and Orientalism in Contemporary Romance Novels." *Journal of Popular Culture* 40 (6): 1032–1051.

El Tawila, Sahar, and Zeinab Khadr. 2004. *Patterns of Marriage and Family Formation Among Youth in Egypt*. Cairo: National Population Council and Cairo University.

Teo, Hsu-Ming. 2012. *Desert Passions: Orientalism and Romance Novels*. Austin: University of Texas Press.

Thomason, Laura M. 2008. "On the Steps of the Mosque. The Legal Rights of Non-Marital Children in Egypt." *Hastings Women's Law Journal* 19 (1) :121–147.

"355% increase in marriages between Egyptians and foreign women in the last 5 years and 17,000 cases in 2010" [in Arabic]. *Al Arabiya*, January 2, 2011, http://www.alarabiya.net/articles/2011/01/20/134332.html.

Al-Tifashi, Ahmad ibn Yusuf. 2001. *Ruju' al-Shaykh ila Sibah fi al-Quwa 'ala al-Ba'h* [The old man's return to his youth in sexual prowess]. Damascus: Dar al-Kitab al-'Arabi.

———. Forthcoming. *Sensual Delights of the Heart: Arab Erotica by Ahmed al-Tifashi*. Translated by Daniel Newman. London: Saqi.

Toudeft, F. 2010. *Étude sur les Connaissances, Attitudes et Comportements des Jeunes Universitaires en Matière de l'Infection à VIH/SIDA: Évaluation des Actions de Proximité* [Study of the knowledge, attitudes and behaviors of university students with relation to HIV/AIDS: assessment of outreach initiatives]. Algiers: AIDS-Algérie.

UNAIDS. 2011. *Middle East and North Africa Regional Report on AIDS 2011*. Cairo: UNAIDS.

———. 2012. *Together We Will End AIDS*. Geneva: UNAIDS.

UNESCO. 2009. *International Technical Guidance on Sexuality Education: An Evidence-Informed Approach for Schools, Teachers and Health Educators*. Vol. 1. Paris: UNESCO.

United Arab Emirates National Bureau of Statistics. 2011. *Marriage Contracts and Divorce Certificates Registered at Courts by Spouse Nationality and Emirate, 2011*.

U.S. Department of State. 2012. *Egypt: Country-Specific Information*. http://travel.state.gov/travel/cis_pa_tw/cis/cis_1108.html#safety.

Wahba, Mamdouh, and Farzaneh Roudi-Fahimi. 2012. *The Need for Reproductive Health Education in Schools in Egypt*. Washington, D.C.: Population Reference Bureau.

Wasfy, Awsam. 2007. *Shifa' al-Hubb* [The cure is love]. Cairo: Awsam Wasfy.

Weeks, Jeffrey. 2007. *The World We Have Won: The Remaking of Erotic and Intimate Life*. London: Routledge.

Welchman, Lynn, and Sara Hossain, eds. 2005. *"Honour": Crimes, Paradigms and Violence Against Women*. London: Zed Books.

Whitaker, Brian. 2011. *Unspeakable Love: Gay and Lesbian Life in the Middle East*. London: Saqi.

Willman Bordat, Susan, and Saida Kouzzi. 2010. "Legal Empowerment of Unwed Mothers: Experiences of Moroccan NGOs." In *Legal Empowerment: Practitioners' Perspectives*, edited by Stephen Golub, pp. 179–201. Rome: International Development Law Organization.

World Health Organization. 2006. *Defining Sexual Health: Report of a Technical Consultation on Sexual Health, January 28–31, 2002, Geneva*. Geneva: World Health Organization.

———. 2011. *Unsafe Abortion: Global and Regional Estimates of the Incidence of Unsafe Abortion and Associated Mortality in 2008*. Geneva: World Health Organization.

World Health Organization, Department of Reproductive Health and Research. 2008. *Eliminating Female Genital Mutilation: An Interagency Statement UNAIDS, UNDP, UNECA, UNESCO, UNFPA, UNHCHR, UNHCR, UNICEF, UNIFEM, WHO*. Geneva: World Health Organization.

World Health Organization Task Force on Psychosocial Research on Family Planning, Special Programme of Research, Development and Research Training in Human Reproduction. 1981. "A Cross-Cultural Study on Menstruation: Implications for Contraceptive Development and Use." *Studies in Family Planning* 12 (1): 3–16.

Wright, Jr., Jerry W., and Everett K. Rowson, eds. 1997. *Homoeroticism in Classical Arabic Literature*. New York: Columbia University Press.

Yosri, Yasmine. 2011. *Mother-Daughter Communication About Sexual and Reproductive Health Matters in Slum Areas in Alexandria, Egypt.* Cairo: Population Council.

Yount, Kathryn M. 2004. "Symbolic Gender Politics, Religious Group Identity, and the Decline in Female Genital Cutting in Minya, Egypt." *Social Forces* 82 (3): 1063–90.

———. 2011. "Women's Conformity as Resistance to Intimate Partner Violence in Assiut, Egypt." *Sex Roles* 64: 43–58.

Youssef, Olfa. 2008. *Hayrat Muslima* [A Muslim woman's confusion]. Tunis: Dar Sahar al-Nashr.

Al-Zahid, Medhat. 2010. *Tijarat al-Jins* [Sex trade]. Cairo: Shehab Foundation.

Zaiem, Mohammed Hedi, and Jalila Attafi. 2010. "Mariages en Tunisie, 1991–2007" [Marriages in Tunisia, 1991–2007]. Paper presented at Youth in a World of Change: Trajectories by Gender. Group on Population and Reproductive Health No. 9/2010. Tunis: ONFP.

El-Zanaty, Fatma, and Ann Way. 2009. *Egypt: Demographic and Health Survey 2008*. Cairo: Egypt Ministry of Health, El-Zanaty and Associates, and Macro International.

Al-Zayyat, Habib. 1956. "Al-mar'a al-ghulamiyya fi al-Islam" [Woman as *ghulamiyya* in Islam]. *Al-Machriq* (March-April): 155–92.

Ze'evi, Dror. 2005. "Hiding Sexuality: The Disappearance of Sexual Discourse in the Late Ottoman Middle East." *Social Analysis* 49 (2): 34–53.

———. 2006. *Producing Desire: Changing Sexual Discourse in the Ottoman Middle East, 1500–1900*. Berkeley: University of California Press.

Znazen, Abir, Olfa Frikha-Gargouri, Lamia Berrajah, Sihem Bellalouna, Hela Hakim, Nabiha Gueddana, and Adnene Hammami. 2010. "Sexually Transmitted Infections Among Female Sex Workers in Tunisia: High Prevalence of *Chlamydia trachomatis*." *Sexually Transmitted Infections* 86: 500–505.

Al-Zubaidi, A. A.. 1993. *Mukhtasar Sahih al-Bukhari* [A summary of authentic hadith according to al-Bukhari]. Beirut: Mu'assassa al-Kutub al-Thaqafiyya.

# Acknowledgments

This book would not have been possible without the participation of Gamal El Feki. Retired neurosurgeon-turned-research associate, he unstintingly shared his knowledge of Egyptian history and society—lived and learned—as well as his informed and insightful interpretations of Islam. Without his expert grasp of Arabic, and his encouragement at every stage of this project, I would have been completely lost in translation. One of the rewards of researching and writing this book was the opportunity of working with him; the fact that he is also my father is my great good fortune. Thanks too to my mother, Gwyneth El Feki, for graciously tolerating years of single-minded conversation as my father and I argued about the finer points of Arab sexuality. It was my mother who, when I was still a child, confidently predicted that I would one day write a book. You were right, Mam, though I'm not sure this is quite what you had in mind.

I am also grateful to my extended family who put me up (and put up with me) during my travels across the Arab region. Particular thanks to Abdel Fatah and Zizi El Feki and their children in Cairo and Dubai; Leila El Feki and family in Alexandria; Ahmed Warda and family in Jeddah; and Bakr and Soheir Nour in Doha. My uncle used to warn me not to talk to people about politics or religion. I am delighted to assure him that I largely followed his advice; fortunately, he never asked me not to talk about sex.

My agent Toby Eady, his associates Jamie Coleman and Zaria Rich, and former colleague Samar Hammam, were indispensable in the writing of this book; their professional expertise, and personal friendship, is greatly appreciated. I would also like to thank my editors at Pantheon and Chatto & Windus, Dan Frank and Becky Hardie. Tim Rostron and colleagues at Random House Canada deserve special praise for their flawless assistance when my manuscript was "lost" en route to New York (that's another story) and weeks of work had to be made up effectively overnight. Wissam Shawkat and Fadila Hannouf also made valuable contributions to the final stages of this book.

I could not have reached the finish without the many people who generously shared their time and expertise. In addition to those already mentioned in the book, I owe a particular debt of gratitude to Khadija Moalla and Ehab El Kharrat, formerly of the UNDP HIV/AIDS Regional Program in Arab States, whose work on the epidemic paved the way for my research. Also in Egypt, I would like to thank Montasser Kamal of the Ford Foundation; Nahla Abdel Tawab, Ali Rashad, and colleagues at the Population Council; Ghada Barsoum at the American University in Cairo; Chafik El-Chazli of Alexandria University; Mahmoud Fathalla of Assiut University; Sany Kozman of Friends of Life;

Mervat Nesseim and colleagues at CDS; Ahmed Ragab, Gamal Serour, and colleagues at Al-Azhar University; Hamidreza Setayesh, formerly of UNAIDS Cairo; Viola Shafik; Cherif Soliman and team at Family Health International; and Mamdouh Wahba of the Egyptian Family Health Society. Thanks also to Iman Ahmed, Carol Ann Clouston, Ismail El Mokadem, Mawaheb El-Mouelhy, Amel Fahmy, Fatma Geel, Abeer Heider, Amal Zakaria Mattar, and Khaled Samy for their insights, and their friendship.

In Tunisia, Sénim Ben Abdallah, Sara Ben Amarra, Monia Arfaoui, Wahid Al Farchichi, Saloua Ghrissa, Selma Hajri, Ridha Kamoun (with ATL), Aida Robanna (with UNDP), Mongia Souahi, and Abdelmajid Zahaf (of ATUPRET) were instrumental in my research. I would also like to thank Hoda Romdhani and her family for their hospitality and a truly memorable Eid al-Adha. In Morocco, I am similarly grateful to Hafida Al Baz (of SolFem); Abdessamad Benalla; Amal Chabach; Azzouz Ettoussi (with OPALS); Soumaya Naamane Guessous; Hakima Himmich, Othman Mellouk, Nadia Rafif, and colleagues at ALCS; as well as Nadia Kadiri and Soumia Berrada (at Ibn Rochd University Hospital). Special thanks also to Chafik Chraibi and Abdessamad Dialmy.

I would like to express my appreciation to Sally Shalabi and Mohammed El Nasser in Jordan; Scander Abdelkader Soufi (with ANIS) in Algeria; Shireen Assaf in the West Bank; and Sanaa Felemban and Abdoo Khal in Saudi Arabia. In Qatar, thanks to Laith Abu-Raddad and Ghina Mumtaz of Weil Cornell Medical School, as well as Yassir and Sufia Khan. In Lebanon, my work would not have been possible without the assistance of Georges Azzi of AFE; Jocelyn DeJong, Faysal Al-Kak, and Brigitte Khoury of the American University in Beirut; Asma Kurdahi, with UNFPA; and Charbel Maydaa, Rabih Maher, and colleagues at Helem. I would also like to thank Chaza Akik, Azza Baydoun, Jad Choueiri, Claire Damaa, Lina Khoury, Nina Lahham, Marwan Nahle, and Nizar Saghieh.

Friends and collaborators further afield include Muhammad Abdel Haleem at SOAS; Janet Afary at University of California, Santa Barbara; Edwige Fortier; Leila Hessini with IPAS; Eszter Kismodi at WHO; Tanya Kisserli, formerly of the International HIV/AIDS Alliance, and colleagues; Mansoor Moaddel at Eastern Michigan State University; Daniel Newman at Durham University; David Patterson at IDLO; Lawrence Pintak at Washington State University; Farzaneh Roudi-Fahimi at PRB; Everett Rowson at New York University; and Diane Singerman at American University. There are many more friends and colleagues to whom I am indebted; a full list can be found at www.sexandthe citadel.com

Finally, there is my husband. When I began this book, he was my fiancé; after all the trials and tribulations of first-time authorship, and the long-distance longing of my years on the road, he was man (or possibly mad) enough to still want to marry me. I am, for once, at a loss for words to express my deep love, gratitude, and appreciation to him.

# Index